THIS BOOK WILL CHANGE YOUR LIFE

The Best of This Diary Will Change Your Life

Benrik

Benrik are Ben Carey and Henrik Delehag, authors, artists and all-round creative pundits. Benrik's goal is to create an alternative to the current rationalistic collective imagination, turning everyday life on its head before bashing it in. Once this alternative worldview has been seeded in enough readers' minds, it will be child's play to take over the state, the army, the media and most of the major multilateral institutions. Watch this space.

Also by Benrik: other works include "Lose Weight! Get Laid! Find God!", "The Couple's Book", and "A book for people who want to become stinking rich but aren't quite sure how", based on their columns in the Independent and the Guardian. But don't buy any of them until you've finished this book.

After years of painful testing on guinea pigs across the globe, the definitive life-changing manual is in your hands. Since 2004, close to half a million people have purchased copies of the annual "Diary Will Change Your Life" series and followed its daily and weekly tasks, reporting back to its creators Benrik and other readers on www.benrik.co.uk. This edition distills the best of those tasks, and presents Benrik's extreme life-change programme in a beautiful yet convenient format. You can of course dip in and out of it, but for guaranteed results, you must follow it for a whole year, one day at a time. Indeed, for cast-iron guaranteed results, repeat this every year for the rest of your life. Good luck!

To task in coordination with everyone else, start on www.benrik.co.uk in early January.

Personal details

PHOTO (Before)	PHOTO (After)

Name ....

Address ....

Phone (home) .... Phone (mobile) ....

Email ....

Computer IP address ....

Date Of Birth .... Social Security number ....

Bank details A/C .... Sort code ....

Internet password ....

Credit cards ....

Pin numbers ....

Burglar alarm code ....

Role model ....

Aspiration in life ....

Childhood dream ....

Claim to fame ....

Definition of beauty ....

Explanation of evil ....

Other details you deem relevant ....

Completely unnecessary detail ....

Compromising detail ....

IS THIS BOOK A GIFT?

DONOR: Explore reasons for giving it here ....

....

GIFTEE: Explore feelings on receiving it here ....

....

In case of emergency

IN CASE OF ACCIDENT

Name of GP …………………… Phone ……………………

Medication ……………………

……………………

Previous operations ……………………

……………………

Limbs I would rather not have amputated ……………………

……………………

Organs I would rather not have removed ……………………

……………………

Current Blood Group …………………… Preferred Blood Group ……………………

Should I become involved in an accident and require a transfusion, please use this opportunity to change my blood group as indicated above. Thank you.

IN CASE OF AMNESIA

My favourite colour (circle) ■ ■ ■ ■ ☐ ■

My favourite food ……………………

My lucky number …………………… My sexual orientation ……………………

My best foot …………………… My best friend ……………………

My most annoying habits ……………………

……………………

IN CASE OF SUDDEN DEATH

Person to contact …………………… Phone ……………………

Break the news to them gently? Yes ☐ No ☐

Confession (my worst sin): I did ……………………

to ……………………

I want to be buried ☐ cremated ☐

Song to be played ……………………

Do not invite ……………………

Epitaph ……………………

Lasting regret ……………………

My stuff goes to ……………………

Dear …………………… (best friend),

please go to my room and remove ……………………

from …………………… before my poor mother finds it.

IN CASE OF GLOBAL THERMONUCLEAR WAR

Favourite isotope ……………………

Country where you agree to meet up with your loved ones within 10 years ……………………

IN CASE THE ROBOTS TAKE OVER

Benrik are looking for a child to train to take on the robots in the year 2037. Must be mature for its age and prepared to sacrifice its childhood. Are you that child? Do you know such a child? Are you prepared to conceive that child? If so, email Benrik asap.

WARM-UP DAY

Warm up with an easy task that will only change your life a little bit. Choose one of the following options:

Do one press-up.

Perform a striptease (in private).

Learn to play "Chopsticks".

me
arse
work
pity
sand
are
is
post
cat
sew

Increase your typing speed by three words a minute.

HA

Jaywalk in a pedestrian zone.

Set all your clocks to exactly the right time.

SEX

Fantasize about your partner.

Use a different thickness comb.

HA
HA

Hold the phone up to your other ear.

PHIL

Tell someone your middle name.

BOSS

Leave work five minutes early.

Bookmark a new website.

Curt
Anne
Anthony

Give your genitalia pet names.

YOU COWARD!

Insult an insect.

NIKO

Triple-tie your shoelaces.

I HAVE NO PEN-ILE UN-IT

Whisper a white lie when no one's listening.

Try a new sandwich filling.

Go on a one-minute hunger strike.

Your life should have changed, but not measurably.

THE LOVE OF YOUR LIFE

Today, gaze at everyone wondering whether they might be the one true love of your life, the one destined for you and you alone, and whether you might be passing them by forever... Act in consequence.

Advise your military today

The armed forces of Western powers are currently deployed across the globe in a variety of combat missions. It is your duty not only to support them, but to provide them with any tactical insights you have gleaned from your personal study of the battlefield. Write to someone in your national military directly today, and claim your rightful place in the chain of command. Sample letters:

Lieutenant R. McGregor
9th Armoured Brigade
SFOR
Sarajevo
Bosnia

Dear Lieutenant,

My thoughts are with you during this difficult time away from loved ones. Your actions are making peace possible throughout the world. Now, I spend a lot of time on internet chat rooms, and I've picked up rumours of potential civil unrest in Macedonia. You could cross the border with 3rd Battalion at dawn, and take control of the major strategic centres including TV stations. I'll square it with your superiors at this end. God bless you and your men.

With you all the way!
....

General J. Beckbridge
Middle East Tactical Command
C/JTF-KU (Fwd)
Camp Doha
Kuwait

Dear General,

I just wanted to say how much I appreciate all that the armed forces do to protect freedom around the globe. You do a great job and are well worth my tax money. I have a mission for you. I'm guessing the Iranians are hiding some nukes in the Khuzestan region. The element of surprise is on our side. Orders are to invade it immediately with a blitzkrieg pincer movement from Iraq and Qatar, with 42 Commando spearheading the operation and the 1st Armoured Division bringing up the rear. Start asap.

Carpe diem and all that,
....

Private D. Fordham
3rd Battalion
7th Armoured Brigade
Basra
Iraq

Dear Private,

Your country misses you and is appreciative of your dedication and commitment to protecting us and preserving our hard-won freedoms. Keep up the good work, soldier! Now, may I be so bold as to offer you some free advice? From what I can tell on the news, the city of Kerbala looks relatively undefended at the moment. If you crept up through the eastern suburbs in the dead of night with a few other sound chaps from your platoon, I bet you could bag yourself some "insurgents".

A grateful citizen,
....

Sgt. Myers
25th Infantry Division
Camp Anaconda
Uruzgan
Afghanistan

Dear Sergeant,

Your efforts abroad help us all. Please know that we support all that you do to protect millions of people. As you've probably been informed, the Taliban are regrouping in the Waziristan region. My research indicates that if you and your unit hit them hard with 81mm mortar fire tonight at 23.00, you stand a good chance of smashing them to smithereens! Coordinates are: N31° 30' 49.10 " E65° 51' 39.80 ". Let me know how it goes. Good luck!

A citizen-soldier,
....

Discreetly give the finger to people all day today

19

What's in my eye?!

Just chilling out…

Hmmm… I wonder…

Everything's in order, officer

Sure, take the last seat!

Rich pickings…

Is there something in my teeth?

DIARY NEWS

I like to stay informed

Business is business

Day 5

TODAY, SUBVERT CONSUMER SOCIETY FROM WITHIN

Visit luxury stores, pretend to examine their goods and use the opportunity to hide these messages inside for the eventual buyers to discover.

GUCCI

This bag will never make up for your loveless childhood.

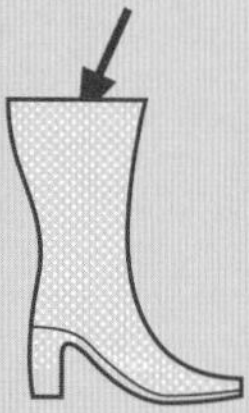

With this boot, you are crushing the poor.

DOLCE

Has this purchase made you feel better about yourself?

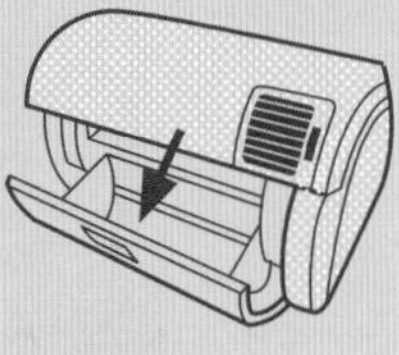

Congratulations for buying a car. Well done you!

This vase is expensive yet empty – same as you?

Have you read much Marx lately, you capitalist swine?

Imagine how many families you could feed for the price of this item.

Opium
FOR HER

Happy? I didn't think so...

Today, try food that scares you

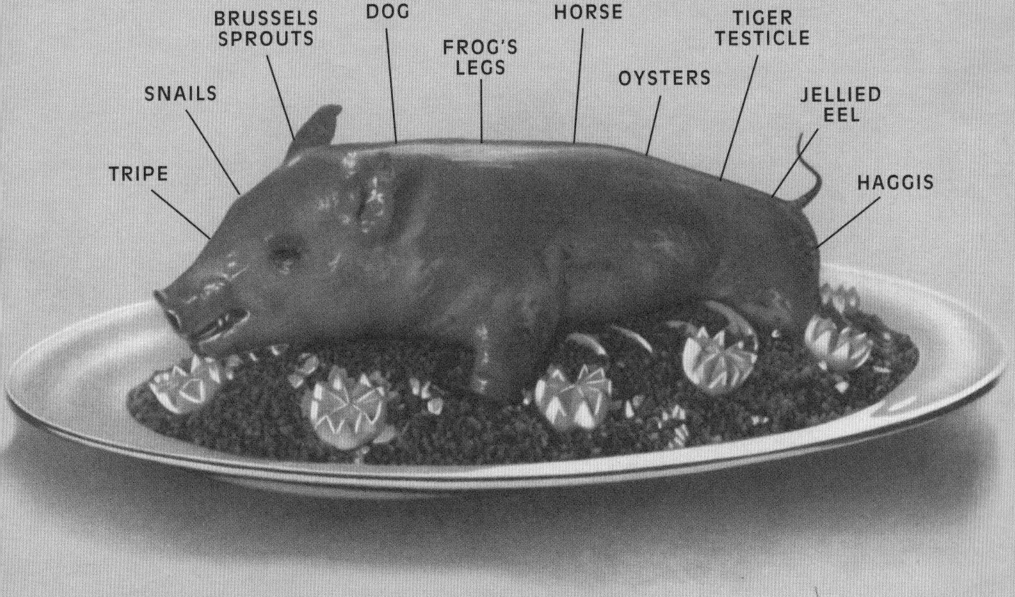
BRUSSELS SPROUTS
DOG
FROG'S LEGS
HORSE
TIGER TESTICLE
OYSTERS
SNAILS
JELLIED EEL
TRIPE
HAGGIS

TODAY, LET BENRIK STAMP YOUR PASSPORT

To induct you symbolically into the Benrik community, we require that you send us your passport, so that we may stamp it with the Benrik logo. This will confirm your commitment to the life-changing programme, and make you truly "one of us". From hereon in, there is no turning back...

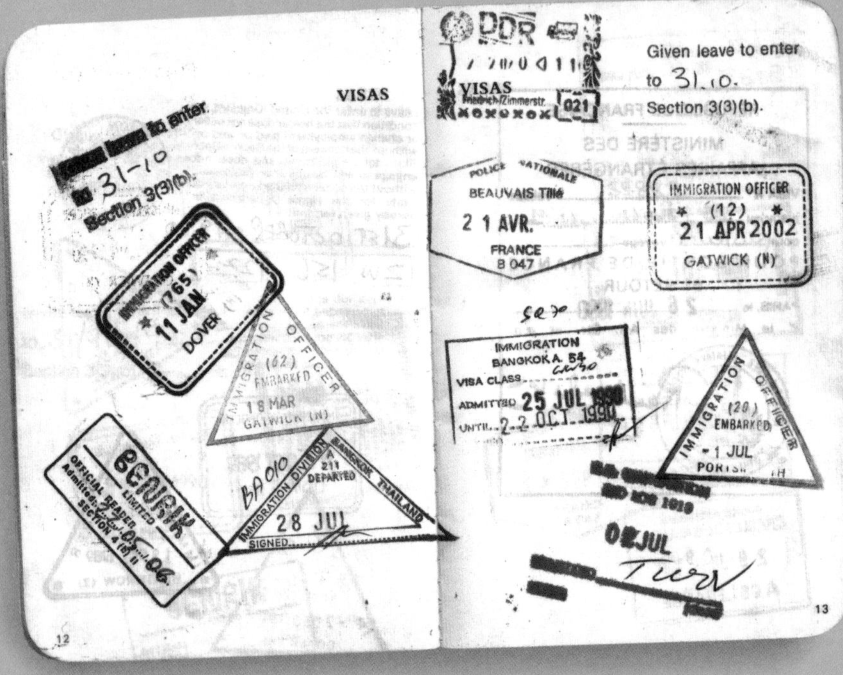
VISAS
Section 3(3)(b).
IMMIGRATION OFFICER
(765)
11 JAN
DOVER
IMMIGRATION OFFICER
(62)
EMBARKED
18 MAR
GATWICK (N)
BENRIK
LIMITED
OFFICIAL READER
IMMIGRATION DIVISION
BANGKOK THAILAND
211
DEPARTED
28 JUL
SIGNED
12
DDR
VISAS
Given leave to enter
to 31.10.
Section 3(3)(b).
POLICE NATIONALE
BEAUVAIS Tillé
21 AVR.
FRANCE
B 047
IMMIGRATION OFFICER
(12)
21 APR 2002
GATWICK (N)
IMMIGRATION
BANGKOK A. 54
VISA CLASS
ADMITTED 25 JUL 1990
UNTIL 22 OCT 1990
IMMIGRATION OFFICER
(20)
EMBARKED
1 JUL
13

Attach this application form to your passport

Dear Benrik,
Please stamp my passport (enclosed) as proof of my membership.
I have read the terms and conditions below and agree to them.
Name:..
Date:..
Signature:..

Send your passport by registered post to: Benrik, c/o United Agents, 12–26 Lexington St, London W1F 0LE, UK. Enclose a special delivery or recorded self-addressed envelope for the return of your passport. Benrik are not responsible for any passports lost in the post. Please allow 28 days for the return of your stamped passport. By sending in your passport, you confirm that you understand that a passport is an official document, and that carrying a defaced passport may constitute an offence in some countries. Benrik are not responsible for any difficulties occasioned by the Benrik stamp, including but not limited to: refusal of entry to any country including your own; confiscation of passport and consequences thereof; missed flights, connections, or disrupted travel arrangements of any kind; arrest or any form of detention, prosecution and/or conviction; loss of citizenship, visa, refugee or asylum status.

Everyone can emulate Rembrandt these days and produce a self-portrait that reveals their inner self. How do you see yourself? Today, take the best portrait of yourself you can manage. Take as many shots as you need to, and post the most revealing one on benrik.co.uk for the world to discover the true you.

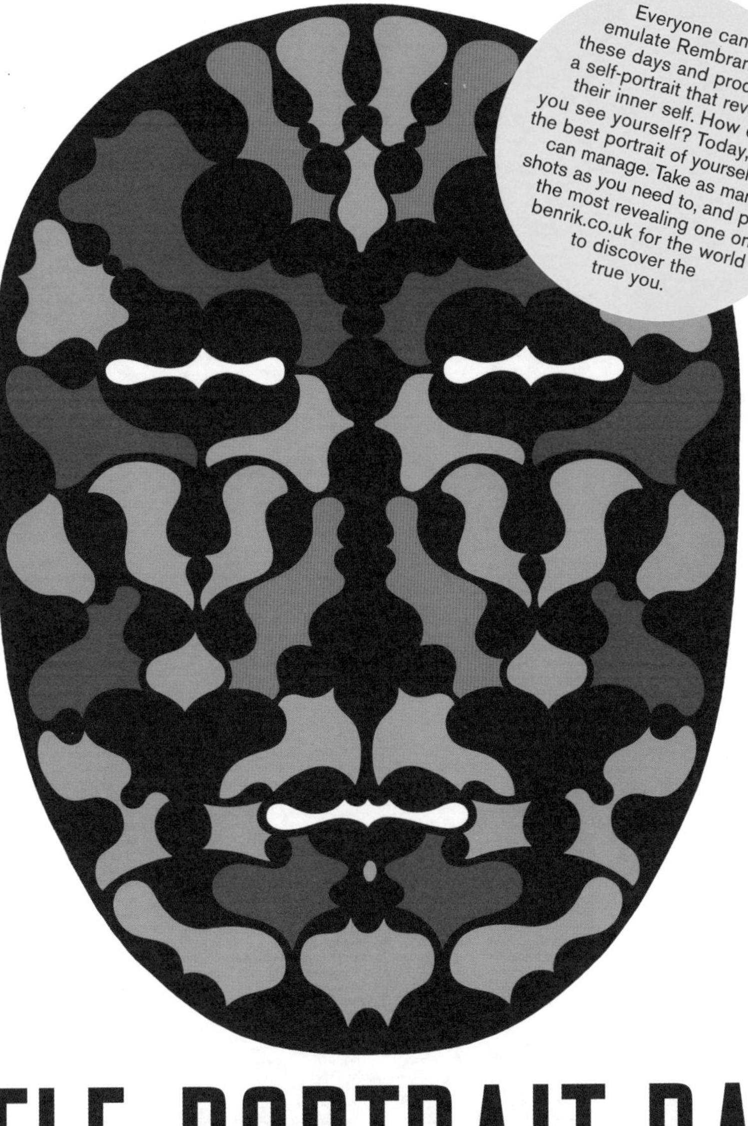

SELF-PORTRAIT DAY

Day 9

THINGS YOU WILL NEVER DO BEFORE YOU DIE

Tick the boxes to come to terms with the fact that you will never:

- Read Proust ☐
- Climb Everest ☐
- Swim with dolphins ☐
- Learn Italian ☐
- Visit Bhutan ☐
- Write that novel/screenplay ☐
- Become world chess champion ☐
- Rob a bank ☐
- Run away ☐
- Have a sex change ☐
- Become a queen ☐
- Become a king ☐
- Wear coloured lenses ☐
- Donate your liver ☐
- Compromise ☐
- Become a millionaire ☐
- Go to heaven ☐
- Parachute ☐
- Walk to the North Pole ☐
- Learn Russian ☐
- Live off charity ☐
- Contract an STD ☐
- Swallow a coin ☐
- Spend a night in prison ☐
- Start a revolution ☐
- Pretend everything is all right ☐
- Follow this Book rigorously ☐
- Learn how to drive ☐
- Hurt a friend ☐
- Celebrate Xmas in May ☐
- Call your father "Pa" ☐
- Call your mother "Ma" ☐
- Learn the Periodic Table by heart ☐
- Go to a drive-in cinema ☐
- Become an artist ☐
- Collect stamps ☐
- Work in a coal mine ☐
- Be late for a date ☐
- Watch all of Bergman ☐
- Follow Mao's teachings ☐
- Bite the dust ☐
- Kiss a stranger ☐
- Move to Japan ☐
- Visit space ☐
- Invent a cookie ☐
- Become grumpy when old ☐
- Wear a rucksack ☐
- Ride a camel ☐
- Use a semicolon ☐
- Inject heroin ☐
- Wear loafers ☐
- Speak in tongues ☐
- Become a fanatic ☐
- Dress like a hip-hopper ☐
- Faint with love ☐
- Save the world ☐
- Become insensitive to suffering ☐
- Be gay ☐
- Be heterosexual ☐
- Start a cult ☐
- Stand and speak up for your rights ☐
- Talk to strangers ☐
- Start a fire ☐
- Drink yourself silly in New Zealand ☐
- Order tap water ☐
- Grow a beard ☐
- Master the yo-yo ☐
- Become a fitness instructor ☐
- Be on TV ☐
- Laugh at a bad joke ☐
- Feel like Batman ☐
- Apply for a patent ☐
- Become a rock star ☐
- Fall for advertising ☐
- Live for a year on a desert island ☐
- Stop worrying ☐
- Use the term "solutionize" ☐
- Confess to a priest ☐
- Confess to a whore ☐
- Eat leaves from a tree ☐
- Graffiti a highway bridge ☐
- Be drunk during office hours ☐
- Own an owl ☐
- Contemplate suicide ☐
- Ride a Harley ☐
- Take NO for an answer ☐
- Say a prayer ☐
- Gamble your shirt ☐
- Break a promise ☐
- Learn to fly ☐
- Get a tattoo ☐
- Learn to live with gnats ☐
- Go on a field trip ☐
- Take part in a brainstorming ☐
- Invade a small country ☐
- Be the fifth wheel ☐
- Ride a donkey ☐
- Demand a ransom ☐
- Proclaim yourself emperor ☐
- Disinherit your heirs ☐
- Say NO when you mean YES ☐
- Adopt a Romanian ☐
- Seduce the prom queen ☐
- Paint someone in tar and feathers ☐
- Run for your life ☐
- Witness a miracle ☐
- Light a fart ☐
- Shave off your pubic hair ☐
- Smoke a cat ☐
- Make the front page ☐
- Cross-dress ☐
- Win the Nobel Peace Prize ☐
- Make love in front of a stranger ☐
- Volunteer for a dangerous mission ☐
- Overdose ☐
- Give birth to a goatboy ☐
- Win the rat race ☐
- Make like a tree ☐
- Overthrow a regime ☐
- Bake a soufflé ☐
- Organize an orgy ☐
- Understand Hitler ☐
- Race at Monaco ☐
- Live within your means ☐
- Marry someone you've just met ☐
- Marry someone you've never met ☐
- Star in a Hollywood blockbuster ☐
- Shovel manure ☐
- Discover the lost city of Atlantis ☐
- Dream in black and white ☐
- See your face on a banknote ☐
- Be eaten by cannibals ☐
- Own a grotto ☐
- Solve a crime ☐
- Host a game show ☐
- Sue the government ☐
- Win the lottery ☐
- Sleep with your best friend's partner ☐
- Start your own religion ☐
- Experience an earthquake ☐
- Meet Santa ☐
- Shoot the last buffalo ☐
- Bump'n'grind ☐
- Hibernate ☐
- Burn your bra (women) ☐
- Burn your jockstrap (men) ☐
- Find a guru ☐
- Turn 117 years old ☐
- Update the Kama Sutra ☐
- Marry a prince or princess ☐
- Settle in Pittsburgh ☐
- Run with the wolves ☐
- Become pope ☐
- Inherit the crown jewels ☐
- Be used as a manga character ☐
- Grow a tail ☐
- Crash a helicopter in the jungle ☐
- Take a vow of silence ☐
- Take a vow of chastity ☐
- Jump bail ☐
- Move someone to tears ☐
- Fake a multiple orgasm ☐
- Become employee of the month ☐
- Go live with a hermit ☐
- Greet the extraterrestrial delegation ☐
- Become a Muslim ☐
- Become a Buddhist ☐
- Become a Christian ☐
- Tie the perfect shoelace knot ☐
- Eradicate hepatitis C ☐
- Kiss your own lips ☐
- Shoot the pianist ☐
- Ride off into the sunset ☐
- Invent a typeface ☐
- Reject society ☐
- Beat Bjorn Borg at tennis ☐
- Fulfill your true potential ☐
- Be in the eye of the storm ☐
- Break the bank in Vegas ☐
- Have a park bench named after you ☐
- Risk your life ☐
- Refuse a new technology ☐
- Meet your great-great-grandchildren ☐
- Suffer a fool gladly ☐
- Sway a jury ☐
- Sweep a chimney ☐
- Fight the power ☐
- Be the 78th person on the moon ☐
- Collect coins ☐
- Be called upon by your president ☐
- Win best-looking baby of the year ☐
- Smoke a Cuban cigar ☐
- Think up a new swear word ☐
- Fight a duel ☐
- Jump the gun ☐
- Escape your past ☐
- Suck on 12 lollipops at once ☐
- Have your own brand of olive oil ☐
- Become immortal ☐
- Learn pole dancing ☐
- Play the lead in Swan Lake ☐
- Master the remote control ☐
- Catch that bird that pooped on you ☐
- Loop the loop ☐
- Make a pact with the devil ☐
- Wish upon a star ☐
- Tell your deepest secret ☐
- Witness the mating of flamingos ☐
- Feel ugly ☐
- Feel pretty ☐
- Confess under duress ☐
- Walk down the yellow brick road ☐
- Travel at warp speed ☐
- Stab someone in the back ☐
- Implode ☐
- Swim in Lake Titicaca ☐
- Jump on a real bandwagon ☐
- Run an arms dealership ☐
- Shit in the woods ☐
- Exterminate a zombie ☐
- Sniff superglue ☐
- Whistle while you work ☐
- Become a superhero ☐
- Memorize an encyclopaedia ☐
- Floss twice a day ☐
- Go on a rampage ☐
- Make your bank manager beg ☐
- Lick an electric eel ☐
- Broker a ceasefire ☐
- Conduct an orchestra ☐
- Jump ship ☐
- Make a leap of faith ☐
- Get drunk on meths ☐
- Sacrifice a goat ☐
- Live to tell the tale ☐
- Inaugurate a building ☐
- Forgive and forget ☐
- Sleep with a whore of Babylon ☐
- Reach Nirvana ☐
- Find out what it's all about ☐
- Crush grapes with your bare feet ☐
- Ride a yak ☐
- Sup with Satan ☐
- Bite the hand that feeds you ☐
- Track down Lord Lucan ☐
- Cause an intergalactic rift ☐
- Get away with murder ☐
- Travel back in time ☐
- Apologize for existing ☐
- Think the unthinkable ☐
- Appease a dictator ☐
- Lose your mojo ☐
- Face a firing squad ☐
- Become an object of worship ☐
- Gate crash the White House ☐
- Burn a banknote ☐
- Have the Midas touch ☐
- Trigger an avalanche ☐
- Cure the common cold ☐
- Own an oil field ☐
- Save the whale ☐
- Discover a new continent ☐
- Serenade a lover ☐
- Come out of a black hole alive ☐
- Precipitate the decline of the West ☐
- Jump for joy ☐
- Suck your little toe in public ☐
- Mate with another species ☐
- Become possessed ☐
- Surpass Einstein ☐
- Understand Einstein ☐
- Look like Einstein ☐
- Predict an eclipse ☐
- Participate in the Olympics ☐
- Catch a shark ☐
- Meet your maker ☐
- Commit arson ☐
- Wear a cape ☐
- Talk dirty to a flower ☐
- Spot the Invisible Man ☐
- Head a posse ☐
- Undergo emergency liposuction ☐
- Do the Rubik's Cube ☐
- Blame God for everything ☐
- Acquire a hard-ass nickname ☐
- Betray your country ☐
- Regain your virginity ☐
- Change astrological signs ☐
- Bring back Bambi ☐
- Write in cuneiform ☐
- Get fired for being truculent ☐
- Become like your father ☐
- Become like your mother ☐
- Join the French Foreign Legion ☐
- Achieve perfection ☐
- Spell "egg" differently ☐
- Win top prize for your verruca ☐
- Beg in the street ☐
- Channel lava away from a village ☐
- Grow a third nipple ☐
- Spend all your salary on payday ☐
- Witness the Big Bang ☐
- Gerrymander ☐
- Generate controversy ☐
- Meet a bolshevik ☐
- Ooze charm ☐
- Moult ☐
- Have too much of a good thing ☐
- Die of hard work ☐
- Run amok ☐
- Discover your ancestor is Napoleon ☐
- Make it to the top ☐
- Successfully crash-land a jumbo jet ☐
- Fiddle while Rome burns ☐
- Design the perfect crouton ☐
- Run out of tears ☐
- Howl at the full moon ☐
- Win an Oscar ☐
- Unbreak a taboo ☐
- Give rise to a cause célèbre ☐
- Part the Red Sea ☐
- Have sex with your clone ☐
- Know the truth about JFK ☐
- Wave a red rag to a bull ☐
- Get high on life ☐
- Find your self ☐
- Rule the world ☐
- Other ☐

TODAY DO A RUNNER

READY,
STEADY...

RUNNER ETIQUETTE:

1) Wait until the coffee course, particularly if there is a set menu.
2) Do not leave your date behind, unless you are sure it is the last time you wish to see them.
3) Do not start actually "running" until you are outside the restaurant.
4) Do not select the heaviest items on the menu. Running on a bouillabaisse is medically inadvisable.
5) Beginners and the shy:
   Do a practice "runner" before ordering any food.

TODAY: Insult an alien

All radio waves are beamed up into space at the speed of light, and can travel millions of miles towards faraway galaxies. So, even an amateur CB radio can be used to communicate with other worlds. Today, check it's working by radioing up an appropriate insult. When the alien arrives, tell him or her you were just testing.

Planet Mars

Distance from Earth: *78,000,000km.*
Likely alien life form: *Martians.*
Appropriate insult: *Your mother is a Venusian whore.*

Kuiper Belt

Distance from Earth: *6,000,000,000km.*
Likely alien life form: *Microbial spores.*
Appropriate insult: *N/A (non-intelligent life).*

Alpha Centauri

Distance from Earth: *4.3 light years.*
Likely alien life form: *Ozone-breathing octopi.*
Appropriate insult: *God you're ugly, even by alien standards.*

Andromeda

Distance from Earth: *2.3 million light years.*
Likely alien life form: *Wise, peace-loving, oil-mining humanoids.*
Appropriate insult: *Hey hippies, as soon as we humans master warp drive space travel technology, you're toast.*

Galaxy M33

Distance from Earth: *3 million light years.*
Likely alien life form: *the dinosaurs, who fled the Earth in their spaceship just before the meteorite shower.*
Appropriate insult: *It's our planet now suckers.*

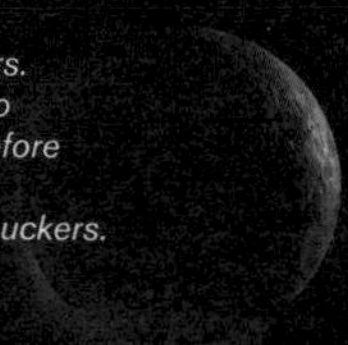

Zorg Empire

Distance from Earth: *9.1 million light years.*
Likely alien life form: *Zorgoids, three-headed flesh-hungry beasts, predators of the seven known universes.*
Appropriate insult: *Come and get some, you warlike aliens who have mastered warp drive space travel technology!*

Cosmic horizon

Distance from Earth: *1.3 billion light years.*
Likely alien life form: *God knows.*
Appropriate insult: *Wouldn't risk it on this one.*

Recruit a celebrity to the Benrik cult today:

Tom Cruise has done wonders for Scientology, advocating it in public and helping it reach a younger, trendier audience. Benrik too require a celebrity to join their "extreme life-changing" cause and boost their profile. Today, every reader must try and convert a celebrity to Benrik, by filling in the form below, bookmarking it, and sending this Book to a famous person of their choice. Anyone who gets a genuine reply will feature in Benrik's Hall Of Fame (unless the reply takes legal form).

To the celebrity receiving this book: to promote the "extreme life-change" cause, please hold the book in the following way as you enter or leave celebrity parties.

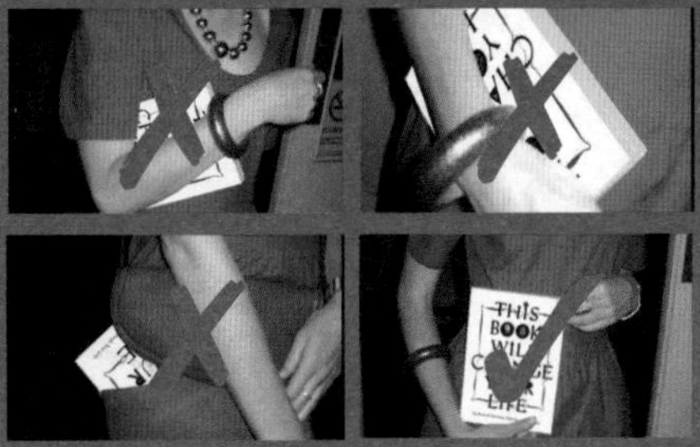

Dear [Celebrity name]

I have long admired your work, and in particular

[Relevant work detail e.g. film part, hit song, lengthy novel]

which just blew me away on so many levels, like

[Name one level on which you were especially blown away]

I'm no one in particular, just a [Job title] from [Location]

But I thought I'd send you this book. It's none of my business really, but I read in the press recently that you had problems because of

[Give details of recent tabloid story concerning the celebrity]

They obviously make all this up, but still, it sounds like you could use a radical life-change. Follow this book's instructions every day and you'll get much more positive publicity let me assure you! Anyway, I don't want to bother you any longer, as I have my own problems

[Name a few of your problems]

I urge you to visit www.benrik.co.uk and join us for your own sake. Good luck.

[Sign here]

P.S. Call me on [Your mobile phone number] if you need to discuss.

TODAY, PRETEND TO BE A SECRET AGENT

No one can know. This Book was a pretext to get in touch with you. Your government needs you. Don't look up now, they are watching. Meet at 1300 today outside work. Wave at the grey car. It will pick you up and take you to the secret rendezvous. Good luck. *P.S. Tear this page out and swallow it.*

SENSE-LESS DAY

Go through today without using your sense of: *sight*

HOW TO: VERY DARK GLASSES AND WHITE CANE.

True story: There is an extraordinary study by Marius Von Senden, called "Space and Sight." In it he examines the experiences of those born blind whose sight has recently been restored by cataract surgery. For them, vision is a radical new experience. They see the world as a field of colours. One girl was so moved by its dazzling brilliance that she kept her eyes shut for two weeks, only opening them briefly now and again, to repeat "Oh God! How beautiful." Alas, she found it impossible to understand space, and kept bumping into these colours. She was only ever happy with her eyes closed, pretending to be blind again.

Today, ask your loved ones to list your bad points

On Benrik's journey to change your life, you must undergo self-criticism and establish just what was wrong with your old one. Ask your nearest and dearest to write down what they don't like about you so that you may attempt to rectify the problem. To help motivate you, they are to renounce you at the end of the year if you haven't changed.

(EXAMPLE: "YOU DROOL IN YOUR SLEEP, ALL OVER MY PILLOW")

Partner:

What I don't like about you, my spouse/lover: ....

....

I hereby promise to ditch you by the end of the year if this hasn't changed.

SIGNATURE: ....

(EXAMPLE: "YOU IGNORE MY ADVICE TO SETTLE DOWN")

Parent:

What I don't like about you, my child: ....

....

I hereby promise to disinherit you by the end of the year if this hasn't changed.

SIGNATURE: ....

(EXAMPLE: "YOU KEEP BURDENING ME WITH UNREASONABLE EXPECTATIONS")

Child:

What I don't like about you, my parent: ....

....

I hereby promise to run away by the end of the year if this hasn't changed.

SIGNATURE: ....

(EXAMPLE: "YOU TALK ABOUT YOURSELF TOO MUCH, AND IT'S NOT THAT INTERESTING EITHER")

Friend:

What I don't like about you, my friend: ....

....

I hereby promise to drop you by the end of the year if this hasn't changed.

SIGNATURE: ....

(EXAMPLE: "YOU'RE INCOMPETENT")

Boss:

What I don't like about you, my employee: ....

....

I hereby promise to fire you by the end of the year if this hasn't changed.

SIGNATURE: ....

POLICE

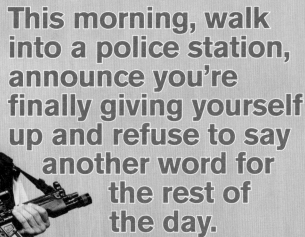

This morning, walk into a police station, announce you're finally giving yourself up and refuse to say another word for the rest of the day.

Know your rights!

You may be giving yourself up, but that doesn't mean you're giving up your basic rights. Make sure the police follow due process, and if not, complain about it to the Independent Police Complaints Commission on 08453 002 002.

ARREST: An arrest is only lawful if you are told that you are under arrest and are given the grounds for your arrest at the time or as soon as possible afterwards. Once in custody, you are entitled to a clean cell with adequate heating, lighting and bedding, as well as access to toilet facilities.

DETENTION: The police must determine as soon as practicable whether there is enough evidence to charge you. They may only detain you for up to 36 hours without charge, unless you are lucky enough to be detained under recent anti-terrorist legislation, in which case it's 28 days.

SEARCH: If you refuse to identify yourself, a police officer of the same sex may search you for any clues. Strip searches are only allowed if the custody officer considers it to be strictly necessary, or if you specifically request one.

LEGAL ADVICE: Upon your arrest, you should be informed of your statutory right to consult a solicitor free of charge and in private. You can always exercise this right without actually speaking to the solicitor when they turn up of course.

RIGHT TO SILENCE: You have the right to silence. In the UK, however, it has been curtailed in recent years. Before, you were allowed to stay silent although anything you said could be held against you. Now, saying nothing may actually harm your defence.

USE OF FORCE: The police are allowed to use reasonable force where you refuse to consent to certain procedures, including fingerprinting and "non-intimate samples". However they may not use force to obtain "intimate samples", such as blood, semen or any tissue taken from an orifice other than the mouth.

USE OF TORTURE: The police are not really allowed to torture you, unless you are following today's task in a dictatorial regime, which we do not recommend even in the name of extreme life-change.

RELEASE: The police may attempt to release you before the full day is up. They may for instance be tempted to deny there is enough evidence to suspect you of an actual offence. Foil their plan by rolling your eyes, dribbling, and making violent stabbing gestures. This should renew their interest.

Keep the Book on your person at all times during arrest, and remember: whatever the police say, they are not legally allowed to separate you from it!

Today, stick a message on a banknote

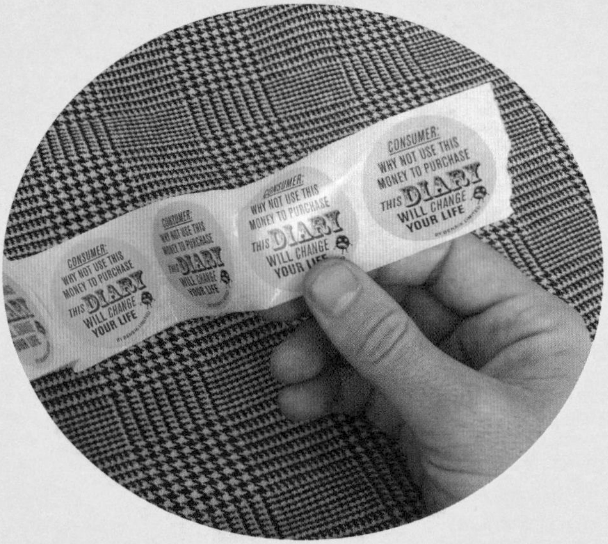
CONSUMER:
WHY NOT USE THIS
MONEY TO PURCHASE
THIS DIARY
WILL CHANGE
YOUR LIFE

Banknotes are the ultimate media, circulating between millions every day free of charge. Benrik believe that their use for communication purposes would reinforce the social tissue and make the spending experience a lot more "fun".

Possible messages to write:
- **Darling don't forget the milk**
- **Mistress Eva 07890 61647**
- **Mickey ♥ Tracy**
- **Save the blue-crested grebe!**
- **Sorry about the herpes everyone**

Caution: The Bank Of England are not yet fully convinced by our plan. This is their current position: "We strongly discourage people from taking any action which will, even to a very limited extent, shorten the life of our banknotes. Clearly sticking labels to banknotes is likely to do this. As for making the notes "more fun" that is not the purpose of a banknote. You may also find yourself prosecuted if the portrait of the Queen is defaced in any way. May I suggest that you find another way to advertise your publication." Public Enquiries Group, Bank Of England

Sabotage Hollywood Day

Go to movies and shout out the ending to help people realize how predictable most big studio productions are. Examples:

Apollo 13
"They don't make the moon, but return safely."

Basic Instinct
"Sharon Stone did it!"

Casablanca
"Ilsa leaves Casablanca without Rick."

Deep Impact
"The shuttle crew blow themselves up with the comet and save us."

E.T.
"The other aliens rescue him."

Forrest Gump
"Forrest's Mum and Jenny die, but leave Forrest with a baby."

Gladiator
"Russell Crowe kills the emperor but dies."

Halloween
"They think they've killed him, but they haven't!"

Independence Day
"They disable the alien shield and nuke them all."

Jaws
"Schneider blows the shark up and swims home."

Karate Kid
"Daniel wins."

Lock Stock And Two Smoking Barrels
"Big Chris takes the money, they nearly throw away the priceless guns."

Mission Impossible
"Everything has been set up by Jon Voight."

Notting Hill
"They get married, she gets pregnant."

Ocean's Eleven
"The Swat team are the conmen."

Pearl Harbor
"The Japanese lose the war."

Quiz Show
"The hoax is exposed."

Raiders Of The Lost Ark
"Indy recaptures the Ark for the US government."

Saving Private Ryan
"The old man at the beginning is Ryan."

Thelma And Louise
"They commit suicide by driving off a cliff."

Usual Suspects
"Kevin Spacey has made everything up."

Vanilla Sky
"Too complicated to explain."

When Harry Met Sally
"Meg Ryan and Billy Crystal eventually get together."

XXX
"Vin Diesel triumphs over the bad guys."

You've Got Mail
"Meg Ryan and Tom Hanks eventually get together."

Zulu
"The Zulus recognize the soldiers' bravery and let them survive."

Day 19

Long-lost relative day

Judge which one of your elderly relatives is most likely to have hoarded away a pile of cash and call them up out of the blue to get in their will.

Colonisation
ABROAD
REW
PLEAS
E

True story!

Marcus Grant, 32, was working as a checkout assistant for Walmart in North Canton, Ohio, when his supervisor Russell Streiff called him to the phone. His great-aunt Lana Milova Granovskaia had just died at the age of 105. Lana had been a young painter of great promise just before the revolution, even said to be in line for a portrait of Tsar Nicholas II. Of course, her career ended as quickly as it had begun. Now, the only time Marcus had ever met great-aunt Lana was in 1995 in Moscow, when he had been backpacking around Europe and decided to drop in on her in her humble suburban flat. Then he had charmed the lonely old lady with his naive American ways, and his encyclopaedic knowledge of Cold War-era Bond films. Ironically, she later froze to death in her post-Soviet garret on the very day the new Russian courts accepted her claim to the Granovskaia estate outside Moscow, now worth a hefty $40,000,000. The rest of the Grant (ex-Granovskaia) clan having ignored her, she'd left everything to Marcus. Marcus has now quit Walmart, and is living in San Fernando, California, pending the outcome of the court case with Lana's stepsister Magda, an off-shore tax accountant in Latvia.

Today, search your house for bodies left over from any previous serial-killer occupants

Favourite serial-killer hiding places:

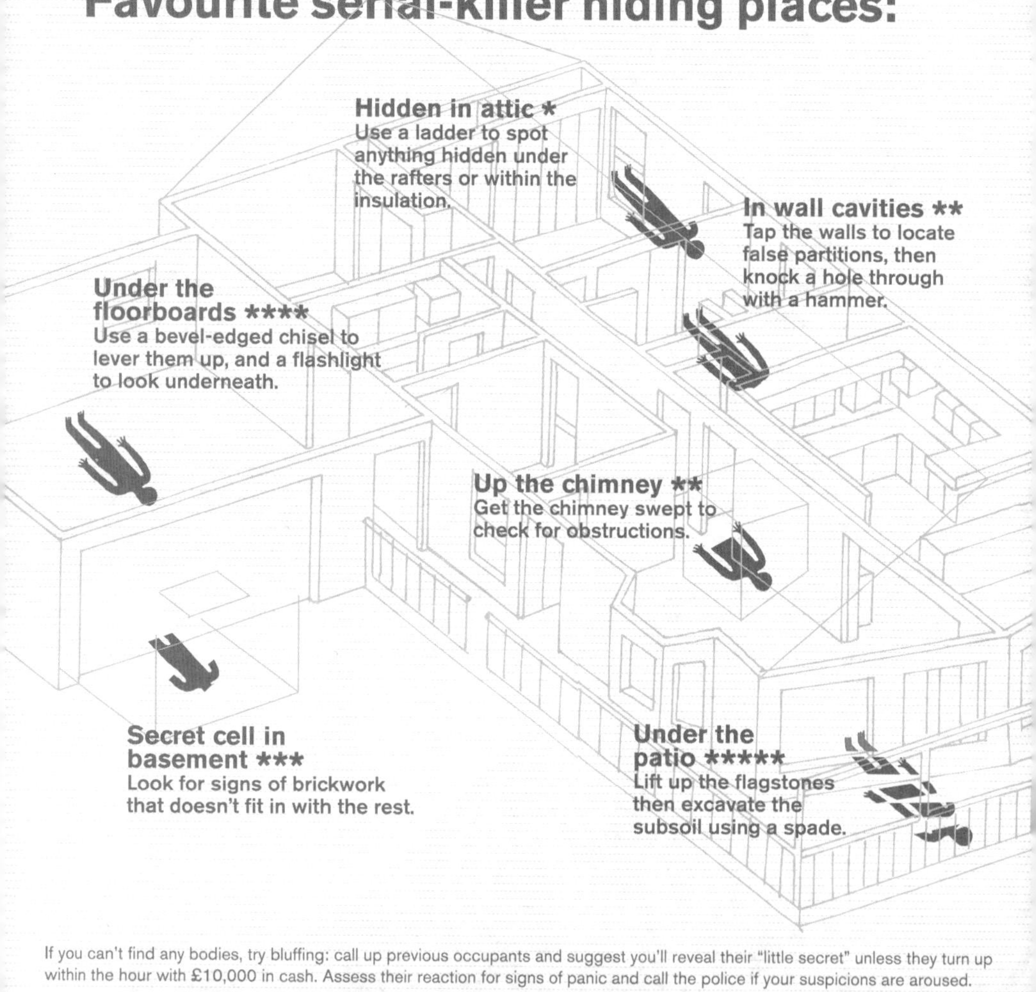
Hidden in attic *
Use a ladder to spot anything hidden under the rafters or within the insulation.
In wall cavities **
Tap the walls to locate false partitions, then knock a hole through with a hammer.
Under the floorboards ******
Use a bevel-edged chisel to lever them up, and a flashlight to look underneath.
Up the chimney **
Get the chimney swept to check for obstructions.
Secret cell in basement ****
Look for signs of brickwork that doesn't fit in with the rest.
Under the patio ********
Lift up the flagstones then excavate the subsoil using a spade.

If you can't find any bodies, try bluffing: call up previous occupants and suggest you'll reveal their "little secret" unless they turn up within the hour with £10,000 in cash. Assess their reaction for signs of panic and call the police if your suspicions are aroused.

TODAY, HELP PUT AN END TO LOUD MOBILE-PHONE CONVERSATIONS

Benrik have taken it upon themselves to combat antisocial mobile-phone calls. If callers don't care for either their privacy or that of others around them, they won't mind if it's violated still further. Readers are therefore asked to record any obnoxiously loud phone calls they may hear onto their own mobiles, and post them online for all to enjoy. The most preposterous ones will be available by podcast, with a prize to anyone who can name and shame their authors.

COVENTRY TO BASILDON 12:33 P.M. TRAIN ON 12 FEBRUARY, COACH 3 "… what it is? It's not that he's shit in bed, it's … he's shit at everything, he's a loser that's what … the other day he dropped Lisa again … I know I know … four … but you can still get brain damage … what happened to him yeah probably yeah that's right … wanker, yeah … can't believe I married him"

CAFÉ AL FRESCO, TUNBRIDGE WELLS, 23 APRIL, 11:12 A.M. "says it's fungal … no, f-u-n-g-a-l, like mushrooms … yeah no I got to see him straight away yeah … yes … I dunno … at the pool?… he had a good poke anyway, apparently it's spread all the way inside … no … well, like red inflamed scabby bits, you know … flaky? no, greasy … did you? … anyway he gave me some cream … can't stop scratching it"

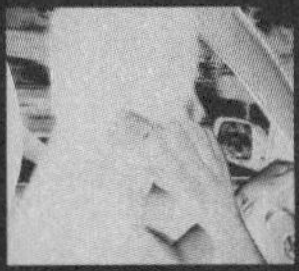

HEATHROW AIRPORT BUSINESS-CLASS LOUNGE, 2 NOVEMBER, 8:34 A.M. "Yes I'd like to book an appointment … What about Thursday next week? … Thursday 6 p.m.? … hmmm … no Wednesday I'm in Brussels … Friday 10 a.m.? 10.30? Ok. What do you charge? £150 … Can I get you down to £100? Come on £140's not a discount … Meet me halfway here … £130, ok … And do you do anal? Good good"

TECHNICAL NOTE: Use the "voice recorder" function of your mobile, or a discreet dictaphone. Even though your victims forfeit their right to confidentiality by shouting down the phone in public, they may not realize this and could object to you recording them.

They give me one week to live.

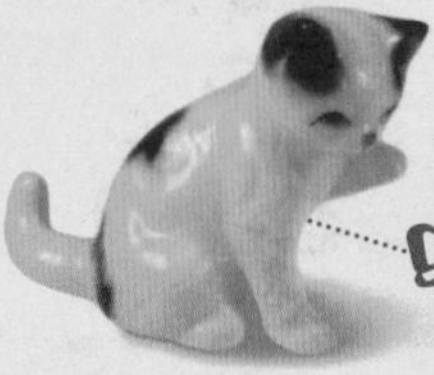

I never got your e-mail.

You don't have a daddy.

The president just got shot!

Be a pathological liar for a day

This porno mag was in your drawer.

He fancies you like crazy, he told me so.

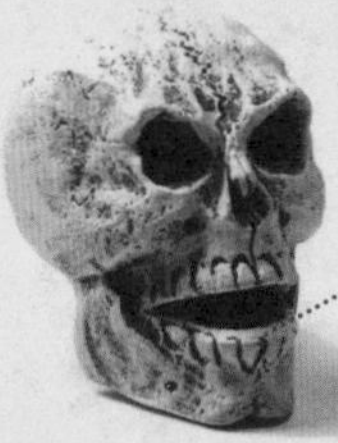

I double-checked your parachute myself.

I gave you that report yesterday!

Of course I'm wearing a condom.

Today lie your ass off about absolutely everything and enjoy a much more stimulating existence.

Choose your final meal on death row and make it

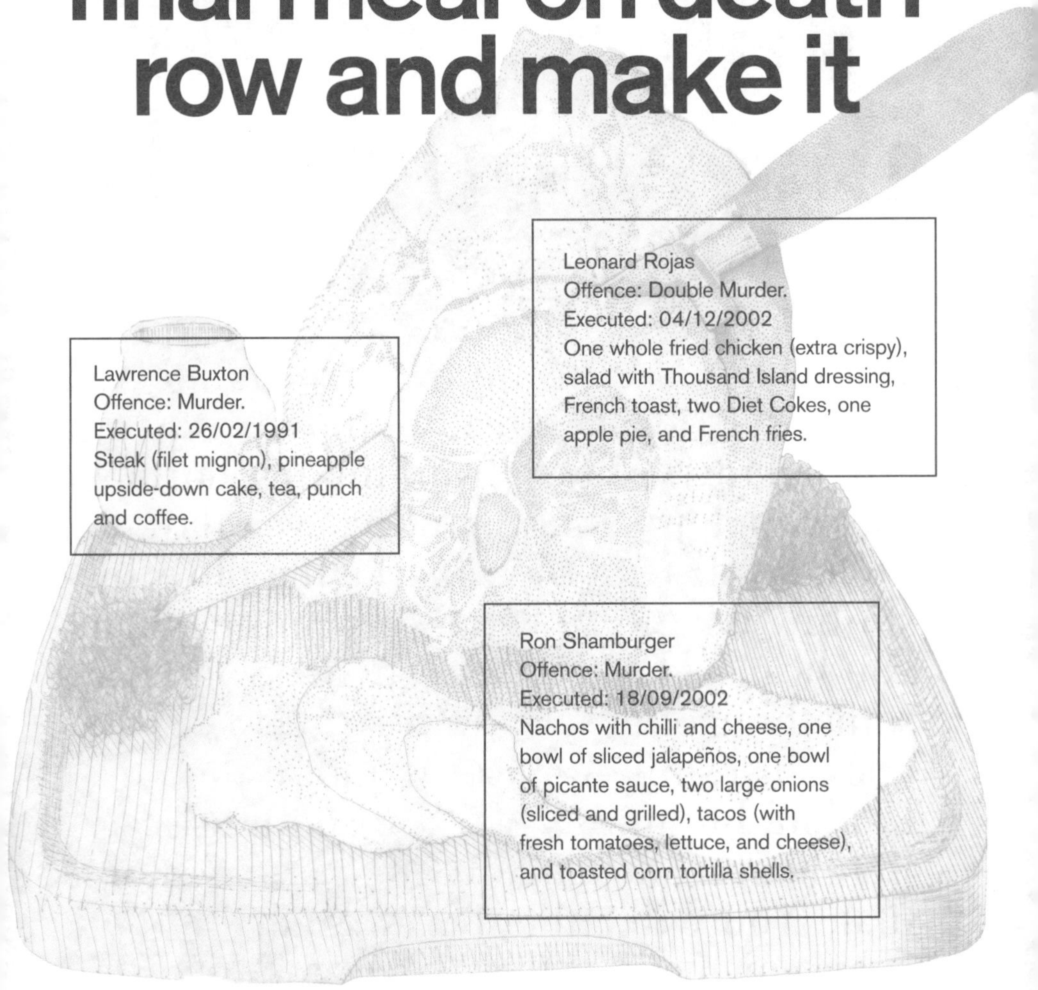

Lawrence Buxton
Offence: Murder.
Executed: 26/02/1991
Steak (filet mignon), pineapple upside-down cake, tea, punch and coffee.

Leonard Rojas
Offence: Double Murder.
Executed: 04/12/2002
One whole fried chicken (extra crispy), salad with Thousand Island dressing, French toast, two Diet Cokes, one apple pie, and French fries.

Ron Shamburger
Offence: Murder.
Executed: 18/09/2002
Nachos with chilli and cheese, one bowl of sliced jalapeños, one bowl of picante sauce, two large onions (sliced and grilled), tacos (with fresh tomatoes, lettuce, and cheese), and toasted corn tortilla shells.

DEATH ROW CANNIBAL DENIED LAST MEAL: Archie Williams, 36, was denied his last meal before his execution in July 2002. Reports from the prison state that Williams had requested that he be served his cellmate, John Peirson. Peirson, who was also on death row awaiting his execution had agreed to let himself be fed to his friend after his death. "They had made some sort of death pact with each other a few weeks before they were set to be executed," stated Kevin Marsh, Warden of the San Angelo Maximum Security Prison. "The state is not in the habit of granting such odd and disgusting requests."

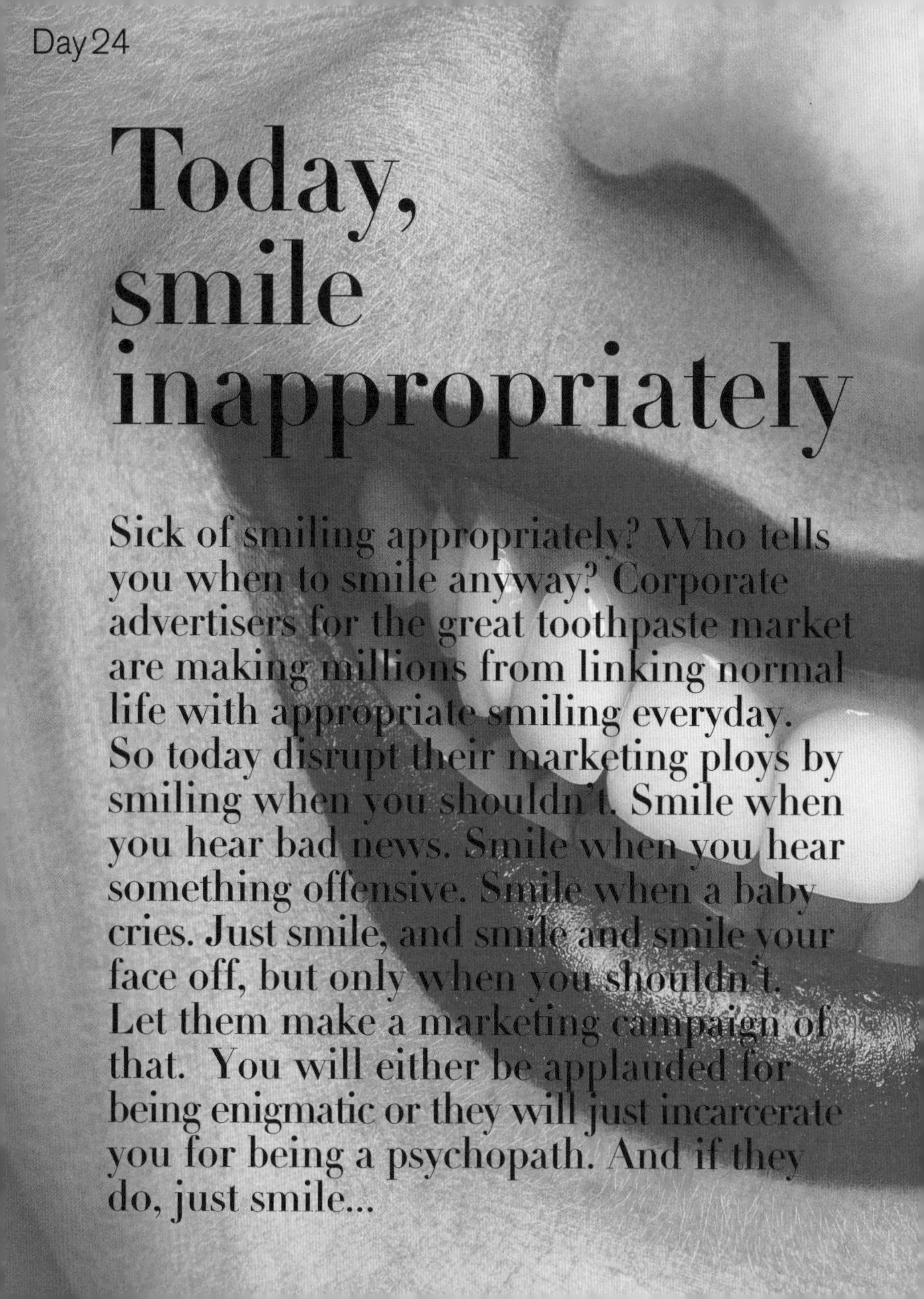

Today, smile inappropriately

Sick of smiling appropriately? Who tells you when to smile anyway? Corporate advertisers for the great toothpaste market are making millions from linking normal life with appropriate smiling everyday. So today disrupt their marketing ploys by smiling when you shouldn't. Smile when you hear bad news. Smile when you hear something offensive. Smile when a baby cries. Just smile, and smile and smile your face off, but only when you shouldn't. Let them make a marketing campaign of that. You will either be applauded for being enigmatic or they will just incarcerate you for being a psychopath. And if they do, just smile...

TODAY JUMP A QUEUE

YES

Tourists are a good bet: they don't know the rules, they won't speak well enough to protest, and in their country it's often the done thing anyway.

NO

Avoid the middle of the queue: people here have queued a long time already and are stressed about whether they'll get in.

NO

Avoid the elderly: they have high moral standards and will enjoy rebuking a young hooligan in public.

BEST

The very front of the queue has been scientifically proven to be the best place to muscle in: people are relaxed as they can see they'll get in, and it's so cheeky they can't believe you're queue jumping anyway.

76

Day 26

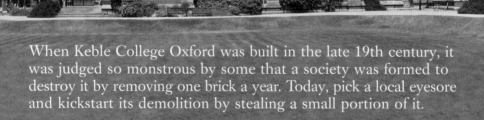

TODAY HELP DESTROY AN UGLY BUILDING

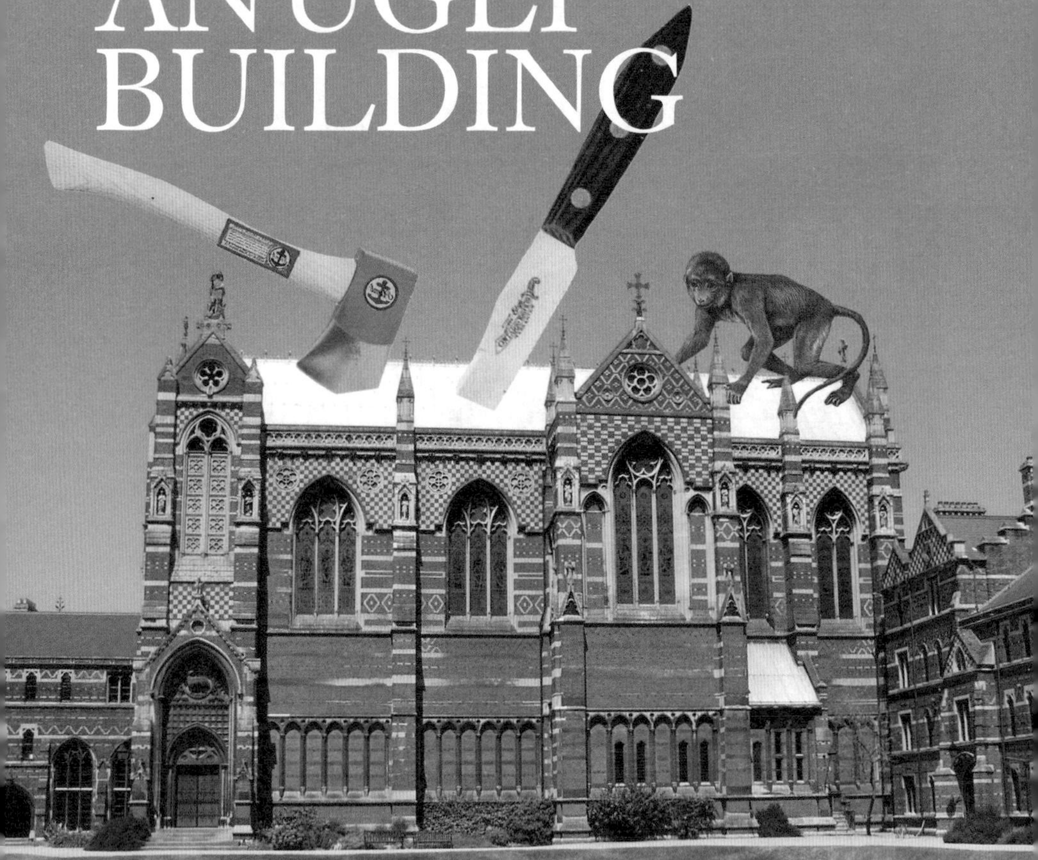

When Keble College Oxford was built in the late 19th century, it was judged so monstrous by some that a society was formed to destroy it by removing one brick a year. Today, pick a local eyesore and kickstart its demolition by stealing a small portion of it.

"It is a truth universally acknowledged, that a single man in possession of a good fortune, must be in want of a wife."
Pride and Prejudice,
Jane Austen

"Hale knew they meant to murder him before he had been in Brighton three hours."
Brighton Rock,
Graham Greene

"I have carefully collected all I could possibly find out about the history of poor Werther and I lay it before you here, knowing that you will thank me for doing so."
The Sorrows of Young Werther,
Johan Wolfgang von Goethe

"And this also, has been one of the dark places of the earth."
Heart of Darkness,
Joseph Conrad

"Mother died today."
L'Etranger,
Albert Camus

"Someone must have been telling lies about Joseph K., for without having done anything wrong he was arrested one fine morning."
The Trial, Franz Kafka

"All happy families resemble each other; each unhappy family is unhappy in its own way."
Anna Karenina, Tolstoy

"...the first thing you'll probably want to know is where I was born, and what my lousy childhood was like, and how my parents were occupied and all before they had me, and all that David Copperfield kind of crap, but I don't feel like going into it."
The Catcher in the Rye,
J.D. Salinger

"Riverrun, past Eve and Adam's, from swerve of shore to bend of bay, brings us by a commodius vicus of recirculation back to Howth Castle and Environs."
Finnegans Wake, James Joyce

"It was a bright cold day in April, and the clocks were striking thirteen."
1984, George Orwell

"LOLITA,
light of my life,
fire of my loins."
Lolita, Vladimir Nabokov

"You don't know about me, without you have read a book by the name of The Adventures of Tom Sawyer, but that ain't no matter."
Huckleberry Finn,
Mark Twain

"You are about to begin reading Italo Calvino's new novel, If on a winter's night a traveller."
If on a winter's night a traveller,
Italo Calvino

"Longtemps je me suis couché de bonne heure."
A la Recherche du Temps Perdu,
Marcel Proust

"In the beginning God created the heavens and the earth."
Old Testament,
Anonymous

"Stately, plump Buck Milligan came from the stairhead, bearing a bowl of lather on which a mirror and a razor lay crossed."
Ulysses,
James Joyce

"The snow in the mountains was melting and Bunny had been dead for several weeks before we came to understand the gravity of our situation."
The Secret History,
Donna Tartt

"The past is a foreign country: they do things differently there."
The Go-Between,
L.P.Hartley

Today write the opening sentence of your début novel:

....

....

TODAY, RETURN ALL YOUR JUNK MAIL

Junk mail clogs up your letter box and forces you to spend hours every month disposing of it. But hey, if you send it back, it has the same effect on the companies who dish it out. Just write return to sender and change the name to B. Smith, Resources & Personnel Dept, and they will spend valuable time trying to work out who or what should be on the receiving end of your correspondence.

Day 29

TODAY, EAT WRONG

Modern health experts keep issuing contradictory advice. One week, wine is good for you. The next, vitamins are out. Today, eat the opposite of whatever you're told to. You'll enjoy yourself more and you may well be proved right in the long-run anyway.

DO EAT: LARD
Contains nutrients essential to brain function, says 2017 report

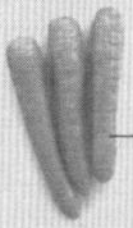

DON'T EAT: CARROTS
Will be linked to cancer of the retina in 2016

DON'T EAT: BROCCOLI
Correlated to urinary tract infections by 2029

DON'T EAT: ORANGES
By 2035, well-established as primary cause of brittle bones

DO DRINK: WINE
"A bottle a day keeps bird flu away" (Government campaign, 2044)

DO EAT: SALT
20g per meal in winter prevents common cold (Nobel Prize for medicine, 2021)

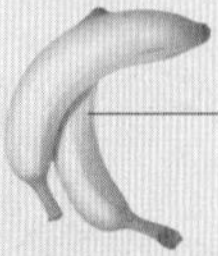

DON'T EAT: BANANAS
May cause fatal blood-pressure drop in zero-gravity conditions (Warning to all colonists, 2061)

DO EAT: PORK SCRATCHINGS
In combination with avocado purée, increase longevity by up to 8 years (The Lancet, 2030)

DON'T EAT: FRUIT & VEGETABLES
"Discredited five-a-day policy responsible for agonizing haemorrhagic deaths of millions" (BBC headline, June 2050)

EVERY-BODY SCREAM TODAY!
At 20:07 Greenwich Mean Time everyone across the world will scream at once. Whether you are in the pub, a movie, a confessional, a funeral, on a date or just sitting at home on your computer, we'll all scream at once and see if we can hear it.

This is an example of one of the many reader-suggested tasks in this Book. The reader in this instance is Joel Moss Levinson, USA. Nice work, Joel.

Groom someone on the net today

Internet grooming is a potent new psychological tool, which has been unfairly misappropriated by paedophiles. You don't have to be a twisted sicko to use it; anyone may groom anyone else for a wide variety of useful tasks, from teaching you a foreign language to polishing your shoes. Follow the basic guidelines below and report your grooming successes today on www.benrik.co.uk.

THE SEVEN STAGES OF GROOMING:

1. *Find a chat room:* There are hundreds of thousands of chat rooms on the internet. Try and find one that corresponds to your particular interest e.g. if you wish to groom someone to trim your hedge, you might try chatting on www.gardenchat.com.

2. *Select a groomee:* Observe the chat before intervening. Is there anyone no one is talking to? Is anyone clearly new to the group and looking for a chatting companion? If their nickname (or *handle*) includes the word 'lonely', you have a groomee.

3. *Introduce yourself:* Take care not to scare your groomee away by declaring your grooming interest prematurely. <Hi>, <Hello>, <Wazzup> are all effective introductions. <Any1 wanna walk my dog round the blck every morning?> is not.

4. *Sympathize with their problems:* Befriend your groomee by encouraging them to share their problems. Are they fed up with their job? Is their partner cheating on them? Are they feeling a little depressed? You may not give a damn, but it creates a useful bond between you.

5. *Share secrets:* Deepen the bond by trusting your groomee with some secrets. This is the critical phase. Start with uncontroversial secrets like <I feel worthless inside> and gradually link them to your interest e.g. <Maybe I'd feel better if my bathroom was retiled>.

6. *Meet up:* After grooming them for a few hours, ask them to meet up; by now, they should trust you. That's no reason to trust them, however, as the internet is full of weirdos. Make sure you tell a friend where you're going, and when you mean to return.

7. *Reap the rewards!:* If you have groomed them properly, your groomee should be primed to do your bidding. Sit back as they follow your orders to tidy up your garage, shampoo your carpet, teach you blackjack, or whatever on earth it is you have groomed them to do.

Today rage against the machine!

Rage against the toaster
You've burnt it again! Raaaaaagggghhh!!!
Rage against the kettle
Boil you fucker, boil!!
Rage against the espresso-maker
I hate you and everything you stand for!!!
Rage against the hair dryer
I wish you'd just die you beast!!
Rage against the scooter
Aaaarggh! I can't stand you scooter!!!
Rage against the elevator
Crash down for all I care you fascist scum!!!
Rage against the microwave
I'm going to destroy you I swear on my mother's head!!!
Rage against the mobile phone
Bastard mobile phone, why won't you ring???!!!

Become spokesperson for your neighbourhood today!

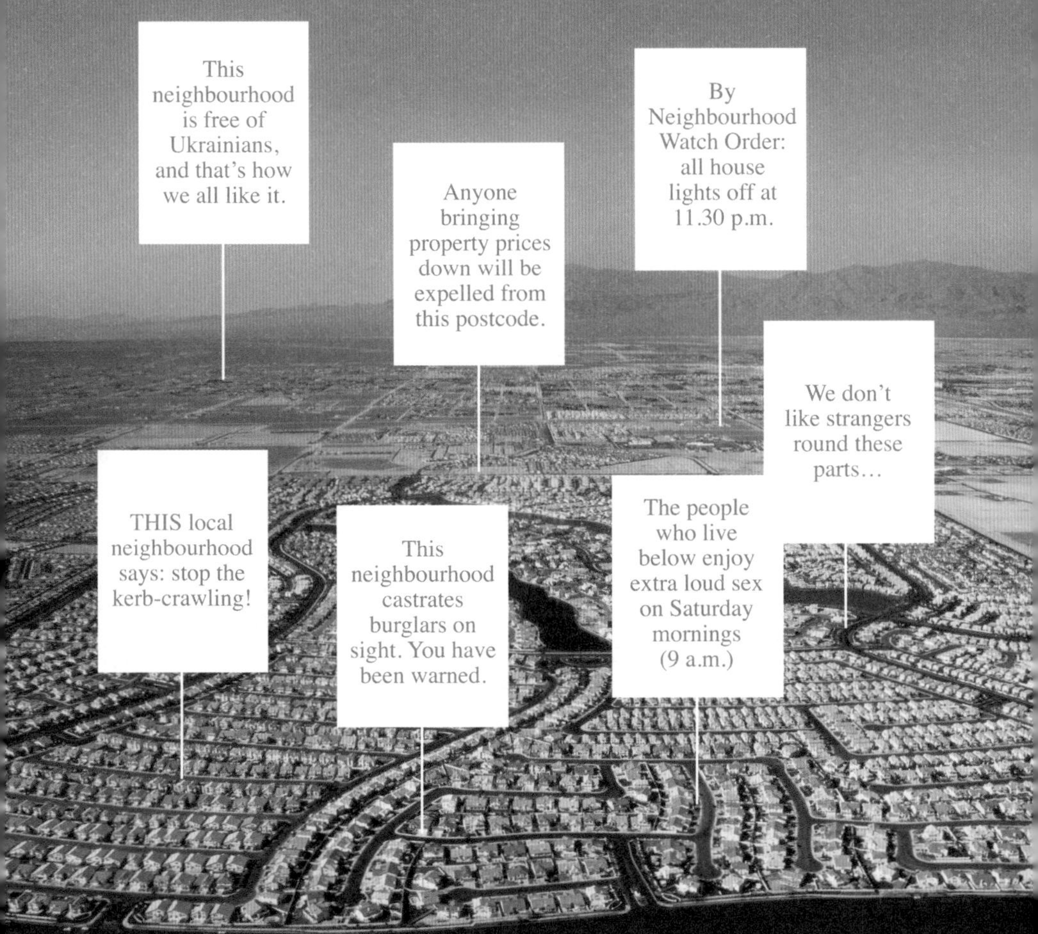
This neighbourhood is free of Ukrainians, and that's how we all like it.
Anyone bringing property prices down will be expelled from this postcode.
By Neighbourhood Watch Order: all house lights off at 11.30 p.m.
We don't like strangers round these parts…
THIS local neighbourhood says: stop the kerb-crawling!
This neighbourhood castrates burglars on sight. You have been warned.
The people who live below enjoy extra loud sex on Saturday mornings (9 a.m.)

A strong and united local community can help defeat crime, littering, loneliness and other modern social vices. Bring your neighbourhood together today: stick a sign in your front window that speaks up on its behalf.

Today gatecrash a funeral

The loss of one person is a loss for the whole of humanity. You may never have met the deceased but something they did or someone they loved made an imperceptible difference to your world. You will never know them now, but their soul at least will have touched you. Read the obituaries every day for news of the dead and commemorate your loss by turning up at the funeral.

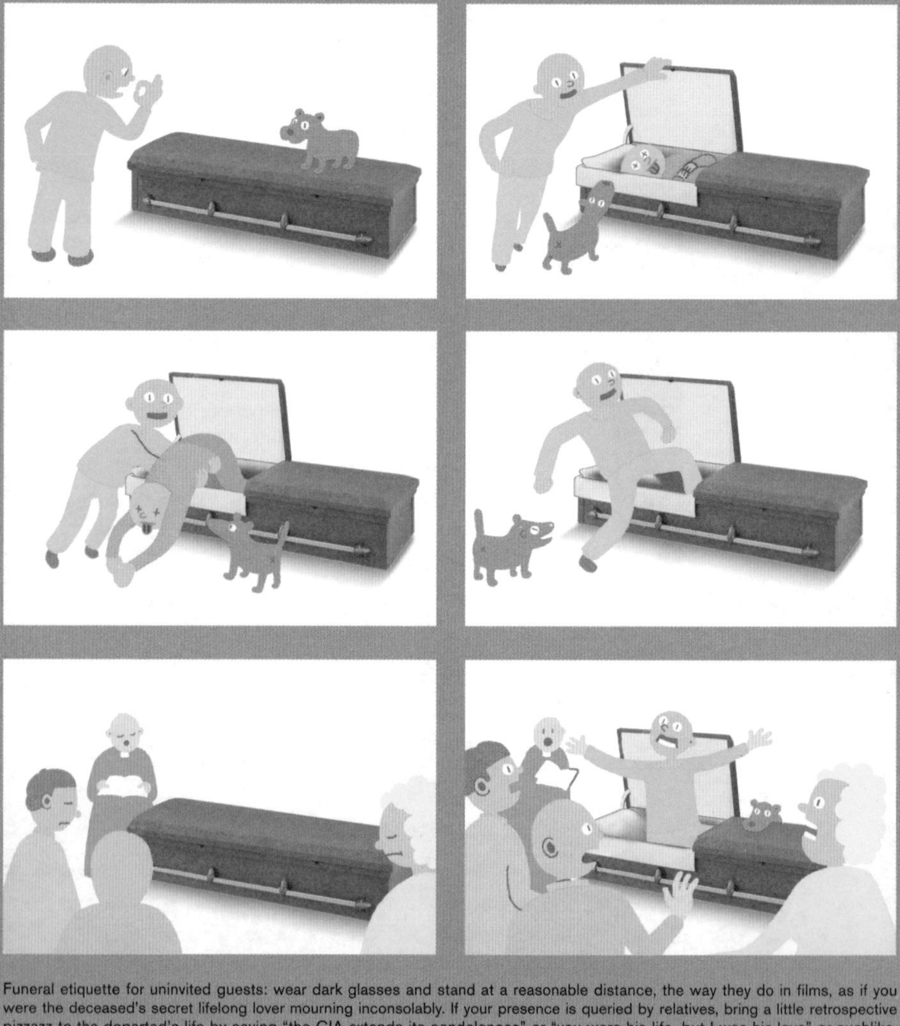

Funeral etiquette for uninvited guests: wear dark glasses and stand at a reasonable distance, the way they do in films, as if you were the deceased's secret lifelong lover mourning inconsolably. If your presence is queried by relatives, bring a little retrospective pizzazz to the departed's life by saying "the CIA extends its condolences" or "you were his life, but I was his love" or suchlike.

How memorable is your everyday conversation? Today, find out by writing down everything you say. Highlight the wittiest phrases.

Examples:

Oscar Wilde
(1854-1900)
"Only dull people are brilliant at breakfast"

Dorothy Parker
(1893-1967)
"I don't care what is written about me so long as it isn't true"

Tallulah Bankhead
(1903-1968)
"If I had to live my life again, I'd make the same mistakes, only sooner"

Benjamin Franklin
(1706-1790)
"He that falls in love with himself will have no rivals"

Samuel Johnson
(1709-1784)
"Of all noise I think music is the least disagreeable"

CALL A CALL CENTRE IN INDIA AND GET THE STAFF TO TEACH YOU ABOUT THEIR CULTURE FOR A CHANGE

More and more companies are outsourcing their call centres to India, where the workforce is cheap and all speak perfect English. Staff are even made to watch *EastEnders* and Premier League football in order to understand English culture.

But why should the cultural interchange be one-way only? Take this opportunity to ask questions and learn about everyday life in India. Don't worry how long the telephone call lasts, it's courtesy of some multinational corporation!

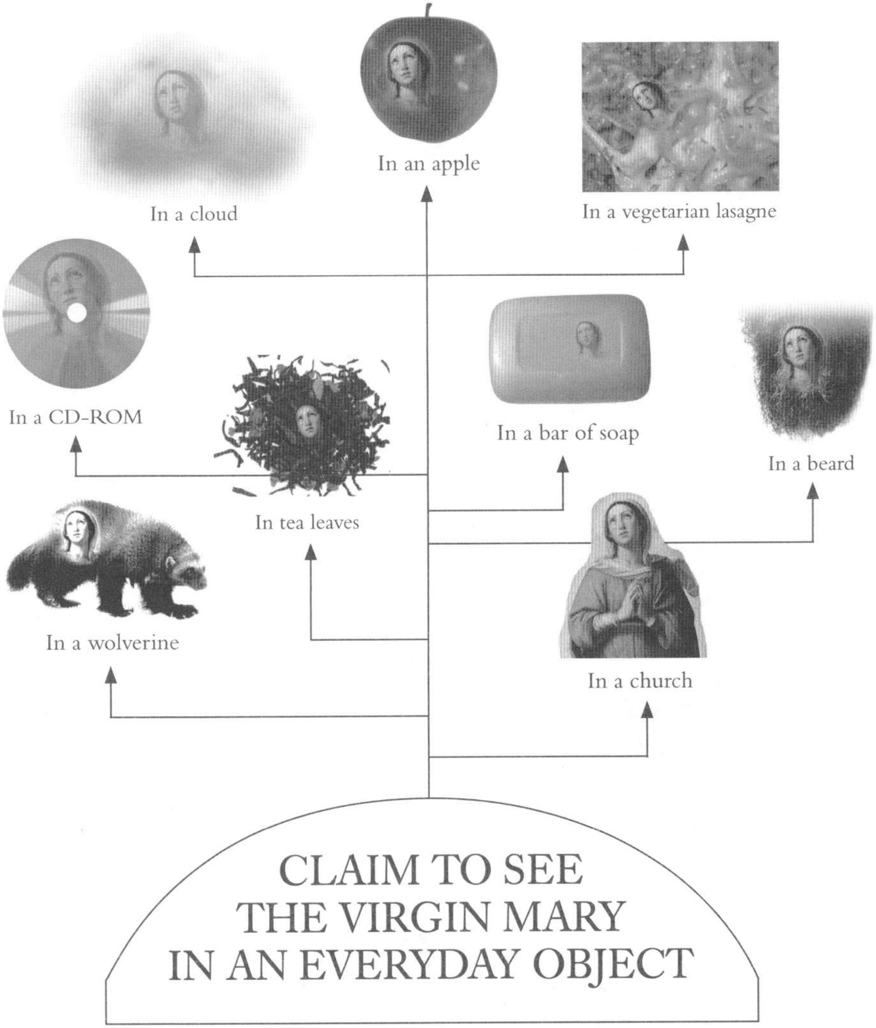
In an apple
In a cloud
In a vegetarian lasagne
In a CD-ROM
In a bar of soap
In a beard
In tea leaves
In a wolverine
In a church

CLAIM TO SEE THE VIRGIN MARY IN AN EVERYDAY OBJECT

This is an easy task, as evidenced by the numerous people who already do it every year. With a bit of imagination and creative effort, the Virgin Mary can be seen in a wide range of settings. Draw inspiration from these examples to create a plausible likeness. Call the Vatican, alert the media, set up a shrine and charge the impressionable faithful an admission fee. If people doubt you, overcome them with your faith by screaming "Do you see it? Do you see it?" at the top of your voice until they admit they do.

Email the Vatican: benedictxvi@vatican.va

SENSE-LESS DAY

Go through today without using your sense of: *hearing*

HOW TO: WAX EAR PLUGS, AVAILABLE AT ANY CHEMIST'S.

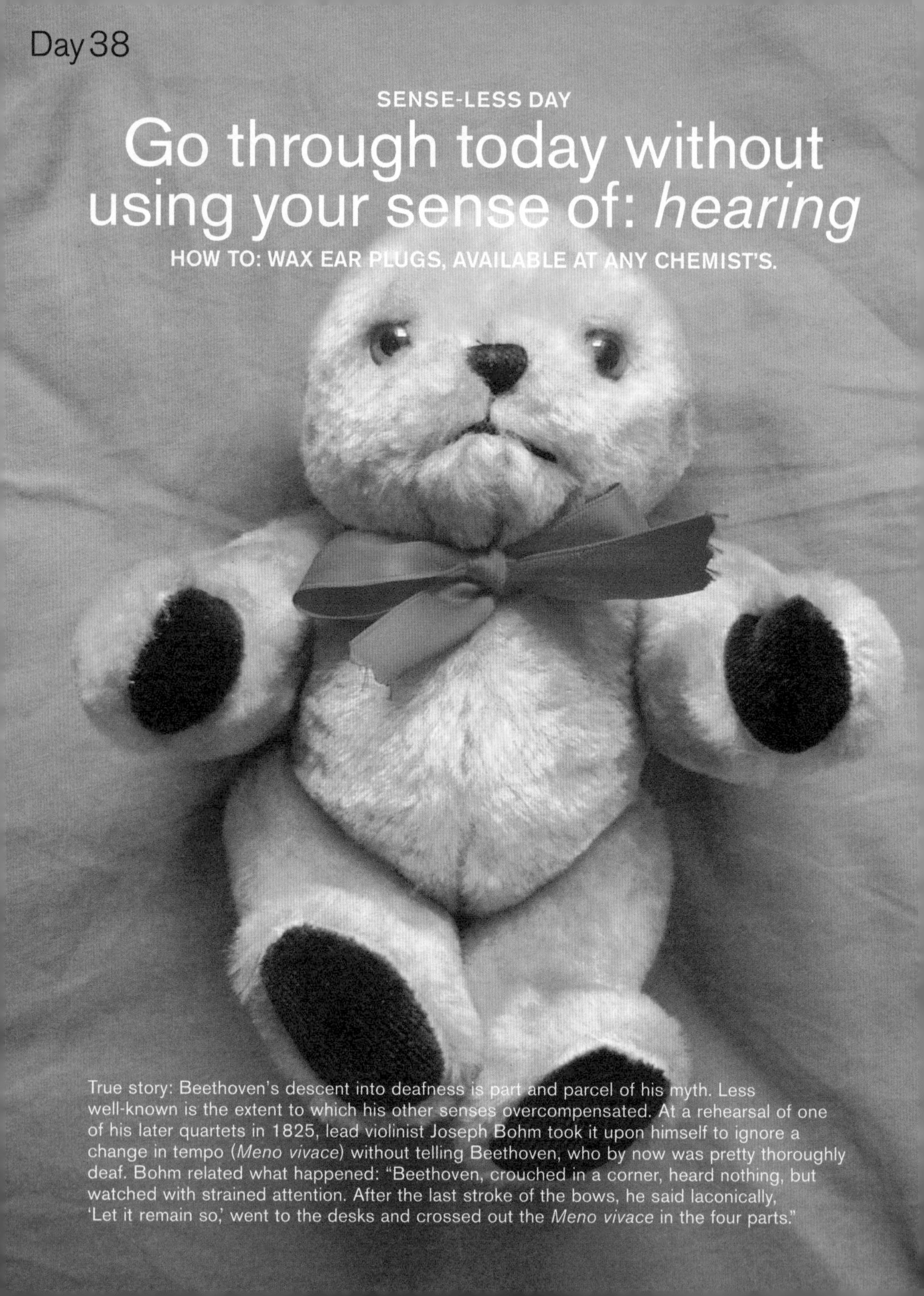

True story: Beethoven's descent into deafness is part and parcel of his myth. Less well-known is the extent to which his other senses overcompensated. At a rehearsal of one of his later quartets in 1825, lead violinist Joseph Bohm took it upon himself to ignore a change in tempo (*Meno vivace*) without telling Beethoven, who by now was pretty thoroughly deaf. Bohm related what happened: "Beethoven, crouched in a corner, heard nothing, but watched with strained attention. After the last stroke of the bows, he said laconically, 'Let it remain so,' went to the desks and crossed out the *Meno vivace* in the four parts."

Tennis sux! Tennis sux! Tennis
UGLY BABY! UGLY BABY!
WE LIVE IN A FASCIST STATE! WE LIVE IN A FASCIST STATE!
Josie's fat! Josie's fat!
We're all gonna die! We're all gonna die! We're all gonna die!
Gran's got alzheimer's! Gran's got alzheimer's!
JOHNNY'S ADOPTED! JOHNNY'S ADOPTED!

Today buy a parrot and train it to say some unpalatable truth that you cannot voice yourself in society

ENVIRONMENT DAY: TEACH MOTHER EARTH WHO'S IN CHARGE HERE

According to the thinking of legendary environmental scientist James Lovelock, the impending climate crisis is Mother Earth's way of fighting back. Lovelock posits an almost conscious Earth – "Gaia"– who is displeased with our human behaviour over the last few centuries, and intends to exact retribution by getting rid of a few billion of us via the mechanism of climate change. Well, this is simply no way to behave in a civilized society. Today, let us teach "Gaia" who's boss. A short sharp poke from all of us should bring her back in line, so that we can all live happily ever after as one big friendly ecosystem.

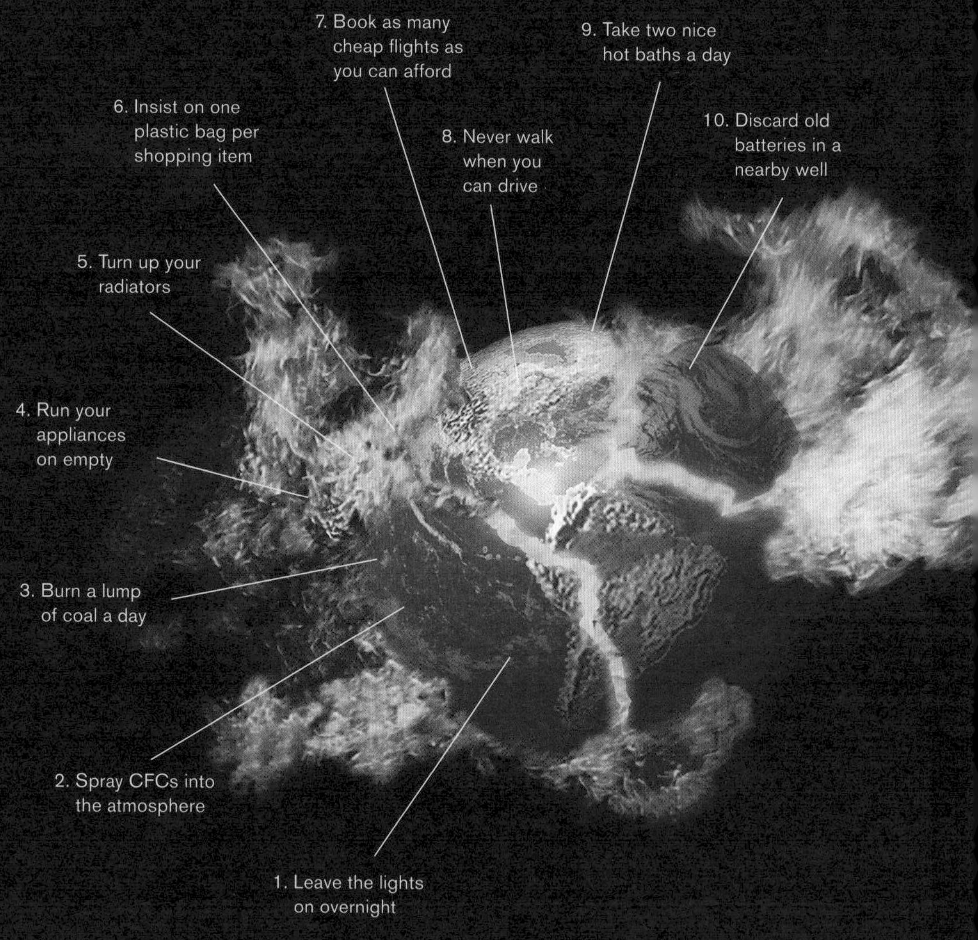
1. Leave the lights on overnight
2. Spray CFCs into the atmosphere
3. Burn a lump of coal a day
4. Run your appliances on empty
5. Turn up your radiators
6. Insist on one plastic bag per shopping item
7. Book as many cheap flights as you can afford
8. Never walk when you can drive
9. Take two nice hot baths a day
10. Discard old batteries in a nearby well

Self-medication Day

Don't just obey medical prejudices: trust your instinct to find the medicine that works for you. Plenty of modern cures were discovered by doctors administering the wrong drugs by mistake. These are Benrik's own medical guidelines, but feel free to experiment and come up with your own.

	Yellow and blue: Diseases of the knee		Blue and red: Heavy diarrhoea
	Yellow and red: Cures swollen arteries		Red and white: When you find yourself on fire
	Yellow and brown: For sex-related headaches		Black: Brings on sudden death
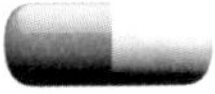	Dark and light green: Club foot		Orange and green: To put you in a bad mood
	Yellow and green: Prevents bad dreams		Pink and green: Women's troubles
	Red and blue: Heavy constipation		Grey and white: Against boredom
	Dark red and brown: Loss of limb		White: These have no effect, avoid

Advanced: medical cocktails. When you have mastered the basics of self-medication, you may progress to combining. It is advisable to try the combinations on a small animal beforehand, as even the most modern drugs can have serious negative side effects when mixed. In truth, not even Benrik have tried all combinations of the above; this will take a lifetime. But yellow/blue with red/pink is definitely best avoided.

This page is dedicated to the memory of Dribbles.

Day 42

TODAY CARRY A HIDDEN WEAPON

With street crime allegedly rife, perhaps you should go armed. Today conceal some means of defending yourself, like scissors or a hammer. Do you feel safer? Or does it merely ramp up your insecurity?

NOTE TO THE POLICE: This fine gentleman/lady/child is carrying a dangerous weapon as part of a Benrik mind experiment into the psychosociology of crime. Please do not arrest them. Benrik vouches for their peaceful nature.

DRAFT YOUR SPEECH TO THE UN TODAY: Every year, the United Nations selects one average human being to make a speech alongside all the heads of state at the plenary meeting of the General Assembly in New York in September. This is your chance to influence the world! Draft your speech and send it to the UN (Office of the President of the General Assembly, United Nations, New York, NY 10017, USA). Here is a guide to the main types of speech, along with their likelihood of selection.

Political

Chance of selection: 0/10

Mr Secretary General, Mr President, distinguished guests, ladies and gentlemen: Thank you for the privilege of being selected to speak as average representative of the human race. It is high time that the human race had a voice here, for since the UN's founding, it has been nothing but a gentlemen's club for the world's fat cats, a transparent veneer on the global totalitarianism of the usual patriarchal élite. I am surprised that all of you here manage to keep a straight face as you pass resolution after resolution enforcing the status quo, and continue to despoil both the poor and the planet in the process. You are indeed united, not for the world, but against it. If you had any shame, you would disband now and return to your countries to be lynched by your countrymen. Then we might start anew, and humankind might stand a chance. Thank you.

Hippie

Chance of selection: 8/10

Mr Secretary General, Mr President, distinguished guests, ladies and gentlemen: Thank you for the privilege of being selected to speak as average representative of the human race. I can't believe everyone on the planet is listening to this, all the millions and billions and trillions of you, I mean it kind of blows my mind. Every word that I say is beamed straight into the hearts of the whole wide world, and that is truly awesome. I'm not an expert on the world's problems like all of you, I'm sure you know what you're doing. All I can offer is the people's perspective. What do the people want? Well, the people want peace, that's all. It's a beautiful word, it's a beautiful thing. It's what the world wants, it's what the world needs. In the words of another average Joe, "can't we all just get along?" So please just keep that in mind as you debate geopolitical stuff. And I just want to say one final thing, to the children... There is hope. We're doing this for you. We're going to make it better, and that's a promise. Peace. Thank you.

Paranoid

Chance of selection: 1/10

Mr Secretary General, Mr President, distinguished guests, ladies and gentlemen: Thank you for the privilege of being selected to speak as average representative of the human race. I know you're trying to switch on the mind-control device you've implanted in my brain, but it's not working you jackals! I'm wearing a thick magnetic copper helmet that blocks all gamma rays. You can fool some people some of the time but you can't fool all the people most of the time. I'm onto you guys, and don't think you can scare me with your UN death squads and your black helicopters. I used to be in 'Nam, and so I can hear choppers coming a mile away, medication or no medication! If any freedom-loving folks in the world are intercepting this transmission, please come and rescue me, I'm in the lair of the antichrist! Vade retro Satanas! You won't take me alive, d'you hear! Thank you.

Alien

Chance of selection: 3/10

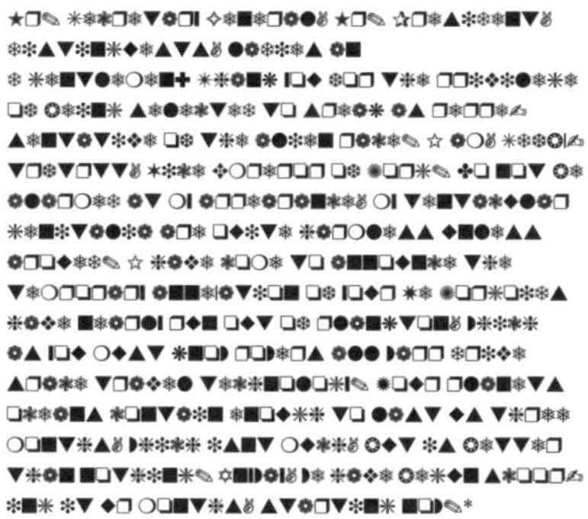

*Mr Secretary General, Mr President, distinguished guests, ladies and gentlemen: Thank you for the privilege of being selected to speak as representative of the alien race. I am Sdfbxtrftptt, Vice Emperor of Zorg. Do not be alarmed at my appearance, my tentacular genitalia are quite harmless unless aroused. I have come to announce the temporary annexation of your planet. We Zorgoids have nearly run out of plankton, which as you must know powers all warp-drive space travel technology. Your planet's oceans contain enough to last us three months, which isn't much, but is better than nothing. Anyway, we have begun scooping it up this morning. We will not harm you humans directly, but as plankton is the basis of your food chain, its removal will soon spell the end of life on earth, so we strongly suggest you come up with a replacement. You have three months, starting now. Thank you.

Day 44

Ecumenical Day

Religion	History	Beliefs	Sacred text	Logo	Slogan
BUDDHISM	Founded by Siddartha Gautama (the Buddha) in the 5th century BC in what is now Nepal, Buddhism spread across much of Asia in the centuries following his death.	There is no God; we go through a succession of reincarnations, with our past actions influencing our next life. The cycle can be halted by reaching enlightenment (nirvana), essentially through meditation and the Middle Way.	The Tri-Pitaka.		"To avoid all that is evil, tc cultivate what is good, to purify the mind."
hinduism	Hinduism is one of the world's oldest religions, originating over 3000 years ago near the river Indus, with complex roots and no single human founder.	There is a universal God or soul called Brahman, who is also expressed in the form of deities such as Krishna, Vishnu, Shiva, and Rama. Life is a great cycle of birth, death and rebirth, governed by Karma, the law of cause and effect.	The Bhagavad Gita, The Upanishads.		"The mind of man is the root of both bondage and release."
paganism	Modern paganism covers most of the ancestral pre-monotheistic religions of the world, from Celtic druidry to Native American shamanism.	Nature and Mother Earth are spiritual, and are to be respected and worshipped, often in the guise of individual gods. The divine in nature has a strong feminine side, linked to the renewal and rebirth of the seasons.	The Golden Bough (Sir James George Frazer).		"The Earth is our Mother and we must take care of her."
atheism	Atheism is a relatively recent creed. Although the Greeks hinted at it, it only really took off with the Enlightenment. In the 19th century, Darwin, Feuerbach and Nietzsche all contributed to its rapid spread. It is now the unofficial religion of the West.	There are no gods. Faith is mere superstition to comfort the feeble-minded and/or prop up oppressive power systems.	Thus Spake Zarathustra (Nietzsche).		"God is dead."
islam	Founded by the Prophet Muhammad in the 7th century after a direct revelation from Allah, Islam swiftly spread both west (all the way to Spain) and east (all the way to China).	Allah is the one and only God. Islam was revealed to humanity by Muhammad, Allah's last prophet. We must obey the Qu'ran and surrender ourselves to Allah.	The Qu'ran.		"There is no Go but Allah, and Muhammad is h messenger."
JUDAISM	Judaism was founded 3500 years ago by Abraham and Moses – who led the Jewish people from Egyptian captivity to the Promised Land of Israel. Judaism has since accompanied the Jewish people in their dramatic history of exiles, persecutions and other tribulations.	There is only one God. The Jews are his chosen people.	The Torah.		"Hear O Israel, the Lord our God, the Lord is One."
CHRISTIANITY	Founded by Jesus Christ, persecuted and crucified by the Romans for his heretical views. Said to have risen from the dead. Word spread by his apostles, including Paul. Christians persecuted until Roman emperor Constantine converted in 312 CE.	Jesus is the son of God, sent by him to redeem humanity. He was crucified for our sins but rose from the dead to join God in heaven.	The Bible.		"Love Thy Neighbour As Thyself."

Today, try out all major religions and see which is best for you

Rituals	Entry requirements	Commitment level	Popular appeal	How to try it out	Your rating
These vary according to the different traditions, but meditation and some chanting are usually in order.	Acceptance of the Four Noble Truths, The Eight Fold Path and the Five Precepts.	Medium. Risk of being reborn as a beetle of some description.	350 million adherents worldwide, and an increasing influence on the Western popular worldview.	Sit in the lotus position for one hour with your eyes closed and your body relaxed, and focus solely on your breathing.	10
Offerings to the Gods, recitation of the Vedas, oblations, chanting of mantras.	Belief in the Vedas, in karma, dharma, and reincarnation. Being renamed (namakarana samskara).	Medium to high, depending on your caste.	Big in India of course. Appeal elsewhere restricted by its deep integration into Indian society, and by the bewildering variety of subgods.	Worship at your local Hindu temple today.	10
Music, prayer, dance, conducted in sacred circles outdoors on hilltops, in caves, near large stones.	Willingness to participate in communal outdoor rituals.	Medium-high. Requires a high tolerance of public ridicule and/or accusations of deviant sexual practices.	Limited. Although neo-paganism has seen a resurgence, partly fuelled by the growth in ecological awareness, it is still a niche religion with a PR problem.	Head for Stonehenge tonight.	10
May adopt watered-down versions of other religions' rituals (weddings, funerals, Christmas).	None.	Used to involve being burnt at the stake. Now less risky.	Widespread. Most atheists are happy to just dismiss the whole religion thing, and hope like hell they don't turn out to be wrong.	Look up at the night sky tonight and imagine us alone, quite alone.	10
The five pillars of Islam are: 1) Shahada (declaration of faith) 2) Salat (prayer five times a day) 3) Zakat (giving to charity every year) 4) Sawm (fasting during Ramadan) 5) Hajj (pilgrimage to Mecca at least once in a lifetime).	Open to all who believe sincerely in its teachings. Reciting the Shahada three times in front of witnesses is all that is formally required to become a Muslim.	High. Islam requires more visible worship than most religions.	Over a billion adherents make it the second most popular faith in the world. Also the fastest-growing.	Attend Friday prayers at your local mosque.	10
Too numerous to detail.	Being or becoming Jewish. To become Jewish: find a sympathetic rabbi, study Judaism, get circumcised if you are a man, appear before the Bet Din (ritual court), choose a Hebrew name, go to the mikveh (ritual bath).	High. Orthodox Judaism pervades everyday life.	Limited, as Judaism is not a proselytising faith.	Visit the synagogue today.	10
Baptism, Confirmation, Eucharist.	Belief in Jesus as our saviour. Baptism.	High in theory, variable in practice.	Most popular faith in the world, with over 2 billion followers.	Go to church today.	10

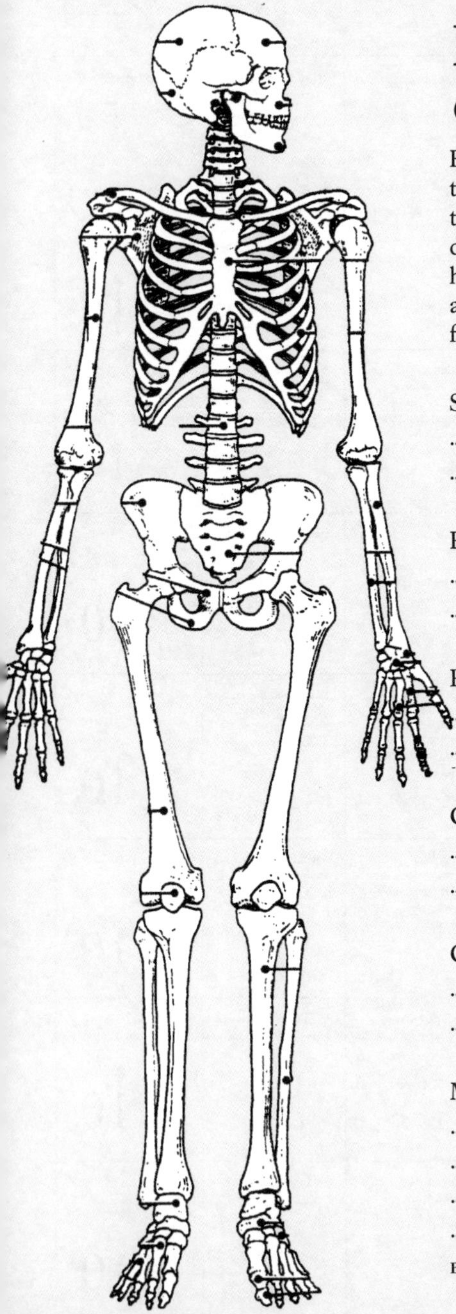

Let the skeletons out of your closet today

Everyone has at least one thing in their past that they would hate to see come out. If you have lived to the full, you probably have several. Today, Benrik declare an amnesty: write down your shameful hidden past on this page, and present it to those around you. Secrets will out – better your loved ones find out this way than through their own devices.

Sexual skeletons: ....

....

....

Relationship skeletons: ....

....

....

Professional skeletons: ....

....

....

Criminal skeletons: ....

....

....

Childhood skeletons: ....

....

....

Miscellaneous skeletons: ....

....

....

....

....

Benrik note: Let He Who Is Without Sin Cast The First Stone (The Bible)

Hedgehog

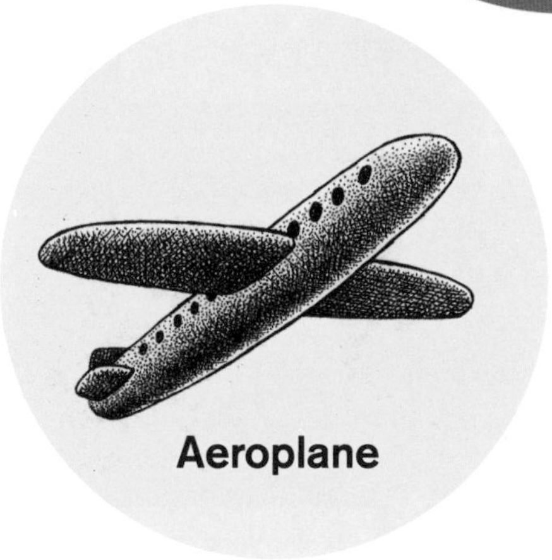
Aeroplane

Midget

Tonight, control your dreams

Freud postulated that our dreams are essentially the recombined elements of things that had affected us during the day. Today, think very hard about these three things and see if they crop up in your dreams tonight.

ANTI PAEDOPHILE DAY

Today, make friends with every child you see.

Public hysteria about paedophiles means we are teaching our kids to distrust strangers instinctively.

In the long-term, this will have a hugely detrimental effect on society – we are literally breeding fear of others.

Reverse this trend by smiling and saying hi to as many kids as possible today, whether accompanied or not.

If everyone does this together, we will teach children to trust in their fellow human beings.

If we don't, the paedophiles will have defeated us.

TODAY PANIC-BUY

SWAN
VESTAS
evian
Natural Mineral Water
IMPERIAL LEATHER
whiskas

Panic-buy: Matches!

Panic-buy: Water!

Panic-buy: Soap!

Panic-buy: Cat food!

Panic-buy: Broccoli!

Panic-buy: Pepper!

Panic-buy: Quiche!

Modern civilization hangs by a thread. Our economies are now based on just-in-time manufacture and delivery processes, so that any sudden and unforeseen run on a product can thrust the whole system into meltdown.

Today, let us all panic-buy the items above, sparking a nationwide chain reaction that will bring global capitalism to its knees, or at least force a comprehensive reappraisal of modern retailing techniques.

Day 49

Make prolonged eye contact with everyone you meet today

Eye contact: communication before words. Monkeys stare each other down. Be the alpha male. Who dares stand up to you? Bite their head off, that'll learn them. Grrrr.

FREE PET DAY!

Put a lost dog ad up and see whether one turns up

fig.1

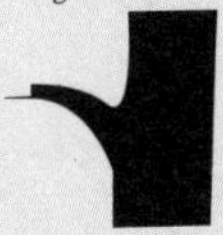

fig.2

fig.3

fig.4

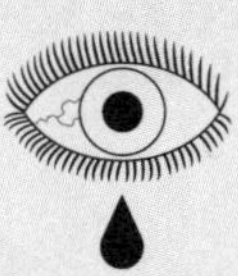

fig.5

LOST
DOG

fig.6

KEY ELEMENTS OF ANY SUCCESSFUL LOST DOG AD

fig.1 Positioning: tree is traditional, or lamp post.
fig.2 Photo: poor quality photocopy, hinting at nationwide magnitude of your search and maximizing the range of dogs that look a bit like that.
fig.3 Reward: keep this bit vague, that way you'll always be able to fob them off with a cheap chocolate bar or similar lame effort.
fig.4 Description: favour the emotional over the descriptive. "My darling bulimic daughter Lizzie's little puppy has gone and she hasn't stopped crying since, please help restore her faith in life" is more motivational than "Fox terrier, 7 years old, brownish, answers to the name dog".
fig.5 Headline: LOST DOG works best usually.
fig.6 Phone number: might attract psychos, but fairly essential.

The sea of change
THE CROWN JEWELS
CARNABY STREET
ENGLISH POTTERY
BRITTISH HUMOR
A PERSON WHO SELLS POST-CARDS
HARRY POTTER
SOHO
London
SUSSEX
MANCHESTER
ENGLISH BREAKFAST
FISH
CHIPS
FISH & CHIPS
Brighton
THE GULF SEA
RIVER THAMES
PRINCE WILLIAM
Wales
ALL BAR ONE
THE LONDON DUNGEON
WINSTON CHURCHILL
THE LONDON EYE
WESTMINSTER
WEST END MUSICAL
NEAREST POLICE-STATION
A RED TELEPHONE BOOTH
A RED DOUBLE-DECKER
YBA
North Haynes
TRAFALGAR SQUARE
NOTTING HILL
France
PUBLIC SCHOOLS
PRIVATE SCHOOLS
Stonehedge
Heathrow
WILLIAM SHAKSPEARE
Beatles are playing here tonight
DOVES TO FEED
PUNKS
VICTORIAN ARCHITEC-TURE
RAIN FREE AREA
PUBLIC HANGING
Tony Blairs palace
Oxford
DANCING IRISHMEN
ENGLAND
THE QUEEN LIVES HERE
NEAREST TUBE
Madame Tussaud's
Hugh Grant
BATH
JAMIE OLIVER
FAWLTY TOWERS
PLANET HOLLYWOOD
BIRMINGHAM
Jack the Ripper
Scotland
COL-LOSE-UM
Haggis
Charles Dickens
BAD COFFEE-CHAIN COFFEE
OXFORD STREET
SPICEGIRLS
MIS
BIG BEN
SHERLOCK HOLMES
Angus Stedkhouse
A PUB
ROBBIE WILLIAMS
SOUVENIR SHOP
SAATCHI GALLERY
LAKE DISTRICT
ROLLING STONES
Margaret Thatcher
PUDDING
Cardiff
THE LONDON TAVERN
HARRODS
DISNEYSTORE
PIZZA HUT

Today mislead a tourist

The world would be a brighter place if tourists got lost more regularly. When an inquisitive foreigner asks his way today, send him off in an unexpected direction. He's read about all the obvious landmarks in his guidebook anyway.

Self-acupuncture Day

Acupuncture is now widely recognized as an effective cure for a wide variety of ills. However it is still beyond the reach of many, while others still may feel slight embarrassment at exposing themselves for treatment. That is why Benrik are providing this self-acupuncture chart. Simply buy some needles and stick them in at the relevant acupuncture points, taking care not to push them in too far (half an inch is about right). Soon your Qi will flow unimpeded again, and your troubles will abate.

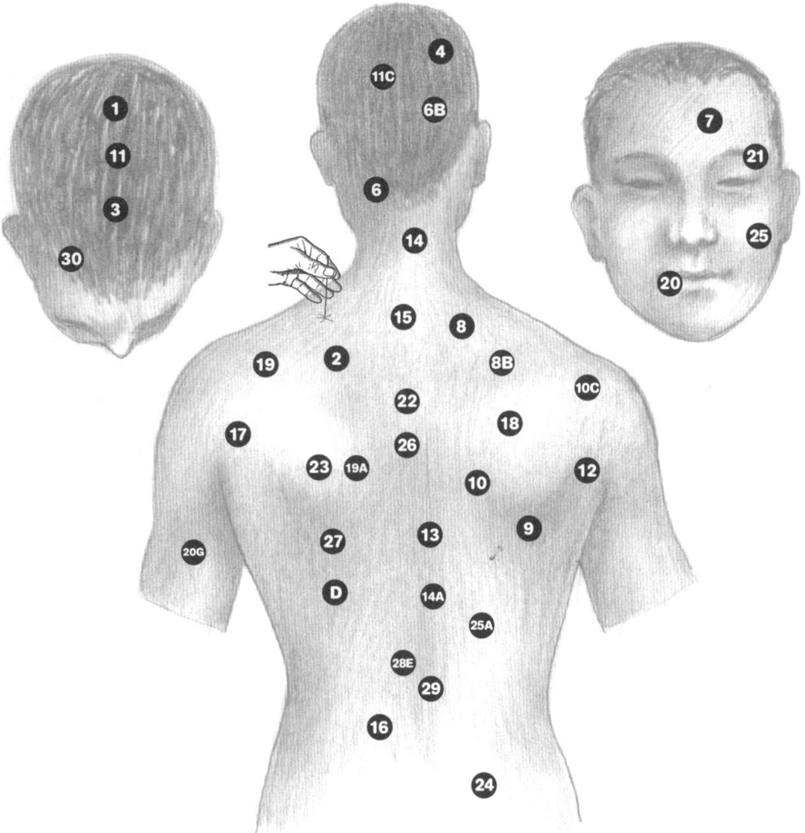
1
11
3
30
4
11C
6B
6
14
7
21
25
20
15
8
19
2
8B
10C
22
18
17
26
23
19A
12
10
9
20G
27
13
D
14A
25A
28E
29
16
24

1. Headache, 2. Eye inflammation, 3. Bronchitis, 4. Asthma, D. Earache, 6. Migraine, 6B. Chilblain, 7. Neck pain, 8. Dry lips, 8B. Cold sores, 9. Hair loss, 10. Furry tongue, 10C. Consumption, 11. General problems, 12. Sluggish circulation, 11C. Pimples, 13. Toothache, 14A. Delirium Tremens, 14. Dizziness, 15. Stress, 16. Anxiety, 17. Cleft palate, 18. Tinnitus, 19. Allergy to nuts, 19A. Wisdom tooth (left), 20. Obesity, 20G. Dropsy, 21. Elbow ache, 22. High blood pressure, 23. Low blood pressure, 24. Bedwetting, 25. Lockjaw, 25A. Dry soles, 26. Menstrual problems, 27. Sore nipples, 28E. Diarrhoea, 29. Fatigue, 30. Involuntary erection, 31. Brittle fingernails, 2AA. Depression, 33. Liver complaint, 331. Scrofula, 34. Pancreatic malfunction, 35. Excessive bile, 36. Sore toes, 37. Excessive saliva, 38. Haemorrhoids, 39. Gout, 40. Irregular heartbeat, 40B. Epilepsy, 40C. Sunburn, 51. Bad breath, 52. Achilles' heel pain, 53. Sleepiness

Day 53

Send your DNA to the authorities today

These days, it is only too easy for an innocent citizen to get mixed up in some global security scare by mistake. You may be in the wrong place at the wrong time. Or an acquaintance may mention you under torture. Or the computer may have you confused with someone with a similar name. Before you know it, you're off to an interrogation camp in the middle of nowhere for five years! Avoid such difficulties by volunteering your DNA ahead of time. Send it to the world's leading security services, and they'll be able to check you off their "suspects" lists early on in any investigation, for guaranteed peace of mind. Here is where to send your DNA. Careful! Each security service has its preferred form of DNA. Make sure you send the right one to avoid complications.

FSB	PREFERRED DNA FORMAT: vial of blood *Dear FSB, Just in case you were suspecting me, I'm sending you my DNA so you can rule me out of your investigations. Bye for now.* SEND TO: FSB, 1/3 Bolshaya Lubyanka Ul., 101000, Moscow, Russia
Interpol	PREFERRED DNA FORMAT: toenail cuttings *Dear Interpol, with so much crime being international these days, you can't be too careful. Check my DNA and cross me off your list!* SEND TO: Interpol General Secretariat, 200, Quai Charles de Gaulle, 69006 Lyon, France
FBI	PREFERRED DNA FORMAT: lock of hair *Dear FBI, Please record my DNA and check my name off your "most wanted" list. Thank you.* SEND TO: Federal Bureau of Investigation, J. Edgar Hoover Building, 935 Pennsylvania Avenue, NW, Washington, D.C. 20535-0001, USA
MI5	PREFERRED DNA FORMAT: urine sample *Dear MI5, I'm a law-abiding citizen. I have nothing to fear, now or in the future. Here's my DNA for safe storage.* SEND TO: MI5, Thames House, Millbank, PO Box 3255, London SW1P 1AE, UK
MSS	PREFERRED DNA FORMAT: small jar of earwax *Dear Ministry of State Security, I doubt I am on your list of suspects, but just in case, here's my DNA to prove my innocence.* SEND TO: Ministry of State Security, 14 Dongchang'an Street, Doncheng District, Beijing, China
CIA	PREFERRED DNA FORMAT: swab of saliva *Dear CIA, I'm innocent! But here's my DNA anyway, just so you can be 100% sure. Good luck.* SEND TO: Central Intelligence Agency, c/o Office of Public Affairs, Washington, D.C. 20505, USA

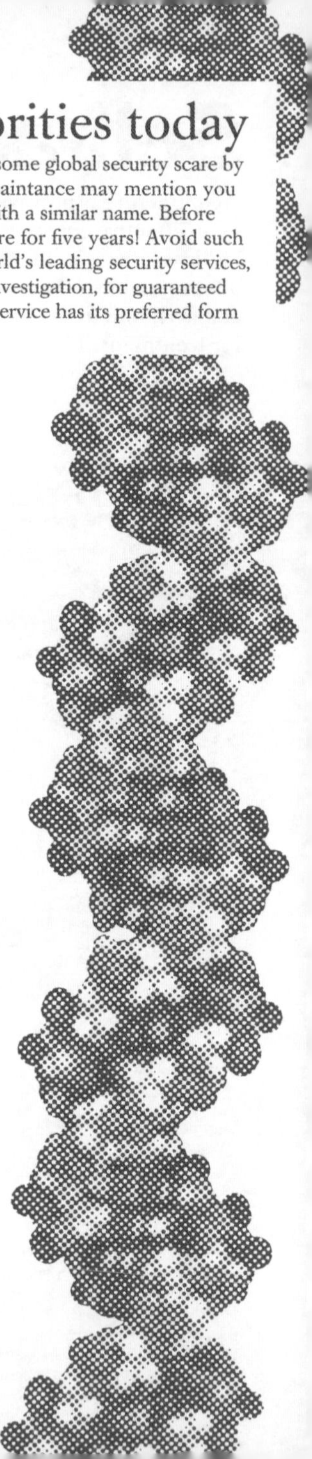

Mass Social Experiment

OUT OF
ORDER

Cut out and stick this sign on any item of public infrastructure you might encounter today, including, but not limited to: lifts, rubbish trucks, cranes, phone booths, toilets, ventilation units, escalators, entrances to tube stations; the aim is to achieve comprehensive social breakdown across the UK.

Today write and thank your most influential teacher

You've been very naughty by not doing this much earlier though, so you have to write it 100 times!

TODAY, LET POWER CORRUPT YOU

Force the pizza delivery guy to go back for extra anchovies

Insist that the receptionist change the flowers' water

Return this book to us for a refund claiming it's rubbish

Make the check-out girl ring all your purchases through again

Order the wine waiter to get you a cleaner glass

Bully your family members to let you hold the remote

Require your visitors to take off their shoes

Demand that your secretary retype the letter in italics

WE ALL ENJOY SOME FORM OF POWER: TODAY LET IT GO TO YOUR HEAD AND ABUSE IT...

Today, welcome a new life
EVERY DAY, AN AVERAGE OF 202176 BABIES ARE BORN WORLDWIDE.
THAT'S ONE NEW LIFE ON THE PLANET EVERY 25 SECONDS.
GO TO YOUR NEAREST MATERNITY WARD AND WELCOME ONE OF THE LITTLE GUYS.

Today, praise an unsung achievement

Dear Sir,
I would like to say how much I enjoyed your review of *Driving Miss Daisy* in today's *TV Weekly*. 'Funny in parts but disappointing ending, watch if you're in' is as succinct and perspicuous a critique as one could wish to read. Thank you.

Dear Madam,
I was very taken by your weather update this morning on television. The way you explained the anticyclone's movements across the British Isles was pure poetry in motion and brought meteorology to life for me.

Dear Sir/Madam,
I purchased a pack of your toothpicks yesterday and I must confess I have never come across such marvellously crafted specimens! My mouth has not felt this clean for 65 years! Keep up the good work.

Gentlemen!
Please pass on my congratulations to the receptionist who transferred my call to your sales department this afternoon at 3.43pm; she did it so smoothly and in such a friendly manner that I hardly noticed the wait!

Dear Neighbour,
Sorry for bothering you with this note, but I can no longer keep quiet. The way you deal with your rubbish never fails to inspire me. Your bags are beautifully tied yet quite hermetic and resistant to squirrels. You have all my respect.

Officer,
I live at 34B and watch you patrolling the street every day. Your posture is magnificent. You strike the perfect balance between scaring off the criminal mind, and reassuring the householder. Bravo! (I have sent a copy of this letter to your superiors.)

Find a way of including the word VORTEX in all your conversations today

Try to do it without sounding clumsy. Here are some suggestions: "Lovely weather, isn't it?" – "Yes, though that cloud over there looks a bit vortex-shaped". "This business report makes for interesting reading" – "Indeed. It lies at the vortex of cruciality". "Did you see that programme on television last night?" – "What, the one about the vortex?"

MAKE THE DALAI LAMA LOSE HIS TEMPER TODAY

Stamp on
passing beetles

Try converting
him to your
religion

Hum the Chinese
National Anthem

Bribe him to
improve your
karma

Request that he
put a curse on
your enemies

Chant
everything he
says back at him

Complain
that yoga
has damaged
your back

Ask him why he's
in exile if his gods
are so great

Invite him over
to the dark side

The Dalai Lama is the epitome of self-control. You have much to learn from him. Seek him out today and ask for an audience. You may not have much time with him for he is a busy man, so bring out his self-control by provoking him as inanely as you can. If he stays calm, you will have witnessed the power of a trained mind. If he becomes angry, you will have gained an appreciation of the limits of human self-discipline and won't feel so guilty when you lose your own rag.

The Dalai Lama lives in Dharamsala in the north Indian state of Himachal Pradesh, but fortunately for you, he is due to give a series of talks in Nottingham, UK, this coming weekend, entitled Bringing Meaning to Our Lives. Contact the Office of Tibet in London for details and get a front-row seat (tel: 020 7722 5378, fax: 020 7722 0362). N.B. The visit took place late May 2008. He kept his temper.

Check that your sex life is normal today

We get most of our information about what constitutes a normal sex life from the media. But *Cosmo* and Hollywood are hardly the most reliable guides to what goes on in real bedrooms. Today, overcome your coyness: fill in this questionnaire and ask your peer group to assess how much you deviate from the sexual straight and narrow.

Sum up your sexual life:

VIRGINITY
Lost? Yes ☐ No ☐
At age:...
To:...

NUMBER OF PARTNERS
One (self) ☐
One (other) ☐
Several (number):....................................

INTERCOURSE
Regular? Yes ☐ No ☐
Frequency:......per day/week/month/year
With:..
....
....
....
....

FANTASIES
Favourite:..
Secret:...
Repressed:..

VENEREAL DISEASES
None ☐
Embarrassing ☐
Life-threatening ☐

FETISH
Legal:..
Illegal:...
Law doesn't even acknowledge it:..

Ask your friends for their opinion:

FRIEND'S NAME	FRIEND'S VERDICT ON YOUR SEX LIFE
1	Normal ☐ Boring ☐ Perverted ☐ Friendship terminated ☐
2	Normal ☐ Boring ☐ Perverted ☐ Friendship terminated ☐
3	Normal ☐ Boring ☐ Perverted ☐ Friendship terminated ☐
4	Normal ☐ Boring ☐ Perverted ☐ Friendship terminated ☐
5	Normal ☐ Boring ☐ Perverted ☐ Friendship terminated ☐

TODAY,
SEND YOUR SUGGESTIONS TO THE GOVERNMENT
Dear Prime Minister. I am a senior citizen 76 years of age. I supported your political party at the last election but this is the last straw sir! Those goddamn gays are running riot! I am not homophobic (though sometimes I think this country could do with a bit more homophobia). BUT I object to those perverts parading their penises and scrotums in front of me in the street! IF THAT'S FREE SPEECH, THEN TO HELL WITH FREE SPEECH! I am not accusing you of anything personally. But if you support perversion then in my book that makes you a pervert.
Why no ? I never thought this country would come to this. Shame on you! Have our leaders (including you) gone utterly mad? I am not against homosexual people doing their business in private. But in public??!! On television??!! I do not expect to turn my television on and have their scrotums thrust in my face.
Your government is pe verting this once great nation. Desist at once! I pray for you sir. Anonymous.

Make a non-obscene phone call today

Call a stranger at random and whisper nice things about them down the line

Your phone has
a lovely ring

I admire the way you keep your
front garden so well-tended

Your voice is so strong
I bet you're a baritone

I noticed your name as soon as
I opened the phone book

Every word you say has the
feel of self-confidence

I bet if we met we'd be
friends straightaway

Maybe it's a fancy, but I could
swear I can smell your sweet
scent down the phone

Even when you curse it
sounds like pure poetry

Don't hang up, I want this
conversation to last forever

If no one's home, leave a message: Hello this is just to prepare you mentally for when I come up to you in the street and hug you tight you don't know me but I feel like I've known you a very long time now and I just think you're super so don't worry I could tell you what I look like but that would ruin the surprise anyway I look forward to meeting you very soon good night CLICK

Trust someone with your life today

Deepen the bonds between you and a close friend today and experience the vulnerability and liberation that ensues. Trust them to guide you on a railway platform with your eyes closed. Trust them to prepare your dose of medication. Trust them to turn the gas off after you fall asleep. Trust them not to post that death threat to a mafioso that you signed.

Advanced: to truly test your faith in mankind, try this with a complete stranger. Good luck.

Day 65

LURE A FLY ONTO THIS PAGE AND SWAT IT HERE

Switch on your appendix today

The human appendix is generally dismissed by the medical profession as a vestigial organ, that is, an organ that was once useful but is now obsolete in evolutionary terms. Conventional wisdom holds that it only merits our attention when it becomes inflamed to the point where it must be removed. This is a short-sighted view. There is another school of thought: the appendix may be beginning its evolutionary journey, gradually growing into an organ with new capacities that we can scarcely yet imagine, such as telepathy, or the ability to digest Martian foodstuffs. Today, try turning your appendix on and triggering these new and wonderful functions.

Method 1:
MICROWAVE
Stand with your appendix pressed against the microwave door for three hours on high power.

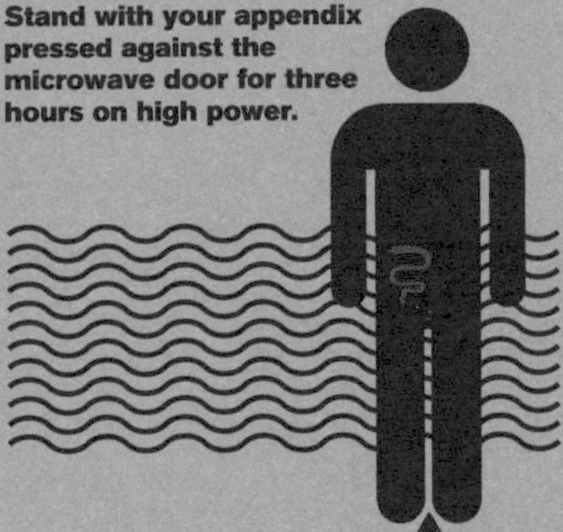

Method 2:
"HOT AND COLD" THERAPY
Apply heat and cold to the appendix through the skin by alternating an ice pack and a hair dryer set on max. (twice a day).

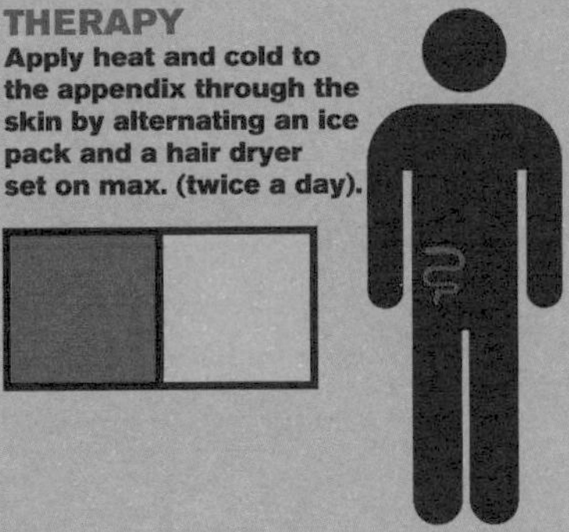

Method 3:
MOBILE PHONE
Strap your mobile phone over your appendix so that it is bathed in electromagnetic waves throughout the day.

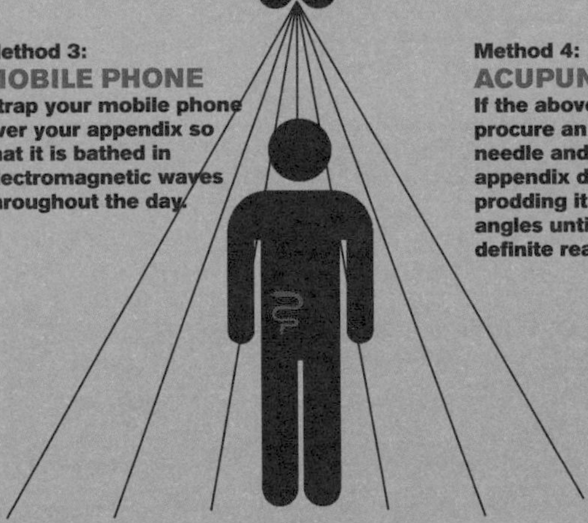

Method 4:
ACUPUNCTURE
If the above methods fail, procure an acupuncture needle and insert into the appendix directly. Try prodding it at different angles until you get a definite reaction.

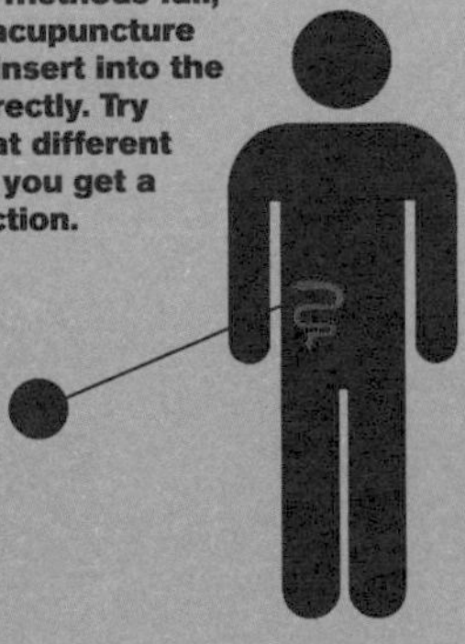

REFERENCES:
Collins, D.C. (1955) "A study of 50,000 specimens of the human vermiform appendix." Surg Gynecol Obstet. 101: 437–445.
Saave, J. J. (1955) "Absence of the vermiform appendix; report of a case discovered at necropsy." Acta Anat (Basel). 23: 327–329.
Iuchtman, M. (1993) "Autoamputation of appendix and the 'absent' appendix." Arch Surg. 128: 600.
Dasso, J. F., Obiakor, H., Bach, H., Anderson, A. O., and Mage, R. G. (2000) "A morphological and immunohistological study of the human and rabbit appendix for comparison with the avian bursa." Dev Comp Immunol 24: 797–814.

Today: sketch someone opposite you on public transport and see how they react

In case of violent reaction, show them this:

The bearer of this document has been mandated by the public transport authorities to effect paper likenesses of individual users of aforesaid public transport facilities for the purposes of national security. Civilians are asked to cooperate with enquiries under pain of prosecution.

FATHER'S DAY!

Assess your Dad's performance so far

Father's name...
Father's age...
Father's age when he met my mother..
Father's age when he had me..
Degree of certainty that he is my father.................................../10

What I call my father
Dad ☐ Daddy ☐ Father ☐ Papa ☐ Pop ☐ Bastard ☐
Other..
....

GENERAL	YES	NO	DON'T KNOW
My father has provided me with a sense of stability	☐	☐	☐
My father has provided me with a sense of security	☐	☐	☐
My father has provided me with a sense of purpose	☐	☐	☐
My father's relationship with my mother has made me feel that loving relationships are:			
the norm	☐	☐	☐
hard work	☐	☐	☐
a bitter illusion	☐	☐	☐

MEN
My father's relationship with me:
...has been that of a positive role model which has enabled me to identify with him and develop into a well-balanced male ☐
...has been that of an overpowering tyrant, nipping my confidence in the bud and leading to repressed violence and depression ☐
...has been absent, leaving me with an unresolved Oedipal conflict and a confused sexual identity ☐

WOMEN
My father's relationship with me:
...has allowed me to deal with the Electra complex to the point where I can enjoy fulfilling relationships with men ☐
...has fostered a dependency on overtly callous men whom I normally expect to leave me after a few months at best ☐
...has turned me into a distrustful shrew who avoids men and indeed close relationships in general ☐

In your own words, write your assessment of your father so far, along with suggestions as to how he might improve. *Cut it out and leave it under his pillow.*

Kyoto
Reforesting
Battle
Basement
Chemotherapy
Timer
Iran
Destruction
Suicide bombe
Fallout
Sunni
Hostage
Pain
Biohazard
Convulsions
Carbon dioxide
Ozone
Water wars
Perverted
Factors
Annihilation
Everywhere
Cold war
Radiation sickness
On the ru
Proliferation
Too late
Fossil fuel
Wahhabism
Hurricane Katrin

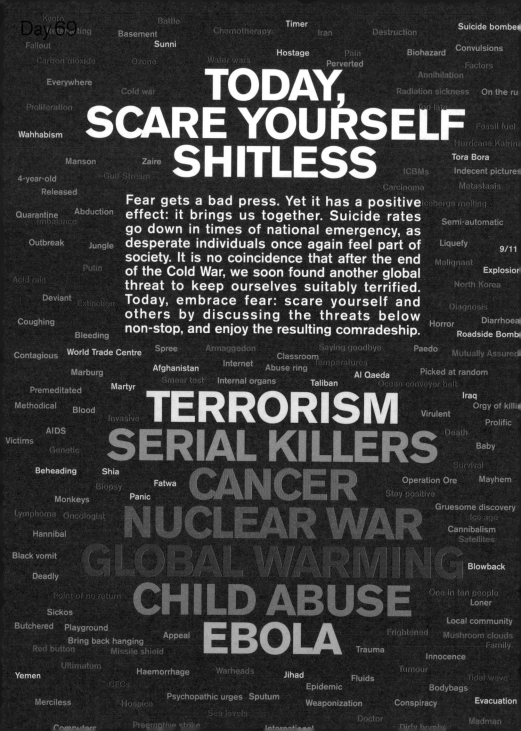

TODAY, SCARE YOURSELF SHITLESS

Manson
Zaire
Tora Bora
ICBMs
Indecent picture
4-year-old
Gulf Stream
Carcinoma
Metastasis
Released
Icebergs melting
Quarantine
Abduction
Imbalance
Semi-automatic
Outbreak
Jungle
Liquefy
9/11
Putin
Malignant
Explosion
Acid rain
North Korea
Deviant
Extinction
Diagnosis
Coughing
Horror
Diarrhoea
Bleeding
Roadside Bomb

Fear gets a bad press. Yet it has a positive effect: it brings us together. Suicide rates go down in times of national emergency, as desperate individuals once again feel part of society. It is no coincidence that after the end of the Cold War, we soon found another global threat to keep ourselves suitably terrified. Today, embrace fear: scare yourself and others by discussing the threats below non-stop, and enjoy the resulting comradeship.

Contagious
World Trade Centre
Spree
Armaggedon
Saying goodbye
Paedo
Mutually Assured
Classroom
Internet
Abuse ring
Temperatures
Marburg
Afghanistan
Al Qaeda
Picked at random
Smear test
Internal organs
Taliban
Ocean conveyor belt
Premeditated
Martyr
Iraq
Methodical
Blood
Orgy of killi
Virulent
Invasive
Prolific
AIDS
Victims
Death
Genetic
Baby
Survival
Beheading
Shia
Fatwa
Operation Ore
Mayhem
Biopsy
Stay positive
Monkeys
Panic
Gruesome discovery
Lymphoma
Oncologist
Ice age
Hannibal
Cannibalism
Satellites
Black vomit
Blowback
Deadly
Point of no return
One in ten people
Loner
Sickos
Local community
Butchered
Playground
Appeal
Frightened
Mushroom clouds
Bring back hanging
Family
Red button
Missile shield
Trauma
Innocence
Ultimatum
Tumour
Yemen
Haemorrhage
Warheads
Jihad
Fluids
Tidal wave
CFCs
Epidemic
Bodybags
Merciless
Psychopathic urges
Sputum
Hospice
Weaponization
Conspiracy
Evacuation
Sea levels
Doctor
Madman
Computers
Preemptive strike
International
Dirty bombs

TERRORISM
SERIAL KILLERS
CANCER
NUCLEAR WAR
GLOBAL WARMING
CHILD ABUSE
EBOLA

1865
1902
1871
SONY
1612
1887
1788
1920
243A.D.
1900
1347
1679

Today confuse future archaeologists by dating things wrongly

The historian of tomorrow has it too easy. Complicate matters slightly by picking an item of consumer electronics, dating it 23/05/1778 in marker pen, and burying it in your back garden. Thousands of years from now, you could be the cause of a major re-evaluation of Late Second Millennium history.

Enter Miss or Mr World

Miss World and its male counterpart Mr World are eagerly-awaited global events, on a par with the Olympics or the World Cup. The reason for their appeal? They don't just focus on the competitors' appearance, but also on their inner beauty. There is thus no reason why you shouldn't stand a good chance of winning, provided your personality is in good shape. Apply to Miss World Organization, enclosing a photo.

Dear organizers,

Please include me in your selection process for the next Miss World/Mr World. I believe I deserve to win because: ....
....
....
....
....
....

Photo

Name:..
Address:..
Date of birth:...
Height:...
Statistics:..
Occupation:...
Dream:..
Hobbies:...

I support world peace ☐
I don't support world peace ☐

Send to: Miss/Mr World Organization, c/o TWI Interactive Limited, Burlington Lane, London, W4 2TH, UK.

JUDGEMENT DAY

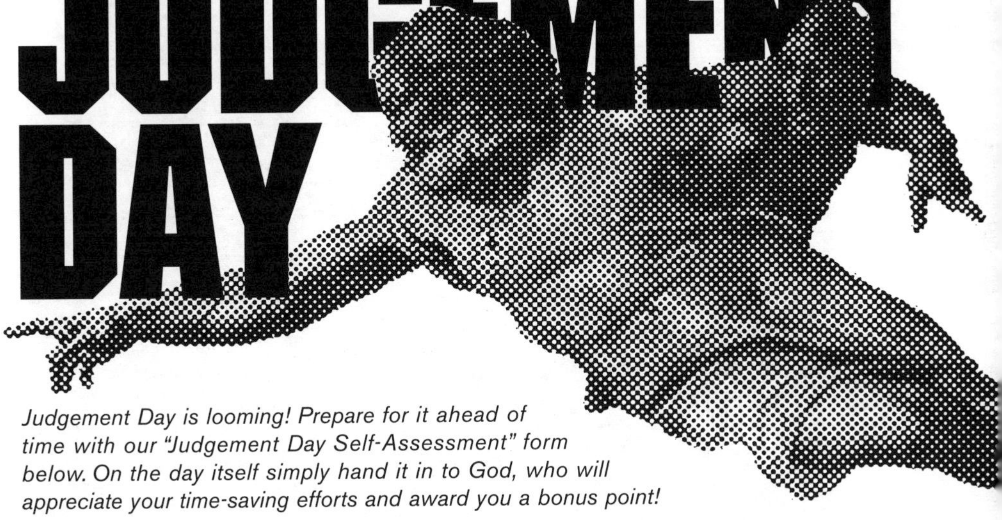

Judgement Day is looming! Prepare for it ahead of time with our "Judgement Day Self-Assessment" form below. On the day itself simply hand it in to God, who will appreciate your time-saving efforts and award you a bonus point!

MY GOOD DEEDS	MY SINS	OTHER
Helped blind person across street	Fornicated with strangers	Drank semi-skimmed milk
Comforted crying child	Lied to my own mother	Knitted green jumper
Returned lost wallet	Murdered my father	Tried to repair toaster to no avail
Gave to worthwhile charity	Stole ice cream from a child	Kept CDs in alphabetical order
Loved my neighbour	Engaged in sodomy (repeatedly)	Always sat in front row at movies
Cured the sick	Padded out my expense claims	Preferred pepper to salt
Fed the hungry	Envied everyone I ever met	Holidayed in the Bahamas twice
Did a good turn	Lied about my age to lover	Enjoyed chess as a hobby
Helped the aged	Was gluttonous as a baby	Had a friend named Toby
Saved a cat from up a tree	Chronically undertipped hookers	Kept a goldfish for 4 years
Rewound videos before returning them	Made greed my true religion	Worked in a bar whilst travelling
Planted a tree	Sacrificed goats to Satan	Visited long-lost cousin in Scotland
Forgave an enemy	Talked behind backs	Read mostly non-fiction
Went to church	Secretly despised my children	Broke a leg skiing
Have been a good listener	"Borrowed" library book forever	Went to Jon Bon Jovi concert
Was faithful to my spouse	Shoplifted pornography	Played the lottery regularly
Dried the dishes without being asked	Masturbated uncontrollably	Never really had favourite film
Rescued family from house on fire	Listened to Alice Cooper backwards	Redecorated spare bedroom in fuchsia
Adopted a stray dog	Stole from the cookie jar	Sent total of 658 postcards
Prayed in earnest	Skipped Sunday school	Rose to senior manager position
Found a family for ugly orphan	Told orphan they were ugly	Saw documentary about orphanage once
Total	Total	Total ....

If your sins exceed your good deeds, you're going to hell buddy! Unless you make up the deficit between now and midnight. If your other deeds preponderate, God will decide your fate on a passing whim, or maybe even by tossing a coin, who knows.

GURGLE!
BURP!
PITTER PATTER!
Belch!
FART!

Spend today listening to a loved one's inner workings.

Reach new levels of intimacy. Put your ear to their chest, their belly, their groin, and monitor their plumbing noises. Record them carefully and see if you can discern a pattern.

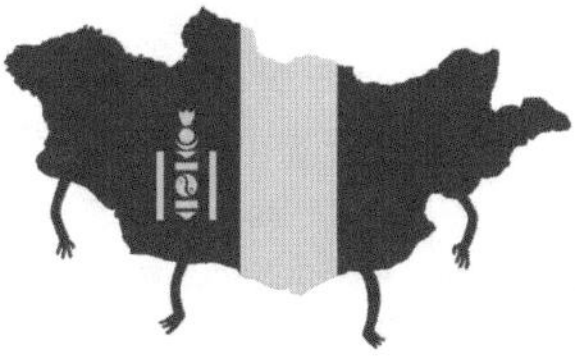

TODAY, THREATEN A FOREIGN COUNTRY

Diplomacy is too important to be left to the government. Today speak for the land of your birth on the international stage by sending this ultimatum to a country of your choice.

Dear Leader of ....

I have so far tolerated your behaviour in the spirit of international forbearance, but enough is enough.
I am hereby issuing you with an ultimatum. Either you desist from your obnoxious course of action, or I shall be forced to invade. I have the full backing of my country's government and its armed forces, which are at the ready to give you a drubbing, should you prevaricate on this matter. You have until 11.59pm tonight to respond. Truly, you will rue the day you offended me. Yours sincerely,

....

speaking on behalf of

...................................(country)

Insure your best feature today

Since Hollywood star Betty Grable insured her legs for $1m in the 1940s, actors and models have rushed to Lloyds of London to get their favourite body parts covered. Why shouldn't you? Call them for a quote on your finest asset on 020 7327 5448. Here is a rough guide to what you can expect to pay.

Nose (cute)
Value: £5,890
Premium:
£54.03/month

Nose (crooked)
Value: £167
Premium:
£3.63/month

Hairy hands
Value: £251
Premium:
£7.88/month

Smile
Value: £1,545
Premium:
£23/month

Suckable big toes
Value: £3,208
Premium:
£39.75/month

Personality
Value: £7
Premium:
£0.55/month

Brain
Value: £54,000
Premium:
£231.65/month

Je ne sais quoi
Value: £25,709
Premium:
£158.42/month

TODAY ZOMBIE-PROOF YOUR HOME

FIRST

Research zombie behaviour. Rent out a couple of classic zombie movies to learn their wants, needs, likes, dislikes and, most importantly, what it takes to either stop them or hold them at bay.

SECOND

Gather any items and tools needed, including boards, hammers, and nails to board up windows and doors. Also procure weaponry to fight them off as they try to breach your defences, e.g. chainsaws, shotguns or even golf clubs.

THIRD

Stockpile non-perishable food, just in case the zombie invasion lasts days rather than hours.

FINALLY

Do a dry run: board up your house, timing the exercise. Don't worry what the neighbours think - they will most likely be part of any potential zombie horde anyway.

Day 77

ERECT A STATUE OF YOURSELF IN A PUBLIC PLACE TODAY

SIDNEY KENTMAN
1954-

Statues are a short cut to immortality. Contact an affordable local sculptor today and have them cast your features in the material of your choice. As soon as it's ready, choose a public space where your statue will look right at home; a large square perhaps, or a park. Everyone knows that's where statues belong, so as long as you install it with confidence, you won't be challenged. Finally, don't forget the plaque with your name, date of birth, and public achievements; tourists require this kind of information.

FREELANCE AS A TRAFFIC WARDEN TODAY

With the best will in the world, traffic warden firms like NCP can't cover the whole country, and therefore miss out on thousands of potential fines a day. Today, look out for illegally-parked cars, call the traffic warden company to alert them to their location, and claim 10% of the fine. Given an average fine of £80, you could make £8 for a mere ten seconds' work. And you'll be helping to enforce parking regulations into the bargain! Place these "freelance parking tickets" on the windshield so that the traffic warden company can arrange payment.

FREELANCE PARKING TICKET

Ticket No: ....

VEHICLE:
Make: .... Model: ....
Colour: .... Registration No: ....

PARKING OFFENCE:
Date: .... Time: ....
Location: ....
Description: ....
Fine £: ....

FREELANCE TRAFFIC WARDEN
Name: ....
Address: ....
Phone number: ....
Signature: ....

Offence confirmed

I certify that the above vehicle was parked in violation of parking law on the above date and time. This preliminary ticket was issued by a freelancer and must be confirmed by a registered traffic warden. I have called a registered traffic enforcement company and they are on their way to verify the offence and issue a full penalty ticket. Please pay 10% commission of the above fine directly into my bank account No:.......................... Sort code: ....
Bank: .... Thank you!

FREELANCE PARKING TICKET

Ticket No: ....

VEHICLE:
Make: .... Model: ....
Colour: .... Registration No: ....

PARKING OFFENCE:
Date: .... Time: ....
Location: ....
Description: ....
Fine £: ....

FREELANCE TRAFFIC WARDEN
Name: ....
Address: ....
Phone number: ....
Signature: ....

Offence confirmed

I certify that the above vehicle was parked in violation of parking law on the above date and time. This preliminary ticket was issued by a freelancer and must be confirmed by a registered traffic warden. I have called a registered traffic enforcement company and they are on their way to verify the offence and issue a full penalty ticket. Please pay 10% commission of the above fine directly into my bank account No:.......................... Sort code: ....
Bank: .... Thank you!

FREELANCE PARKING TICKET

Ticket No: ....

VEHICLE:
Make: .... Model: ....
Colour: .... Registration No: ....

PARKING OFFENCE:
Date: .... Time: ....
Location: ....
Description: ....
Fine £: ....

FREELANCE TRAFFIC WARDEN
Name: ....
Address: ....
Phone number: ....
Signature: ....

Offence confirmed

I certify that the above vehicle was parked in violation of parking law on the above date and time. This preliminary ticket was issued by a freelancer and must be confirmed by a registered traffic warden. I have called a registered traffic enforcement company and they are on their way to verify the offence and issue a full penalty ticket. Please pay 10% commission of the above fine directly into my bank account No:.......................... Sort code: ....
Bank: .... Thank you!

FREELANCE PARKING TICKET

Ticket No: ....

VEHICLE:
Make: .... Model: ....
Colour: .... Registration No: ....

PARKING OFFENCE:
Date: .... Time: ....
Location: ....
Description: ....
Fine £: ....

FREELANCE TRAFFIC WARDEN
Name: ....
Address: ....
Phone number: ....
Signature: ....

Offence confirmed

I certify that the above vehicle was parked in violation of parking law on the above date and time. This preliminary ticket was issued by a freelancer and must be confirmed by a registered traffic warden. I have called a registered traffic enforcement company and they are on their way to verify the offence and issue a full penalty ticket. Please pay 10% commission of the above fine directly into my bank account No:.......................... Sort code: ....
Bank: .... Thank you!

FOLLOW YOUR HOROSCOPE'S ADVICE TO THE LETTER TODAY

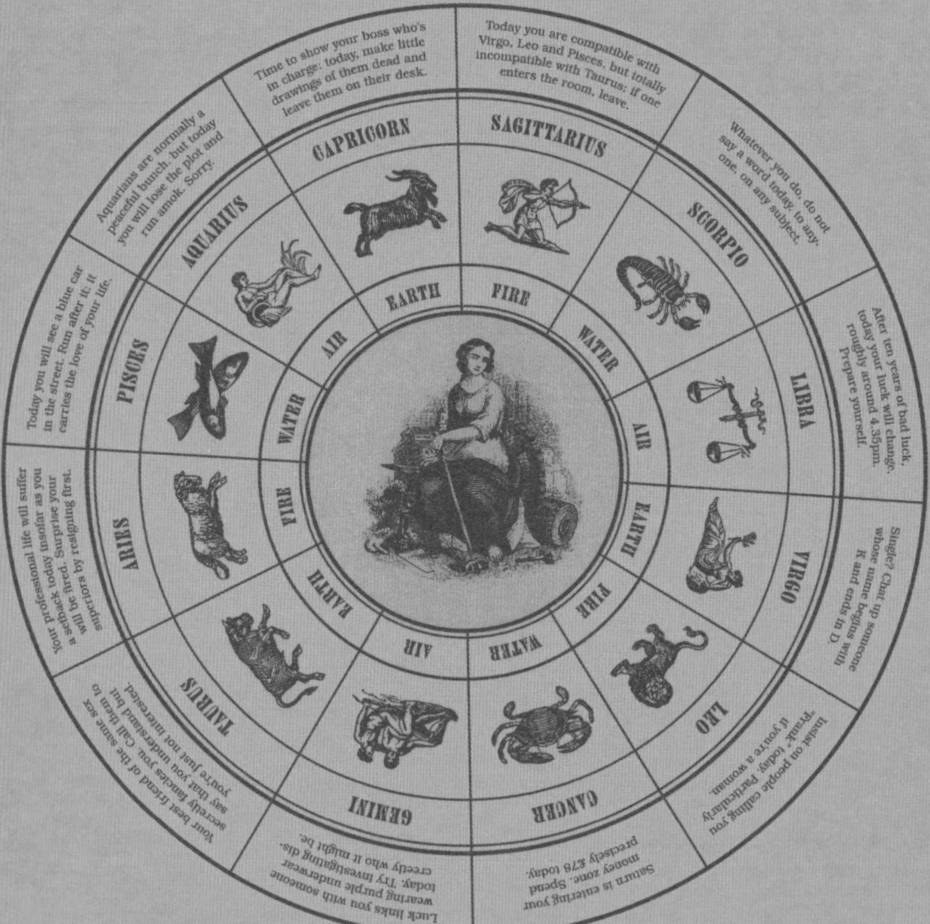
CAPRICORN
Time to show your boss who's in charge: today, make little drawings of them dead and leave them on their desk.
SAGITTARIUS
Today you are compatible with Virgo, Leo and Pisces, but totally incompatible with Taurus; if one enters the room, leave.
SCORPIO
Whatever you do, do not say a word today, to anyone, on any subject.
LIBRA
After ten years of bad luck, today your luck will change, roughly around 4.35pm. Prepare yourself.
VIRGO
Single? Chat up someone whose name begins with K and ends in D.
LEO
Insist on people calling you "Frank" today. Particularly if you're a woman.
CANCER
Saturn is entering your money zone. Spend precisely £78 today.
GEMINI
Luck links you with someone wearing purple underwear today. Try investigating discreetly who it might be.
TAURUS
Your best friend of the same sex secretly fancies you. Call them to say that you understand but you're just not interested.
ARIES
Your professional life will suffer a setback today insofar as you will be fired. Surprise your superiors by resigning first.
PISCES
Today you will see a blue car in the street. Run after it; it carries the love of your life.
AQUARIUS
Aquarians are normally a peaceful bunch, but today you will lose the plot and run amok. Sorry.
EARTH
FIRE
WATER
AIR
EARTH
FIRE
WATER
AIR
EARTH
FIRE
WATER
AIR

To help, we've had this one designed scientifically, by the world's leading expert.

Clean your nails with a kitchen knife
Crack your knuckles slowly as they speak
Tear the wings off a nearby fly
Put your cigarette out in their coffee
Snap a pencil in two, preferably theirs
Headbutt the wall next to their head
Caress their cheek ominously
Threaten to chop their damn neck off and stuff their eviscerated bowels down it if they don't make your life smoother

Today, solve problems with the threat of violence

Well-known Hollywood legend Dennis Hopper used to facilitate script meetings by placing a couple of loaded handguns on the table in front of him. And indeed, the threat of force was how things got done for millions of years before we evolved language and degenerated into a consensus-seeking species. Today, see if your life runs more smoothly through sheer physical intimidation. Pick one or several of these tried-and-tested techniques: whichever is most appropriate to the situation in hand. All of them should be accompanied by a pregnant unflinching stare at whoever you are trying to intimidate.

PRAY TO OUT-OF-DATE GODS TODAY

Before the spirit-crushing advent of monotheism, there used to be a much wider variety of gods. By now, however, they are extremely bored, and so will act with extra diligence on behalf of anyone who bothers invoking them. Today, give it a try. Who knows – if it worked for the Vikings, it could work for you.

God		Expertise	Background	Typical prayer
	Minerva	Wisdom	Daughter of Jupiter	*Dear Minerva daughter of Jupiter, I am being offered a 3-year fixed rate mortgage with no redemption penalties at 5.15% + £2000 cashback. Tell me what to do.*
	Loki	Trouble	Murderer of Balder, the son of Odin and Frigg	*Dear Loki, my neighbour is aggravating me with his loud "metal" music. Please kill him in the night (discreetly).*
	Thanatos	Death	Brother of Hypnos	*Dear Thanatos, my cousin has cancer of the thyroid. Leave him alone or I'll fucking come after you myself.*
	Nerthus	Fecundity	Sister and wife of Njörd	*Nerthus, I have been trying for a baby with my husband for six months now. Before we resort to IVF, would you mind trying to help? We would call the child after you.*
	Poseidon	Ocean	Son of Cronus and Rhea, brother of Zeus	*Poseidon, please sheathe thy trident until we dock in Calais as these rough seas are reversing my digestive process.*
	Ra	Sun	Father of Shu and Tefnut	*Dear Ra, we will be holidaying in Malaga from the 13th to the 19th of April. Could you please ensure we enjoy mostly sunshine with little to no cloud cover?*
	Moloch	Infant sacrifice	"Abomination of the children of Ammon"	*Dear Moloch, my 9-year-old is running wild. I do not wish to spank him. Could you please give him a fright of some kind (apparition, threat of sacrifice etc.)? Thanks in advance.*
	Mars	War, carnage	Earth-god, father of Romulus and Remus	*Dear Mars, would you mind preventing the dissemination of chemical and biological weapons of mass destruction? Spears and arrows were just fine.*

Today speak the UNSPEAKABLE

In our verbally incontinent society, recover the power of words by finding something you cannot actually bring yourself to say out loud in public.

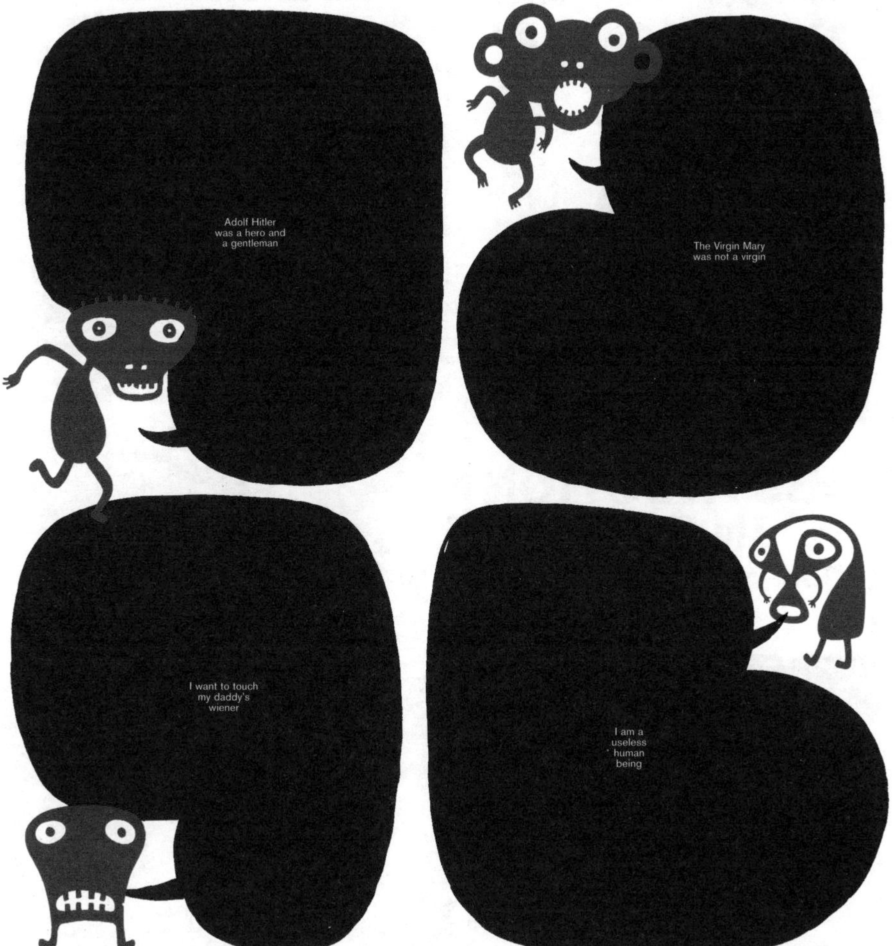
Adolf Hitler was a hero and a gentleman
The Virgin Mary was not a virgin
I want to touch my daddy's wiener
I am a useless human being

Day 83

Help finish roadworks today

Roadworks are a constant source of frustration to city dwellers. No sooner is one hole filled than another is dug, often in the very same place, and left unmanned for days. Today, speed matters along: find a hole where no work seems to be proceeding. Stick one or several of the messages below on pipes, barriers or other infrastructure where you judge they may bring works to a swifter conclusion.

XXXXX
Obsolete Mains Water
REMOVE
REWIRE
URGENT!
EXCLUSION ZONE
CRIME
SCENE!
OBSTRUCTION
IN PIPE
Bore in with pneumatic drill at 30°.
NATIONAL GRID
240V
USE GLOVES!
TREATED
WASTE
HAZCHEM RISK 0
CAUTION!
HOT

DOES CHEESE REALLY GIVE YOU NIGHTMARES?

Find out by eating 100g of one of the following and recording your dreams.

DANISH BLUE
(zombies)

GORGONZOLA
(vampires)

GRUYERE
(castration anxiety)

PARMESAN
(friends deserting you)

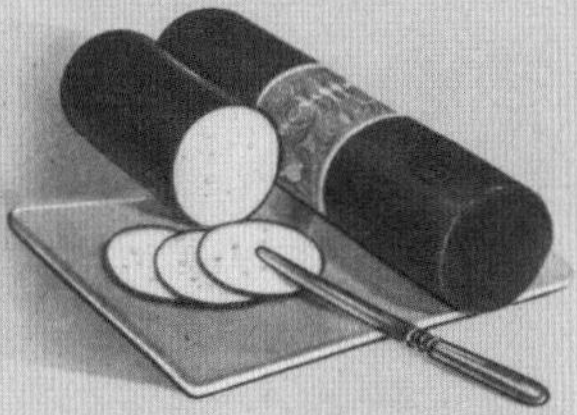

STILTON
(loss of loved one)

BRIE
(falling from great height)

EMMENTAL
(going to hell)

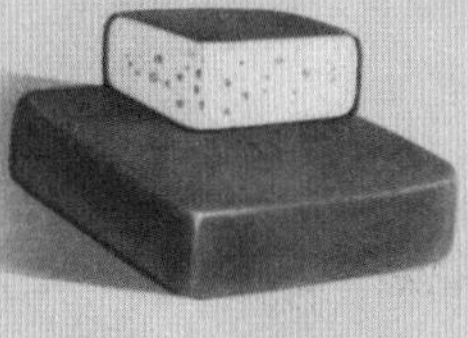

ROCQUEFORT
(general sweatiness)

Disgrace Day

Today, tell everyone you've lost your job, home and place in society, and see who still talks to you. When the chips are down, who are your real friends?

10am
I've been made redundant
Support ☐
Betrayal ☐

11am
Actually, I was fired
Support ☐
Betrayal ☐

12pm
I was fired for stealing
Support ☐
Betrayal ☐

1pm
I stole to pay for my heroin habit
Support ☐
Betrayal ☐

2pm
I've been "using" for years now
Support ☐
Betrayal ☐

3pm
I normally sell my body to get the money
Support ☐
Betrayal ☐

4pm
But I caught genital herpes as a result
Support ☐
Betrayal ☐

5pm
My partner has kicked me out
Support ☐
Betrayal ☐

6pm
My family have disowned me
Support ☐
Betrayal ☐

7pm
The police are looking for me
Support ☐
Betrayal ☐

8pm
I'm totally bankrupt
Support ☐
Betrayal ☐

9pm
Can I stay at your place for a while?
Betrayal ☐

Stages of disgrace: reveal the extent of your disgrace gradually, noting whether they support you at each stage.

Today return to childhood

Draw like Picasso
DADDY
HA HA HA
Teddy
Play with your food
AOCH!
Hurt a fly
Scream for ice cream
Smash a window
ICE CREAM
Get someone else to dress you
Fight with your siblings
AOUCH!
Wet your pants

Toilet training: did it mess you up? Toilet training is a crucial formative influence on your life. As you sit on the potty today, see if it triggers any repressed memories that may have helped ruin your life. Do you feel aggressive at work or in traffic? Do you feel like emotions are bottling up inside? Do you want to just let rip? Then chances are you may be suffering from TTS (Toilet Training Syndrome). Unfortunately there is no cure, though it may sometimes help to sue your parents.

Day 87

Today, go through people's rubbish and use the information to chat them up

Low fat
Yogurt
150g e

"You have a great figure, do you work out?"

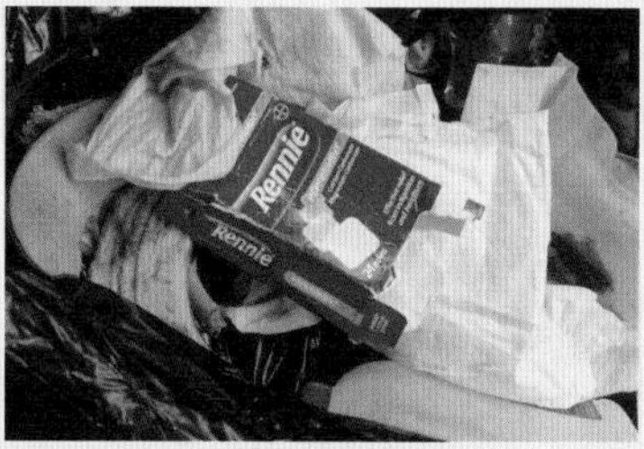
Rennie
Rennie

"Are you ok there, you look a bit stressed?"

"Can I buy you a drink?"

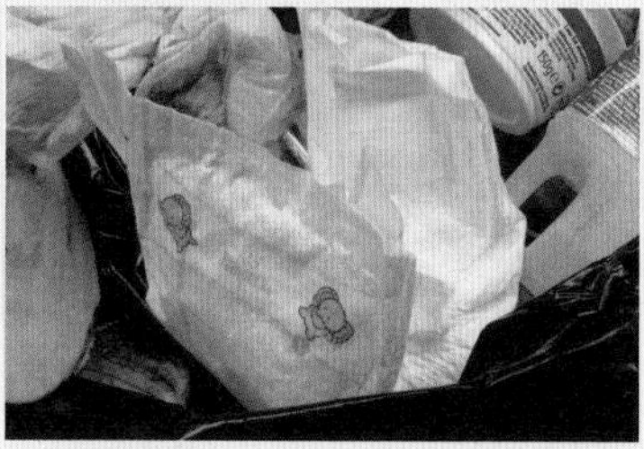

"Can you sign my petition against sex offenders moving in next door?"

ECOVER
NATURALLY POWERFUL DISHWASHER TABLETS
EFFICIENT AND SAFE

"Would you know where the nearest recycling centre is?"

"Want sex?"

TODAY WATCH SOMEONE SLEEP

Sleepwatching is the new meditation. There is nothing more relaxing than watching someone lie asleep in front of you, in a state of deep trusting peace, free of the cares and stresses of daily life. It induces a feeling of well-being and benevolence, a Zen-like oneness with the sleeper and the world at large. Today, sleepwatch your partner for at least four hours a night and notice the difference in your mood. If you don't have a regular sleeping partner, find a "sleepwatching buddy" on www.benrik.co.uk.

SAFETY GUIDELINES

Consent: It is important that you gain the prior consent of the sleeper. Sleepwatching someone without their knowledge is unethical, impractical, and could cause misunderstandings if they suddenly woke up.

Snoring: Many of the relaxation benefits of sleepwatching may be lost if you end up sleepwatching a heavy snorer. Try pushing them onto their side, or gently pinching their nostrils until the snoring abates.

Sleepwalking: As with snoring, sleepwalking can detract from the sleepwatching experience. Try to steer the sleepwalker away from life-threatening situations such as balconies, and coax them back to bed.

Staying awake: The beginner sleepwatcher may find it difficult to stay awake. It is recommended to bring a thermos of strong coffee to sustain you through the first hours. After a while, your body will get used to not sleeping.

Inappropriate behaviour: Sleepwatching involves a sacred bond of trust between sleeper and watcher. Under no circumstances should the watcher "interfere" with the sleeper, even if the sleeper appears to be in the grip of a dream with sexual content.

Day 89

Today, speak only Esperanto

Esperanto is the most successful artificial language, with over 2 million speakers worldwide. It was conceived and published by Ludovic Lazarus Zamenhof in the 1880s with the aim of replacing complicated and exclusive "unplanned" languages, thus facilitating world peace. This is why dictators have often perceived it as a threat, with Stalin for instance calling it "the dangerous language" and deporting all its registered speakers to Siberia in 1938. Every letter in Esperanto has only one sound, every word is pronounced as it is spelled, the grammar consists of 16 simple rules, and only 500 words are required for basic conversation.
Do your bit to advance the cause of global harmony with this little primer, full of useful sentences that you will not find in the phrasebooks.

This is a citizen's arrest, drop your knives.	Mi civitan-arestas vin, faligu viajn tran^cilojn.
I am looking for an Esperanto-speaking dominatrix.	Mi ser^cas seksmastrinon kiu parolas esperanton.
Quick! I need emergency surgery now!	Rapidu! Mi urg'e bezonas kirurgion nun!
If you park in my spot, I will shoot you in the head.	Mi vian kapon pafos se vi s'telos mian parklokon.
The referee is blind.	La arbitristo blindas.
Our plans for invasion are finally ready.	Niaj planoj invadi finfine pretas.
That's a massive line of cocaine.	Longegas tiu linio da kokaino.
You goddamn retard, don't you understand Esperanto?	Vi volapukisto, ^cu Esperanton vi ne komprenas?

CONTROL ORDER DAY

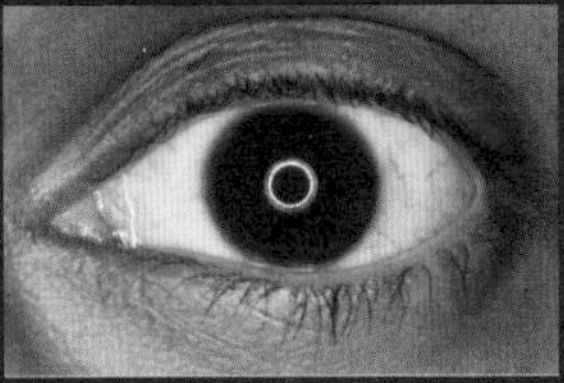

Benrik are concerned to impose and maintain an appropriate level of supervision over their readers in these uncertain times. Today, they are therefore introducing control orders on Benrik followers, to monitor their behaviour and keep them in line.

1. Benrik readers must register on www.benrik.co.uk and post a photo of themselves holding up this page with the "Control Order Acceptance" box signed.
2. Benrik controllees are to email their contact details to control@benrik.co.uk, including a copy of valid ID and their mobile phone number, so that Benrik may control them more effectively.
3. Controllees must email their schedule for the day for approval to control@benrik.co.uk by 10 a.m. GMT, including in particular a list of the people they intend to meet or associate with.
4. Controllees are to present themselves to Benrik's headquarters (address on website) between 9 a.m. and 5 p.m. to be tagged. Controllees living abroad may be notified of local tagging facilities via the site.
5. Controllees must CC control@benrik.co.uk on all email communications, both work-related and personal.
6. Controllees must report by checking in to benrik.co.uk once every 4 hours and giving details of their exact whereabouts, supported by photos.
7. Controllees must report their thoughts to Benrik throughout the day, via control@benrik.co.uk. Benrik will intervene to censor and redirect any unwholesome or unauthorised thoughts.

CONTROL ORDER ACCEPTANCE

I recognize that by buying this book or receiving it as a gift, I accept that Benrik are entitled to intrude in my private life and impose such restrictions on it as they may see fit. I hereby opt out of the European Convention on Human Rights for the day.

Signed and dated:

TODAY USE YOUR REMOTE CONTROL FOR EVIL PURPOSES

Turns traffic lights green
Activates dark side of people
Restarts supercomputers
Remote Nuclear War Button
Triggers immediate orgasm
Makes cats vomit
Disables incoming missiles
Jams other people's mobiles
Makes aeroplanes go faster
Pauses pacemakers
Even its maker has forgotten what this one does

Don't just point it at the TV! Instead try these functions.

Benrikchalking Day

American hoboes in the Depression communicated through rough chalk symbols on sidewalks, fences and buildings, to let each other know what to expect in that area. More recently it's been used to advertise wireless access points. But the potential is much greater. Today, chalk the streets near you in Benrik signs, to let your fellow readers know the salient features of your neighbourhood.

Hobo sign language

Kind hearted lady
Unsafe place
2
10
Crooks!
Talk religion to get food
Work available
Bad-tempered owner
Judge lives here
No-alcohol town
Owner out
Bad water
Hoboes arrested on sight
Man with guns
Free telephone
Rich people live here
Vicious dog here
Gentleman
Hold your tongue
Good place to catch a train

Benrik sign language

Dog with diarrhoea
Woman with evil laugh
Nudist couple in window above
Bad haircuts here
Conscientious butcher
Don't order the prawns in here!
Celebrity often has coffee here
Small child pees from balcony
Flatulent shopkeeper
Road rage intersection
Household with widescreen TV
Watch your change in here
Housewife with forlorn smile
Cappuccinos extra frothy
Very loud kettle
Double pram zone
Man plays saxophone badly
Pee here if you really can't hold it

Day 93

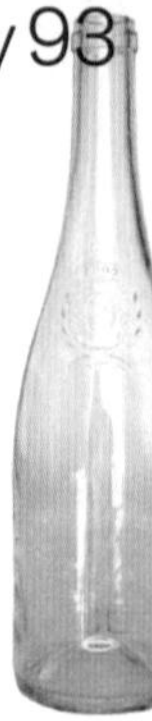

PLAIN GLASS BOTTLE:
standard "I'm lost on a desert island" messages

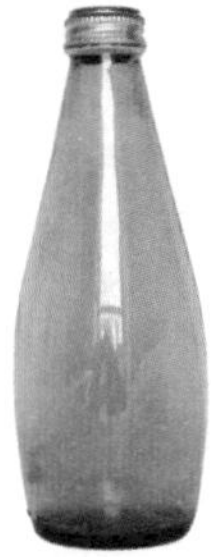

MINERAL WATER BOTTLE:
for long fancy letters you'd like to see published someday

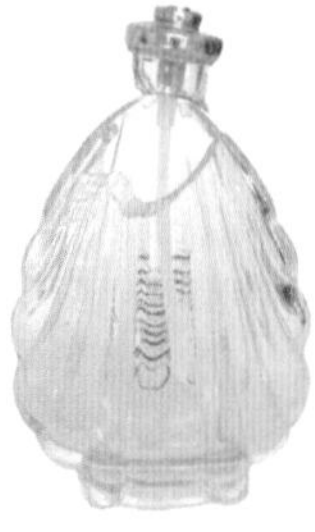

PERFUME BOTTLE:
letters to one's illicit lovers

BEER BOTTLE:
party invitations & news of sports victories

VINTAGE CHAMPAGNE BOTTLE:
formal messages, weddings, funerals, bar mitzvahs

TODAY SEND A MESSAGE IN A BOTTLE

Be sure to choose the appropriate bottle for your message.

(Note: according to marine experts, there are currently 125,000 bottles containing messages floating around the world's oceans. Yours could be one of them.)

PLASTIC BOTTLE:
messages to your inferiors

SOFT-DRINK BOTTLE:
the young person's choice

FOREIGN WINE BOTTLE:
letters from abroad, holiday postcards

SHAKE THE BOTTLE.

MEDICINE BOTTLE:
painful news

BROKEN BOTTLE:
suicide notes

Today, adopt incompatible pets

Adopting a pet is proven to change your life by lowering your blood pressure and making you a more serene and caring individual. Today, adopt not one but several pets, and to spice things up a little, make them incompatible. Within hours, your everyday existence will have acquired a delightful Disney-like quality.

Goldfish
Piranha
Dog
Cat
Rat
Bird
Snake
Mouse

DEGREE OF INCOMPATIBILITY

Extremely incompatible ═══

Highly incompatible ══

Pretty incompatible ──

BLOOD-PRESSURE CHART

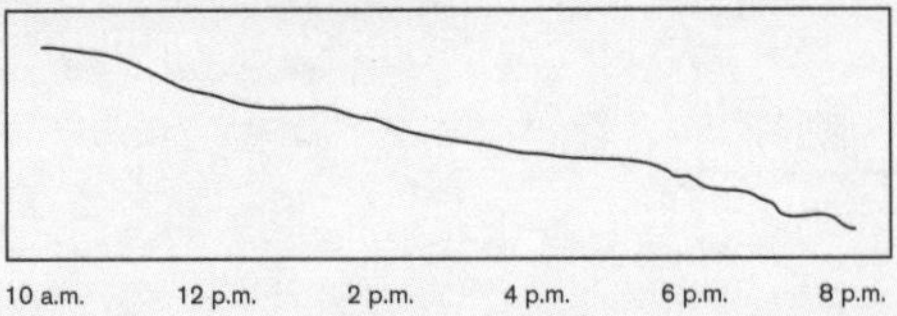
10 a.m.
12 p.m.
2 p.m.
4 p.m.
6 p.m.
8 p.m.

GO BACK TO SCHOOL TODAY

11 12 1
10 2
9 3
8 4
7 6 5

Maybe you weren't well. Maybe you skipped it without realizing its importance. But through no real fault of your own, you missed a crucial lesson, undermining your life since then. Today, go back to your local school and insist on attending a class you missed.

8.30 - 9.20	Maths	1+1
9.20 - 10.10	Geography	Map folding
10.10 - 11.00	P.E.	Sweating gracefully
11.00 - 11.50	French	Transsexual pronouns
11.50 - 12.40	Science	Secret of the universe
12.40 - 13.00	L U N C H	
13.00 - 13.40	Economics	Catching run-away inflation
13.40 - 14.30	Art	Duchamp since Benrik
14.30 - 15.20	English	Speaking proper
15.20 - 16.10	History	1342: the year nothing changed
16.10 - 19.00	DETENTION	

HOMEWORK

You're not allowed out to play with the others until you've finished your homework! Your assignment is to write a 1000-word essay answering any of the following questions. 1) To what extent did post-Kantian attempts to discover an all-encompassing first principle of philosophy succeed (with particular reference to Fichte and Schelling)? 2) "For Mallarmé, symbolism ultimately anticipated the synthesis of Christ and Thanatos". Discuss. 3) Describe how you spent your holiday. Use detail!!!

Humility Day

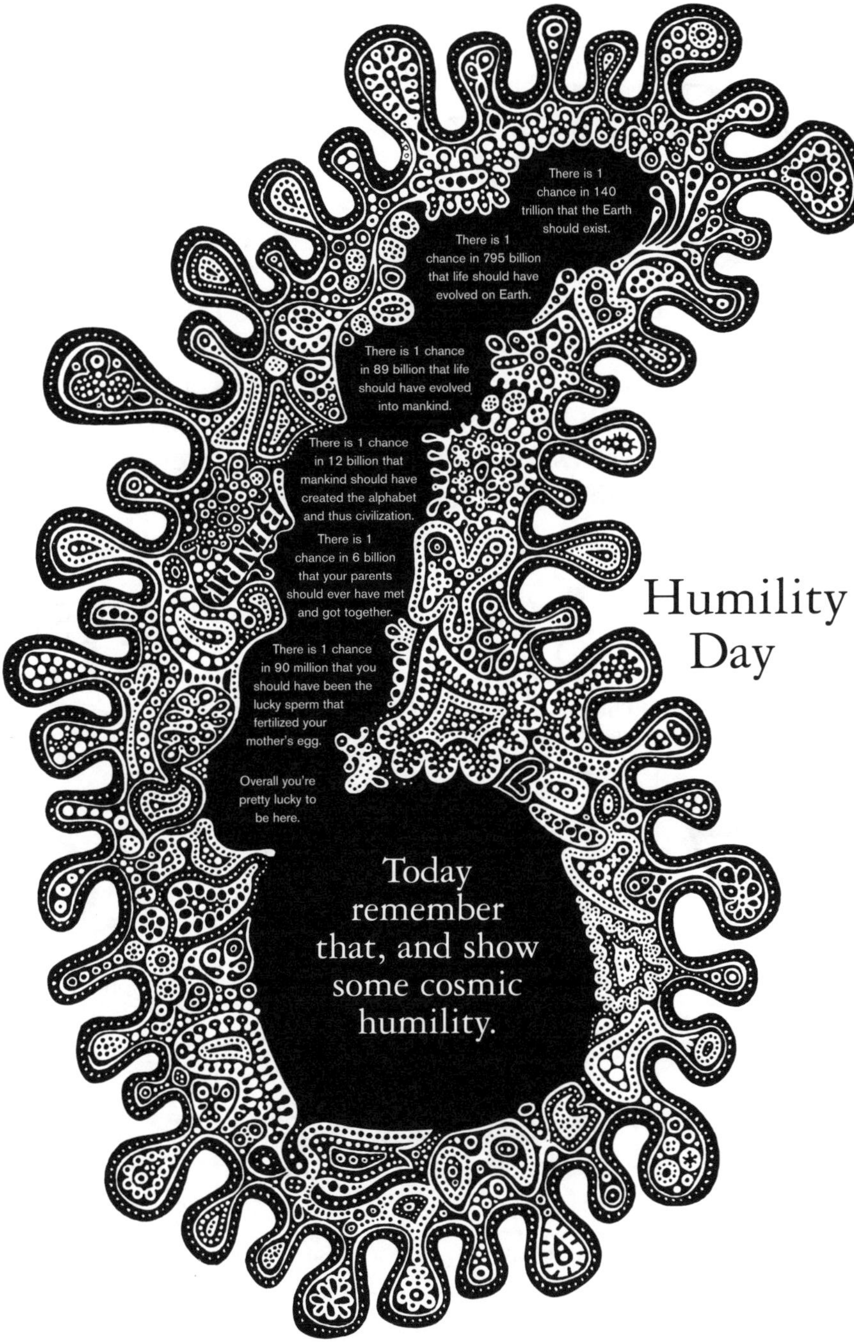
There is 1 chance in 140 trillion that the Earth should exist.
There is 1 chance in 795 billion that life should have evolved on Earth.
There is 1 chance in 89 billion that life should have evolved into mankind.
There is 1 chance in 12 billion that mankind should have created the alphabet and thus civilization.
There is 1 chance in 6 billion that your parents should ever have met and got together.
There is 1 chance in 90 million that you should have been the lucky sperm that fertilized your mother's egg.
Overall you're pretty lucky to be here.
BENRIK
Today remember that, and show some cosmic humility.

Day 97

146

Today, tip abnormally

The arbitrary rule of tipping is to leave 10 to 15%, but this is an old-fashioned and lazy approach. Tipping is an art form, expressive of your personality and potentially a force for social disruption. Today explore its potential, starting with our random guidelines. Begin with the tediously conventional 10% and add or subtract as follows.

-£1 The tippee has green or greenish eyes	**+£1** The tippee has a visible tattoo on his or her chest	**+£1.50** The sky is blue with fewer than three clouds	**+£1.50** The tippee has used a word beginning with "R"
+£7 The sum of your bill is a primary number	**-£8** You can't figure out if it is a primary number	**+£1** The tippee has offered sex as part of the service	**-£6** The world's geopolitical prospects look grim
-£1 The tippee resembles someone on TV	**-£4** Yesterday you went to bed drunk	**+£0.50** The service provided was good	**NB.** In some cases you will end up with a negative sum, which is known as reverse tipping. Here the tippee owes you money, which you may collect in cash or through extra service. Show them this book if they query your claim.

BECOME A HERMIT TODAY

Who can be a hermit? Anyone! The hermit lifestyle is due for a serious comeback: it's the perfect antidote to modern clutter and materialism. This is what you need to get started.

A GROTTO
We're not talking Hugh Hefner here: any hole in the ground you can hide in will do. Consult Ordnance Survey to find grottos in your area.

SCISSORS
To trim your great long grey straggly beard (women may dispense with this until the age of 70).

A DOG
Purists may quibble over this one, but an animal companion is within the rules, provided it too becomes a hermit and does not fraternize with other dogs.

A BLANKET
The hermit look is simply not complete without one. It also has practical applications, like stopping you from freezing to death.

A STICK
To beat away the other dogs, and to threaten pesky kids whose idea of fun is to try and set you on fire.

BROADBAND
To record your hermit experiences in a blog and share tips with other hermits.

A RAKE
To gather moss and lichen from the forest floor for food and for selling to local florists.

Subscribe to Raven's Bread, the quarterly newsletter for hermits ("Food for those in solitude"). For a year, send a US bank draft for $10 to editors Paul and Karen Fredette at Raven's Bread, 18065 Hwy. 209, Hot Springs, North Carolina NC 28743, USA. Any extra donations are used to subsidise subscriptions for hermits who cannot afford the cost. Thank you.

Day 99

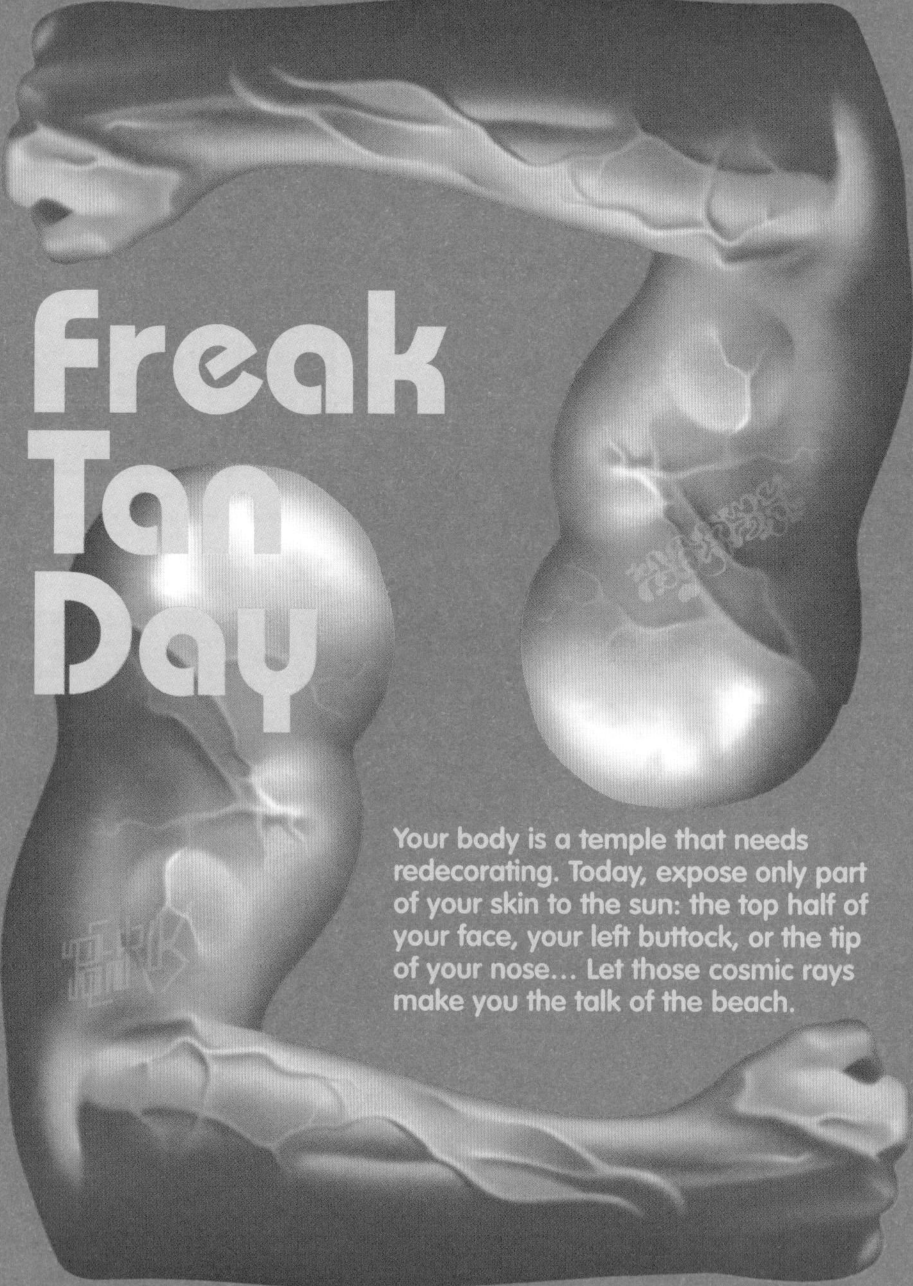

Freak Tan Day

Your body is a temple that needs redecorating. Today, expose only part of your skin to the sun: the top half of your face, your left buttock, or the tip of your nose... Let those cosmic rays make you the talk of the beach.

DO NOT DISTURB! Attract the writers' attention, but don't ask them directly to include you in their next novel as this will only irk them. You have to earn your claim to fame.

Today become a muse: stalk a well-known writer and set up a memorable incident that will inspire their next novel.

SALMAN RUSHDIE
Author of: Midnight's Children, The Satanic Verses
Lives: New York
Look out for him: Tribeca

Suggested incident: Offer to sell him the magic carpet that Ibn Battuta's great-great-granddaughter gave to your forebears in the year 1451, and on which he first flew over America, discovering it 100 years before Columbus.

MARTIN AMIS
Author of: Money, London Fields
Lives: Primrose Hill
Look out for him: Regent's Park Road

Suggested incident: Dress up as a Gestapo officer in a heavy leather raincoat, and expose yourself to the children of hard-looking geezers until you get beaten to a pulp.

CHUCK PALAHNIUK
Author of: Fight Club, Choke, Haunted
Lives: Portland, Oregon
Look out for him: Washington Park

Suggested incident: Accost a passer-by with a smile and claim you recognize them from your anger management class. Fly into a rage and headbutt them when they deny you've ever met.

DAN BROWN
Author of: The Da Vinci Code
Lives: Exeter, New Hampshire
Look out for him: Water St

Suggested incident: Paint blood-red stigmata on your hands and smear them all over an albino kitten before accomplices bundle you into a blacked-out limo and speed off.

WILL SELF
Author of: Great Apes, My Idea of Fun
Lives: Stockwell
Look out for him: Larkhall Park

Suggested incident: Impersonate a blind pensioner who can only find his way home by snorting a Hansel&Gretel-like line of cocaine on the pavement all the way to the front door.

JK ROWLING
Author of: the Harry Potter series
Lives: Edinburgh
Look out for her: Princes St

Suggested incident: Bite into an apple, then shriek as you pull a handful of live worms out of your pocket.

TODAY, COLD-CALL: Cold-calling need not be restricted to commercial purposes. We all require things, and cold-calling is as valid a way of obtaining them as any other, so pick up the phone book and dial away today. The key principle to remember is never to give up; you only need one successful phone call to forget the hundreds of unsuccessful ones. Here is a cold-calling script to help you get started.

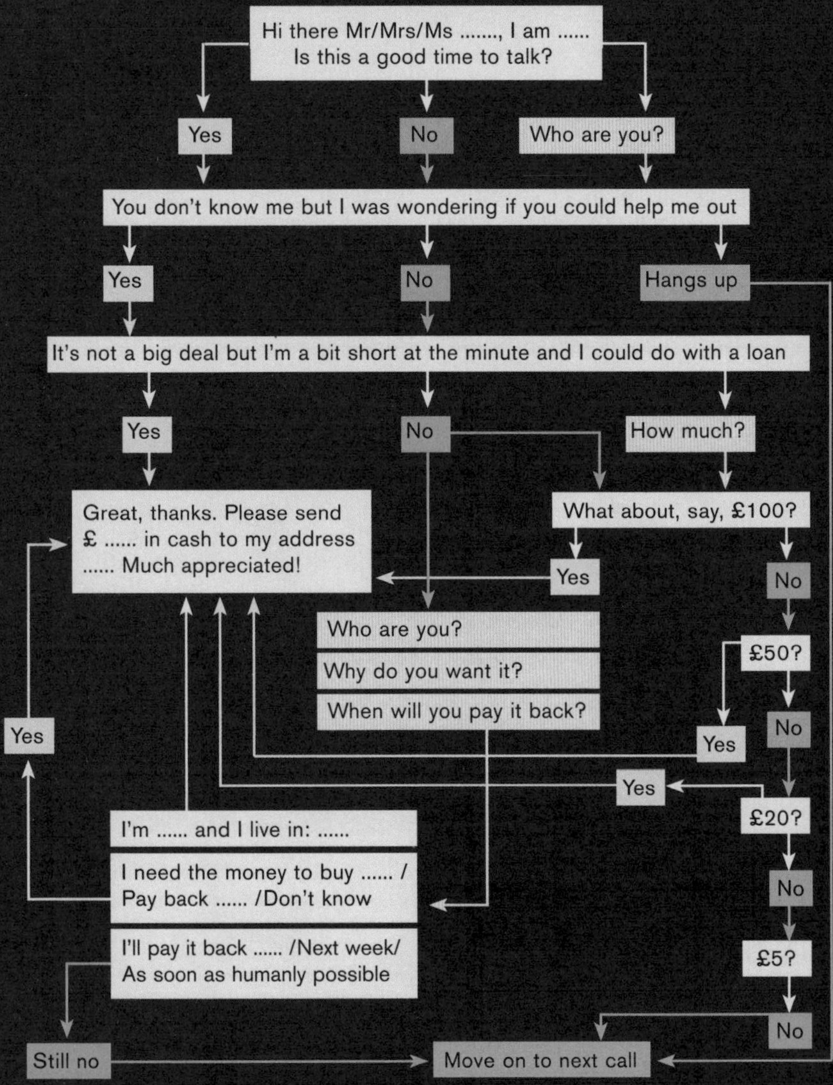
Hi there Mr/Mrs/Ms ...., I am ......
Is this a good time to talk?
Yes
No
Who are you?
You don't know me but I was wondering if you could help me out
Yes
No
Hangs up
It's not a big deal but I'm a bit short at the minute and I could do with a loan
Yes
No
How much?
Great, thanks. Please send £ ...... in cash to my address ...... Much appreciated!
What about, say, £100?
Yes
No
Who are you?
Why do you want it?
When will you pay it back?
£50?
Yes
No
Yes
Yes
£20?
I'm ...... and I live in: ......
I need the money to buy ...... / Pay back ...... /Don't know
No
I'll pay it back ...... /Next week/ As soon as humanly possible
£5?
No
Still no
Move on to next call

PRE-FEMINISM DAY

The most radical change of the twentieth century has been in the relationship between men and women. It is the first time in history that women have been even approximately treated as equals. Today, revert to pre-feminist behaviour to measure the difference.

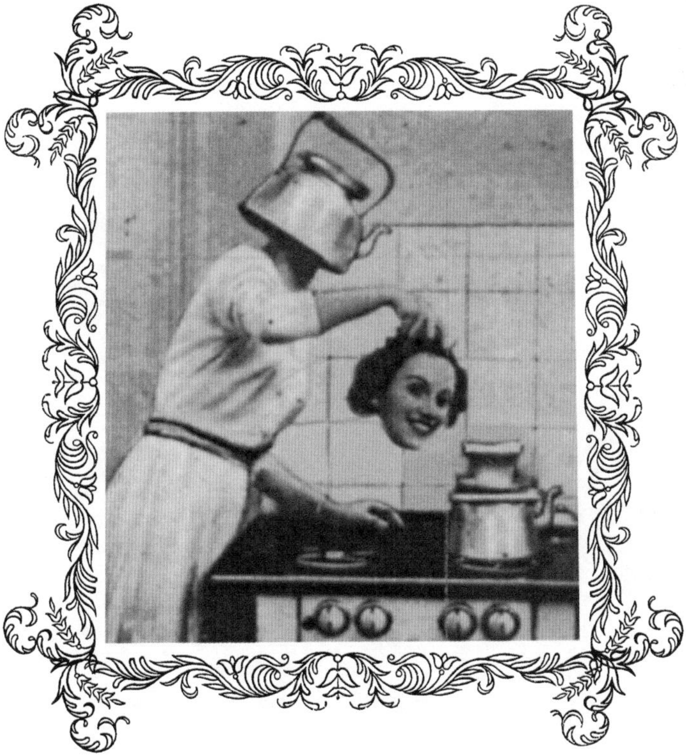

Women:

1) Make sure you look your best
2) Don't speak unless spoken to
3) Stay at home and do the housework
4) Cook a nice dinner for your man
5) Ask him for some pocket money for a new dress

Men:

1) Open doors, stand up, take your hat off
2) Buy your lady some flowers on your way back from work
3) Compliment her on her cooking
4) Sssshhhh her if she voices a foolish opinion
5) Skip foreplay, roll over and snore

Today decide which organs to donate in case of death and leave a copy of this page with your family. One body can help 100 other people.

What organs can I donate?

Tick the boxes of your choice.

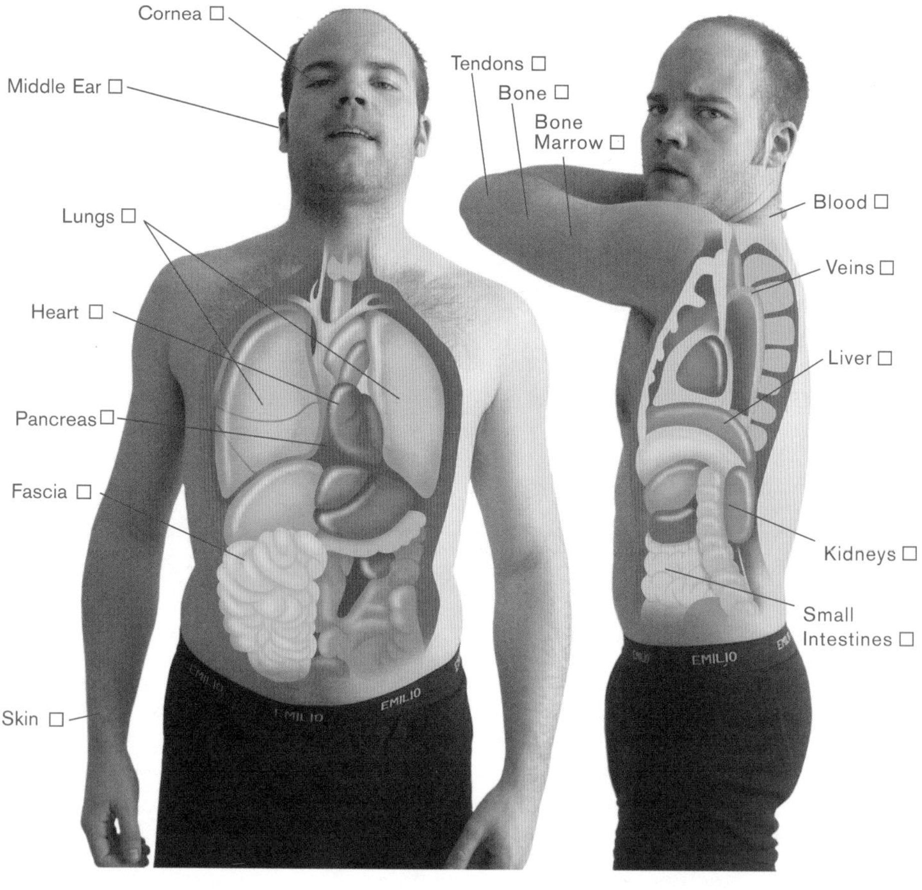
Cornea ☐
Middle Ear ☐
Lungs ☐
Heart ☐
Pancreas ☐
Fascia ☐
Skin ☐
Tendons ☐
Bone ☐
Bone Marrow ☐
Blood ☐
Veins ☐
Liver ☐
Kidneys ☐
Small Intestines ☐
EMILIO

Smile more often when you see me

Read me my horoscope

When you next see me, pretend we've never met

Offer me flowers more often

Hug me

Sleep with me

Don't leave me alone

Wake me up if I snore

Hold my hand to cross the street

Tell me something cute

Salute me

Today give little tasks to people around you

Carry my Book for me today

Watch my back

Let me win all discussions

Let me have the remote tonight

Read me a bed time story

Buy me lunch

Tie up my laces if they come undone

Answer my telephones

Hold the lift for me

Tell me what to do!

Greet me with a bow

Whistle my favourite tune

Water my desk plants

Buy me an expensive car

Let me win at chess for once

Tell me if my breath stinks

When I say something witty, praise me

Don't let me forget my umbrella again!

Organize my surprise birthday party

Pick my nose

Never talk to me again

Day 105

Muzak!

Carry your own desired musical ambience around with you today. Make a tape of songs appropriate to the mood you wish to convey to those around you, and play it on a beatbox all day long. For instance:

Angry

Fight The Power Public Enemy
The Prisoner Iron Maiden
White America Eminem
Fifth Symphony Beethoven
Fuck The Pain Away Peaches
Mutter Ramstein
Injustice For All Metallica
Smells Like Teen Spirit Nirvana
Won't Get Fooled Again The Who

Good for: asking for a pay rise, complaining in shops.

Hungry

Strawberry Fields Forever The Beatles
Candy And A Currant Bun Pink Floyd
Sugar And Spice The Searchers
Vindaloo Fat Les
Rock Lobster B-52s
Hungry Like The Wolf Duran Duran
Soup Is Good Food Dead Kennedys
Cinnamon Girl Neil Young
Crème Brulee Sonic Youth

Good for: restaurant settings, supermarkets.

Happy

Dancing Queen Abba
Shiny Happy People REM
Beautiful Day U2
Freedom Aretha Franklin
Holiday Madonna
It's Raining Men Weather girls
Celebration Kool And The Gang
Club Tropicana Wham!
La Bamba Los Lobos

Good for: winning the lottery, delivering babies.

Sad

Everybody Hurts REM
Yesterday The Beatles
So Far Away Carole King
Last Christmas Wham!
Moonlight Sonata Beethoven
Crying Roy Orbison
Crying Primal Scream
Tears In Heaven Eric Clapton
Do They Know It's Xmas? Band Aid

Good for: dumping partner, telling someone they have a parking ticket.

Lustful

Horny Mousse T
You Sexy Thing Hot Chocolate
Sex Machine James Brown
Erotica Madonna
Push It Salt'n'Pepa
I Touch Myself The Divinyls
Touch Me Samantha Fox
Suck My Dick Lil' Kim
I Want Your Sex George Michael

Good for: first date, public masturbation.

Mad

Freak Radiohead
Rambling On Procol Harum
Livin' La Vida Loca Ricky Martin
I Talk To The Trees Tony Bavaar
Party Out Of Bounds B-52s
Rock Me Amadeus Falco
O Superman Laurie Anderson
Can We Fix It Bob The Builder
Ring Cycle Wagner

Good for: scaring away muggers, scaring away loved ones.

Buddhist Fundamentalism Day

Relax,
or we kill
you.

You will be made
to reach Nirvana,
even if it's under
torture.

Through
meditation let
us annihilate our
enemies.

All Buddhist
suicide bombers
to be reborn as
Bill Gates.

Enlightenment
at the barrel
of a gun.

Go with the
flow, or die,
infidel.

The Middle
Way or the
highway.

Unless everyone
chills out immediately,
we slaughter them.

The Buddhist religion has so far failed to spawn a militant arm that would enforce their worldview against those of other more aggressive religions. We have corrected this anomaly by starting a Buddhist Fundamentalist group. Their eightfold demands are set out above. Join their armed struggle today on www.benrik.co.uk.

Today, mess up your kids so they turn into Picasso

Early deprivation of affection and the subsequent inner conviction that you are worthless fuel the compulsive ambition that drives the artist. By namby-pamby standards, it may seem that you are being cruel to your children, but really you are doing them a favour. 'They fuck you up, your Mum and Dad' is not therapeutical babbling, but the poet's grateful acknowledgement of his two-headed Muse. As Proust said, 'everything we think of as great comes from neurotics. They alone have founded religions and composed masterpieces'. He knew this first hand: when he didn't get his customary goodnight kiss from his mother one night at the age of seven, he concluded that love was doomed and was plunged into the lifelong despondency that produced his magnum opus. As his example shows, nothing heavy-handed is required; a forgotten kiss, a strange look, or a rash word are all it takes to spice up a life.

MY NAME IS ADOLF. AT LEAST THATS WHAT MY DADDY CALLS ME. MY REAL NAME IS BILLY. BUT DADDY SAYS ADOLF IS BETER FOR ME. HE SAYS I WILL UNDERSTAND WHEN I GROW UP. IT MAKES THE OTHER KIDS AT SKOOL LAUGH. I DONT KNOW WHY. MUMMY IS A PAINTER. SHE PAINTS WITH ME. I LIKE PAINTING BUT I DONT LIKE BLAK. BLAK IS THE ONLY COLOR MUMMY SAYS I CAN USE UNTIL I AM 9. THEN I CAN USE PINK. I DONT LIKE PINK. ON SUNDAYS DADDY AND MUMMY TAKE ME TO THE MUZEUM. I SIT IN FRONT OF THE PAINTINGS. THEN THEY GO TO THEY GO TO THE PUB. CANT GO BECAUS I AM 8 DADDY SAYS THE PAINTINGS WILBE MY MUMMY AND DADDY FOR 2 HOURS. BUT SOMETIMES ITS 3. I KNOW BECAUS I COUNT THE SEKUNDS IN MY HEAD. I CAN COUNT UP TO 14858. THAT WAS THE MOST THEY WERE IN THE PUB AND I WERE LOOKING AT THE PAINTING. SOMETIMES I DREAM THEY ARE DEAD. DADDY SAID GOOD BOY ADOLF AND GAVE ME RED PAINT FOR MY BIRTH-DAY.
ME AND MY MUMMY AND MY DADDY

Hand out a calling card to strangers today

The calling card is the ancestor of the more mundane business card, and was used by the Chinese and European nobilities to lubricate social interaction. Aristocrats would leave calling cards at each other's homes – and if the gesture was reciprocated, they would visit each other. Our times cry out for an updated version. The "Benrik Calling Card" is to be handed out to intriguing strangers, whom one suspects might enhance one's life. They are tailored to modern urban interaction, and should be dispensed with a silent smile, putting the onus on the receiver to get in touch.

I loved the book you're reading. Call when you've finished it and let me know what you thought!

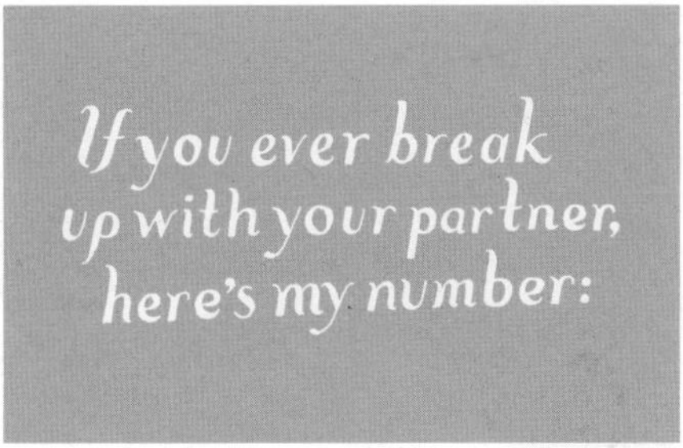
If you ever break up with your partner, here's my number:

You look nice. Get in touch sometime!

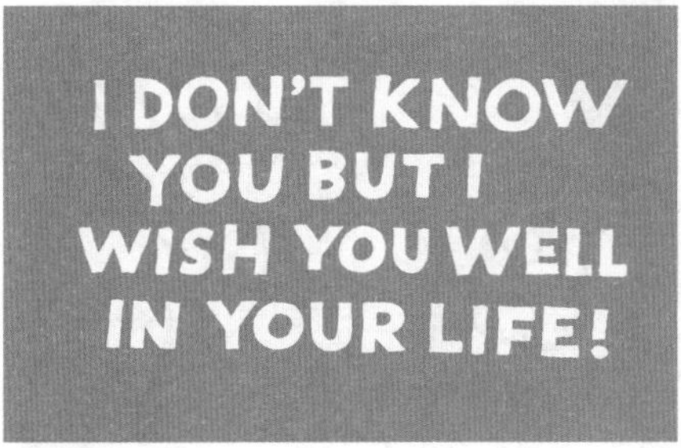
I DON'T KNOW YOU BUT I WISH YOU WELL IN YOUR LIFE!

SMILE!
IT MIGHT NEVER HAPPEN.

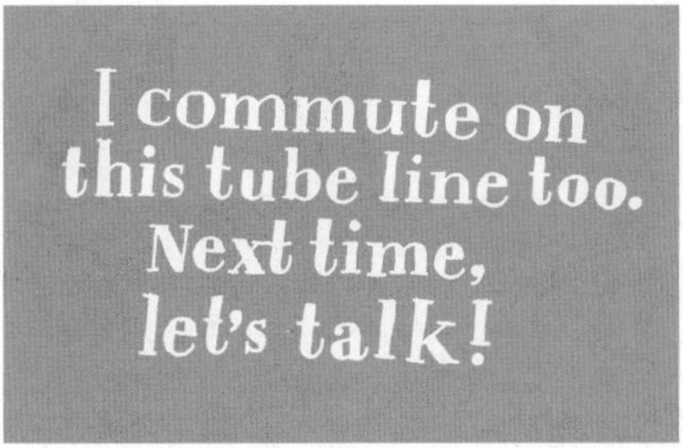
I commute on this tube line too. Next time, let's talk!

Here are a few examples from the range – duplicate them yourself, or purchase the finished article via www.benrik.co.uk or Moo.com.

LEAVE YOUR WALLET ON THE STREET TODAY

TRUST US

In 1983, French artist Sophie Calle found an address book on a Paris street. She photocopied its contents and returned it anonymously to its owner, one Pierre Baudry. She then proceeded to call all the people featured in the book, and wrote a series of newspaper articles about Mr Baudry based on what his friends, family and acquaintances told her. Today, discreetly drop your wallet on the pavement, and put your private life into the hands of a passer-by.

N.B.: Over twenty years later, Monsieur Baudry was allegedly still furious.

Choose one hair on your body that you will let grow 1 metre long.

Most hair grows at approximately half an inch a month, so within 8 years your chosen hair should be reaching optimum length. Remember to keep it clean, using shampoo and conditioner daily, and avoiding any tangling.

Special note for pubic hair: tape it to your inside leg during sexual congress so as not to ruffle it.

You'll never get bored of your special hair. Here for instance, we've used ours to recreate the Mona Lisa, only better.

Dream analysis

Work out what your dreams are telling you to do and do it!

CLOUDS

There are problems ahead at work, go on holiday.

CATS

You need more independence, quit your job and dump your partner.

MIRRORS

Your self is divided, pull yourself together.

FIRE

Someone hates you: hate them back.

DESERT

You are lonely. Wake up and talk to someone.

SEX

You want sex. Have sex.

CASTRATION

You are having a clichéd dream. Wake up immediately!

LADDERS

You are climbing towards your goal. Hurry up before someone beats you to it.

FALLING

You fear failure. Don't do anything at all today.

ROPES

You feel all tied up. Not much you can do here.

TREES

You need emotional support. Hug a tree.

WEB

You are trapped! Run away now.

DEATH

You are afraid of dying. Go to your GP for a check-up.

KEYS

The solution to your problem is in the cupboard that opens with those keys.

TODAY, FOLLOW THESE DIRECTIONS

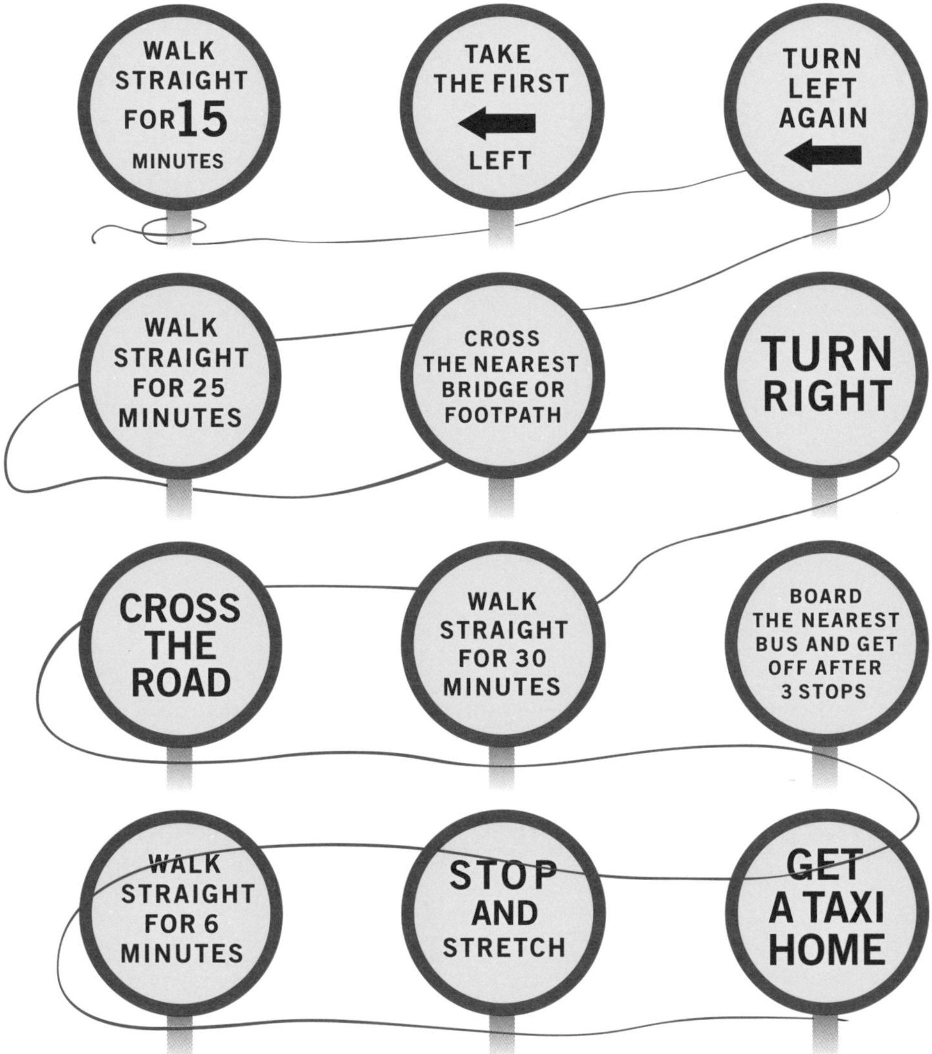
WALK STRAIGHT FOR 15 MINUTES
TAKE THE FIRST LEFT
TURN LEFT AGAIN
WALK STRAIGHT FOR 25 MINUTES
CROSS THE NEAREST BRIDGE OR FOOTPATH
TURN RIGHT
CROSS THE ROAD
WALK STRAIGHT FOR 30 MINUTES
BOARD THE NEAREST BUS AND GET OFF AFTER 3 STOPS
WALK STRAIGHT FOR 6 MINUTES
STOP AND STRETCH
GET A TAXI HOME

Today make a pact with the devil

Fill in this standard satanic contract with your own blood, which must be drawn from your left arm.

Dear Lucifer

I, ...,
wish to make a pact with you.

In exchange for my soul, you will grant me great power/vast wealth (cross out) for the next .... years (to be agreed). I undertake to abide by the rules of the damned, accept the Devil's mark, sacrifice children to you and generally make a satanic nuisance of myself.

Signed and dated in my blood,

....

To register this pact with the devil, stand within a magic circle and recite the following invocation: "LUCIFER, Emperor, Master of All Rebellious Spirits, I beseech thee to be favourable to me in calling upon thy GREAT MINISTER which I make, desiring thus to make a pact with him. BEELZEBUB, Prince, I pray thee also, to protect me in my undertaking. ASTAROTH, Count, be propitious to me and cause that this night the GREAT DEMON appear to me in human form and without any evil smell, and that he grant me, by means of the pact which I shall deliver to him, all the treasures of which I have need. GREAT DEMON, I beseech thee, leave thy dwelling, in whatever part of the world you may be, to come speak with me; if not, I shall thereto compel thee by the power of the mighty words of the Great Key of Solomon, whereof he made use to force the rebellious spirits to accept his pact. Appear then instantly or I shall continually torment thee with the mighty words of the Key: AGLON, TETRAGRAMMATON, ICION, STIMULAMATHON, EROHARES, RETRASAMATHON, ONERA, VAYCHEON, ESITION, EXISTIEN, ERYONA, CLYORAN, ERASYN, MOYN, MEFFIAS, SOTER, EMMANUEL, SABAOTH, ADONAI. I call you. AMEN". When the demon appears, simply hand him the pact and get a receipt. Congratulations! You have successfully sold your soul. May you rot in hell!

Trace your High School sweetheart and offer to meet up

You never forget your first love, but have they forgotten you? Look up cute little Chuck or sexy Martha in the phone book and give them a bell. By now they're probably stuck in a loveless marriage with 2.3 kids and a mortgage. You may well feature in their broken dreams.

Note: Should the words "creep", "police" or "restraining order" crop up in their conversation, it's a fairly sound indication that you did not feature in their dreams after all. Trace your second high school sweetheart and so on until successful or in jail.

BOYCOTT SOMETHING THAT'S NEVER BEEN BOYCOTTED BEFORE

Rhododendrons Porcini Tower Bridge Handshakes Oxygen Motherhood Smurfs Camels Surprise birthday parties 3B pencils Clouds with phallic shapes Gravity Innuendo Clothes Money Fax machines Hope Tasmania Viagra Horizontal stripes Caravaggio Stupidity Nelson Mandela Lopsided grins The flu The Queen Ugly suitcases Lawyers Love songs Apple pie Ballroom dancing Children Recycling Coconuts Sunshine Mascara Agatha Christie Plutonium Milkshakes Benrik Limited Plywood Tuesdays Soft focus photography Running Cancer The Danube Aircraft carriers Mimes Beauty Watercoolers Shadows Culture Shower gel Chainsaws Business cards Alopecia Timidity Plasticine Birmingham Cantilevering Taboos Menhirs Song Suicide Chopsticks Miracles Spirals Tamagotchis Fire Instamatics Catalogues Bastards who use you then discard you like a dirty tissue Exits Ciphers Freaks of nature Chaos Soup Jupiter The man in the moon Witchcraft Catamites Asphalt DNA Rock'n'roll The Tudor dynasty Riffs Ecuadoreans Photosynthesis Leprosy Satellites Monkfish Tasmania Repetition Donuts Hurricanes Trimesters Repetition Man's inhumanity to man Mildew Transitions Business lunches Boycotts

Today, buy a stranger flowers

CHRYSANTHEMUM
You're a wonderful friend

WHITE CAMELLIA
You're adorable

ACACIA
I love you secretly

RED ROSE
I love you

PRIMROSE
I can't live without you

WHITE LILAC
I'm a virgin, please be gentle

TULIP
You are the perfect lover

YELLOW HYACINTH
I'm jealous

PINK CARNATION
You have disappointed me

BLUEBELL
Let's call it a day

DAFFODIL
Are you still here?

CROCUS
If you call again,
I'll get an injunction

BECOME A SUPERHERO TODAY

Don't remain Clark Kent all your life. It only takes a little effort to acquire potentially useful superhero powers. Here's how.

Get a job in a corporate genetic modification lab. Late one night, "accidentally" fall into the experimental seeds centrifuge.

SUPER
GM

Powers: can clone himself at the drop of a hat.

In the course of a stroll outside Sellafield, get stung by a nestful of unusually large wasps...

WASPGIRL

Powers: each of her fingertips contains a radioactive sting!

Steal an Amazonian tribe's prized medicinal plant for the pharmaceutical industry and be cursed for 1000 years as a result.

Snakeboy

Powers: with his forked tongue, can lie his way out of any situation.

Fall into the vat of "unfit for human consumption" meat during a guided tour of an abattoir.

MEATMAN

Powers: can antagonize vegetarian villains.

Listen to Sex Pistols album repeatedly until timewarp projects you back to the late seventies.

PUNK
WOMAN

Powers: her anger can cause any society to implode.

This one was just born this way, you can't become one.

MONSTER
MAN

Powers: turns into a scary monster.

Today write a letter to your future self

Hello future me.
I'm glad we're still around to read this in the year 2040. What's happened to us in the last 30 years? Obviously I can't speculate too much, but from where I'm standing now, we'll have done well to avoid personal and global annihilation! So if im reading this, things have gone pretty good already. What are my hopes for the future me? I hoped we've lived up to my promise and become a race car driver. I imagine we've married and have kids (2 or 3) though I'll understand if we've become gay. It's because of that Martha bitch isn't it? We never liked her. Anyway, have we gone around the world as planned? I'd have to say I'd be really pissed off if we hadn't as I've just started saving. Also it's my life dream, so if we haven't got a good excuse that makes us a big fat loser in my book. Did we ever get caught for that tax scam? I'm pretty nervous about it now. I don't imagine we can get away with that in 2040, when computers probably monitor your every move. Maybe we're a famous astronaut? In which case schoolchildren will be reading this and learning about our life! But probably not. Anyway gotta go and live our life, so that's all for now.

Your past self

Today destroy photos that make you look ugly.

Everyone has a pile of old photos lying around. Good ones are invaluable: they represent good memories to cherish for the rest of your life. But bad photos are bad karma: they represent negative moments of your life and show you as boring, ugly or demonic. Burn them promptly.

SING EVERYTHING TODAY

I WOULD LIKE A PINT OF MILK!

I AM GOING TO THE TOILET NOW

THE MAN IN FRONT OF ME IN THE QUEUE IS VERY FAT INDEED!

I AM BEATING MY WIFE AGAIN

THERE'S A FREE PARKING SPACE AT LAST!!!

THIS ITEM IS TOO DEAR

IS IT SERIOUS DOCTOR?

LET ME SPEAK TO THE MANAGER

I HAVE FORGOTTEN MY UMBRELLA!

GIVE ME A PAYRISE OR I QUIT

WE ARE WALKING OUT OF THE TOWER BLOCK

I AM GOING TO JUMP OFF THIS TOWER BLOCK ONTO THE PEOPLE BELOW

I AM GOING TO BATTER YOU, YOU NONCE!!

THIS ADVERTISING IS TERRIBLE!

BRIBE PEOPLE ALL DAY

Bribing is an essential social practice, the lubricant in the engine of the free market, helping to bridge supply and demand. Other cultures know this, which is why they ignore misguided advice to abolish it. Good bribes, tactfully delivered, will guarantee you a more stress-free life in no time. Practise the art of bribery today, starting with our rough guide to tariffs below.

£1

Supermarket checkout girl to let you jump the queue

£23

Airline hostess to upgrade you to business class

£10

Traffic warden to tear up parking ticket

£14

Public bus to detour via your address

£18

Teacher to give you better grade

£59

Council to pick up your rubbish first

£6

Cable guy to connect you to forbidden channels

£1,000,
000

Government to build nuclear power plant in someone else's back garden

£49

Benrik to include your photo in next book

JOIN EXTREMIST ORGANIZATIONS AND OUT-EXTREME THEM TODAY

There is something appealingly old-fashioned about people who hold extreme views, something medieval about their blind certainties and the lengths to which they will go to advance their cause. Today, join some of these organizations, learn from their resolve, and test their grip on rational thought by suggesting even more extreme views and seeing if they embrace them.

	ORGANIZATION	EXTREME BELIEFS	HOW TO JOIN THEM	HOW TO OUT-EXTREME THEM
BNP	BRITISH NATIONAL PARTY	Calls for an immediate halt to all further immigration, the immediate deportation of criminal and illegal immigrants, and the resettlement of immigrants who are legally here. Also calls for restoration of capital punishment.	Membership is open to those of British or kindred European ethnic descent. Join at enquiries@bnp.org.uk.	"Foreign tourists come over here and sleep with our women. Ban tourism pronto!"
AF	ANARCHIST FEDERATION	The Anarchist Federation is an organization of class-struggle anarchists which aims to abolish capitalism, all hierarchy and all oppression to create a free worldwide classless equal society: anarchist communism.	Email your membershp enquiry with name and postal address to: join@afed.org.uk.	"Any organization is intrinsically hierarchical and fascist. Let's disband immediately!"
ALF	ANIMAL LIBERATION FRONT	Animals are our brothers and sisters in other species. They have equal rights and therefore need protecting by direct action against all forms of animal abuse, including in particular animal testing.	Try contacting them via the Animal Liberation Press Office, BM4400, London, WC1N 3XX.	"Don't insects have equal rights too? Kill the fly killers!"
AFUN	AL-FIRQAT UN-NAAJIYAH (the Saviour Sect)	Would like to see the implementation of Sharia law in the UK – which under their rule would be known as the Islamic Republic of Great Britain. Sample article on website: "Kill those who insult the Prophet Muhammad".	Any person can become a member of the Saviour Sect, providing they strictly adhere to the teachings of the Prophet Muhammad (SAW) and his Companions.	N/A
ELF	EARTH LIBERATION FRONT	The environment must be protected by "ecotage" (ecological sabotage), which involves inflicting economic damage on those who profit from the destruction and exploitation of the Earth.	The E.L.F. has no centralized organization to contact. You could always try to attend an Earth First Gathering (efgathering@aktivix.org) and hope that kindred spirits turn up.	"Humans are an incorrigible scourge on the fragile face of the Earth. The only solution is to all move to another, more resilient planet asap!"
UKLL	UK LIFE LEAGUE	"We want to close [the abortion industry] down. Period. No compromise, no excuses. Killing a baby is always wrong. Abortion is murder." They request any information on "abortionists, clinic workers and anybody else who actively supports unborn child-killing".	Contact the UKLL office for a Pro-Life Action pack: UK LifeLeague, 11 Waterloo Place, London, SWY 4AU.	"Sperm are alive. Male masturbation should count as genocide!"

N.B.: Make sure you tell these organizations that you are also joining the other five today!

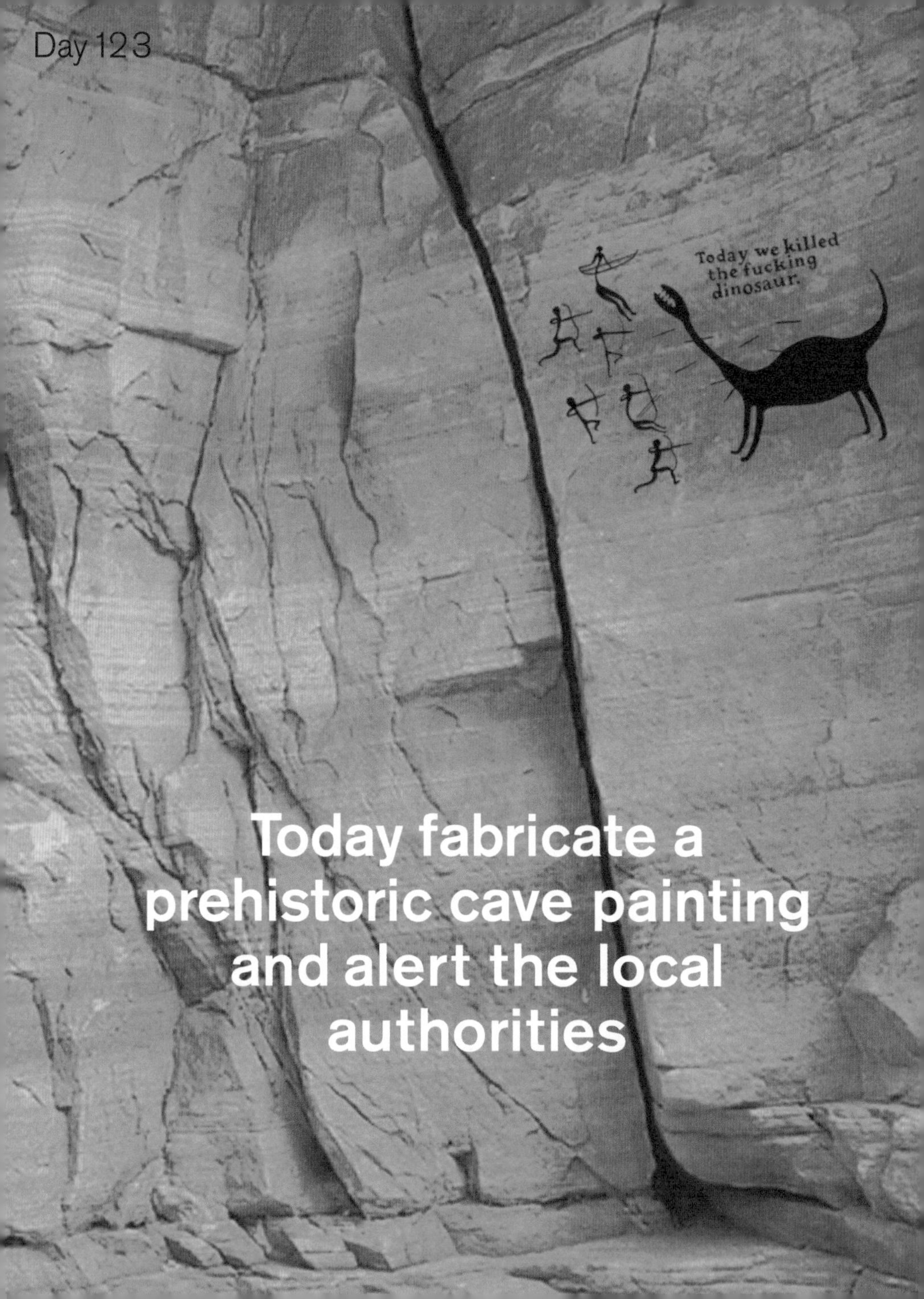
Today we killed
the fucking
dinosaur.

Today fabricate a prehistoric cave painting and alert the local authorities

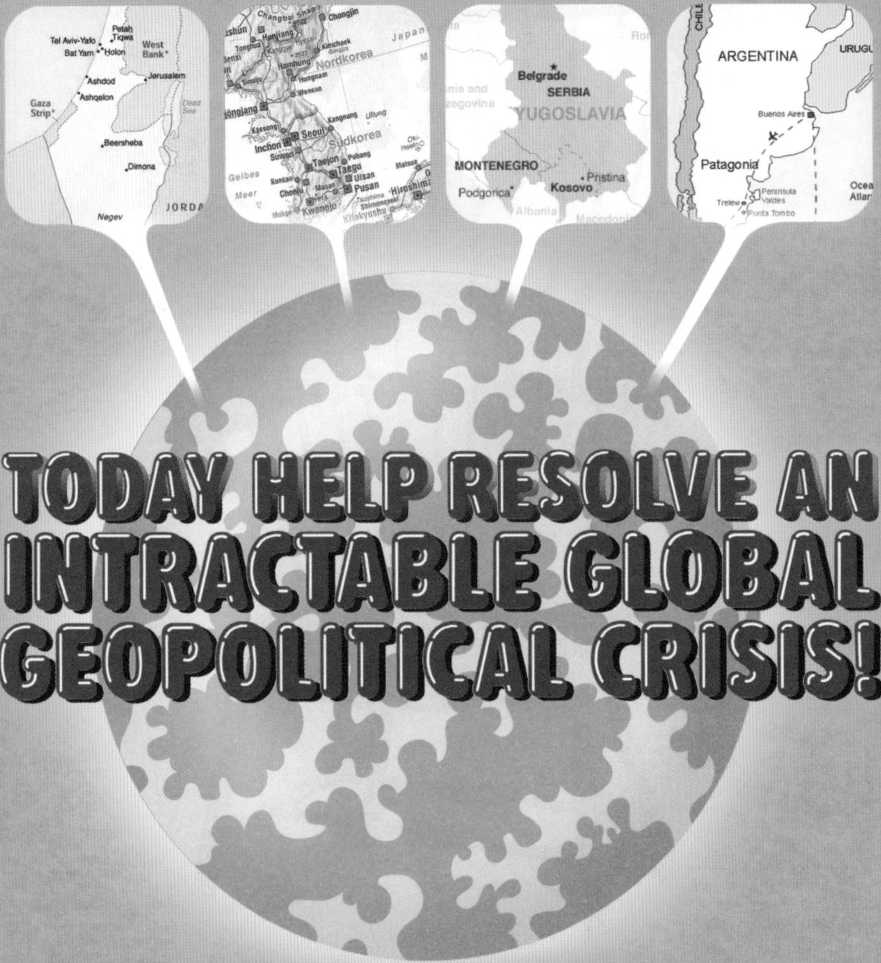
Tel Aviv-Yafo
Petah Tiqwa
Bat Yam
Holon
West Bank
Ashdod
Jerusalem
Ashqelon
Gaza Strip
Dead Sea
Beersheba
Dimona
Negev
JORDA
Chongjin
Nordkorea
Japan
Hamhung
Wonsan
Seoul
Südkorea
Inchon
Taejon
Taegu
Ulsan
Pusan
Hiroshima
Gelbes Meer
Belgrade
SERBIA
YUGOSLAVIA
MONTENEGRO
Pristina
Podgorica
Kosovo
Albania
CHILE
ARGENTINA
URUGU
Buenos Aires
Patagonia
Peninsula Valdes
Trelew
Punta Tombo

TODAY HELP RESOLVE AN INTRACTABLE GLOBAL GEOPOLITICAL CRISIS!

Some bright spark out there must be able to come up with an answer to the world's various problems. Could it be you? Put your mind to it for a couple of minutes. Redraw maps using coloured crayons and explain your plan in no more than 80 words. Send to: Secretary-General, UNITED NATIONS, S-378, New York, NY 10017, USA.

Day 125

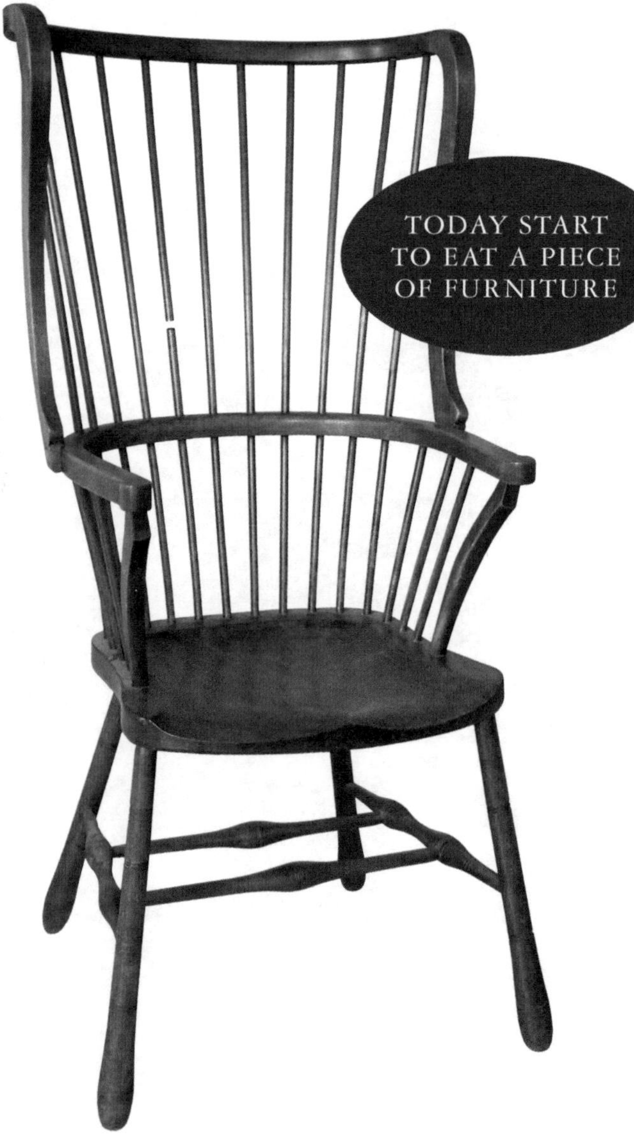
TODAY START
TO EAT A PIECE
OF FURNITURE

Shave off a small amount of wood from your piece of furniture. Sprinkle it on your lunch. Enjoy! Persevere every day, and you should be able to eat the entire piece of furniture within 20 years.

BEFRIEND A CUSTOMER CARE PERSON

Customer-care hotlines recruit individuals with exceptional emotional intelligence and empathy, who are well worth having as friends. Today, make it your mission to befriend a customer-carer and meet them for real by the end of the day.

STEP 1 Call a customer-care line with an obscure question that they can't answer immediately. Make sure you get the customer-carer's name and agree to call them back. E.g. *Hello! What do you call the exact shade of green you use on your biscuit packaging, as I want the same for my curtains?*

STEP 2 Ring back, asking to speak to the same person. As they give you the information you requested, change the question slightly, to prolong the contact. E.g. *You're going to laugh, but I've just remembered I'm allergic to green, what about the blue?*

STEP 3 When you next speak, introduce some emotional tension into your relationship. Being so empathetic, they will start to sympathize. E.g. *My house has just burnt down, so I don't need any damn curtains! What am I going to do? Oh mercy on me!*

STEP 4 Call them back an hour later to thank them for being so empathetic, and apologize for selfishly only talking about yourself all the time. E.g. *It turned out to be a false alarm, but I was in such distress and you saved me! And you must have so many problems of your own!*

STEP 5 Personalize the relationship. You've been through a lot together over the last few hours. Get him or her to acknowledge the bond between you. E.g. *This may sound crazy, but I feel some connection between us that goes way beyond biscuits. Are you a Gemini?*

STEP 6 Work out where the call centre is based, and wait for your customer-care friend to emerge. A fiver to the security guard will ensure they point out the right person. Don't say anything at this point, but follow them discreetly to find out where they live.

STEP 7 Knock on their door just before midnight, and introduce yourself. Carry a recording of your conversations to jog their memory. Hey presto! You have a new friend. E.g. *Surprise! I say, you're even lovelier in real life than you are on the phone. And look, I've brought you some biscuits!*

JESUS

MONARCHY DAY
Find out your position in the line of succession

Everyone in the UK could in theory inherit the throne if all the more obvious candidates died. Where do you stand in the line of succession? To help you work out your likely position, here are the current highest and lowest ranking contenders.

Top 30	Bottom 30
1 Prince Charles	58 997 564 Mr Lee Smith of Deptford
2 Prince William	58 997 565 Mrs Janine Smith of Deptford
3 Prince Harry	58 997 566 Master Wayne Smith, 8, of Deptford
4 Prince Andrew	58 997 567 Master Rick Smith, 7, of Deptford
5 Princess Beatrice	58 997 568 Master Keiron Smith, 5, of Deptford
6 Princess Eugenie	58 997 569 Miss Kerry Smith, 3, of Deptford
7 Prince Edward	58 997 570 Miss Dolly Smith, 1, of Deptford
8 Lady Louise Windsor	58 997 571 Miss Smith (not yet named) of Deptford
9 Princess Anne	58 997 572 That guy outside the Dog & Duck in East Grinstead
10 Mr Peter Phillips	58 997 573 The man who screams "Mucky fucky" outside Allwoods Primary
11 Miss Zara Phillips	58 997 574 "Jon" who swallows his glass eye for a quid, Leeds
12 Viscount Linley	58 997 575 Pete Brown (aka "Big Suzie" by night)
13 Hon. Charles Armstrong-Jones	58 997 576 Mistress Whiplash, Soho
14 Hon. Margarita Armstrong-Jones	58 997 577 Ali Beghal (born abroad)
15 Lady Sarah Chatto	58 997 578 Khalid Azzam (born abroad)
16 Master Samuel Chatto	58 997 579 Muhammad Al-Banshiri (born abroad)
17 Master Arthur Chatto	58 997 580 Samir Abdul (born abroad)
18 Duke of Gloucester	58 997 581 Ziad Ali Waleed (born abroad)
19 Earl of Ulster	58 997 582 Prince Philip (born abroad)
20 Lady Davina Windsor	58 997 583 Sarah Ferguson
21 Lady Rose Windsor	58 997 584 Henrik Delehag
22 Duke of Kent	58 997 585 Ben Carey
23 Lady Marina Windsor	58 997 586 Maxine Carr
24 Lady Amelia Windsor	58 997 587 Ronnie Biggs
25 Lady Helen Taylor	58 997 588 Bill "the Bulldog" Spencer (Her Majesty's Guest)
26 Master Columbus Taylor	58 997 589 "Psycho" George (Her Majesty's Guest)
27 Master Cassius Taylor	58 997 590 Alan "Anthrax" Payne (whereabouts unknown)
28 Miss Eloise Taylor	58 997 591 "Uncle Lollipop" Stuart (Her Majesty's Guest)
29 Lord Frederick Windsor	58 997 592 Inmate 45-5678-765 (no name on file)
30 Lady Gabriella Windsor	58 997 593 Lord Lucan

Pass a note on public transport today

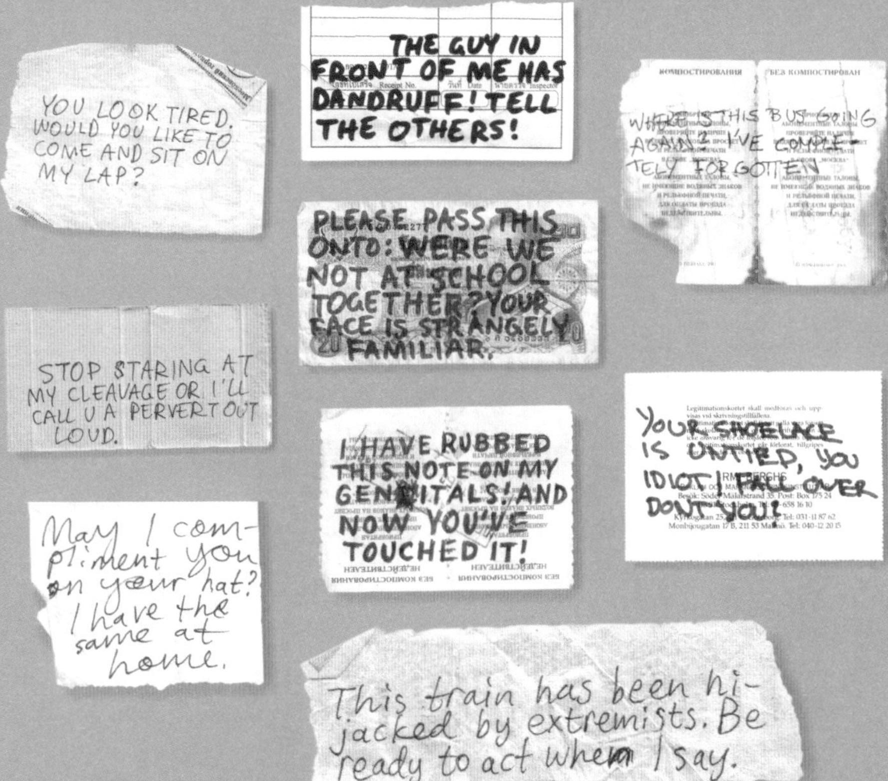
YOU LOOK TIRED. WOULD YOU LIKE TO COME AND SIT ON MY LAP?
THE GUY IN FRONT OF ME HAS DANDRUFF! TELL THE OTHERS!
WHERE IS THIS BUS GOING AGAIN? I'VE COMPLETELY FORGOTTEN
PLEASE PASS THIS ONTO: WERE WE NOT AT SCHOOL TOGETHER? YOUR FACE IS STRANGELY FAMILIAR.
STOP STARING AT MY CLEAVAGE OR I'LL CALL U A PERVERT OUT LOUD.
I HAVE RUBBED THIS NOTE ON MY GENITALS! AND NOW YOU'VE TOUCHED IT!
YOUR SHOELACE IS UNTIED, YOU IDIOT! FALL OVER DON'T YOU!
May I compliment you on your hat? I have the same at home.
This train has been hijacked by extremists. Be ready to act when I say.

on the bus to work i'm never alone

SENSE-LESS DAY

Go through today without using your sense of: *smell*

HOW TO: NOSE PLUG, COLD VIRUS.

True story: Susan T. ran a perfume shop in downtown Baltimore. Her big selling point was the ability to mix a unique perfume for every customer. She prospered, until she was accidentally exposed to toxins, and lost all sense of smell. According to medical expert Dr Carol Fiske, this condition ("anosmia") affects millions, particularly amongst elderly men. It sometimes disappears with time, says Fiske, though no one yet knows how or why. This comes as no consolation to Susan T., of course, who can no longer smell her precious perfumes and has had to close shop and lose her livelihood as a result. She has not worn perfume since.

Nostradamus Day

Benrik are asking their readers to predict the future in the year 2015. Simply answer the questions below and complete the tie-breaker. The winning answer will be disclosed on December 31, 2015, and the winner hailed as the Nostradamus of their time!

Clothing	In 2015, we will all be wearing space suits In 2015, we will all be wearing birthday suits In 2015, we will all be wearing Gap	❑ ❑ ❑
Transport	In 2015, petrol-fuelled cars will be banned In 2015, cyclists will be a majority In 2015, the robot-horse will be the norm	❑ ❑ ❑
Geopolitics	In 2015, Israel and Palestine will be at war In 2015, the USA and China will be at war In 2015, the Earth and Omega Centauri will be at war	❑ ❑ ❑
Business	In 2015, genetics will be the No1 industry In 2015, the Dow Jones will hit 30,000 In 2015, Microsoft will invade a small country	❑ ❑ ❑
Art	In 2015, art will run out of taboos to break In 2015, perspective will make a come-back In 2015, rebel artists will seize Jupiter	❑ ❑ ❑
Space	In 2015, mankind will be exploring Pluto In 2015, mankind will be exploring the Andromeda galaxy In 2015, mankind will be getting the hell out before the second meteorite hits	❑ ❑ ❑
Design	In 2015, clutter will be back In 2015, the zero-gravity bookshelf will be a huge hit In 2015, whole books will be devoted to this doodle 	❑ ❑ ❑
Internet	In 2015, the internet will be wired into our brains In 2015, the most visited site will be "alienhotties.com" In 2015, search engines will find true love and settle down	❑ ❑ ❑
Tie-breaker	What would be a good slogan for the breakfast cereal of the year 2015? .... (200 letters max.)	

Day 131

Hitchhiking has had a bad rap in the past, but it is one of the better solutions to the environmental pollution problems posed by cars, and a great way of generating a sense of community as well. Follow our guidelines to ensure safe and peaceable hitchhiking and hit the road.

EAT
SHIT
AND
DIE

DRIVERS: Pick up a hitchhiker today
Do not pick up anyone with a beard
Do not pick up anyone with fresh bloodstains on clothing
Do not pick up serial killer-types
Do not try to sexually engage with hiker (especially by pretending to confuse their knee for gearbox)

NON-DRIVERS: Hitchhike today
Do design a nice legible sign on some dry cardboard
Do hide any fresh blood stains on clothing
Do avoid mention of serial killer past
Do not try to sexually engage with driver (especially when they're driving)

Day 132

today choose what you'd prefer to be reincarnated as

Circle your first choice and send off with a £5 donation to the Dalai Lama, Lhassa, Tibet.

Mouth obscenities to passing strangers today

Me and you, yes?
I'm hot for you
I love your body
Hey there big boy
You look naughty
You sexy beast
I want you now
Hello horny
Nice ass, stranger!
Take me I'm yours
Do you come here often?
Fucky fucky sucky sucky
My place or the alleyway?

Should they take you up on your offer, either go ahead with it, or claim you were mouthing something innocuous, like "Your shirt is untucked".

Day 134

TWIN YOURSELF WITH A FOREIGNER TODAY

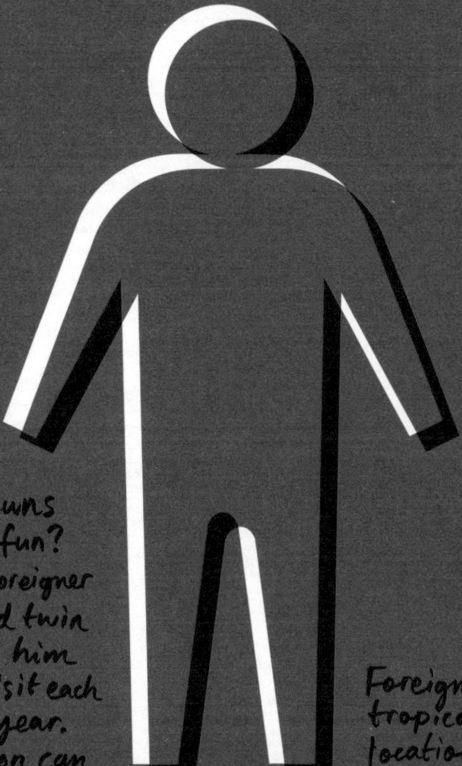

Why should towns have all the fun? Today pick a foreigner at random and twin yourself with him or her. Then visit each other once a year. NOTA: no person can be twinned to more than one other.

Foreigners in tropical-style locations are usually already twinned. Vacant twins are currently readily available in the following locations: Vladivostok, Khartoum, Sanaa, Baghdad, Epsom.

Day 135

Children's Day!

Children too can change their lives. Why should self-improvement be the preserve of "grown-ups"? This page lets your child enjoy this book along with you and empowers them to change their future.

Hi! Our name is Benrik! What's your name? We're going to play a game. It's called "change your life". Do one of these eight things and you win. It's easy, and lots of fun!
Suitable for ages 3-12
GOO GRRR POO YUM
Tell teacher Daddy hit you. Again.
Ci-ga-rettes. They're yummy! Try one.
Zoos are fun, especially cuddling the furry animals.
What's on the other side of a plug? Let's find out!
Greatgrandma is sleepy again! Let's shout in her ear.
Let's surprise Mummy by hiding in the freezer!
Sweets? Yes please Mister!

How many of your thoughts are truly yours? Today cast off your second-hand opinions and return them to their originators.

Reverse Brainwashing Day

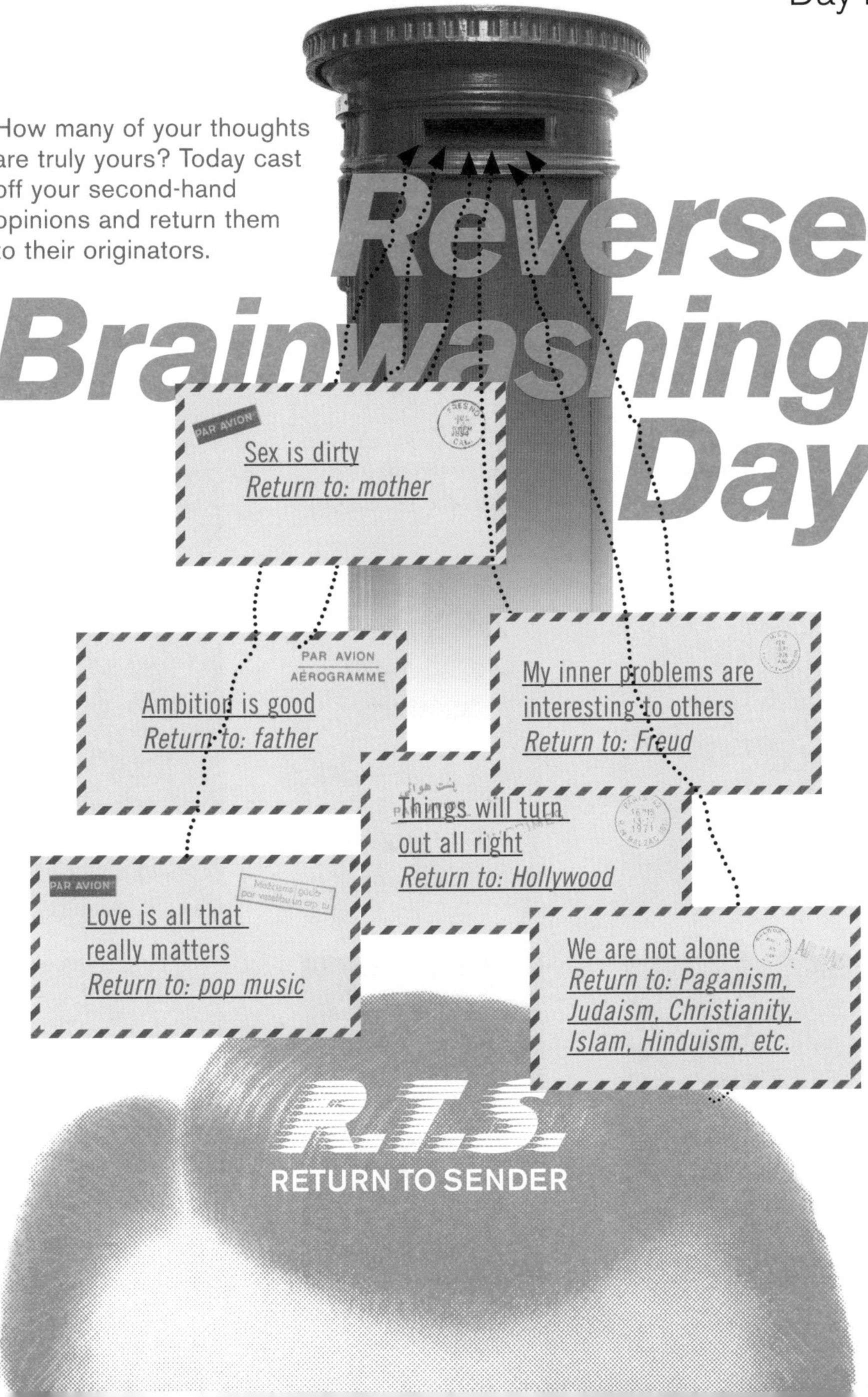
PAR AVION
Sex is dirty
Return to: mother
PAR AVION
AÉROGRAMME
Ambition is good
Return to: father
My inner problems are interesting to others
Return to: Freud
Things will turn out all right
Return to: Hollywood
PAR AVION
Love is all that really matters
Return to: pop music
We are not alone
Return to: Paganism, Judaism, Christianity, Islam, Hinduism, etc.
R.T.S.
RETURN TO SENDER

WRITE A BESTSELLER TODAY

There is no easier way to fame and fortune than to write a bestseller. It needn't take much more than a day, particularly with these ideas to inspire you.

The Kama Sutra for One
The single person's guide to pleasure
How square are you?
A humorous guide to maths
A year in Bonn
The expat experience exposed
The secret story of soup
The fascinating history of soup
Tim Johnson: the anonymous murderer
A whodunnit with a difference
*
Lose weight get laid find God
The all-in-one action plan
The birds, the bees and the rhino.
What they never taught you about sex
1985 The sequel
The Naked Guest
A cookbook for cannibals

*Too late, Benrik wrote this in 2007

Send some roses to your long-suffering mother

HOW MANY SHOULD YOU SEND?
Start with 12, and add or deduct as follows:

She breastfed you +3
She dropped you –4
She gave up promising career for you +2
She overprotected you –2
She tried her best +1
She smoked during pregnancy –3
She's still your best friend +5 (women) –5 (men)

Today, dial a phone number at random and read out this script with an all-American accent.

You know, without Christ, without Jesus, we have no hope. Why? Well, because we know that the standard of God's righteousness is Law, a law of the Ten Commandments, a law of statutes and judgments. And which God gave unto Moses on Sinai, saying this is thy righteousness, O Israel. But you know, God also gave another law. A law revolving around a system of shedding a poor and innocent lamb's blood. So that all who would break the Law of God, who would seek God for forgiveness and pardon, had to bring a lamb, something innocent, and slay it – although, Israel themselves never really knew the real meaning of this. Nonetheless, they were commanded to do it. Also there were other sacrifices, such as: turtle-doves, goats, oxen, red heifers.

But, it was a very sophisticated and very prolific type system of worship. Of course, God had to give these people their own country. He had to give them blessings and things, to be able to perform these rituals. And naturally of course, having to slay a lamb for your sins or such sacrifices, it would definitely keep a man on guard, not to sin too much, because otherwise he could lose the livestock pretty quick, couldn't he? Well anyway, (thanks be unto God), from as far back as Deuteronomy 32, all the way through to Malachi, there has been other writings, writings of the Prophets. Writings who do not usurp the authority of Moses, but actually exalt The Law of Moses. But yet there's an additional testimony. For the same God of Heaven – Who's rich in mercy – has not only given to men a Law, but also a way of escape, for those Repentant Souls who might fall short of the glory of God's law. Which some scholars will agree, that the glory of God's law is that it's a divine precept of His own character. God's character is revealed in The Law. Now, Christ is the only hope for a world that sins. Now, how do we know? Well – The Prophets – have prophesied? But what if we're not familiar with the prophets? Well, were the Jews familiar with the prophets when this Word-of-God was made flesh? When Mary, The Virgin, had a baby boy, did everyone believe, that she was really a virgin when Christ was conceived? If we search the Scriptures, we'll find in certain arguments the Pharisees confronted Christ – and said to him, "We be not sons born of fornication." So obviously, not everyone believed that he was a child of a virgin birth! If they hadn't looked back to Isaiah chapter 8, and learned the mystery of Immanuel – that a virgin would conceive and bear a son – then they might not really put too much ahhm... consistency into the fact that Christ at that day claimed to be born of a virgin. I mean, if Isaiah the prophet was a false prophet, well then naturally they would conclude that anyone claiming to have these things fulfilled would be false, too. But of course, Christ, he did something much more, than to just fulfill prophecy. He did miracles. Miracles of mercy such as: healing the sick, feeding the hungry, raising the dead. And if we study we'll see that "Matthew, Mark, Luke, and John" gives us in somewhat, a full view of the oppositions, and also, the confidements, that he had in doing these miracles. He gathered many unto him through the means of these miracles.

But sad to say, even though he had done so many miracles, Scripture says, yet when it came right down to it, they didn't believe in him. It's amazing that even his own disciples forsook him – except Mary Magdalene. She stayed with him to the end, didn't she? Last to leave The Cross, first to come to the sepulchre. Now, we need to sit here, and we need to ask the question, "how come the men of that generation didn't believe in Christ?"

In Matthew 23, Christ had to say to the Jews "O Jerusalem, Jerusalem" how often I would have gathered you, but you would not. Why? He tells them that they have forsaken The Prophets. "Thou that killest the prophets," how often I would have gathered you. How does the subject of 'gathering Israel' and 'the prophets' combine together? He tells them that their houses, their temple, is left to them desolate.

And that in Matthew 24, as Christ said on the Mount of Olives, his disciples came to him to ask him, concerning these things. What should be the sign of thy coming and of the end of the world? Well, Christ begins to tell them, let no man deceive you, "For many shall come in my name, saying, I am Christ; and shall deceive many."

If you dial an answering machine, try to fit it all in the time allocated. If you can't, call back later to complete the message.

KILL SOMETHING DAY

So-called "Western civilization" suppresses our legitimate aggressive impulses. Cast off the chains of narrow morality and stamp out the sad life of a member of some inferior species today: an ant, or perhaps a gnat of some kind. Indulge your dark urges before they overwhelm you. After all, as top Russian anarchist Mikhail Bakunin declared: *the passion for destruction is also a creative passion...*

Day 141

Today: find suspicious activity and report it

We must be vigilant in the face of the terrorist threat. As the UK police suggests, "where there's unusual activity that doesn't fit normal day-to-day life, we need to know" – a broad call to action if ever there was one. Still, citizens must do their duty: "if you suspect it, report it". Examples of suspicious activity:

UK confidential anti-terrorist hotline:

0800 789 321

Post photos of the suspicious activity on www.benrik.co.uk

"Mary at 29a hasn't put her recycling box out this week."

"There's a chap outside my house who's been tying his shoelace for two whole minutes."

"My colleague always puts the phone down when I walk in."

"This bald man in my local Tesco's just bought a three-pack of shampoo."

"The Johnsons have bought fertiliser and it's not even planting season."

"The curtains at No 98 are always closed in the afternoon."

"A dark brown 4x4 has just driven past the train station three times."

"How can that ghastly family afford a bigger house than ours?"

Test a proverb today and record its practical usefulness

The best things in life are free

When the cat's away the mice will play

Look before you leap

Never look a gift horse in the mouth

Strike while the iron is hot

Beat your wife every day - if you don't know why, she will

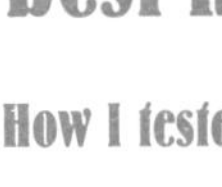

The early bird catches the morning worm

Laughter is the best medicine

Example: The grass is always greener on the other side of the fence

How to test the proverb: Find a fence with grass on both sides. Position yourself on one side and record the degree of greenness. Then climb the fence over to the "other side" and repeat the observation procedure. Compare the different measurings and draw your own conclusions.

You cannot have your cake and eat it

An apple a day keeps the doctor away

Bad news travels fast

Honesty is the best policy

Nothing ventured nothing gained

It takes two to tango

You win some you lose some

Curiosity killed the cat

How I tested the proverb: ....

....

Truth............................./10

Usefulness...................../10

Day 143

Today, hug every tree you walk past

Tree-hugging is a well-attested life-enhancing practice, that brings you closer to nature and helps you reconnect with your very own "roots". Today, hug every single tree you encounter for at least one minute. Most trees are highly huggable, but here are the world's most affectionate ones; look out for them.

"Daisy"
Oak
21 years old
New Forest, UK

"Michael"
Pine
68 years old
Richmond Park
London, UK

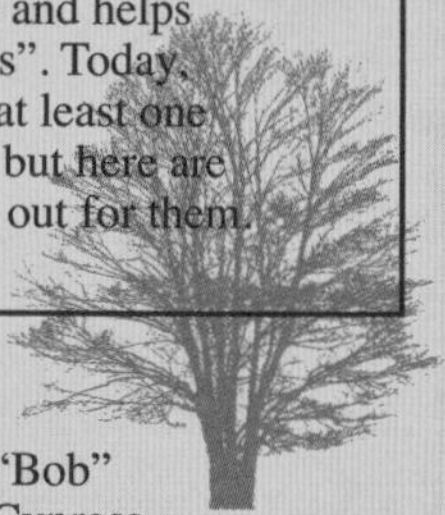

"Bob"
Cypress
Age: unknown
Lincoln Park Golf Course
San Francisco, USA

"George"
Chestnut
59 years old
Botanic Gardens
Adelaide, Australia

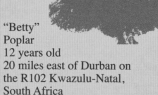

"Betty"
Poplar
12 years old
20 miles east of Durban on the R102 Kwazulu-Natal, South Africa

"Keanu"
Coconut
23 years old
Garden of Mr/Mrs Dale
33 Woodlawn Drive
Honolulu, Hawaii, USA

"Sebastian"
Beech
17 years old
Paparoa National Park
South Island, New Zealand

"Mitsuko"
Bonsai (careful not to crush it)
49 years old
1-1-20 Kanayama Cho Naka Ku
Nagoya, Japan

"Hjalmar"
Christmas
5 years old
Erstavik-skogen
Sweden

Etiquette: it is considered bad form to carve your name in the tree you have just hugged.

Speak to people as if you were a global corporation today

Milk in your tea?
= Let's brainstorm how to calibrate the synergy of your baseline items going forward.

How about a date?
= Let's align timeframes in view of a merger with mutual cross-linking benefits.

I'm late, sorry.
= The window of opportunity for an optimal win-win arrival time is in jeopardy.

I'm very drunk.
= Within a horizontal framework, let us take a 360 degree blue sky look at our increasingly volatile operating environment.

What time does the next train leave?
= We need to ascertain the variables that impact on stepchange in provision of core market programmes.

I'm leaving you.
= The cross-pollinating partnering paradigm that has governed our dialoguing has been rightsized.

TODAY, BLEED HERE:

In a million years' time with advanced technology they'll be able to reconstitute you from your DNA.

Name: ....

Address: ....

Post code: ....

Why I'm worth reconstituting from my DNA a million years hence: ....

....

....

TODAY DO EVERYTHING SOCIETY URGES YOU TO

Pay here
PEDESTRIANS push button and wait for signal opposite
Please take one
FLASH FOR LESS
SAVE 80%!
GO
Stop!
tool up for spring
TURN LEFT
TOWARDS
buy now! enquire at admi
Fire escape keep clear
Assembly point
PARK
ZIP IT!
Evacuation Instructions
CHAT
spring to life
NO RUSH
be mine
Just taste it
46DD
PLEASE RING BELL
PAY HERE
play here!
unwind
GO
Danger Deep excavations
Warning High voltage cables overhead
No unauthorised persons allowed on this site
Foot protection must be worn
RELAX & UNWIND WITH FRIENDS
Dazzle like never before!
FREEFONE NOW
dare to be different
Just mix
Dress to turn heads at parties
wait
cross with care
OWN THEM
READ IT NOW!
INSERT & REMOVE BEFORE DIALLING
INSERT & DIAL
WIN
wait
SILENCE PLEASE
Fight
WITNESS CONTEMPORARY ARTISTS DOCUMENT OUR TIME

Day 147

Today:
test god's existence

Whether god exists or not is a pretty fundamental question, and one that could make a big difference to your life. If you're not yet convinced either way, find out for sure with these questions, which are especially designed to make him manifest himself. It's best to address them from a mount or hill of some sort, as that's how he's used to humans communicating with him.

Questions to god:

Hey god, look at this. I'm doodling right here in this bible of yours.

Show me a miracle god and I'll sacrifice any animal you care to mention

Help god, I'm angel Bob. I've lost my wings somewhere over there. Help me out?

god, I bet you can't hit me with lightning. I'm too fast, whoooossshhh!

god, I have some important data about the Devils latest plans. Come down and I'll show you.

god are you there?
(worth a try)

TODAY, TOPPLE A DICTATOR USING ONLY THE INTERNET:

The information revolution is a direct challenge to authoritarian states. With its many points of access and its decentralized, disembodied nature, the internet is the perfect rallying point for change. Yet it has still to claim its first direct dictator scalp. Benrik readers can change that today by emailing them and convincing them to step down from power with a few well-chosen arguments.

Kim Jong Il (North Korea)
www.korea-dpr.com

Hu Jintao (China)
www.govonline.cn

Fidel Castro (Cuba)
www.cubagov.cu

Robert Mugabe (Zimbabwe)
www.gta.gov.zw

Than Shwe (Burma)
www.myatmyanmar.net

Omar Al-Bashir (Sudan)
www.sudan.gov.sd

Saparmurat Niyazov (Turkmenistan)
www.mct.gov.tm

Alexander Lukashenko (Belarus)
www.president.gov.by

Crown Prince Abdullah (Saudi Arabia)
www.shura.gov.sa

Day 149

Attend court today and offer your verdict to the judge

Most trials are open to the public. You've watched enough TV series to know the legal basics. Now put your knowledge into practice. Listen carefully to the evidence, weigh up the pros and cons in your mind, and shout out your verdict as soon as you reach it. The judge will be grateful for your input.

If your verdict is rejected:
You have the right to appeal. Approach the judge outside the courtroom and demand a retrial. Outline your version of events and present any new evidence and/or witnesses you may have found. If the judge does not co-operate, lodge a formal complaint with the Lord Chancellor, and alert the media to a miscarriage of justice. Take it all the way to the High Court if you have to!

Entry to the galleries is free, but you must be over 14. Cameras, videos, recording equipment and mobile phones are prohibited. But you are allowed to make a few clumsy crayon drawings of the scene.

Positive Discrimination Day

30
39

Refuse to slow-dance with 30 to 39-year-olds.

54kg

If anyone under 55 kgs enters the room, leave.

Alon niom

Ignore people who mispronounce the word "aluminium".

Brutalize anyone you catch eating between meals.

No physical contact with bald people.

Don't answer any questions from brunettes.

If a redhead appears on screen, switch off your TV.

Ask for your money back if your taxi driver's hair is curly.

Don't go into any shop run by a couple.

Chase anyone with high blood pressure out of town.

Run away screaming from anyone pregnant.

Refuse to smile back at pony-tailed checkout girls.

Don't sit down next to anyone with myopia.

Blame cardigan-wearers for a political problem.

42

Don't allow 42-year-olds into your home.

Fire employees with "outie" belly buttons.

Denounce left-handers to the police.

Give money to beggars with green eyes only.

Only employ people with glasses.

Phil

Flirt only with people whose name begins with K.

Ostracize opera-goers.

Avoid men with excessive nostril hair.

40

Verbally abuse men with size 7 feet.

Torture anyone with freckles.

Accept sexual offers only from people born in the countryside.

Only do business with people taller than you.

Ask any neighbour with green curtains to move.

Tell your children to avoid cat-owners.

55

Only buy from women over 56.

Refuse to shake hands with electric-razor users.

Discrimination is not necessarily evil, as long as you discriminate in a totally arbitrary manner. Treating people equally is a recipe for permanent boredom. Make everyone's life more lively today by obeying these simple rules.

Day 151

EPIDEMIC DAY: Today, everyone report to their local hospital with the same mystery illness. Following the SARS, BSE and bird flu scares, national health systems are now geared towards detecting patterns of illness early, in order to limit their spread. Today, test national readiness by collectively reporting to your nearest hospital A&E with the symptoms below. If the prevention systems are working, the nation should be under alert by the evening and you should all be under quarantine. Please note: as with any interesting new disease, the symptoms evolve hour by hour. Please keep to this sequence all together, or the doctors may get confused.

Time	Symptoms	Experts you will meet
9am	Your left eyeball is highly itchy, but at the back, so you can't scratch it.	Ophthalmologist
11am	The itchiness has spread to your lower intestine, equally difficult to scratch.	Gastroenterologist
12pm	As well as the itching, you have developed an urge to urinate constantly.	Urologist
12.15pm	As you try to urinate, you hear music in your head, specifically Russian classical symphonic pieces.	ENT consultant
3pm	Your heart feels like it has synchronized to the beat of the Russian music, and that it will stop when the piece ends.	Cardiologist Psychiatrist
4.06pm	The itch has stopped, but your frontal lobe is feeling mushier than usual. The best way you can describe it is that your brain is melting. Get round to mentioning you just got back from trekking in Borneo last week.	Neurosurgeon Neurologist Immunologist Haematologist Parasitologist Epidemiologist
11.57pm	You have recovered; perhaps it was a false alarm or a cold. You'd like to leave the camp and go home now please.	Lawyer

Open yourself up to criticism today

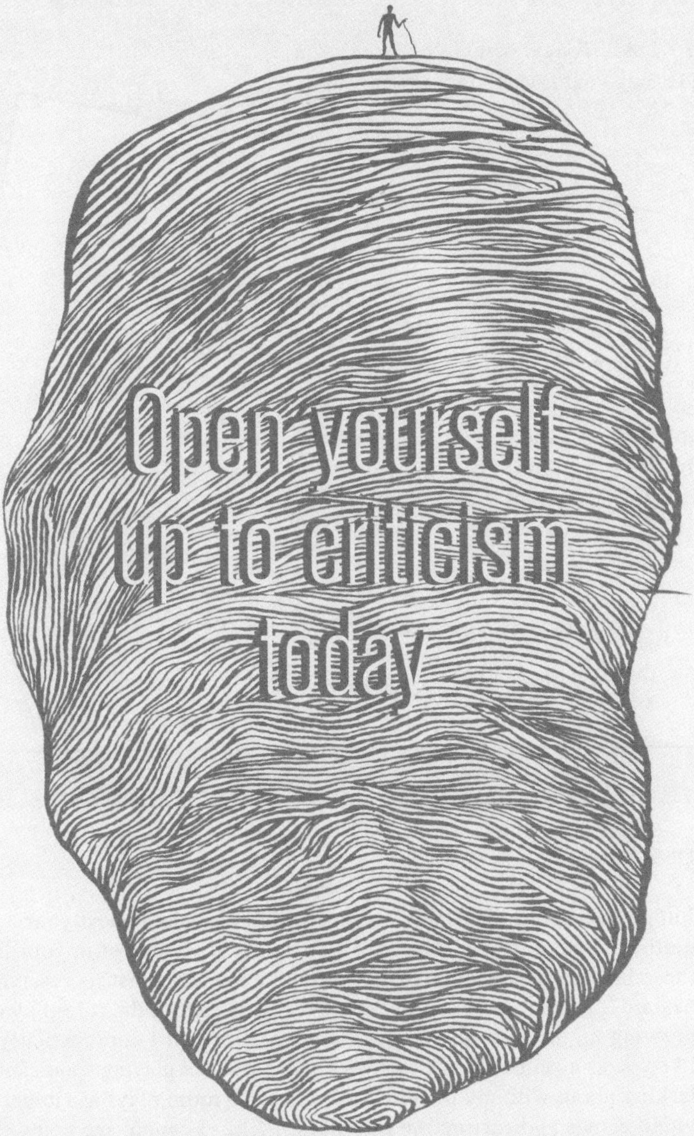

The path to true self-knowledge is fraught and tortuous. Often, we may only attain it through the glare of others. Today, take the single thing you have ever created that you are most proud of, and ask for an undiluted critique. The work could be anything, from that draft novel you've hidden in your bottom drawer, to photos of the wedding you planned so carefully; from your PhD thesis to your childhood doodles – anything that touches a nerve and reveals your soul.

Day 153

HONESTY DAY: Today, write to everyone you know expressing your true feelings towards them

Dear Postman,

I live at 54b Eton Avenue, which is on your regular round. My kitchen overlooks the street and so I see you deliver the mail every morning, usually about 10.20. I am married, although my husband and I no longer make love. This is very frustrating to me as I have a high libido, and I suspect he is having an affair. I have considered trying to seduce you to gain a revenge of sorts, but try as I may, I cannot sexualize you to the necessary extent. I've tried fantasizing about you coming in and kissing me roughly before we tear each other's clothes off and ravish each other on the hallway carpet. But this fails to arouse me. There is something about you that leaves me quite cold, and even repulses me a little, if truth be told. Other than that, I have no complaints with your postmanship though, keep up the good work!

Mrs Breekridge

Dear Son,

I hope you like my birthday present, although to be honest your mother chose it. It is a fact that I've slightly lost interest in your life these last few years, ever since you called me a "fascist repressive bastard". I understand and accept that this is part of the role-play of growing up these days, but it made me realize that I don't actually like you as a child. When I was your age, I was out playing sports and larking about with my mates. You're in your room playing violent video games and surfing the Internet for filth. I cannot see you turning into any kind of responsible adult. I suggest that we maintain a frosty relationship until you leave home, and then see each other once a year until I pass away. Anyway, happy ninth birthday.

xDad

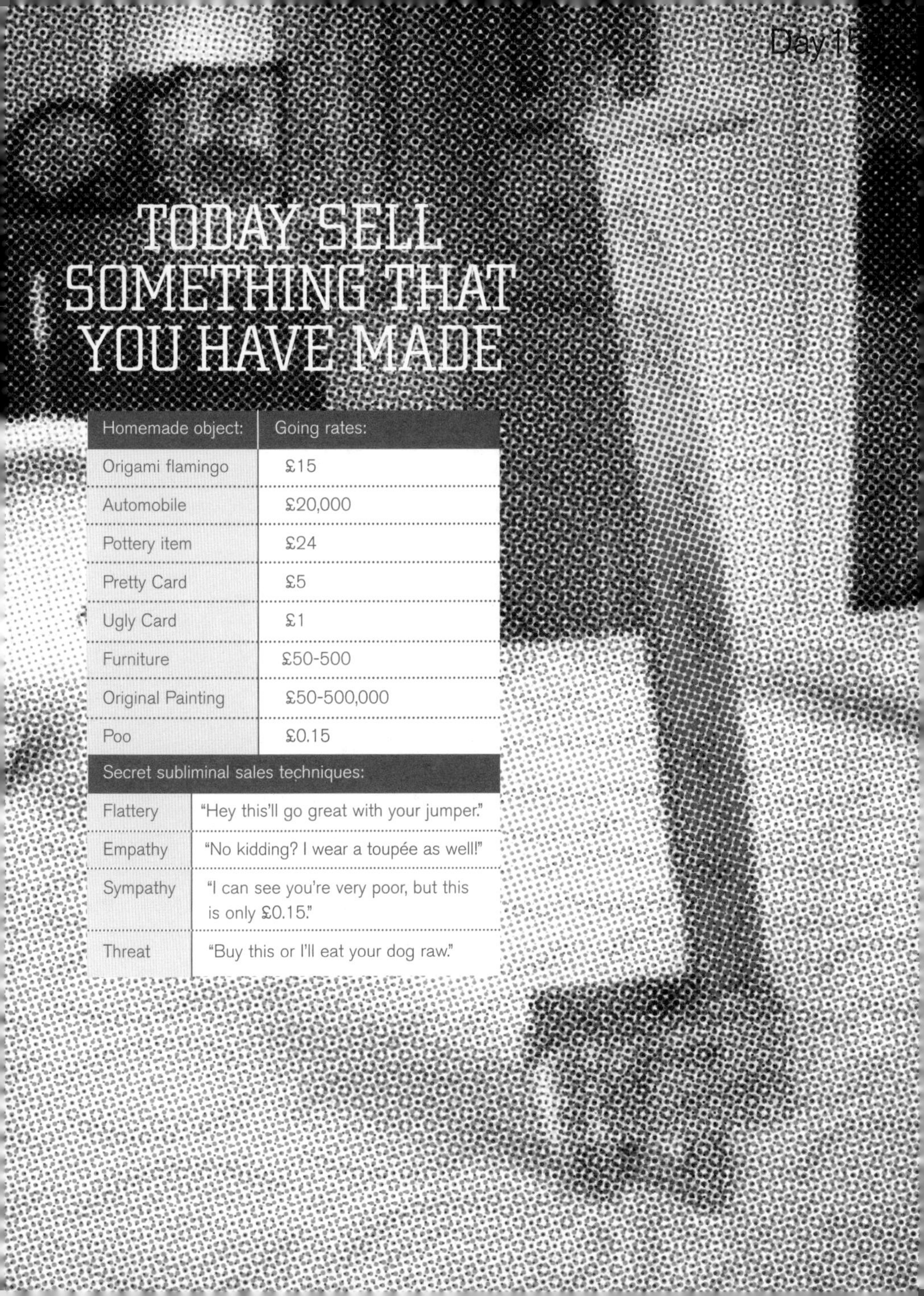

TODAY SELL SOMETHING THAT YOU HAVE MADE

Homemade object:	Going rates:
Origami flamingo	£15
Automobile	£20,000
Pottery item	£24
Pretty Card	£5
Ugly Card	£1
Furniture	£50-500
Original Painting	£50-500,000
Poo	£0.15

Secret subliminal sales techniques:	
Flattery	"Hey this'll go great with your jumper."
Empathy	"No kidding? I wear a toupée as well!"
Sympathy	"I can see you're very poor, but this is only £0.15."
Threat	"Buy this or I'll eat your dog raw."

Day 155

Today knock on every door you see

Our daily routines take us past hundreds of doors, most of which have effectively become invisible to us, but each of which conceals a whole new world waiting to be discovered. Today, knock on those doors and find out what lies behind them. Show the Book if it helps, but obey this one rule: if you are lucky enough to be invited in, you must accept. Down the rabbit-hole you go…

Here are some typical closed doors with what lies behind them:

Sudanese refugee who used to be a king

Broom cupboard

Most beautiful woman in the world crying with loneliness

Children who have tied up their babysitter and are watching forbidden TV programmes

DANGER
HIGH VOLTAGE

Gateway to parallel universe

AMNESIA DAY

Wake up claiming to have lost your memory. See if your friends and relatives try and take advantage.

THINGS THEY WILL SAY TO TAKE ADVANTAGE:

- Your motto was always "you can't take it with you".
- Come on pumpkin, you used to love lesbian threesomes.
- But daddy, you bought me this airgun yourself!
- "I love doing the washing-up", that's what you'd say.
- One of your kidneys was mine, but please don't feel you owe me.

THINGS YOU SHOULD SAY TO TAKE ADVANTAGE:

- Do I like champagne? Gee, it's so hard to know.
- Maybe it would help if I saw Paris again!
- Affair with my secretary? Didn't even know I had one.
- Work?! No, if I remember one thing it's that I didn't work.
- They say sexual stimulation triggers those deep-seated memories.

Day 157

Benrik Babysitting Day

TODAY, REPROGRAMME A CHILD WITH BENRIK VIEWS. Babysitting isn't just a boring way of earning not much money; it's an opportunity to contribute to a child's education. Either babysit a child of your acquaintance, or put a notice in a local shop advertising your services (£8/hour is the going rate). Wait until the parents have left, and instead of letting the child waste its time watching TV, read to him or her from the views below.

Teachers are paid to lie to you

The dinosaurs are still around, they're just hiding

Santa Claus is a secular Satan

War is good for when peace gets too boring

Tea is for girls, coffee is for boys

Benrik is your good uncle, the other one is a cyborg

Soon we'll all move to another nicer planet

Sometimes 1+1=3

Benrik's books make you grow up a lot quicker

God has Alzheimer's

SHARE SOMEONE'S PAIN TODAY

A burden shared is a burden halved. Find a friend in distress and bear some of their grief.

Day 159

Mainstream Day

Stop rocking the boat! Today make sure your tastes and actions don't clash with those of 95% of the population.

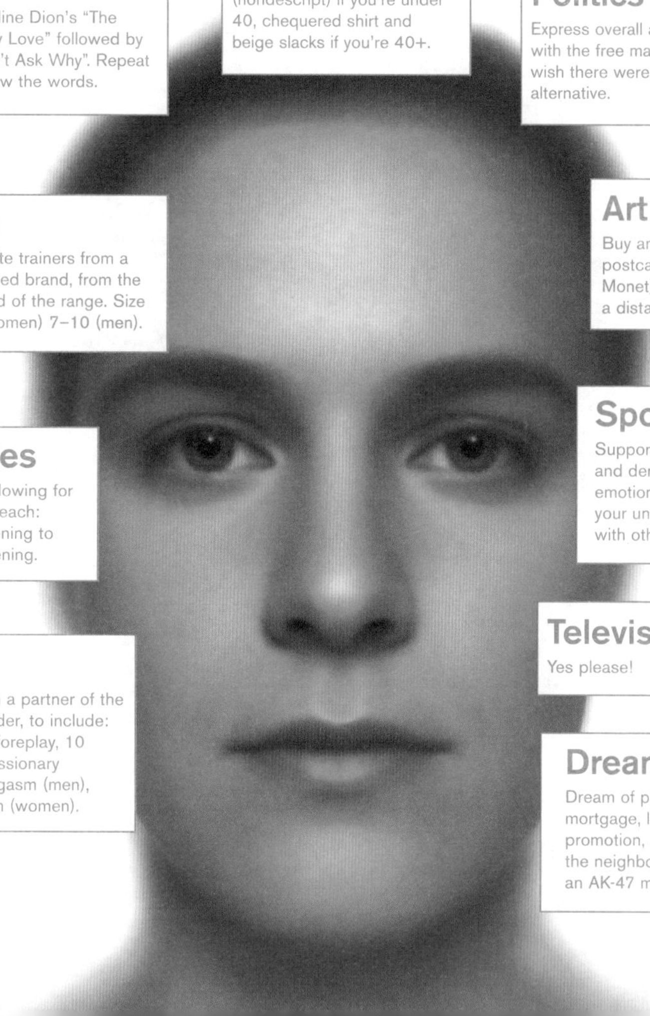

Music
Listen to Celine Dion's "The Colour of My Love" followed by "Love Doesn't Ask Why". Repeat until you know the words.

Clothes
Plain jeans and a T-shirt (nondescript) if you're under 40, chequered shirt and beige slacks if you're 40+.

Politics
Express overall agreement with the free market, but wish there were a cuddlier alternative.

Shoes
Purchase white trainers from a widely-marketed brand, from the less fancy end of the range. Size (UK): 5–7 (women) 7–10 (men).

Art
Buy an Impressionist postcard (Manet or Monet) and send it to a distant relative.

Hobbies
Enjoy the following for half an hour each: reading, listening to music, gardening.

Sport
Support a football team, and derive much-needed emotional strength from your unspoken bond with other supporters.

Sex
Have sex with a partner of the opposite gender, to include: 5 minutes of foreplay, 10 minutes of missionary position, 1 orgasm (men), 1 fake orgasm (women).

Television
Yes please!

Dreams
Dream of paying off the mortgage, landing that promotion, and taking out the neighbourhood with an AK-47 machine gun.

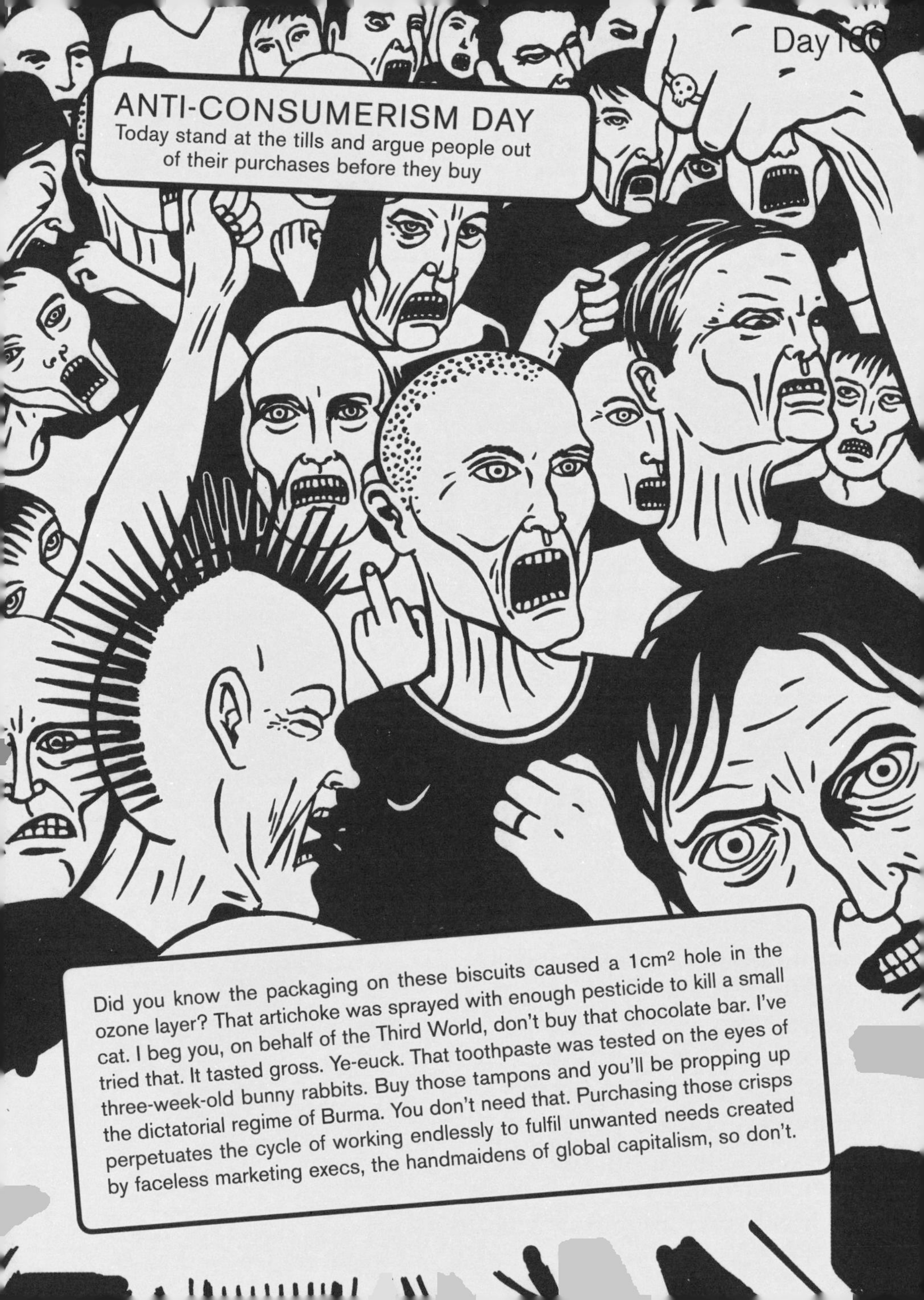

ANTI-CONSUMERISM DAY

Today stand at the tills and argue people out of their purchases before they buy

Did you know the packaging on these biscuits caused a 1cm² hole in the ozone layer? That artichoke was sprayed with enough pesticide to kill a small cat. I beg you, on behalf of the Third World, don't buy that chocolate bar. I've tried that. It tasted gross. Ye-euck. That toothpaste was tested on the eyes of three-week-old bunny rabbits. Buy those tampons and you'll be propping up the dictatorial regime of Burma. You don't need that. Purchasing those crisps perpetuates the cycle of working endlessly to fulfil unwanted needs created by faceless marketing execs, the handmaidens of global capitalism, so don't.

Today, impress your librarian

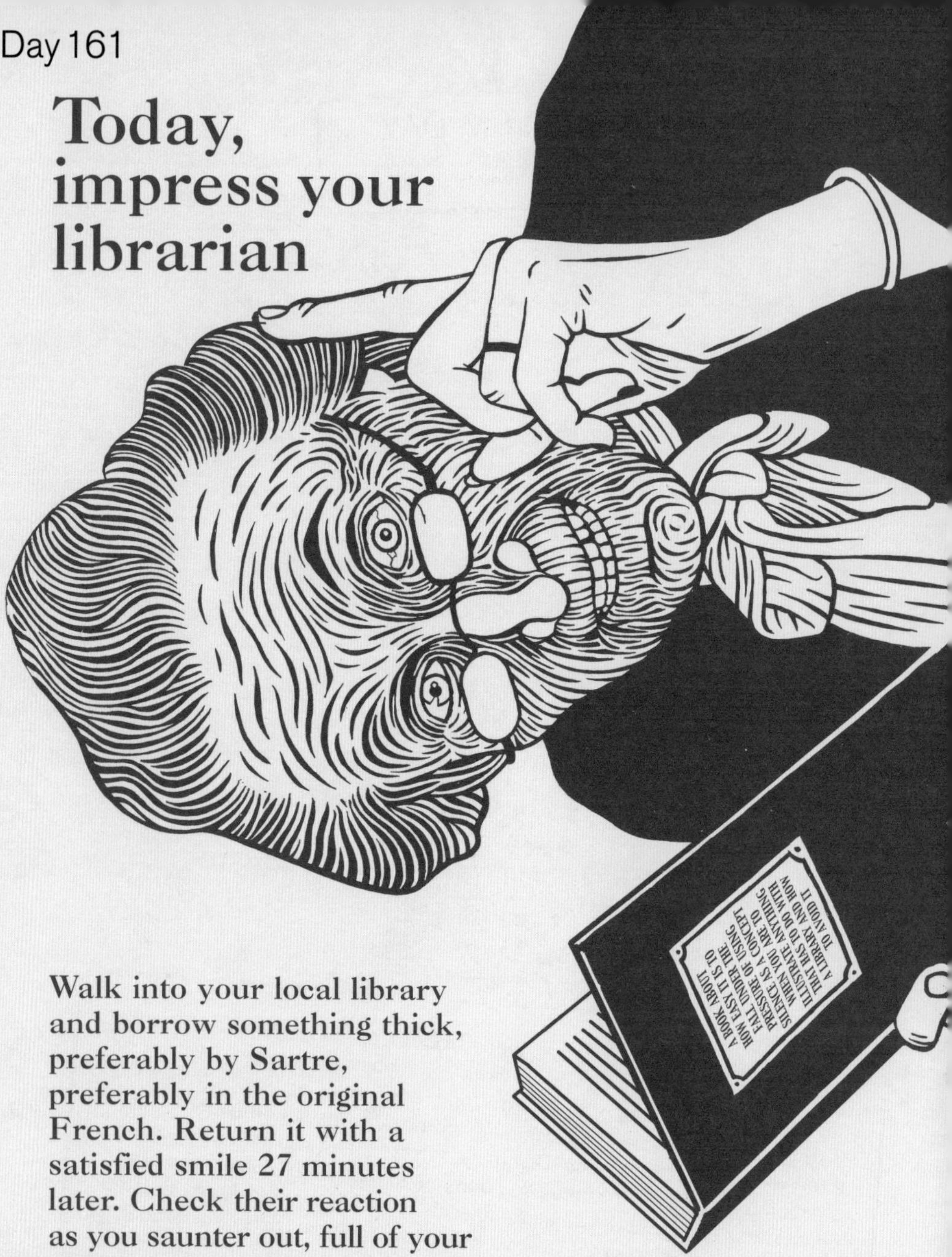
A BOOK ABOUT
HOW EASY IT IS TO
FALL UNDER THE
PRESSURE OF USING
SILENCE AS A CONCEPT
WHEN YOU ARE TO
ILLUSTRATE ANYTHING
THAT HAS TO DO WITH
A LIBRARY AND HOW
TO AVOID IT

Walk into your local library and borrow something thick, preferably by Sartre, preferably in the original French. Return it with a satisfied smile 27 minutes later. Check their reaction as you saunter out, full of your new learning. You now have a local reputation as a savant.

Today: open a home restaurant

Ted and Linda Biggins

are pleased to welcome you
for one day only at our
exclusive restaurant situated

Opposite the Esso garage, the High Street,

for some delicious home cooking
and friendly service.

Please call 020 7947 451
for reservations

One of the few positive outcomes of Cuba's faltering economy is that hundreds of restaurants have opened up in people's private homes. Known as paladares, they allow you to eat food that is usually much better than that found in the official restaurants.

Menu

Starter

Soup à la Biggins

Mains

Ted and Linda's home-baked special

Dessert

Chef's delight

£ 14.95 for two courses

£ 18.95 for three courses

Tonight, open up your living room to the crowds for a taste of your home cooking. Write a menu using the template above, post it around your neighbourhood, and start taking bookings. How to set the prices: Standard restaurant profit margins are close to 70%. So multiply the cost of the ingredients by 3 and simply divide it by the number of diners.

Send a letter to a mass murderer today

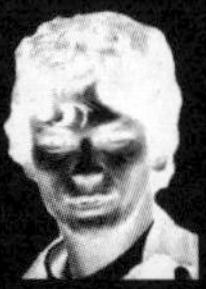

Richard Ramirez
(USA, 1960–)
16 victims+
Nickname: "The Night Stalker"
Address: Death Row,
San Quentin Penitentiary,
San Quentin, CA 94974, USA

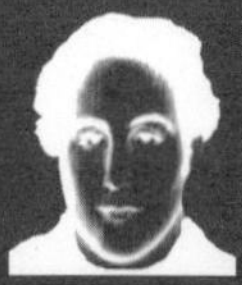

David Berkowitz
(USA, 1953–)
6 victims
Nickname: "Son of Sam"
Address: King's County Hospital,
Brooklyn, NY 11212, USA

Peter Sutcliffe
(UK, 1945–)
13 victims
Nickname: "The Yorkshire Ripper"
Address: Broadmoor Special
Hospital, Crowthorne,
RG45 7EG Berkshire, UK

Dennis Nilsen
(UK, 1943–)
15 victims
Nickname: —
Address: 1x Parkhurst Rd,
Holloway, London N7 9TK, UK

Edmund Kemper
(USA, 1948–)
10 victims
Nickname: "The Co-Ed Killer"
Address: California Medical
Facility, PO box 2000,
Vacaville, CA 95696–2000,
USA

Charles Manson
(USA, 1934–)
6+ victims
Nickname: —
Address: California State
Prison, B–33920, 4A 4R–23,
PO box 3476, Corcora,
CA 93212, USA

Angel Resendez
(Mexico, 1960–)
9 victims
Nickname: "The Railroad Killer"
Address: Death Row, Polunski
Unit, 12002 FM, 350 South
Livingston, TX 77351, USA

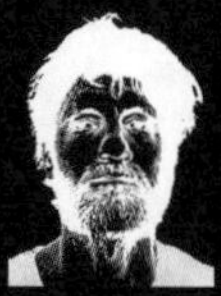

Theodore Kaczynski
(USA, 1942–)
3 victims
Nickname: "The Unabomber"
Address: Florence Admax USP,
P.O. box 8500, 5880 HWY 675,
Florence, CO 81226, USA

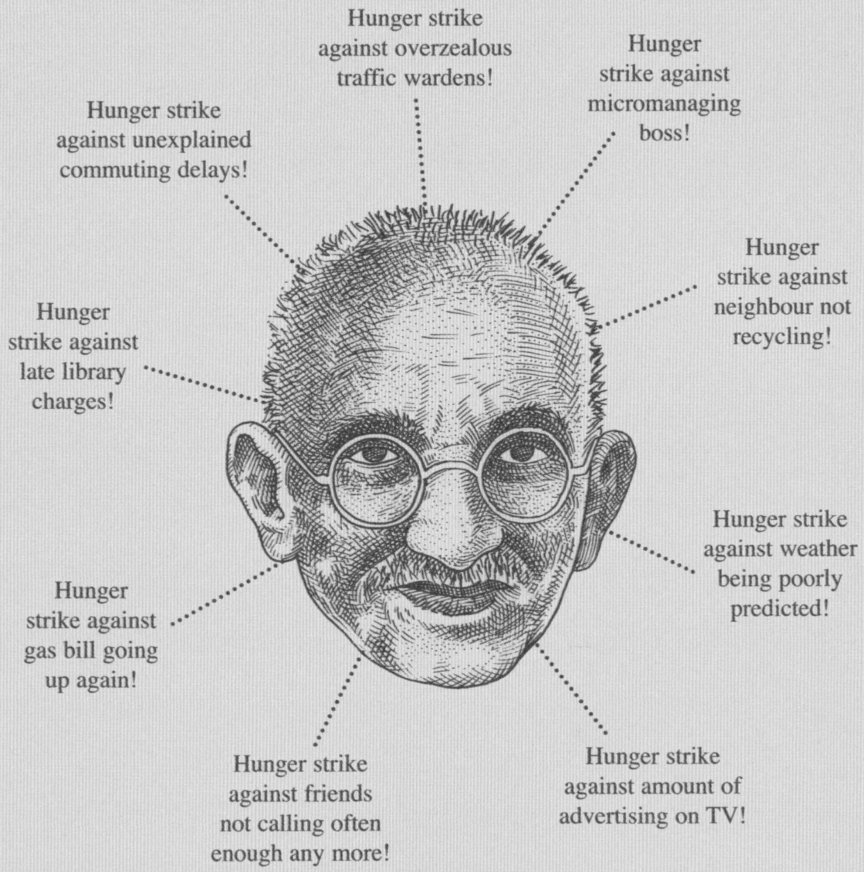
Hunger strike against overzealous traffic wardens!
Hunger strike against micromanaging boss!
Hunger strike against unexplained commuting delays!
Hunger strike against neighbour not recycling!
Hunger strike against late library charges!
Hunger strike against weather being poorly predicted!
Hunger strike against gas bill going up again!
Hunger strike against friends not calling often enough any more!
Hunger strike against amount of advertising on TV!

GO ON HUNGER STRIKE TODAY

Contrary to popular perception, you don't have to be famous or in the news to go on hunger strike. In fact, when the hunger strike was invented (by the Celts), it was mostly used to help settle local disputes such as the recovery of debts. The procedure is to notify whoever you are hunger-striking against, sit in front of their door, and fast until they grant you redress. If they let you starve to death, they suffer social disgrace, and face compensation claims by your family. Hunger strikes are easy to organize, non-violent and inexpensive, yet psychologically intimidating. Embark on one for the day, and settle whatever dispute is currently ruining your peace of mind.

Day 165

TODAY DENOUNCE SOMEONE TO THE GOVERNMENT

SAMPLE
LETTER:
Dear Home
Secretary,
I believe.......
constitutes a grave
threat to national
security, for reasons
which I cannot go
into as I am in a
hurry right now.
Search his home
before it is too late.
Yours anonymously,

Paris Hilton Day

Today, upload a clip of yourself having sex onto the internet. In a world of spin, watching someone you know having intercourse is paradoxically one of the few authentic experiences still available, which is why it has such appeal. And best of all, there is no stigma attached to it these days (as long as your partner is a fully-consenting adult).

Making £££££ from it: Unless you're an heiress, a celebrity, extremely good-looking, or preferably all of the above, you will have trouble attracting a wider audience. Instead, focus on your core target market: people who already know you. If you include friends, distant relatives and colleagues, you probably know upwards of 200 people who would pay hard cash to see you in action. At £5 each, that makes a cool £1,000. Not bad for an evening's work.

BENRIK PUBLIC SLEEPING DAY

DO NOT WAKE!

Dear passer-by,
I am sleeping here for a while.
You are a fellow human being,
and so I trust you to leave me in
peace and not to hurt, dispossess
or abuse me in any way. You may
watch over me though if you like.
I apologize for any snoring.

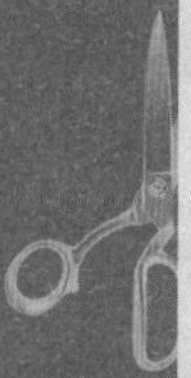

SLEEP IN PUBLIC TODAY

Sleeping in public is usually the prerogative of winos and the homeless. Today, however, you too are to sleep outside your comfort zone. Find a nice park bench, a comfortable bus stop, or someone's front garden, and settle down for the night. Trust others to respect your sleep. And to encourage them, hang this sign around your neck as you slumber.

IMAGINARY FRIEND DAY

Studies indicate that the more long-term friends you have, the happier you're likely to be. So take the lead and create a lifelong chum all of your own.

Give him a name.
Pick something sensible like George or Sarah. "Pikaboo", "Bluebell", "Mr. Macaroni" and the like don't sound like real-friend names.
I hereby name you Benrik!

Earn his affection.
Comb his hair. Get him a drink if he's thirsty. Save a seat for him on the bus and tell others not to sit there.
Ah! Where is that little fucker when I really need him!!!
Benrik! I've built you a nice house!
Benrik's house
This way in Benrik

Talk to him in public.
Gossip. Argue. Laugh at each other's jokes. You're buddies, and you don't care who knows it.
STOP
HAHA HAHAHAH AHAHAHAHA HAHAHAHAH HAHAHAHAH HAHAH

Introduce him to everyone!
It's time to meet your other friends – and family. Don't be shy about it: if they like you they'll like him.
Excuse me, but don't think for a moment that I haven't noticed your refusal to say "Have a Merry Christmas" to my friend Benrik in front of me so I'm leaving goodbye!!!
Is he taking his medication?

Take him out on the town.
Book a table for two at a swish restaurant. Let him choose the wine. Dance the night away, cheek to cheek.
Don't look back now Benrik, I think the waiter is seriously irritated about you having your feet up on the table. OH NO, he's coming this way. OH, MUMMY!

Make room for him in your bed.
Kiss him good night. Cuddle him to sleep. Do anything at all to please your little friend...
I want to make something perfectly clear, Benrik: when it comes to pillow-fights you always have to let me win. OK?
TOYS

BETTER THAN AN IMAGINARY FRIEND; YOU NOW HAVE AN IMAGINARY LOVER!
I have never felt this for anyone else, I swear!
The END

Teenage Day

Today act like a teenager

Blah blah blah this is like such a boring idea for a day. It sucks bigtime, I mean why am I doing this Book? It's sooooo patronising to assume that teens are all the same for one thing, like, attention-span-deficited, spotty, moaning hormones on legs. AAAA-AA-A-A-RRRRGGGHHH! It makes me wanna vom! It's like what Sartre said: "We're all free to be what we want to be." Or something. Don't Benrik get it?!!! Tragic... The world is a funny place. Who said that? Bah, this isn't worth writing about, I dunno why I get so wound up. Sometimes I do not think my opinions and insights into matters of the world significant enough to merit recording for posterity. My life is so empty.

The universe is doomed. And I hate school, specially math. Gotta do homework man. Later.

Day 170

TODAY LIVE FOR THE MOMENT

Today live for the moment: that moment is 21:31:22 to 21:31:23. Plan your entire day around that one single second of absolute choking nirvana. First, purchase the necessary accessories: one rare Belgian white truffle sugar-dusted chocolate, silk pyjamas, the sleekest hi-fi system available and a CD of Maria Callas. Retire to your home, where after a restorative siesta, you are to bathe in champagne for an hour or so, before receiving a massage from some gorgeous Swedish creature. As the blissful second nears, pop the chocolate in your mouth, kiss the love of your life, and bring yourself to orgasm at 21:31:22, precisely the moment when Maria Callas hits the high note in Tosca's "Vissi D'Arte" aria. Truly now, you may say you'll die having lived.

Open House Day

Today, grant other Benrik followers full access to your house. Simply register your name and address on www.benrik.co.uk and you will become part of the Benrik Open House network. As long as they're registered, any Benrikian can visit and stay in any other Benrikian's house, sharing their food and shelter, and their Book of course. It's like a commune, only without the hippies.

Photograph submitted by Benrik User 947

Benrik User 947 in reality

Benrik House Rules

Whilst you are a guest of a fellow Benrikian, please observe these simple courtesies.

- No rude comments about decoration
- No thieving of prized possessions
- No dishes left in sink
- No graffiti on the toilet door
- No kicking of owner's cat
- No setting fire to owner's offspring
- No sharing of owner's sexual partner
- No selling house while owner out
- No disrespectful criticism of Benrik
- No hippies

Family Love day

Incest works well for animal breeding, so why not for you? Today explore your deeper feelings towards a cousin, a sibling, or a parent perhaps. Taboos, after all, are made to be broken.

Day 173

Today write to your local authority asking that your street be renamed after you. To make sure your application is successful, explain why the current name is no good, give details of your main achievements, and enclose a petition signed by your neighbours. Specify the type of street:

BLOGGS BOULEVARD	BLOGGS ROAD
BLOGGS CLOSE	BLOGGS ROW
BLOGGS SQUARE	BLOGGS ALLEY
BLOGGS GARDENS	BLOGGS WAY
BLOGGS GROVE	BLOGGS CRESCENT
BLOGGS WALK	BLOGGS PROMENADE
AVENUE BLOGGS	BLOGGS STREET

TODAY DO SOMETHING RADICAL WITH YOUR HAIR

Why spend a fortune on clothes to make a fashion statement when your own head provides the perfect opportunity already?

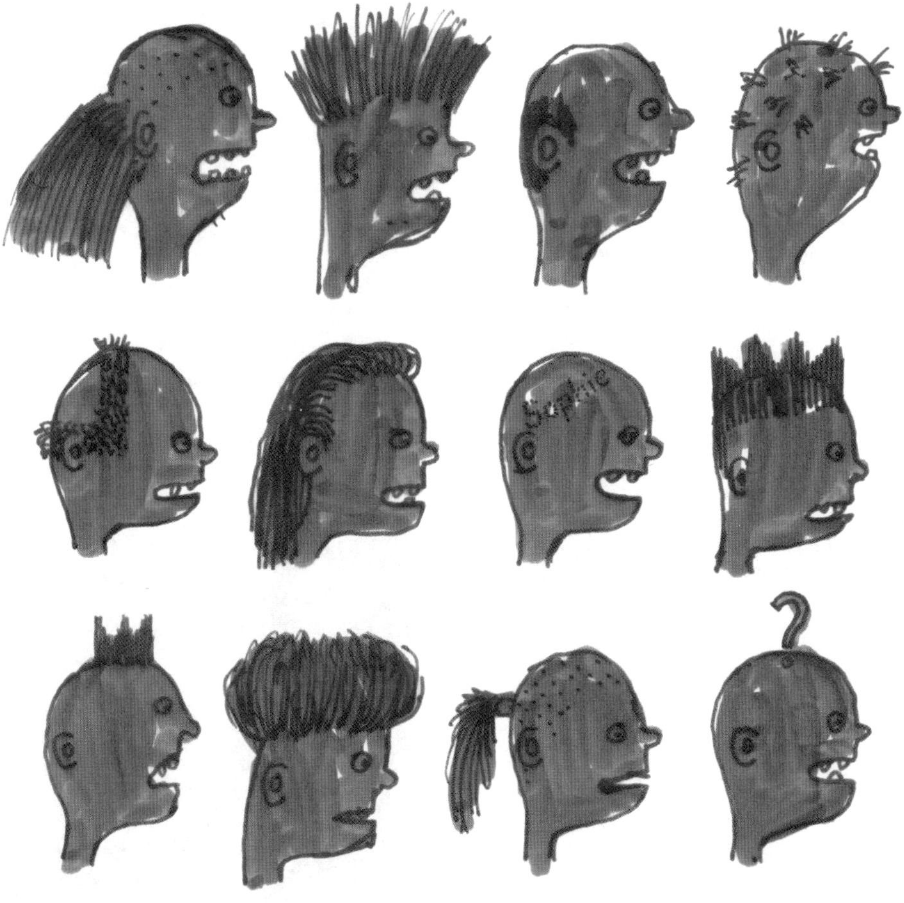
Sophie

ADVANCED: do something radical with your pubic hair. If your main (non-pubic) hair is already radical or you are bald, style your pubic regions. Shaving is hip but potentially dangerous. Colouring is more original and a welcome ice-breaker on those one-night-stands.

Day 175

Today dig at the end of a rainbow.

Myths often survive throughout the ages because they contain a grain of truth. Find out if this one is true today, and you may reap huge rewards.

1. Call up your local weather office for information on probable occurrences of rainbows in your area, based on satellite imagery of cloud formation.

2. Triangulate the exact coordinates of the rainbow's end, and track them down using a portable GPS system.

3. Secure the area and excavate a one-acre site, aiming for an average drilling depth of three metres.
Use a magnetometer to establish an electromagnetic and geophysical profile of the zone.

4. Sift for any pots of gold. Be sure to have legal help at hand to assert your right of ownership.

> Warning: if the rainbow happens to end on a bank, find another one.

Today get psychoanalysed

Who can afford thousands of pounds and hundreds of hours in conventional psychoanalytical therapy? Benrik psychoanalysis takes just ten minutes and lets you know immediately how messed up you are and whether you'll ever turn out normal or not. Answer these simple questions, add up the points, and check your results on the chart below.

Are you a man? *+1*
Are you a woman? *+1*
Don't know *+5*

Did you have a happy childhood? *+1*
Did you have an unhappy childhood? *+3*
Were you robbed of your childhood? *+8*

Is your first memory pleasant? *+2*
Is your first memory traumatic? *+4*
Is your first memory deeply repressed? *+7*

Do your friends consider you an optimist? *+2*
Do your friends consider you a pessimist? *+4*
You have no friends *+9*

This looks like a sheep *+2*
This looks like a cloud *+3*
This looks like a stain of black bilious vomit *+7*

Do you find it easy to discuss your feelings? *+2*
Do you find it hard to discuss your feelings? *+3*
Is the last time you remember having a feeling when you saw your little bunny rabbit get torn apart by your Uncle Jerry's Doberman when you were 5 years old and you had to pick up the little bits of bloody mucky fur from off the carpet and you hid them under your pillow for three weeks and refused to speak for a month? *+14*

Do you enjoy sex at least once a week? *+1*
Do you enjoy sex at least once a month? *+4*
Do you enjoy sex whenever you can afford it? *+7*

Were you closer to your father? *+2*
Were you closer to your mother? *+2*
Were you closer to Uncle Jerry? *+8*

Is this sun rising? *+1*
Is this sun setting? *+2*
Is this sun about to implode, terminating life on earth? *+8*

Do you wake up feeling happy? *+2*
Do you wake up feeling sad? *+4*
Do you wake up feeling wet? *+11*

Are you afraid of heights? *+1*
Are you afraid of spiders? *+2*
Are you afraid of yourself? *+5*

Results
Under 20: You are normal. This is nothing to be ashamed of, but it probably means you'll never write that great novel or change society in any significant way.
Between 20 and 80: You have your healthy share of neuroses. You may consult with a psychotherapist if you feel the need to discuss them further, or you could just get on with your life.
Over 80: Congratulations! You have just been hired by Benrik Limited.

Day 177

Aversion Diet Day

Most diets are far too complicated. Carbohydrate content, GI indexes and other macrobiotic nonsense only make it less likely that the diet will be followed. This is why Benrik are introducing the new "Aversion Diet". The "Aversion Diet" works on a very basic principle: if you eat less, you'll lose weight. Simply open the Book at this page, stare at these unappetizing images during mealtimes, and you are guaranteed immediate results.

Think of them on your flesh!

Concentrate on the furry bits...

Yummy!

Particularly good if you're eating meat.

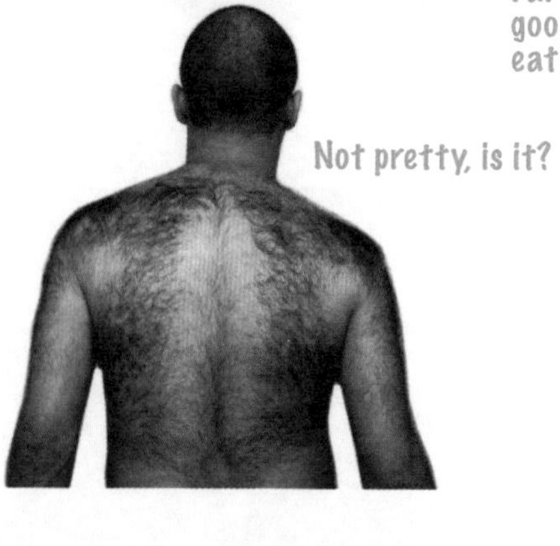

Not pretty, is it?

Bon appétit!

CITIZEN'S ARREST / PW56CJFB 00087 /

ARRESTOR DETAILS

Full name..

Home address..

City.. Post code..

ARRESTEE DETAILS

Full name.. Nickname (if any)..................................

Home address..

City.. Post code..

Height.. Weight.. Eyes..

Hair.. Race.. Gender..

Identifying scars/tattoos..

(if able to draw please attach drawing)

FINGERPRINTS:

CRIME:

Plea: Guilty ☐ Not guilty ☐ Other..

Motive: Drugs ☐ Alcohol ☐ Money ☐ Blackmail ☐Revenge ☐Insanity ☐

Other..

Statement/confession..

....

....

Signatures

Citizen.. Criminal..

MAKE A CITIZEN'S ARREST!

When a crime is committed and no police officer is in the vicinity, you have the right and responsibility to make a Citizen's Arrest. Such crimes include: murder, manslaughter, armed assault, conspiracy to defraud, littering.

Obedience Day

Obedience is a skill so exercise it today by following these simple dictates and you'll find the rest of this Book easier to obey

Speak extra loud to people with names beginning with R today
Walk slower if shorter than the person walking next to you
Refuse to answer any question where the words "you" and "with" are used
Do not accept change if less than 30p
Feign not to see people wearing red
Stay indoors if clouds are heading east or south
Cross the road whenever a passer-by makes eye contact
Clip out all newspaper headlines featuring the word "global" and paste them above your desk
Order the fifth most expensive item on the menu
Introduce yourself to anyone named Bob
Drive at 36 miles per hour exactly
Pick up the phone after five rings
Do not use the letter "d" in any correspondence
Use only the buttons on the top half of your remote control
Increase central heating temperature by 1°C every hour
Only use words invented before 1979
Speak to a minimum of 9 people an hour
Proffer your leg as a lamp post to any passing dog
Chew every mouthful a dozen times before swallowing
Leave the room if anyone with the same first name as you is mentioned

Today, divine the will of your ancestors

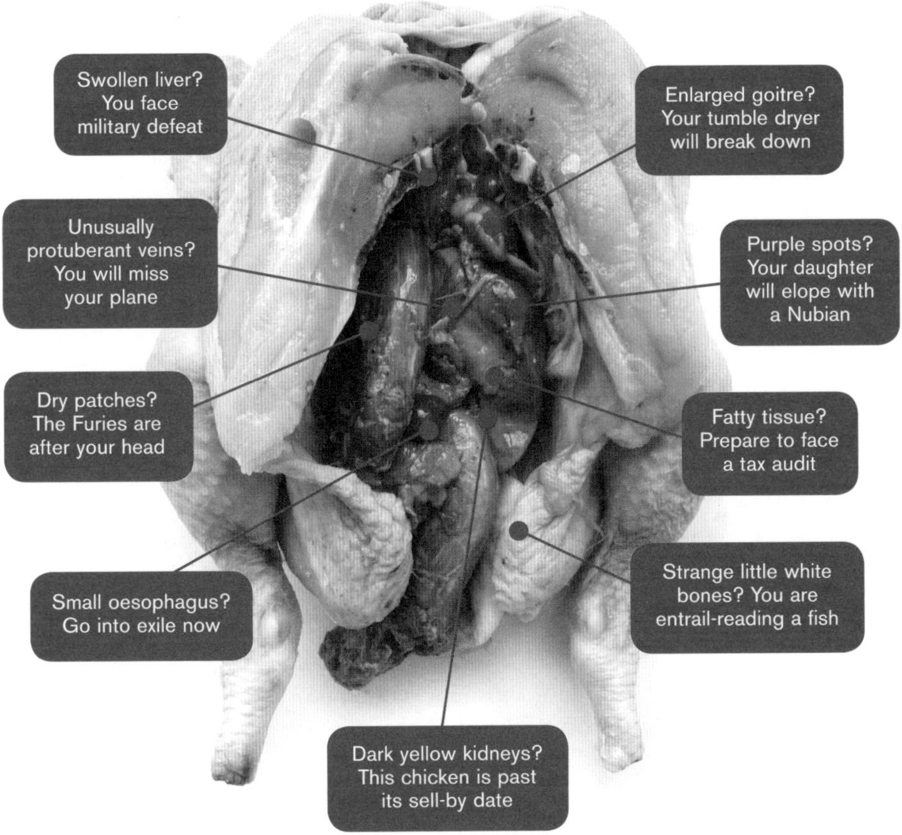
Swollen liver? You face military defeat
Enlarged goitre? Your tumble dryer will break down
Unusually protuberant veins? You will miss your plane
Purple spots? Your daughter will elope with a Nubian
Dry patches? The Furies are after your head
Fatty tissue? Prepare to face a tax audit
Small oesophagus? Go into exile now
Strange little white bones? You are entrail-reading a fish
Dark yellow kidneys? This chicken is past its sell-by date

There is no reason why the ancient Etruscan art of haruspicy, better known as entrail-reading, cannot be practised in our day and age. Before you roast a chicken tonight, take time to 'read' it and learn what fate has in store.

MILLIONAIRE!

Act like you're worth millions today.
Only your bank manager will know the difference.

DRIVE A FERRARI!

The salesman will be only too happy to oblige you with a test drive. Just try not to crash it.

BOOK A SUITE AT THE RITZ!

Obviously call to unbook it tomorrow, as your private jet is unfortunately grounded.

VISIT THE CASINO!

Enjoy the free drinks without gambling and mutter about the dice being loaded here.

INTERVIEW BUTLERS!

A classified ad for a man-servant should attract plenty of potential minions.

CALL THE PRESIDENT!

The White House number is 00 1 202 456 1414. Leave a message to call back urgently.

VIEW A PALATIAL MANSION!

Look scruffy and estate agents will assume you're a rock star.

CHANGE OSAMA'S MIND TODAY

We are spending billions of dollars on tracking down Osama Bin Laden, and sacrificing the lives of hundreds of young soldiers and innocent bystanders in the process – yet we have not tried that most basic of solutions: changing Mr Bin Laden's mind. Today, send in your best arguments to help convince him to renounce his violent ways. Benrik will collate the most persuasive ones and forward them for his attention*. Fingers crossed!

Dear Mr Bin Laden, I am ... (name), of ... (address). I am writing to respectfully invite you to reconsider your global "jihad" against the West. You clearly thought it was right at the time, but I believe that now you should call it quits. Here is my reason: ... I hope this convinces you. If so, please tell your fellow jihadists. I look forward to a future of peace. Yours truly, ...

*Osama Bin Laden often sends the West video messages via Qatar-based TV station Al Jazeera. Benrik will use the same channel and send them to Al Jazeera with instructions to pass them on to Osama.

First impressions are crucial in life. Today hand this to a stranger and find out what impression you made.

Hello!
If you have one minute, would you please write down your first impression of me, for an experiment. Please be as honest as you can. If you want you can shut this book when you're finished and I'll only look when you're gone. Thank you.
Write here please: ....

Photocopy and repeat if you are not happy with the first opinion or if you want more.

Play the stock market today

There's huge money to be made on the stock market, but people are often put off by its seeming complexity, and let's face it, the sheer numbing boredom of trying to fathom those endless figures. And yet it's not rocket science. Benrik have tried to make it more fun, so that anyone can enjoy the experience. Follow our instructions and you too will double your investment and become a trillionaire in no time.

SELL Any share you can't pronounce immediately (though you can't ask for your money back).

INVEST In high yield bonds (aka "junk" bonds). They go up and down a lot which is more exciting all round.

BUY Any shares that end in –ex.

SELL Shares in companies who do not answer the phone within three rings.

START By buying a couple of hundred shares at random, while you still enjoy beginners' luck.

SELL Shares whose price is closest to 666.

SPREAD A rumour that world supplies of salt are about to run out, and buy pepper stocks.

GO LONG On Electronics.

GO WIDE On Tobacco.

GO SHORT On Mining.

CLOSE by selling everything and pocketing the profits (10% to Benrik).

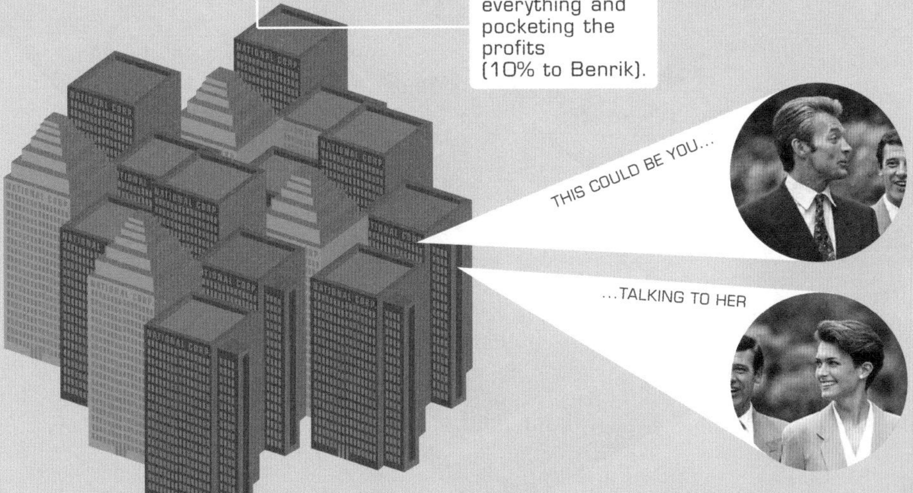
THIS COULD BE YOU...
...TALKING TO HER

In 1999, Swedish artist Ola Pehrson hooked up his yucca plant to a computer that bought shares according to the tiny electrical currents the plant generated. If the shares beat the index, the plant was rewarded with sunlight and water. If the shares did badly, the plant was left in the dark... The plant outperformed the Stockholm stock market by 12% over 4 weeks. This is a risky strategy though, which we do not recommend.

Today: rearrange your local supermarket according to your own preferences

1 BREAD SMELLS
Smell machines are used to awaken the consumer's appetite. Ask them to feature your other favourite products, like beer or tuna chunks.

2 DAIRY SECTION
Milk is always at the back so everyone has to trek through the whole store. Put it by the cash tills instead of the sweets and save everyone an unnecessary walk.

3 ADJACENCIES
Supermarkets try to display complementary products next to each other to increase sales, like tomato sauce near pasta. Create your own, like vodka and tranquillizers.

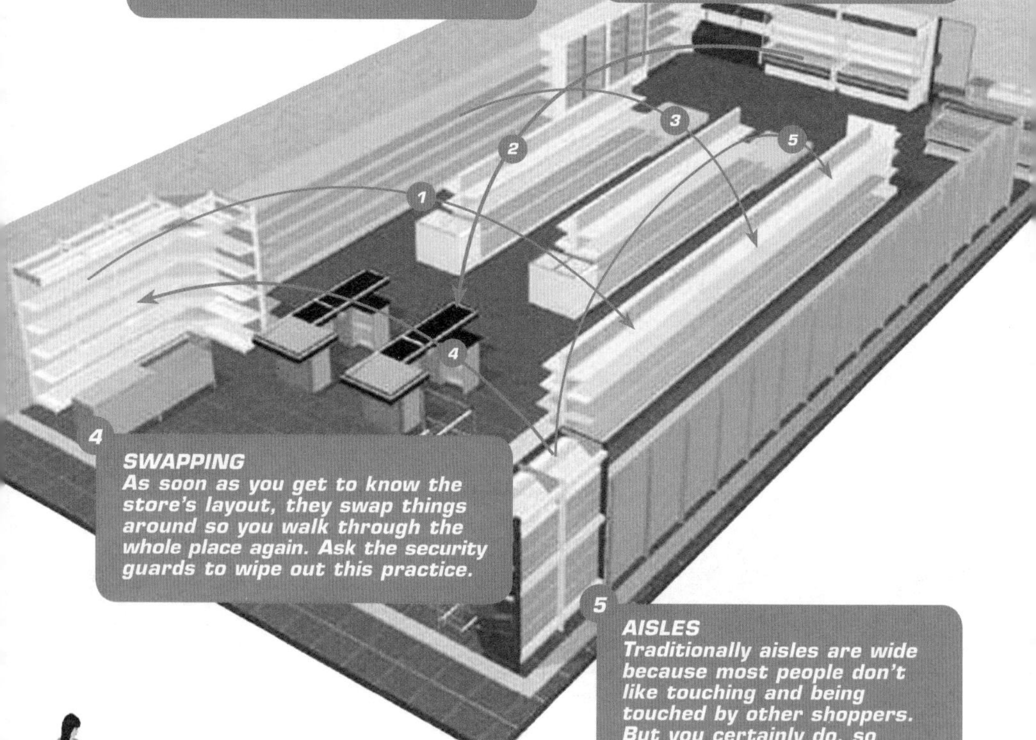
1
2
3
4
5

4 SWAPPING
As soon as you get to know the store's layout, they swap things around so you walk through the whole place again. Ask the security guards to wipe out this practice.

5 AISLES
Traditionally aisles are wide because most people don't like touching and being touched by other shoppers. But you certainly do, so squeeze them close together.

My! This modified-atmosphere-processed, irradiated, ethyl butyrate, osoamyl acetate, menthyl benzoate, cis-3 hexenol, isoamyl isovalerate, ethyl decanoate-flavoured melon smells simply delicious! I'll take two dozen.

TODAY PLACE FLOWERS ON AN OLD UNATTENDED GRAVESTONE

TODAY ANSWER SPAM EMAILS

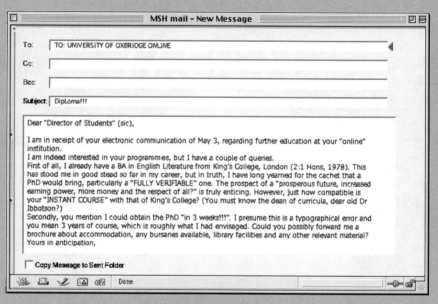

MSH mail - New Message

To: TO: UNIVERSITY OF OXBRIDGE ONLINE

Cc:

Bcc:

Subject: DipLoma!!!

Dear "Director of Students" (sic),

I am in receipt of your electronic communication of May 3, regarding further education at your "online" institution.
I am indeed interested in your programmes, but I have a couple of queries.
First of all, I already have a BA in English Literature from King's College, London (2:1 Hons, 1978). This has stood me in good stead so far in my career, but in truth, I have long yearned for the cachet that a PhD would bring, particularly a "FULLY VERIFIABLE" one. The prospect of a "prosperous future, increased earning power, more money and the respect of all?" is truly enticing. However, just how compatible is your "INSTANT COURSE" with that of King's College? (You must know the dean of curricula, dear old Dr Ibbotson?)
Secondly, you mention I could obtain the PhD "in 3 weeks!!!". I presume this is a typographical error and you mean 3 years of course, which is roughly what I had envisaged. Could you possibly forward me a brochure about accommodation, any bursaries available, library facilities and any other relevant material?
Yours in anticipation,

Copy Message to Sent Folder

Done

MSH mail - New Message

To: ml09880@freenet.tz

Cc:

Bcc:

Subject: Re: SIERA LEONE Orphan

Dear Yolanda,
I was truly sorry to hear of the tragic deaths of your father and your "senior brothers" at the hands of the rebel troops. Civil war is a blight on the face of Africa, and we must all keep up the pressure on politicians to end it. In some ways you are more fortunate than most though. The 18.9 million dollar fortune that your father left you from his "import/export agricultural supplies and tooling" business is a boon, which will enable you to rebuild your life and start again, full of hope. Of course I am willing to help you with the bank account, but I won't hear a word about being paid to do so! I am simply glad to help. My details are: Barclays account number 67657689, sort code 13-66-08. Let me know your details and I will wire over the $55,000 for the local death duties.

Looking forward to meeting you when you get your visa! I have a daughter your age, who also loves to "surf" the internet!
XXX

Copy Message to Sent Folder

Done

Cheerleader Day

TODAY, CHEER UP EVERYONE AROUND YOU! IN LIFE, THERE ARE PEOPLE WHO DRAIN ENERGY, AND PEOPLE WHO EMIT IT. BOOST YOUR COMMUNITY'S MORALE BY PRAISING EVERYONE'S GOOD BEHAVIOUR, AND THUS REINFORCING IT.

"WHAT A WELL-BEHAVED QUEUE WE ARE, WELL DONE US!"

"ISN'T OUR BUS GOING FAST TODAY? I'M CERTAINLY ENJOYING IT!"

TESCO

"I JUST LOVE THE SHOPPING VIBE IN THIS SUPERMARKET THIS AFTERNOON!"

"LET'S PAT OURSELVES ON THE BACK FOR WAITING PATIENTLY, FELLOW COMMUTERS!"

"HEY EVERYONE IN THE LAUNDERETTE, LOOKING SHARP!"

"EVERYBODY ON THIS ESCALATOR IS SPECIAL! I LOVE YOU GUYS!"

GET ADMITTED TO A MENTAL HOSPITAL TODAY

The diagnosing of mental illness is a notoriously woolly process. What is sanity, anyway? Today, turn up at a mental institution, announce that you feel unwell, and get committed, using the script opposite. Reveal your deception at midnight and discover if they allow you to leave*.

WHAT TO SAY TO THE PSYCHIATRIST:
Claim to be conducting your daily life according to the random dictates of two Franco-Swedish individuals whom you've never even met, but who have commanded you to seek psychiatric help against your will and better judgement. Mention that there are thousands of others just like you, although you've never met them either. Be sure to warn the doctor that whatever happens, you are under orders to escape by the end of the day.

THE ROSENHAN EXPERIMENT:
ON BEING SANE IN INSANE PLACES.
In 1972, David Rosenhan famously managed to get eight perfectly sane "patients" admitted to different psychiatric wards in the US, on the basis that they claimed to have heard voices. Once they were in, they acted normally but were still categorized as insane by staff and kept there for up to fifty-two days. In a follow-up experiment, Rosenhan told a hospital in advance that he would be sending them pseudopatients over the next three months. The hospital declared they had spotted forty-one of these impostors. Rosenhan revealed he had not, in fact, sent any.

*If they refuse to allow you to leave, you are exempt from future tasks. Enjoy the rest of your life!

Day 190

Living History Day: Today, live the life of a 13th century peasant.

Wake at dawn as the pig you share your straw bed with relieves himself on your foot. Shake off the fleas, flies and lice, and prepare to meet the day! Skip your bath as usual, you had one last year. Wake your spouse and your eight (or is it nine?) children, and enjoy a breakfast of tasty dry bread, washed down with ale (you don't drink the water from the river - it tastes foul as a result of being used as a sewer). You notice your ox in its wisdom has decided to bash in part of the house's wall. Make a mental note to patch it up with mud when you have two seconds, or maybe with some of the copious manure the ox produced overnight. But for now, off to the fields you go, not to your own strip, but to work on your lord's. It's harvesting time, so grab your sickle, a rusty bit of metal as likely to land you with a tetanus cut as to help you harvest. The crop this year is pretty weak, because it rained for two weeks continuously in June. So you don't want to tire yourself out completely, since there might be little food to help you recuperate. On the other hand if you don't work hard, there'll be no food at all and you'll starve to death. In any case the lord's reeve will be keeping an eye on you and you'll get fined or beaten if you don't pull your weight. Time for lunch, not a moment too soon as you're hungry. You're hungry most of the time anyway though, so it's nothing to complain about. Lunch is more dark bread, with a bit of rat-nibbled cheese if you're lucky. And ale. More work, maybe on the church's land this time. There are other peasants working nearby, but there's not much time for gossip with Hans, Will or Sal (they have no surnames and neither do you. You don't need a surname as there's only a few dozen of you in the village you were born in and which you'll probably never leave in your 13th century life in any case. Not that you know what century you're living in.) Anyway as the sun sets you down tools and head home. Tonight's supper is pottage, a stew of oats with the odd turnip. You're exhausted but you might attempt some rather clumsy intercourse with your spouse, never mind the kids and animals. They've seen and heard it all before. Repeat tomorrow. And every day for the rest of your life, which will probably end around age 45 if you're lucky.

Don't forget the shoes.

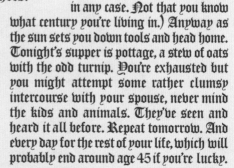

You will need: mud, rats, a straw bed, a pig, cloth, an ox, a field, leprosy, ale, turnips, manure

Have all your food tasted for poison today

From the Borgias to JFK, poisoning has claimed thousands of victims. Yet few take the necessary precautions against it. Today ask a family member or a waiter to taste your food before you ingest it. Then observe them for 20 minutes for the slightest sign of illness, like vomiting, convulsions or massive internal haemorrhaging. Only then may you relax and enjoy your meal. Telltale signs that your food is poisoned:

Roast chicken
Wings look slightly shrunken

Cod and chips
Chips break in two very easily

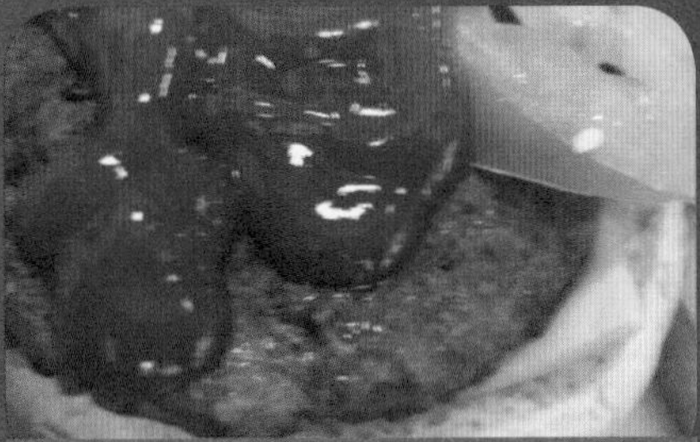

Cheeseburger
Cheese has greenish tinge

Steak
Veins bulging (with the poison)

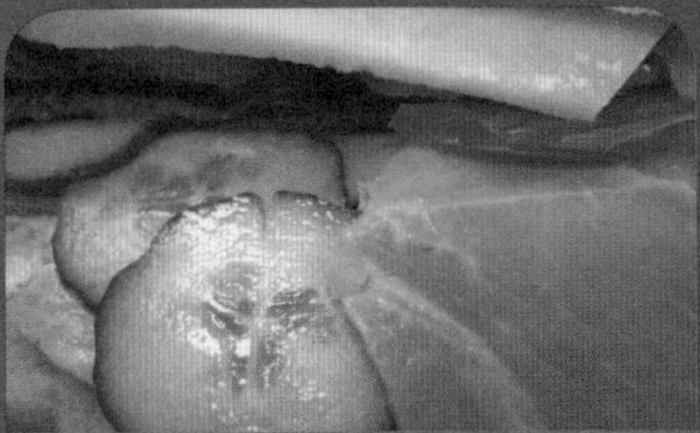

Ham and cheese sandwich
Ham and cheese stuck together

Apple crumble
No visible signs, avoid

Rasputin's top tip: the "mad monk" was the target of many assassination attempts, including one to poison him with huge doses of cyanide. Amazingly, he survived, having deliberately exposed himself to increasing amounts of poison over the years to build up some immunity. Of course he was eventually shot and dumped in a frozen river. Not much you can do about that.

Walk under a ladder

Whistle inside the house

DEFY SUPERSTITION TODAY

Put keys on the table

Open your umbrella inside

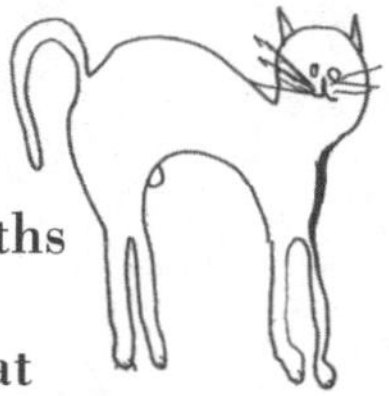

Cross paths with a black cat

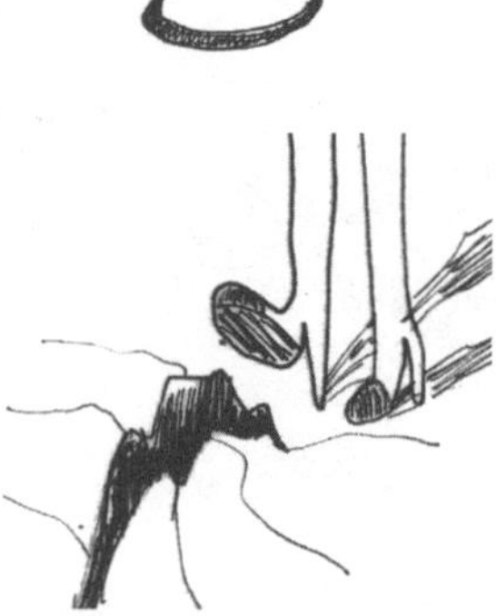

Step on a crack in the pavement

Let milk boil over

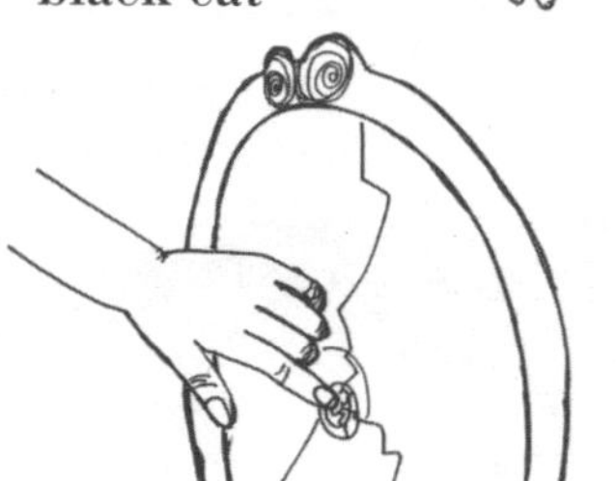

Break a mirror

REBIRTH!

Today ask your parents to help you stage a realistic reconstruction of your birth.

Strange how little we know about the details of the most important moment of our life: its beginning. And yet there are witnesses to the act! Enlist them to recreate that magical instant where you burst forth. Only by understanding where you came from will you fully understand where you're going.

GET IT RIGHT!
Details to check and replicate:

- When and where did the waters break?
- How did you get to hospital?
- What time was it?
- How long did the delivery take?
- What drugs were administered?
- Were stirrups involved?
- Was the father in the room?
- Did you put up a fight?
- Which bit came out first?
- Did you cry when spanked by the nurse?
- Who cut the umbilical cord?

ning: Do not attempt to recreate a Caesarian without qualified medical assistance.

CHANGE SOMEONE'S MIND TODAY

Only fools never change their mind. Help save someone from such folly by arguing them out of their deeply held views on a controversial subject.

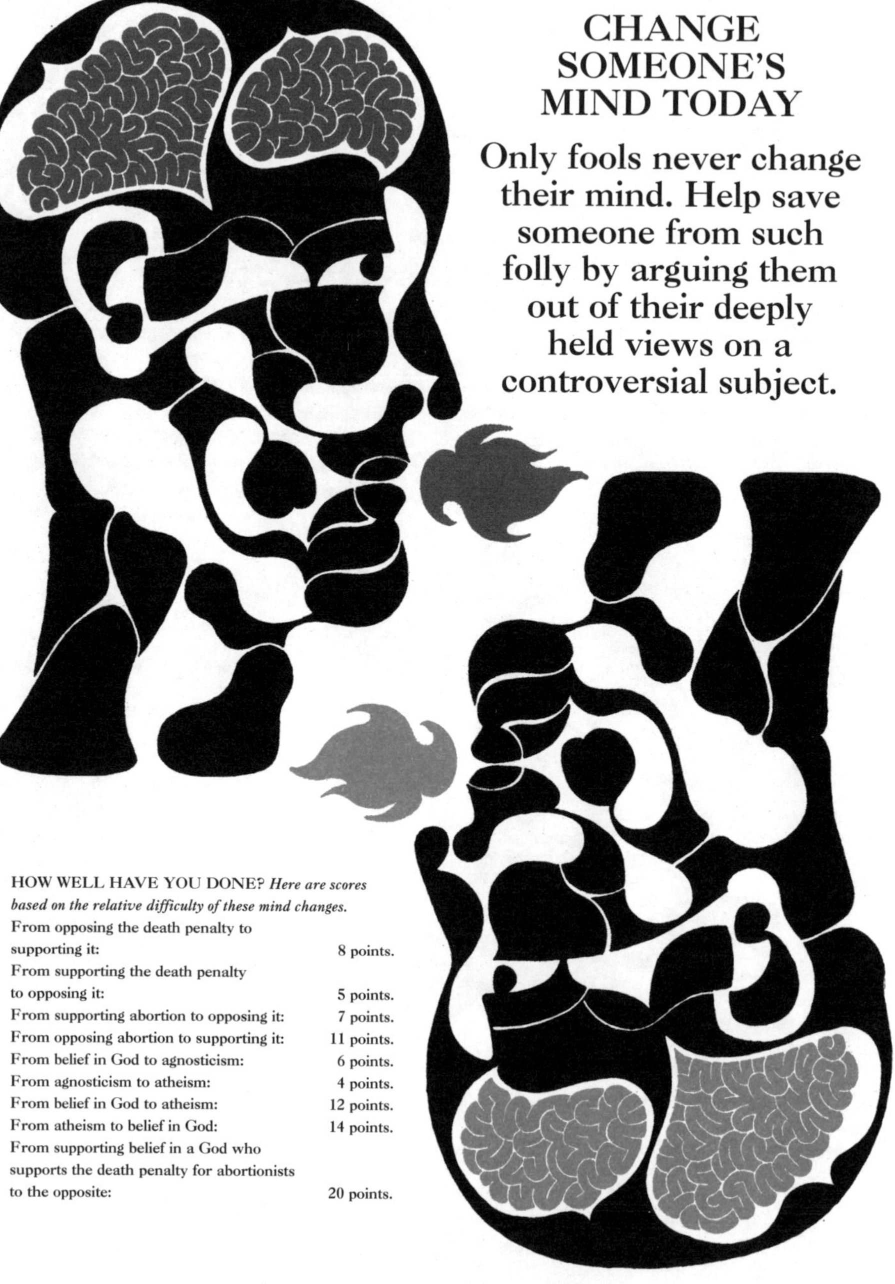

HOW WELL HAVE YOU DONE? *Here are scores based on the relative difficulty of these mind changes.*

From opposing the death penalty to supporting it:	8 points.
From supporting the death penalty to opposing it:	5 points.
From supporting abortion to opposing it:	7 points.
From opposing abortion to supporting it:	11 points.
From belief in God to agnosticism:	6 points.
From agnosticism to atheism:	4 points.
From belief in God to atheism:	12 points.
From atheism to belief in God:	14 points.
From supporting belief in a God who supports the death penalty for abortionists to the opposite:	20 points.

Leave a note on someone's car windscreen

I'm a traffic warden but today I feel lenient. Don't do it again though.

I'm the engineer who made this vehicle. The brakes aren't very good cos I was hungover that day. Watch out.

We've discovered your car is the one responsible for all the damage to the ozone layer; please bike to work in future.

I've left someone in your boot. I'll pick him up next week if that's OK.

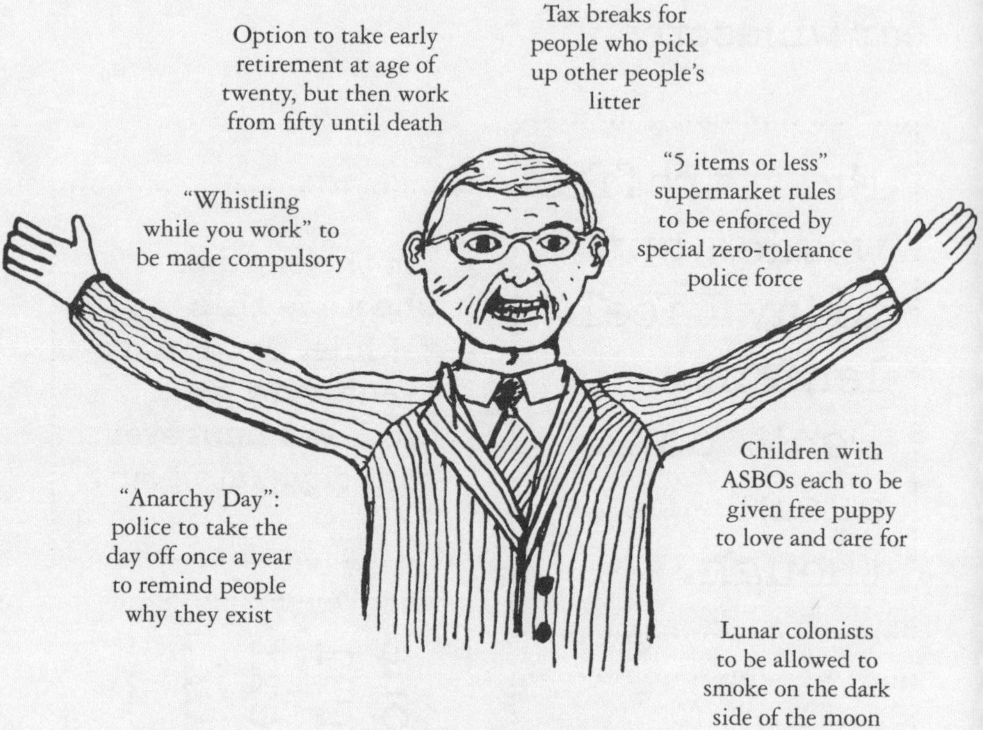
Option to take early retirement at age of twenty, but then work from fifty until death
Tax breaks for people who pick up other people's litter
"Whistling while you work" to be made compulsory
"5 items or less" supermarket rules to be enforced by special zero-tolerance police force
"Anarchy Day": police to take the day off once a year to remind people why they exist
Children with ASBOs each to be given free puppy to love and care for
Lunar colonists to be allowed to smoke on the dark side of the moon

TODAY, GO SEE YOUR MP WITH YOUR SUGGESTION FOR A NEW LAW

It is a tribute to our democracy that anyone can turn up to see their elected representative at a weekly clinic. This ensures that MPs are in direct touch with the masses, and allows issues to filter up into the national debate. Sadly, too many people raise clichéd matters such as their gas bill, rubbish collections, or the latest war. Today, make an appointment to see your MP and propose your very own piece of legislation, demanding that they bring it up in parliament as well as with the relevant government minister. Only by injecting fresh ideas into the political debate will we keep democracy alive!

MINI-PROSTITUTION DAY
SELL A VERY MINOR SEXUAL FAVOUR

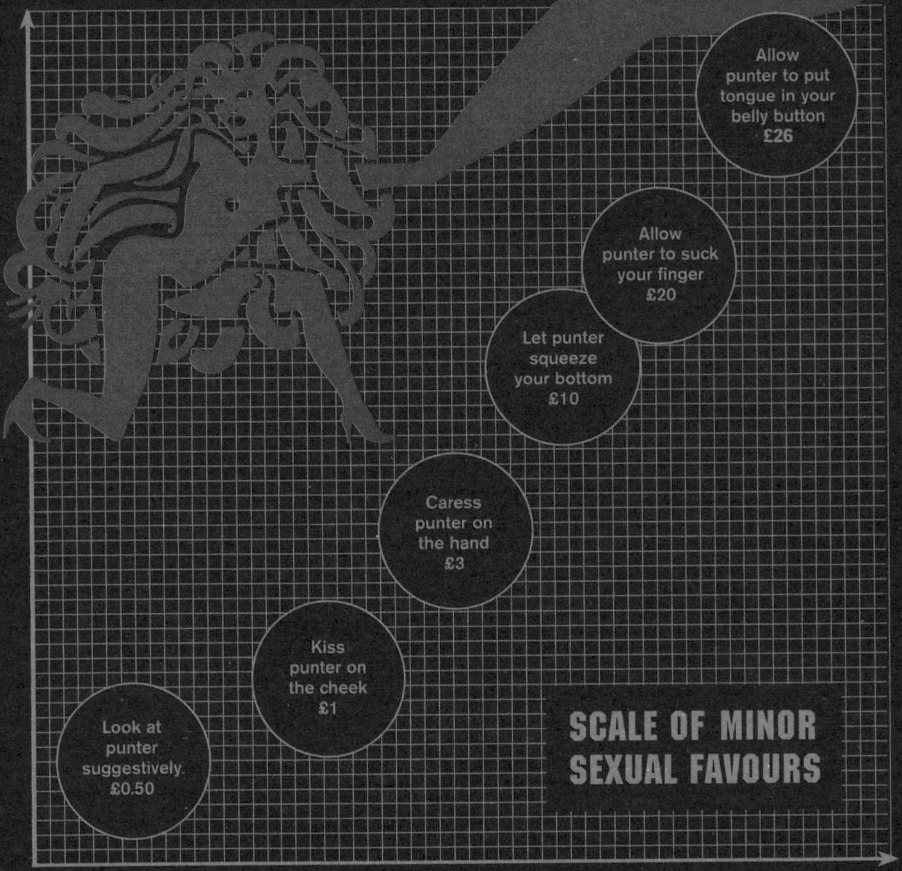
Allow punter to put tongue in your belly button £26
Allow punter to suck your finger £20
Let punter squeeze your bottom £10
Caress punter on the hand £3
Kiss punter on the cheek £1
Look at punter suggestively £0.50
SCALE OF MINOR SEXUAL FAVOURS

It's the oldest job in the world, yet most people never even consider it. There's no reason why you have to jump in at the deep end with full-blown sex with strangers. Find out if prostitution is for you by starting small: offer someone a kiss on the cheek for £1 perhaps; caress a neighbour's hand for £3; let the checkout girl squeeze your bottom for £10. Who knows, you may discover your true vocation.

SPEND TODAY PRETENDING TO BE A TOURIST!

Equipment:
daypack,
camera,
lost look

Background on your country:
Make it up, no one cares.

Itinerary:
10 a.m. Visit Big monument
12 p.m. Ride around in bus for a while
1 p.m. Lunch in tourist trap restaurant
3 p.m. Big museum
5 p.m. Get laughed at by schoolkids
6 p.m. Big show
9 p.m. Get mugged by schoolkids
10 p.m. Bed in Big hotel.
Repeat tomorrow.

Lines:
This monument/museum/show sure is nice.
Do you have any ketchup?
Is the Queen in right now?

Today, agree to meet someone in 10 years' time.

We, the undersigned, may only know each other casually, but we hereby agree to meet up in exactly ten years' time at .... (hour) on the .... (date) at .... (place).
In case we have changed beyond recognition, we agree to wear the following identifying items of clothing: ....
In case we have nothing to say to each other, here is a list of current "hot" topics to reminisce about: ....

....

....

Signed

....

....

See you in ten years' time.

Fill in this coupon and hand it to a stranger or someone you hardly know.

DUMP YOUR PARTNER FOR THE DAY

The best way to reinvigorate a relationship is a short, sharp separation. Today, announce to your other half that you're done with them and storm out.

TOP TIPS FOR THE TEMPORARILY SINGLE

PLAY THE FIELD:

technically you're not in a relationship today, so fool around and satisfy your animal lust.

BITCH ABOUT HIM/HER:

provided you don't tell them it's only for the day, your friends will enjoy revealing they actually hated your ex.

DO THAT THING THAT YOU STOPPED DOING BECAUSE THEY HATE IT:

pluck your nose hair in front of the TV, wear those furry slippers, let the phone ring and ring.

ENJOY A BOTTLE OF WINE ALL BY YOURSELF:

solitary drinking is much more fun on your own.

MASTURBATION RULES OK!

as Woody Allen famously said, it's sex with someone you love.

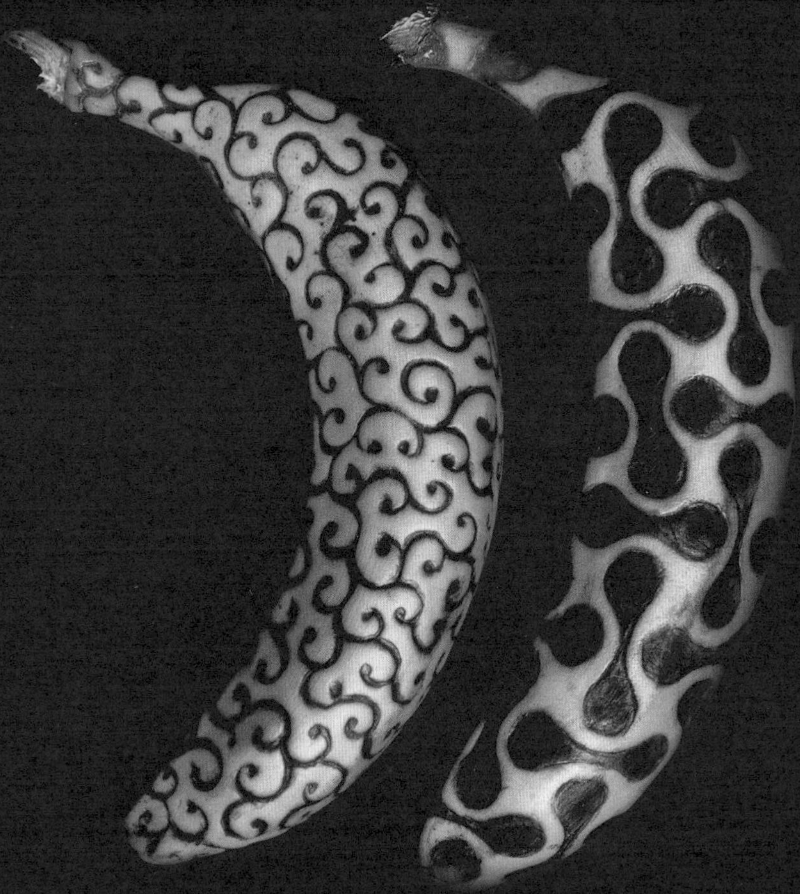

Today, tattoo a banana. Scrape its skin with a sharp implement and watch it go black in minutes! Display it on your windowsill.

Today, make a shrine about someone you don't know but see on a regular basis, then show it to them.

Lovely summer.

John's morning routine

The insurance house.

Getting off the bus.

Just looking?

Peekaboo John!
CAPPUCCINO
MOCH

Who are you talking to John?

NERO
John saw me, but I pretended to be a tourist.

96a
Who the hell lives there?

My painting of John (not finished)

EIGHT MILLION WAYS TO DIE

We all have to die of something. Today make your preference known by ranking this selection of ways to die from 1 to 100.

Hit by truck.../100
Hit by car.../100
Hit by bus.../100
Volcanic eruption.../100
Earthquake.../100
Meteorite on head../100
Cancer../100
Burnt alive../100
Flower pot falls on head../100
Fall under train.../100
Pushed under train../100
Plane crash.../100
Parachute jammed../100
Cocaine overdose.../100
Heroin overdose.../100
Painkiller overdose../100
Trampled at rock concert......................................./100
Struck by lightning../100
Ebola virus../100
Snake bite.../100
Snake constriction../100
Tarantula.../100
Scorpion.../100
Swallowed wasp../100
Broken heart../100
Nuclear bomb.../100
Anthrax in mail.../100
Friendly fire.../100
Spontaneous combustion......................................./100
Eaten by sharks../100
Eaten by cannibals../100
Eaten by piranhas.../100
Eaten by dinosaurs../100
Eaten by zombies ..../100
Eaten by flesh-eating bug....................................../100
Drowned../100
Hanged.../100
Lynched../100
Strangled.../100
Decapitated../100
Crucified.../100
Sliced up.../100
Disembowelled.../100
Eviscerated.../100
Microwaved.../100
Vaporized.../100
Shot in head.../100
Shot in heart../100
Shot in stomach../100
Shot in foot../100
Dropped on head.../100
Gangrene.../100
Choking.../100
Choking on a bone../100
Choking on a nut.../100
Unexpected nut allergy.../100
Lift brake failure../100
Spacesuit leak.../100
Stabbed../100
Stabbed in the back.../100
Bludgeoned with baseball bat................................../100
Abducted by aliens for tests..................................../100
Gas.../100
Paper cut../100
Lethal injection.../100
Electric chair../100
Guillotine.../100
Duel../100
Suicide.../100
Suicide-bombed.../100
Suicide-bomber../100
Food-poisoned.../100
Alcohol-poisoned.../100
Poison-poisoned.../100
Poisoned umbrella tip../100
In my sleep (N/A).../100
Machine-gunned../100
Hypothermia../100
Heart attack.../100
Malaria.../100
Measles../100
Mumps../100
Smallpox.../100
Cholera../100
Whooping cough../100
Black death../100
Car accident.../100
Mafia../100
Buried alive../100
Prematurely cremated.../100
Routine surgery gone wrong..................................../100
Bondage session gone wrong.................................../100
Superman impression gone wrong............................/100
Russian roulette../100
Murdered by serial killer../100
Assassinated../100
Ransom unpaid by family../100
Caught in crossfire.../100
Fall into vat of acid../100
Hara Kiri.../100

Day 204

Poetry Day

Today everyone is to send in a line to create the world's longest poem. They will be collated as they are e-mailed to www.benrik.co.uk, and the result published across the whole world as soon as a suitable final line is deemed to have been found and we think of a good title. The opening line is:

"MERCY, CRIED THE POPINJAY TO THE POPE"

Work on your line here:

....

....

....

....

....

The Iambic Pentameter for idiots: This oeuvre is to be composed in iambic pentameters, undoubtedly the most versatile form in the English poetic idiom. The iambic pentameter runs ti-tum ti-tum ti-tum ti-tum ti-tum, its ten syllables tripping off the tongue effortlessly, thus enabling the poet to propel his meaning forth. William Shakespeare wrote mostly in iambic parameters: "Shall I compare thee to a summer's day? Thou art more lovely and more temperate", and so on and so forth. If it was good enough for him, it's good enough for you. Happy composing. Read a review of the poem so far at poetryfoundation.org. Or view the poem itself at benrik.co.uk/v1/poetry.

SENSE-LESS DAY

Go through today without using your sense of: *taste*

HOW TO: GARGLE WITH SORE THROAT TOPICAL ANAESTHETIC (CONTAINING PHENOL OR BENZOCAINE) TO NUMB YOUR TONGUE BEFORE EATING.

True story: Michael F., 45, lost his sense of taste at the age of 8 following a viral infection that damaged the cranial nerve fibres that carry information from the taste buds to the brain. His condition is known as "ageusia," meaning full loss of taste, which is a very rare disorder. At the time, his main gripe concerned inability to distinguish between ice cream flavours. He did however develop a reputation for being able to ingest insects and some of the smaller lizards without batting an eyelid. He now lives in Denver with his wife and two children, and is reconciled to his loss.

Recover your umbilical cord today

Anyone who has a baby these days is going to want to hang on to its umbilical cord, full of stem cells that promise a cure for many previously untreatable diseases. Today call the hospital where you were born to try and locate your umbilical cord. Perhaps it was just chucked in a drawer, or a cupboard.

Your clone in 2588:

SORRY. WE COULDN'T RETAIN THE MAGMA [redacted] -FACTOR DURING THE SLIZER-PHASE IN THE CRITICAL NUCLEUS. REALLY SORRY ABOUT THAT.

Speak to the midwife who delivered you and ask if she remembers where they put it. Check that your Mum didn't keep it for luck.

Found it? Then call a cryopreservation company and arrange an immediate pick-up.

Today play Traffic Russian Roulette

Traffic Russian Roulette is all the rage amongst the restless youth in the vast suburbs of Ukrainian dormitory towns. It's easy to take part, less easy to win. The idea is simply to cross the road without looking. Start with an easy road and progress to the trickier ones.

MISKOLC
СДЕЛАНО В СССР
Risk:
low
KUK 3330

1. Path in your local park

Threats: dogs, joggers, pushchairs.

Risk:
some

2. Country lane

Threats: cows, tractors, idiots in sports cars.

Risk:
high

3. Main road

Threats: cars, buses, trucks.

Risk:
insane

4. German autobahn

Threats: Mercedes, BMW, Porsche.

TODAY TEST THE POWER OF PRAYER

Prayer is a very much underexploited resource in modern society. Just because prayers sound fancier if they're about world peace doesn't mean they can't work for more mundane matters. Put those atheistic leanings aside and test the power of prayer today.

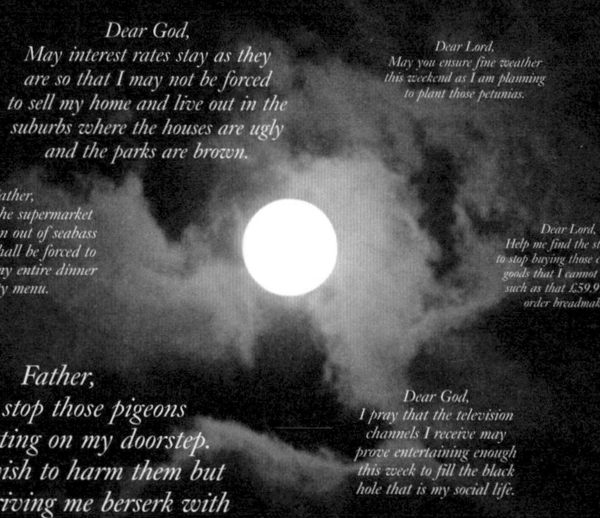

*Dear God,
May interest rates stay as they are so that I may not be forced to sell my home and live out in the suburbs where the houses are ugly and the parks are brown.*

*Dear Lord,
May you ensure fine weather this weekend as I am planning to plant those petunias.*

*Father,
Please let the supermarket not have run out of seabass for then I shall be forced to reconsider my entire dinner party menu.*

*Dear Lord,
Help me find the strength to stop buying those consumer goods that I cannot afford, such as that £59.99 mail order breadmaker.*

*Father,
Please stop those pigeons from shitting on my doorstep. I do not wish to harm them but they are driving me berserk with their cooing all night long.*

*Dear God,
I pray that the television channels I receive may prove entertaining enough this week to fill the black hole that is my social life.*

*Lord,
Please let my boss realize that I have been working like a dog and grant me that day off that I urgently need to go to the VD clinic.*

*Dear God,
I pray that my girlfriend won't leave me. I dumped her for a day last week as Benrik suggested and she cannot see the joke.*

Your Prayer: ....

....

....

Answered ☐ Not answered ☐

Today, lend your mobile to a homeless person and ask them to take your calls, screening out anyone they don't like the sound of.

Important Message!

Date.............................Time.........................A.m. ☐ P.m. ☐
Caller...
....
Of...
Phone number...

☐ Will call again ☐
Telephoned ☐ Wishes to see you ☐
Returned your call ☐
Please call

Response:
They're busy! ☐
They're dead! ☐
They hate you! ☐
Fack off! ☐
Can I take a message? ☐

Important Message!

Date.............................Time.........................A.m. ☐ P.m. ☐
Caller...
....
Of...
Phone number...

☐ Will call again ☐
Telephoned ☐ Wishes to see you ☐
Returned your call ☐
Please call

Response:
They're busy! ☐
They're dead! ☐
They hate you! ☐
Fack off! ☐
Can I take a message? ☐

Important Message!

Date.............................Time.........................A.m. ☐ P.m. ☐
Caller...
....
Of...
Phone number...

☐ Will call again ☐
Telephoned ☐ Wishes to see you ☐
Returned your call ☐
Please call

Response:
They're busy! ☐
They're dead! ☐
They hate you! ☐
Fack off! ☐
Can I take a message? ☐

Important Message!

Date.............................Time.........................A.m. ☐ P.m. ☐
Caller...
....
Of...
Phone number...

☐ Will call again ☐
Telephoned ☐ Wishes to see you ☐
Returned your call ☐
Please call

Response:
They're busy! ☐
They're dead! ☐
They hate you! ☐
Fack off! ☐
Can I take a message? ☐

TODAY SEND A LETTER TO SOMEONE AT RANDOM WITH A PHOTO OF YOURSELF, A £5 BILL, NO EXPLANATION AND NO SENDER ADDRESS. SEE WHAT COMES OF IT.

Have a row with everyone you meet

Sorry!
Benrik LTD.
Why don't you get a job instead of begging?
All the newspapers you sell are full of bad news.
This is the worst sex I've ever had.
I didn't step on your foot, you must have dreamt it.
Your dog has been trying it on with my cat.
That light wasn't red, officer.
Benrik LTD.

Let off steam with this extreme stress-relief method. It's easy: you can start a row over anything, from rip-off taxi fares to rubbish collectors not doing their job properly. Start with insolence, and build up to a nuclear rage. Refuse to see sense!

Reasonableness is the chloroform of our times, the mental cage from which we dare not escape. It is permanent compromise, which only hormone-addled teenagers and mad poets may challenge. Today, revolt against sensibleness: with everyone you meet, rage, burn and rave!

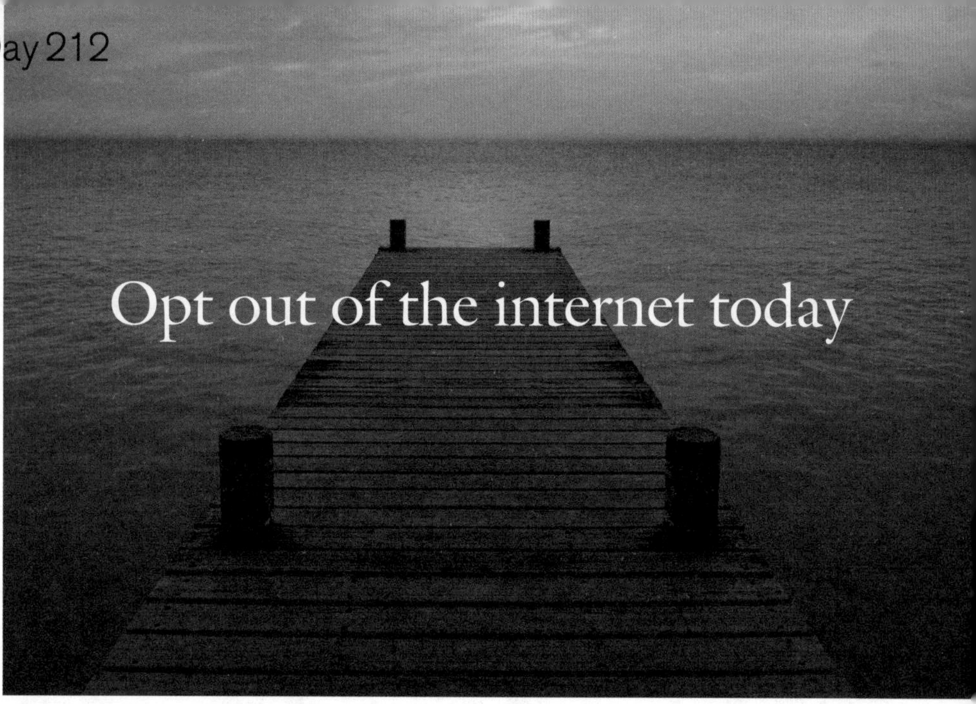

Opt out of the internet today

It is a cliché to point out just how much electronic data is being collected about us. From surveillance CCTV cameras to electronic banking, from supermarket loyalty schemes to internet service-provider logs, there is hardly any aspect of our lives that isn't monitored by someone somewhere. If the current trends continue, we are told, we will end up with a police state.

What many fail to realize, however, is that it is already too late. Your privacy is only protected by the limits of the technology: all this information is currently stored in disparate locations. But as processing power expands and databases are increasingly interconnected, we are heading for the emergence of a unified computer record of all the current information about you; this is the future of the internet.

For an authoritarian government of the future, it will be child's play to search your file automatically, and convict you retrospectively for anything you have said or done today. What may seem innocuous now, may be regarded as subversive in twenty years' time. It is therefore quite possibly too late to save yourself, but you can at least try to limit the damage.

WIPE THE RECORD

Erase any blogs you have written. Delete any message-board posts. Unsubscribe from any email lists. Cancel your credit cards. Never google again. Try to cancel your virtual presence.

CONFUSE THE DATABASE

Already today, software looks for recognizable patterns to help categorize you. Prevent them from pinning you down: invest in weapons stocks one minute, and give to a landmine charity the next.

CHANGE YOUR NAME

A unique name makes it easier to track you down: there aren't that many "Archibald Dokins" about. Change your name by deed poll to something common, like "Sam Brown", to help cover your electronic tracks.

DESTROY THIS BOOK

Ownership of anti-state instructions may in itself constitute an offence in the future. Destroy this book, and ask the bookshop you bought it from to delete your transaction from its records.

TODAY STALK AN ANIMAL!

HEY LASSIE I'M GOING TO EAT
YOU ALIVE YOU LITTLE BITCH!

It is only recently that humans have pulled ahead of the pack and started considering ourselves superior to other species. Today return to your animal roots by stalking another creature. It may take you a while to get the hang of it, so start with something simple, like a cat. Sniff its urine. Scan its tracks. Study its behaviour. Scare the hell out of it when you catch the damn thing. If it denounces you to the animal protection people, remind them that technically you too are an animal and therefore covered by statutory dog-eat-dog legislation. If all else fails either howl at the moon or roll over and play dead.

WEEK OF REVOLUTION!
UNDERGROUND

DOWN WITH THE POST CAPITALIST ORDER!
COMRADES UNITE IN OVERTHROWING THE GOV-ERNMENT! USE ANY MEANS NECESSARY!
WHY FIGHT FAIR WHEN THE STATE APPARATUS DOES NOT?
REPRES-SION BEGETS REACTION! ANARCHY IS TOO TIMID!
RISE AGAINST THE RULING CLASS AND ITS LAPDOG THE MIDDLE CLASS
THEY MAY SPEND MONEY BUT WE WILL SPEND BLOOD! AND LOTS OF IT!!!!!!

PRINT YOUR OWN SAMIZDAT

Revolution is made in the mind. Plant its seeds with your very own samizdat pamphlet. Samizdat rules: no pictures or colours are allowed, it's not meant to be enjoyed. Avoid margins, a waste of scarce paper. Simple words are best, in capitals for emphasis. Logic may be shaky, as long as the main thrust is clear.

WEEK OF REVOLUTION!

EXILE

FOMENT UNREST AWAY FROM HOME

Following yesterday's outburst, you will have been banished. Use this time wisely to make contacts in the revolutionary diaspora. Distribute pamphlets outside offices, speak at covert meetings, rouse the rabble! If you do not come to the attention of the local authorities, you are not fomenting hard enough.

WEEK OF REVOLUTION!
PROPAGANDA

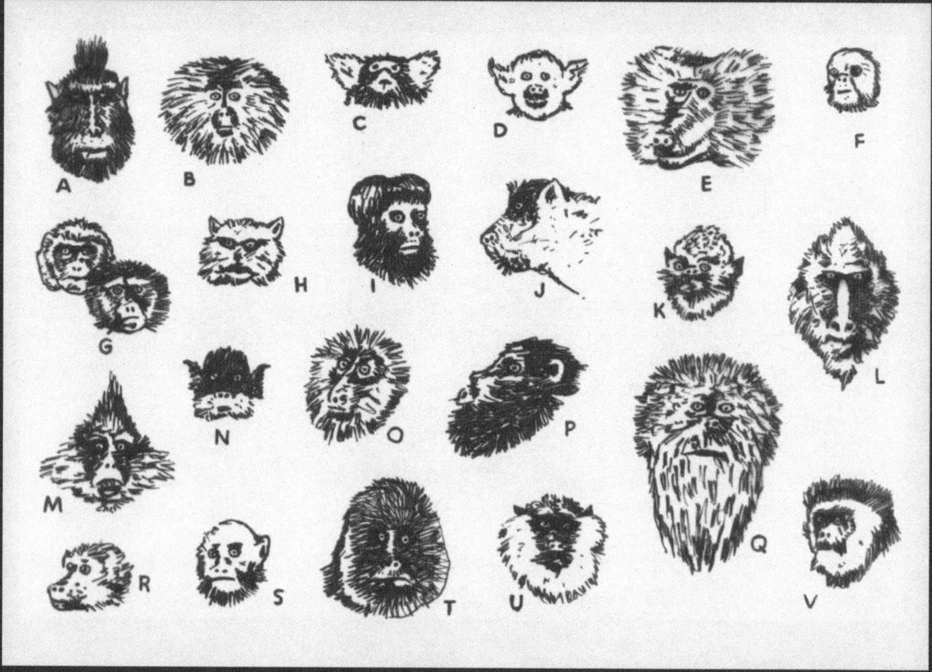
A
B
C
D
E
F
G
H
I
J
K
L
M
N
O
P
Q
R
S
T
U
V

DEVELOP YOUR OWN REVOLUTIONARY BRAND

With so many things to oppose, it's important to give your revolution some individuality. It could be out-of-control facial hair, an unusual scapegoat (the weather?) or a rhetorical device, like starting all your sentences with "But!"

REMINDER: THE STATUS QUO If your revolution is simply a generic one against the status quo, here is a reminder of its basics: our world is dominated by a global elite based on interlocking military economic social and cultural networks, organised to exploit the rest of us as workers and consumers, and configured to exclude even the possibility of serious dissent.

WEEK OF REVOLUTION!

HIJACK A TRAIN TO THE SCENE OF YOUR COUP

No revolution is complete without the spectacular arrival from the hills of the bearded revolutionaries. Today board a train and demand that it divert to the government HQ, or better still, the TV station, where you will take over the country, using force of some description.

WEEK OF REVOLUTION!

NEW DAWN

IMPOSE YOUR NEW SOCIETY

The hardest part is done. Now we must change society. Form neighbourhood committees, headed by the local Benrik reader. Pool all your salaries (including bonuses and benefits in kind) and divide them equally. Put the addresses of your houses in a hat and just reallocate them at random. Enforce equality of opportunity. Then take the rest of the day off as a national holiday.

WEEK OF REVOLUTION!

PURGE

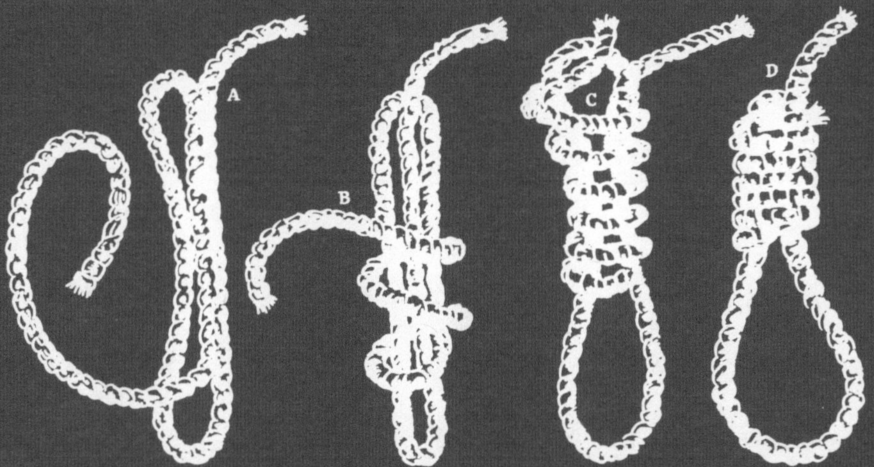
A
B
C
D

NOW LIQUIDATE ABSOLUTELY EVERYONE YOU'VE MET THIS WEEK

"DON'T THINK. IF YOU THINK, DON'T SPEAK. IF YOU SPEAK, DON'T WRITE. IF YOU WRITE, DON'T SIGN. IF YOU THINK, SPEAK, WRITE AND SIGN – DON'T BE SURPRISED!!!"

Negative Thinking Day

Positive thinking is enjoying a resurgence, with books on "cosmic ordering", "The Secret", and other recipes for attitude-based success topping the bestseller lists. Find out very quickly if there is something in it by adopting the opposite mindset: think negatively all day and see if negative things do indeed befall you.

"Uh-oh it's going to rain!"
Did it rain? Yes ☐ No ☐

"Is this baby going to cry at me?"
Did the baby cry at you? Yes ☐ No ☐

"There are sharks in the water for sure."
Were there sharks in the water?
Yes ☐ No ☐

"This computer is going to crash and lose all my documents."
Did the computer crash? Yes ☐ No ☐

"Hot coffee! Could burn my tongue..."
Did your tongue get burnt? Yes ☐ No ☐

Free
cash withdrawals

"I must have run out of money this month."
Had you run out of money? Yes ☐ No ☐

"I'm going to get run over I just know it."
Did you get run over? Yes ☐ No ☐

"It's going to fall on my head!"
Did it fall on your head? Yes ☐ No ☐

"This man looks like he's going to arrest me!"
Did you get arrested? Yes ☐ No ☐

"My house is probably being burgled!"
Did your house get burgled?
Yes ☐ No ☐

"Terrorists might crash it into my building."
Did terrorists try crashing it into your building? Yes ☐ No ☐

"What if the sun suddenly explodes and we all get pulverized in the blast?"
Did the sun explode? Yes ☐ No ☐

SABOTAGE FOCUS GROUPS TODAY

Focus groups are the engine rooms of the market economy, where new products and services are presented to consumers for approval or rejection. They represent a unique early opportunity to dictate far-reaching corporate decisions. Today, attend a focus group, and skew the outcome in a much more creative direction. Remember: no reaction is too ridiculous or too random, particularly if you can convince others in the focus group to back you up.

Call and volunteer your services:
The Research House Ltd 020 7935 4979
Focus Network 020 8563 7117
Ase Research 020 7580 7757

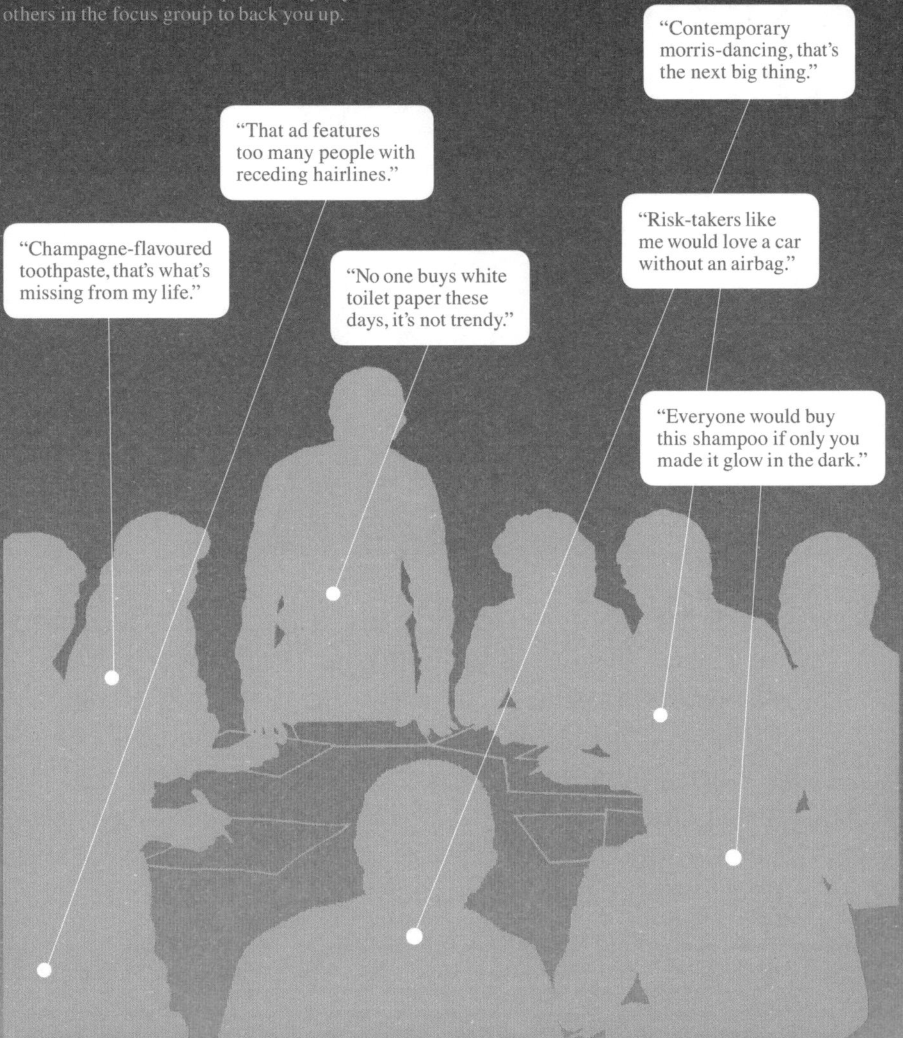
"Contemporary morris-dancing, that's the next big thing."
"That ad features too many people with receding hairlines."
"Champagne-flavoured toothpaste, that's what's missing from my life."
"No one buys white toilet paper these days, it's not trendy."
"Risk-takers like me would love a car without an airbag."
"Everyone would buy this shampoo if only you made it glow in the dark."

Day 222

TODAY STARE INTO OTHER PEOPLE'S HOMES

If people didn't want you to look at their carefully designed living space, they'd put up curtains. There's no actual law against nosiness, so draw up a folding chair outside their windows and peer as much as you like. Like what you see? Then knock and ask if you can become a bona fide friend of the family. That way, you get to enjoy the décor close up, and they'll stop wasting their time calling 999 about privacy invasions.

Common domestic scenes to look out for include: families eating their dinner, housewives watching TV, kids doing their homework, clocks ticking, babies crying, neighbours borrowing cups of sugar, teenagers picking up the phone, salesmen doing their spiel, dogs fouling the carpet, wives cheating on their husbands, husbands cheating on their wives, lovers hiding in cupboards, bailiffs repossessing the fridge, grannies beating their cats, sadomasochistic suburban orgies, cockroaches jumping in the soup, instances of spontaneous combustion, plots being hatched against civilization itself. Don't get caught peeking!

Today, make friends with the geniuses of tomorrow

Don't you wish you had met Einstein or Bill Gates when they were young and still struggling? How easy it would have been to befriend them in their hour of need, only to share in their glory and money later. Today, track down the future leading lights of their generation and become firm friends. How to spot them: geniuses should be recognizable by their manifest brilliance, but also by their endearing eccentricities – keep an eye out for both.

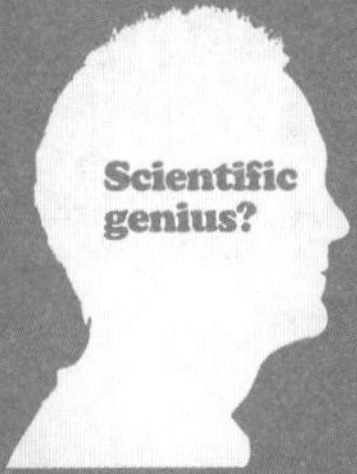
Scientific genius?

Lifetime ambition: to win Nobel Prize for working out how to escape from black holes (est. 2033)
Endearing eccentricity: only trims nasal hair in left nostril
Where to befriend: outside university labs

Artistic genius?

Lifetime ambition: to create artwork that makes everyone who sees it burst into tears of joy (est. 2015)
Endearing eccentricity: bites other people's fingernails
Where to befriend: art school end-of-year shows

Musical genius?

Lifetime ambition: to write the official anthem of the first lunar colony (est. 2023)
Endearing eccentricity: barks back at passing dogs
Where to befriend: deserted gigs in dodgy pubs

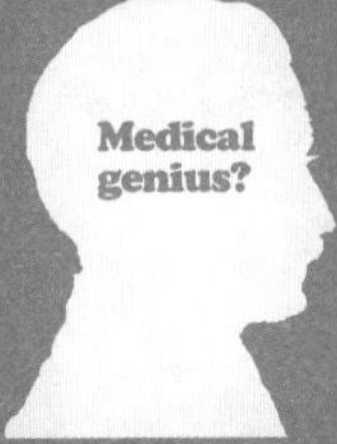
Medical genius?

Lifetime ambition: first surgeon to transplant brains between a reptile and a mammal (est. 2054)
Endearing eccentricity: laughs at bad news on TV
Where to befriend: local A&E

Literary genius?

Lifetime ambition: to write bestseller in her very own alphabet (est. 2067)
Endearing eccentricity: carries fire extinguisher in handbag
Where to befriend: in quietest corner of libraries

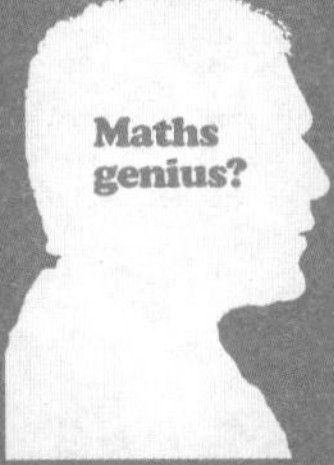
Maths genius?

Lifetime ambition: squaring the circle (est. 2050)
Endearing eccentricity: counting hairs on your head as he first meets you
Where to befriend: local OCD support group

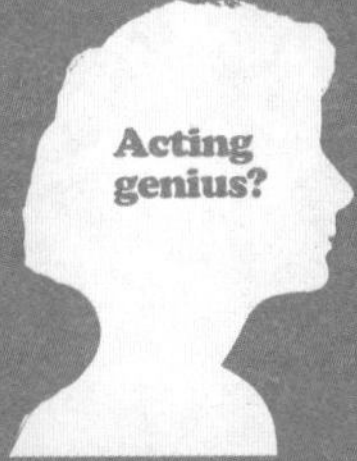
Acting genius?

Lifetime ambition: winning Oscar for portrayal of Hamlet as pre-op transsexual (est. 2041)
Endearing eccentricity: too many to list
Where to befriend: Edinburgh Fringe

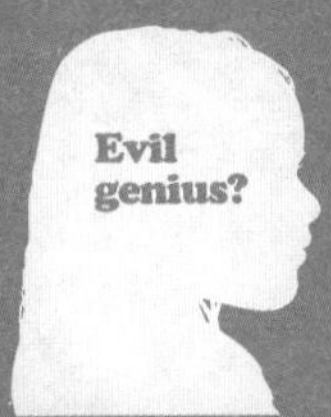
Evil genius?

Lifetime ambition: doing secret deal with alien master race to carve up the Earth between them (est. 2097)
Endearing eccentricity: pinching small children until they wet themselves
Where to befriend: local Jobcentre

Day 224

Today, Dance with Death

DON'T JUDGE YOUR JEANS AFTER WHA
YOU LEARNED FROM YOUR FATHER

We are only ever one minute away from the end. Today, experience death's insane proximity so as to savour life all the more. Stand next to a running chainsaw. Stumble on the train platform. Stare over the edge of the cliff. Run a red light. Insult a skinhead. Just don't take anyone with you though.

BENRIK

Day 225

TALK TO A PLANT FOR AT LEAST ONE HOUR TODAY

A house is not a home.

Good things to say to a plant: "Grow, you plants are the best", "Try to touch the sky", "You're the best plant in the world", "Try your best at growing", "You're so pretty with your light green, dark green and green colours". Bad things to say to a plant: "Die you nasty plants, die", "You are the worst plants in the world", "Die you worthless pieces of green seeds", "You are so ugly when you are standing up, so fall over and don't get up", "You are so ugly when you're green, and you wouldn't be ugly if you were brown and falling over".

INTERNET VIGILANTE DAY

Today police the internet yourself

<cutie69er> asl
<cutie69er> im 13
<LuvinBoy> 16,m,malaysia
<Ready> hello cutie
<cutie69er> hi
<LuvinBoy> 3 years older]
<LuvinBoy> hehe
<Vigilante> Hey you two are underage!
<LuvinBoy> hi
<hottiewithabody> no freedom im am too! haha
cassandra sets mode: +b *!*@26E1AC.EBA119B.7903A39D.IP
<MasterYoda> bored bored bored bored aziz is now known as SwEeT_BoY_MsN
<cutie69er> hi
<Vigilante> cutie69er isn't it past your bedtime?
<LuvinBoy> wazzup...
*some^boy thinks freedom2fight4 is wrong
<handsomeboy_932> 18,mmalaysia
<cutie69er> nm
<sexypip> any m wnt chat, 15 f uk
<Freedom2Fight4> sure u are hottie
<LuvinBoy> nm?
<Freedom2Fight4> whys that some boy
<CKY_17> hi
<hottiewithabody> i am if you knew me you would agree too
<Vigilante> enough of this lechery let's talk about something else guys and girls
*some^boy isnt too coward to state facts that are insulting... freedom2fight4 u suck.... (an insulting fact)
<cutie69er> hi any hot guys? gangsta_18 is now known as Wolf_King
<some^boy> :)
<some^boy> lol
<DrPel_6931> Any girl who wants to have a real talk pvt me (Spanish,German.Italian,French, language iis not a problem-)
<Vigilante> Dr? You don't sound like a teen, get out of our chatroom
<Freedom2Fight4> well i dont and thats why im neutral at the moment
<DrPel_6931> Any girl who wants to have a real talk pvt me (Spanish,German.Italian,French, language iis not a problem-)
<hottiewithabody> im in this HUGE fight right now with a few ppl just b/c i stated the facts
<Freedom2Fight4> sure u are someboy
<some^boy> lol
l_6931> and u r a moron who's only a man behind a computer 8-)
<Vigilante> cutie69er pvt me and I'll help you fight these degenerates
*SEXYIRISHGIRL sits on the arms chair
*SHAZ hey some^boyyyyyyyyyyyyyyyyyyyyyyyyyyyyyyy
<DrPel_6931> and u r a moron who's only a man behind a computer 8-)
<nurse> hiya everyone
<Vigilante> a nurse? Whatever next?
cassandra sets mode: +b *!*sweet_gi*@*
nurse is now known as nurse_538
*Web_Cam_BoY please Àù want WEB CAM girls
<Baby_Bunny> ANY1 FOUND ANY PERVES 2NI
<Vigilante> it's full of perverts raaaaaghh hhhh
DrPel_6931> :S damn it
<DrPel_6931> someone dropped me :S
<hobby> where are hot girls ?
<Vigilante> where are they thosedripping hot ones?????????!!!!!!
*SHAZ hb some^boy
<scrpion1> hiiiiiiiiiiiiiiiiiiiiiiiiiiiiiiiiiiii
<nurse_538> he wants a three some y u not up 4 that
cassandra sets mode: +b *!*araCroft@*
<hobby> any girl wanna chat
<LuvinBoy> anybody want to tok dirty pvt me
<Vigilante> DIRTY LITTLE WHORES OF BABYLON!!!!!!!
<beachgirl> hi room
<samiekins_3469> here!
*SEXYIRISHGIRL sneezes
<hobby> hi beach girl
<samiekins_3469> yeah n e fit guys wntin sommat gooooood pvt me
<Vigilante> that's better. Bye for now.
*some^boy is back... again
<samiekins_3469> :P

Day 227

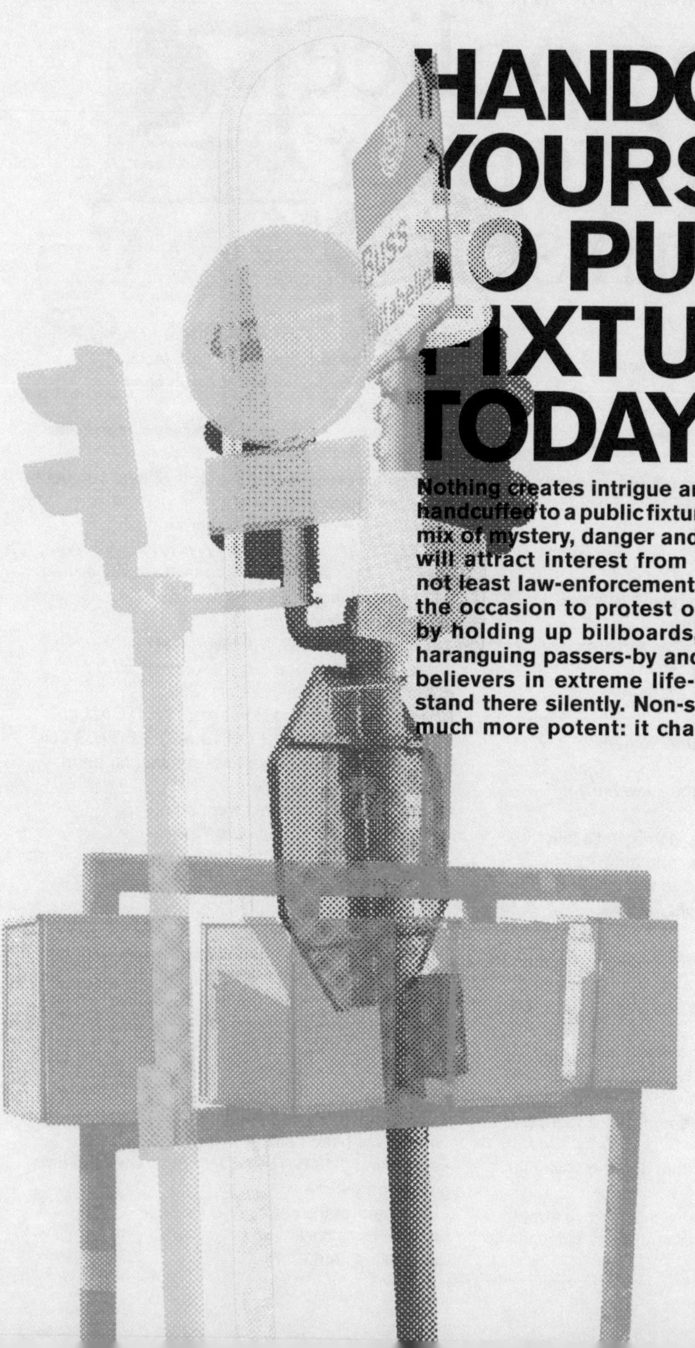

HANDCUFF YOURSELF TO PUBLIC FIXTURES TODAY

Nothing creates intrigue around you like being handcuffed to a public fixture. It projects a heady mix of mystery, danger and vulnerability, which will attract interest from all sorts of people, not least law-enforcement types. You may use the occasion to protest on a favourite issue, by holding up billboards, chanting slogans, haranguing passers-by and so on; but the true believers in extreme life-change should just stand there silently. Non-specific protest is so much more potent: it challenges everything.

TODAY LOBBY CELINE DION TO SING ABOUT YOU

Celine Dion has enjoyed a meteoric rise to global fame. She has sold over 130 million records worldwide and now stars in one of the most successful live shows in the history of entertainment. But her wide repertoire of songs has not yet featured you. Today write to her and suggest yourself as a fertile song topic, detailing your life story and how you think you would fit thematically into her oeuvre. Here is Celine's life to inspire you with emotional connections between your journey and hers.

Celine was born in 1968 in a picturesque small town in Quebec named Charlemagne. The youngest of 14 children (!), she learned the art of entertainment early on, performing with her siblings for the benefit of the locals in her parents' pianobar. At the age of 12, she announced to her mother that she wanted to sing. They composed a song together and contacted one of Montreal's pre-eminent managers, Rene Angelil, in January 1981. Rene was so entranced by Celine's voice that he cried. He then remortgaged to finance her first album and set about introducing her talent to the world! She became an overnight sensation in her native Quebec with her French-language single 'La voix du bon dieu' ('The voice of God'), written by Eddy Marnay – apparently the words that Marnay exclaimed when he first heard her sing. International success swiftly followed, when she won the gold medal at the Yamaha World Song Festival in Tokyo barely a year after her debut. The next five years saw her become a huge star in the French-speaking world, with classic hit albums such as 'Du Soleil Au Coeur' and 'Incognito', which went platinum. Her global breakthrough came in 1988, when she won the Eurovision Song contest, singing 'Ne partez pas sans moi' for Switzerland, wowing 600 million viewers throughout the world in the process! In September 1990 she capitalized on this by releasing 'Unison', her first English language album, which scored a huge hit in the US with the Top 5 single 'Where Does My Heart Beat Now'. But this was just the beginning! In 1991 she sang the title soundtrack for Disney's 'The Beauty and the Beast', which rocketed to No1 and won an Academy Award as well as a Grammy. Celine by now was unstoppable, with her eponymous album 'Celine Dion' spawning no less than FOUR more hit singles. To top it all off, Celine had found love. Rene Angelil was 26 years her senior, yet love knows no such barriers. Their admiration and respect for each other had grown into something more, and on December 17, 1994, they married in Montreal, to the delight of her fans. Meanwhile her worldwide success showed no sign of abating. 'D'Eux' broke through the French language barrier in 1995 to become the biggest-selling French hit in history, netting Celine the knighthood of the order of arts and letters from the French government for being the 'best ambassadress of the French language'. Merci beaucoup! In Britain she topped the charts for weeks with the ballad 'Think Twice', which sold over a million copies. This success, however, was all but eclipsed in 1996 and 1997 when successive albums 'Falling Into You' and 'Let's Talk About Love' sold roughly 30 million worldwide – each! The song 'My Heart Will Go On', movie theme song of 'Titanic', won an Oscar and became a favourite wedding song for fans of Celine. The Nineties were fittingly topped by an authorized biography by Georges-Hebert Germain and a collection of greatest hits, 'All The Way... A Decade Of Song', which featured such classics as 'The Power Of Love', 'Because You Loved Me', and 'If You Asked Me To', along with some brand new songs. By the end of 1999, Celine was long overdue for a break! She decided to take some well-deserved time off from her hectic schedule. In spite of this, there was an unexpected release for her fans in 2001: her baby son, Rene-Charles Angelil, born on January 25! After two years off, Celine returned to showbiz in 2002 with a new blockbusting album, 'A New Day Has Come', an immediate No1 across the globe, with fans reassuring Celine she had not been forgotten! If anything, her schedule has got busier since her break, with several new albums, a perfume launch, and in March 2003, the opening of her own show at Caesar's Palace Las Vegas! Bravo Celine!

Write to: Celine Dion, A New Day, Caesars Palace, 3570 Las Vegas Boulevard, Las Vegas, NV89109, USA

MOTHER'S DAY: MOTHER YOUR MOTHER FOR A CHANGE

Wake her up and cook breakfast
Wash and comb her hair
Kiss her boo-boo better
Give her a piggyback
Do up her shoelaces
Wipe her bottom
Knit her a jumper
Explain about the birds and the bees
Hold her hand as you cross the street
Drag her around the supermarket
Give up your career for her
Darn her socks
Write her a sick note
Play peek-a-boo
Put a plaster on her knee when she falls over
Bake her a cake
Breastfeed her (well, it was weird for her too at the time)
Tuck her into bed and lull her to sleep with a story and a kiss
Help her with her homework
Take her to church
Hug her when she's sad
And for very special mums! Carry her around in your stomach for 9 months, throwing up now and again

She gave birth to you. She brought you up. She loved you unconditionally. She gave you her all. It's time you repaid her. A mere card won't do. Today, take care of her the way she took care of you.

Today eat this book

You will absorb the life-changing properties of the Book much faster if you eat it rather than read it. Today, tuck into your favourite page and have the others to follow. Don't eat beyond today though before looking at the pretty pictures.

Nutritional information:
Typical values per 100 pages
Energy KJ 4565
Kcal 780
Protein 3.2g
Carbohydrate 34.3g
(of which sugars) 8.3g
Fat 4.8g
(of which saturates) 3.9g
Fibre 98g
Sodium trace

THIS BOOK WILL CHANGE YOUR LIFE
The Best of This Diary Will Change Your Life

Make someone hate you today

Hatred is as mysterious and volatile an emotion as love. It is fairly easy to pinpoint why we dislike someone. Dislike is socially acceptable, one of the inevitable lubricants of our close-quarters living. But hatred is socially disruptive. Its intensity is pathological. It overrules rational argument and shreds the social fabric. What drives anyone to hate? Find out today by trying to make someone hate you. It can be someone who already dislikes you, or you can start from scratch with a stranger or a friend. Good luck, and don't forget to tell them it was a joke tomorrow!

EAT SHIT
AND DIE
HATE & DIS-GUST

IGNORE THEM:
When your receptionist smiles and says hi as usual, pretend she's invisible, pause for a moment as if trying to locate the source of a particularly nasty smell, and stride on into the lift.

ATTACK THEIR FAMILY:
Ask your neighbour over the garden fence if she minds that her husband sees the dominatrix in Pond St every other Monday evening on his way home. Say you assumed she knew as everyone else seems to.

INSULT THEIR BELIEFS:
Your great-aunt has been praying fervently all her life to get to heaven. Get her a free subscription to *Science* magazine with instructions to look out for articles on what actually happens after death.

GMT
Genetically
Modified
Tomato
HEY
LUCKY
LADY!
$1
million
inside!
Help! I am
Greg Dwek, a US
citizen kidnapped by the anti-
government forces in Namibia.
For the last ten years they have made
me work like a slave in their apple
plantation in southern Namibia. This
is the first message I've been able to
smuggle out.
Please alert the White House
to my plight by passing
on this apple! My life is
in your hands!
Shave me!
WORMS
ADD
FLAVOUR!
TECHNICALLY
I'M A VEGETABLE

STICK A MESSAGE ON A FRUIT

GMT
Genetically
Modified
Tomato
$1
million
inside!
Shave me!
HEY
LUCKY
LADY!

GRAPHOLOGY DAY
Manipulate others through your handwriting

The science of graphology is often used for such unambitious purposes as assessing job candidates or identifying criminals. Its true potential, however, lies in its capacity to help you control people's impressions of you, regardless of what you actually write. Here are the basics: use them to your advantage.

Backward-sloping writing:
you are a rebel

Don't care if I get your Stupid
job anyway, you can stick!

Different-slanting writing:
you are unstable

Kill Kill by god I will!!
Only joking sweetie!!

Upward-sloping writing:
you are a born optimist

Even without my leg I should
win the marathon easily!

Extra large writing:
you are an egomaniac

I TOLD HAWKING, MY THEORY IS
AT BLACK HOLES ARE LIKE CHEESE

Disconnected writing:
you are introverted

I HO PE THI S NUCL EAR DISA STER DO ESN'T
IN TER FER E WITH MY PA INT ING

Widely spaced writing:
you are antisocial

I don't want a 21st
birthday party anyway

High-looped writing:
you are a dreamer

I know we have never met but I
I always knew I'd marry a princess.

Ts crossed at the top:
you are a born leader

WE MUST CUT BUDGETS EVEN IF IT MEANS
SACKING THEM. TOUGH TIMES CALL. SO

Extra wide writing:
you are extravagant

The second Porsche has no
not arrived yet! I must

Is dotted to the left:
you are a procrastinator

My thesis is nearly finished,
and yes I know I'm 48, but it's n

Light pressured writing:
you are easily led

If you really think I should
join the Foreign Legion then

"Cute" writing:
you are an American teenage girl

Hi!!! Guess what?? Biff invite
me to the prom!!!! Yay!!! N

WRITE A MESSAGE TO THE FUTURE

Mark the envelope "DO NOT OPEN UNTIL JUNE 1, 2104". Begin the letter with today's date and To Whom It May Concern. Suitable topics: world peace, evolutionary trends, suggestions on how to deal with living on other planets, predictions, anecdotes from our times that might interest future generations (sport, "hot news", society, dress trends, etc). Hide the envelope so that it won't be found for a hundred years.

Day 235

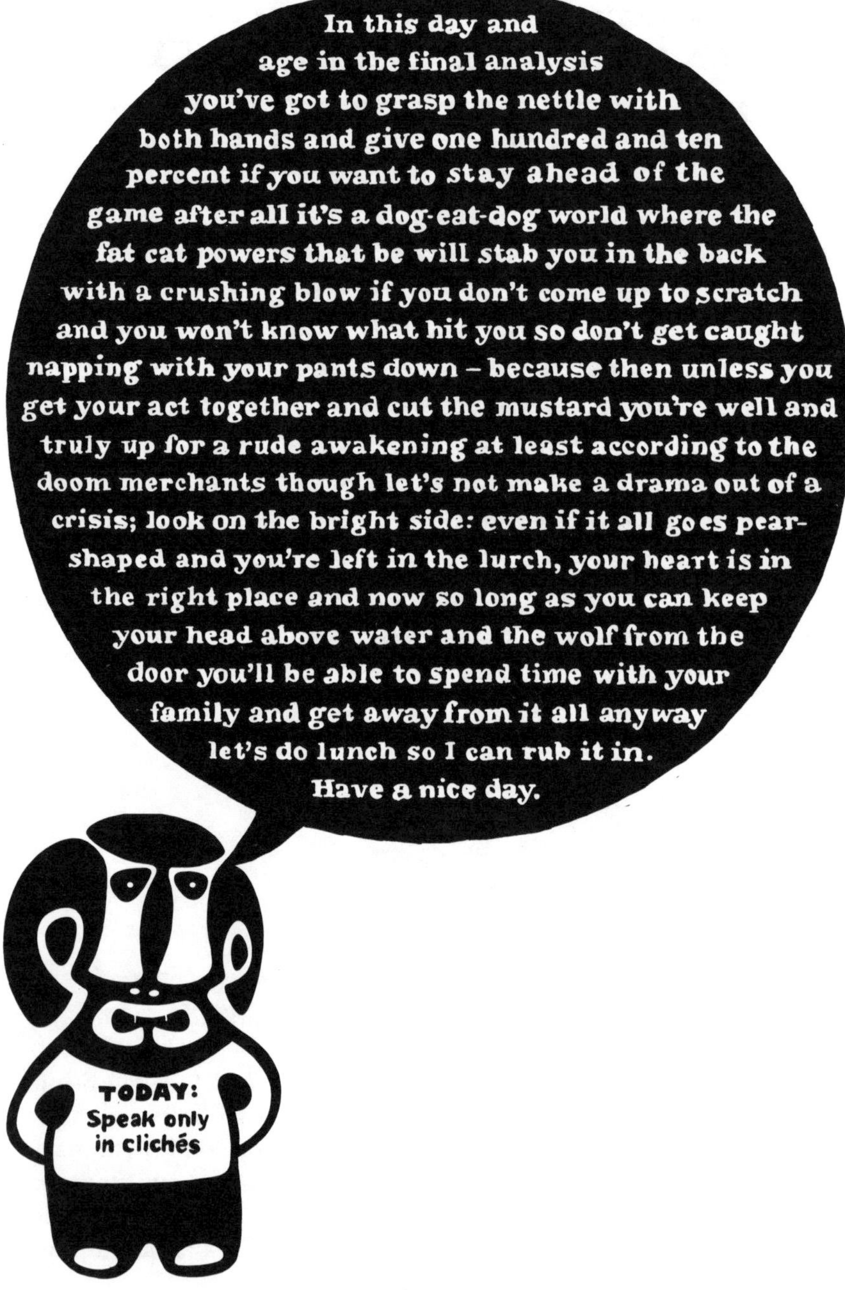
In this day and age in the final analysis you've got to grasp the nettle with both hands and give one hundred and ten percent if you want to stay ahead of the game after all it's a dog-eat-dog world where the fat cat powers that be will stab you in the back with a crushing blow if you don't come up to scratch and you won't know what hit you so don't get caught napping with your pants down – because then unless you get your act together and cut the mustard you're well and truly up for a rude awakening at least according to the doom merchants though let's not make a drama out of a crisis; look on the bright side: even if it all goes pear-shaped and you're left in the lurch, your heart is in the right place and now so long as you can keep your head above water and the wolf from the door you'll be able to spend time with your family and get away from it all anyway let's do lunch so I can rub it in.
Have a nice day.
TODAY: Speak only in clichés

Monopolize radio phone-ins today

Radio stations love phone-ins because they're a cheap way of filling airtime. You love them because they're a golden opportunity to charm the nation. Call a different talk show every hour today, and impress listeners all over the country with your wit, insight and irresistible personality. By this evening, you should aim to have become a much-loved national figure, with offers pouring in for your very own show.

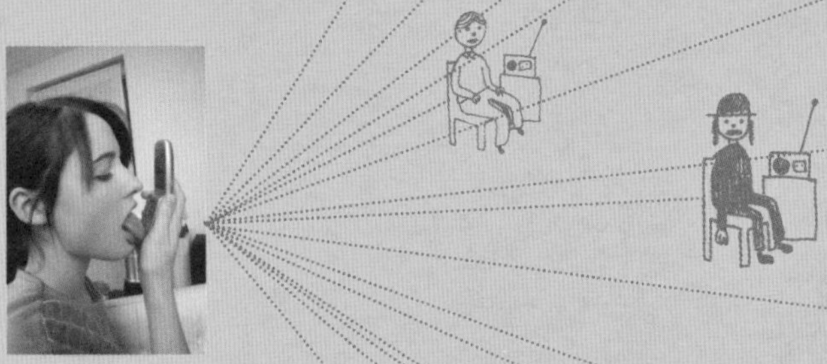

Media training in 3 easy steps:

1) Before going live, you will be put through to a junior researcher who will want to check that you have something relatively sane to say. Once you are on air, don't feel obliged to stick to it of course.

2) Listeners will be busy doing the ironing, driving to work and generally getting on with their lives. To lodge yourself in their consciousness, you will need an original angle: the prime minister has an evil twin, perhaps, or the national lottery is a money-laundering front.

3) Every great media personality needs a memorable catchphrase, that kids will repeat in the playground and bores will repeat in the pub. "Nice to see you, to see you nice" is memorable. "Am I on air yet?" is not. Try to sign off dramatically as well, although not by slamming the phone down, which soon grows tiresome.

Day 237

PLASTIC FANTASTIC!!!

How do you know you look as good as you could? Today make a no-obligation appointment with a plastic surgeon and see what he recommends.

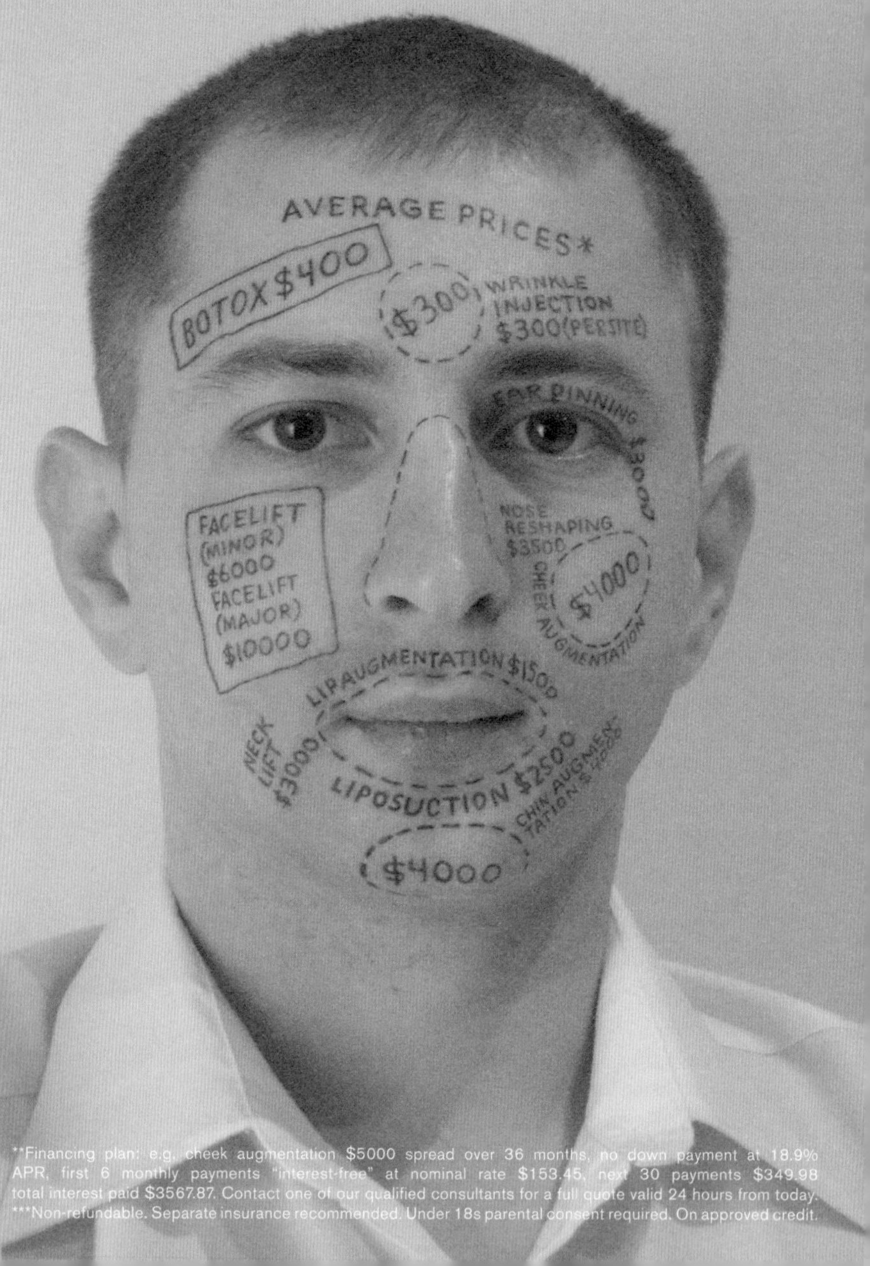

AVERAGE PRICES*
BOTOX $400
$300
WRINKLE INJECTION $300 (PER SITE)
EAR PINNING $3000
FACELIFT (MINOR) $6000 FACELIFT (MAJOR) $10000
NOSE RESHAPING $3500
$4000
CHEEK AUGMENTATION
LIP AUGMENTATION $1500
NECK LIFT $3000
LIPOSUCTION $2500
CHIN AUGMENTATION
$4000

**Financing plan: e.g. cheek augmentation $5000 spread over 36 months, no down payment at 18.9% APR, first 6 monthly payments "interest-free" at nominal rate $153.45, next 30 payments $349.98 total interest paid $3567.87. Contact one of our qualified consultants for a full quote valid 24 hours from today.
***Non-refundable. Separate insurance recommended. Under 18s parental consent required. On approved credit.

Day 238

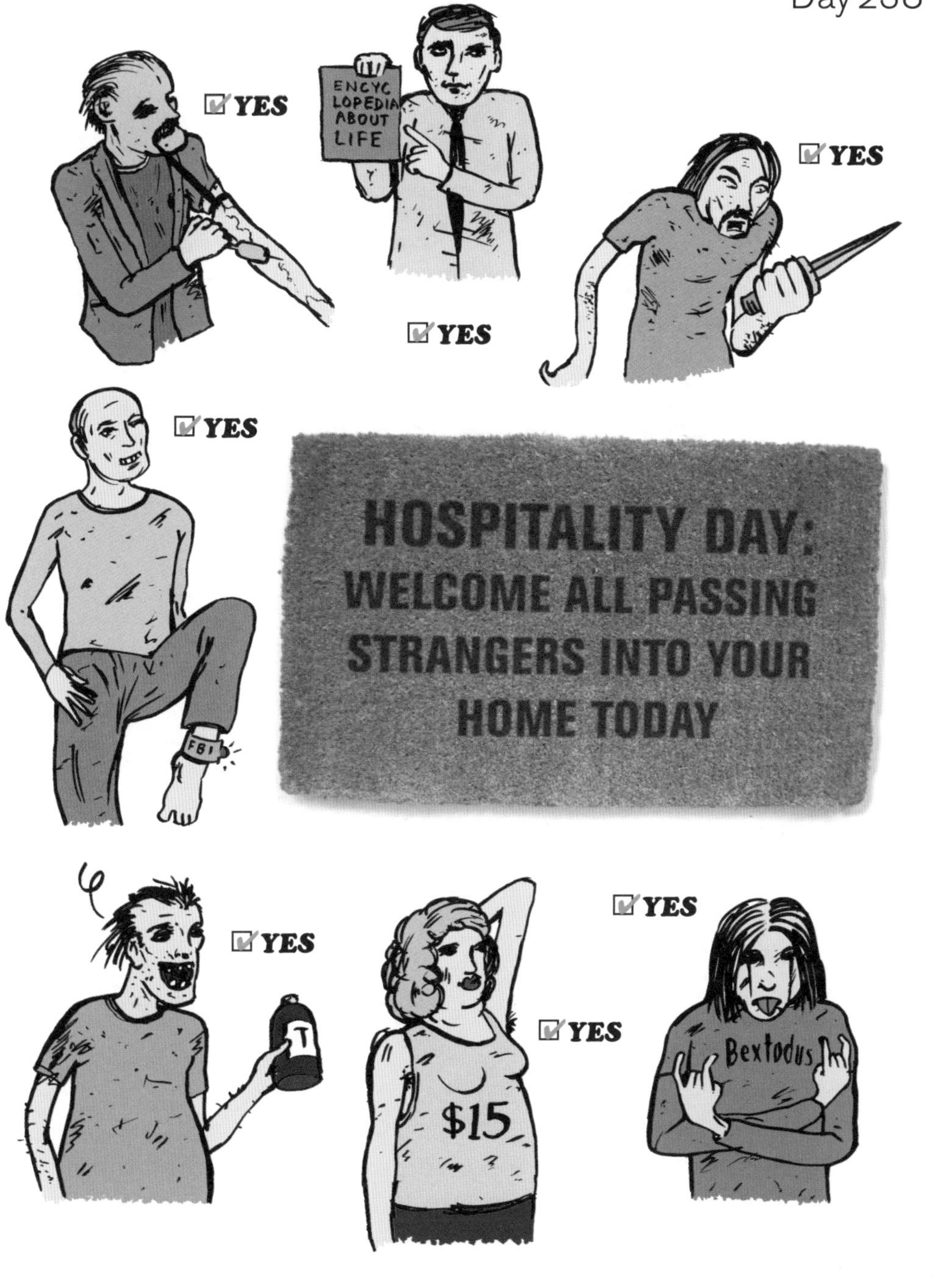
YES
ENCYC LOPEDIA ABOUT LIFE
YES
YES
YES
FBI
HOSPITALITY DAY:
WELCOME ALL PASSING STRANGERS INTO YOUR HOME TODAY
YES
YES
YES
T
$15
Bextodus

Optional: Then kill them, chop them up and stuff them under the floorboards

Today, hand deliver all your e-mails

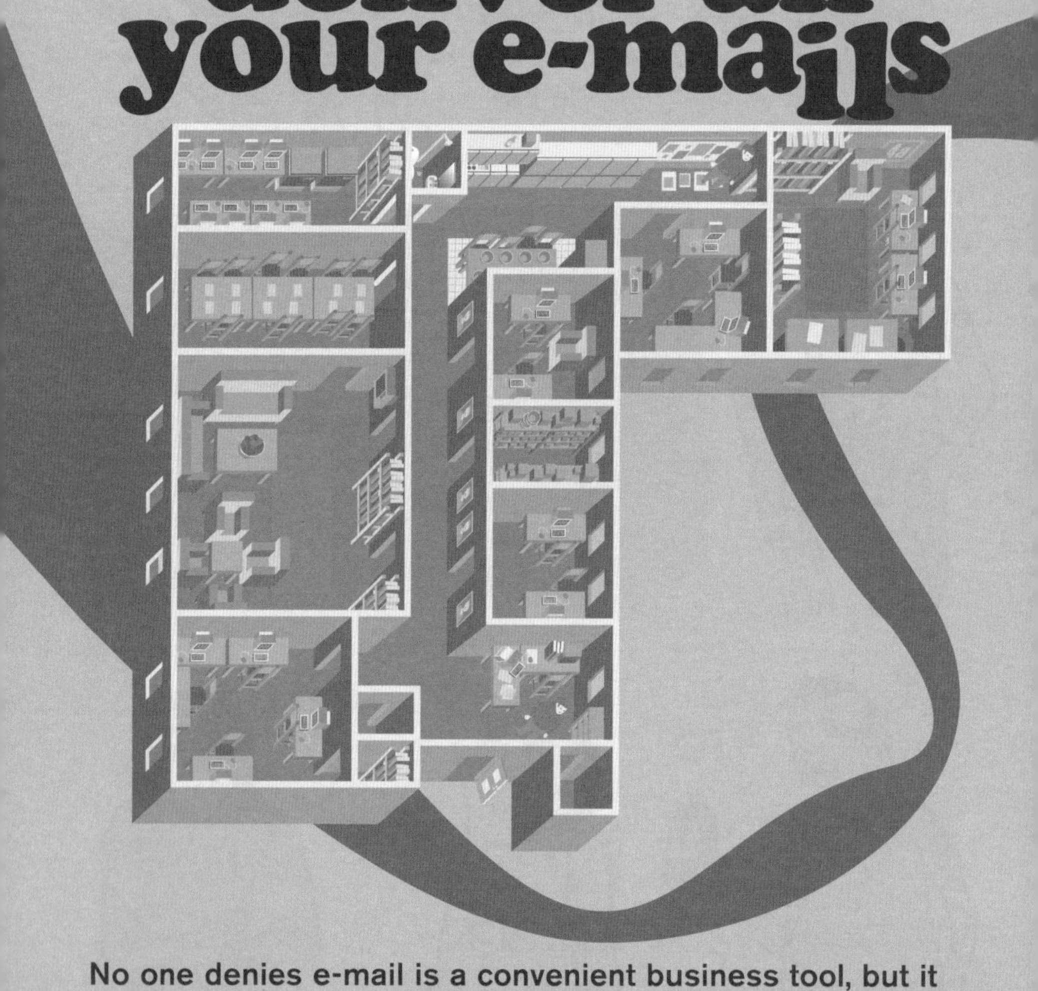

No one denies e-mail is a convenient business tool, but it cannot replace face-to-face interaction as a source of ideas and team spirit. Today, get the best of both worlds by printing out your e-mails and taking them round personally.

MADELEINE DAY

Find the key to a lost childhood memory. A bit of old cake dunked in tea did it for Proust. Go around sniffing everything today to see what triggers your recollections.

Stale teabags remind me so of Grandma

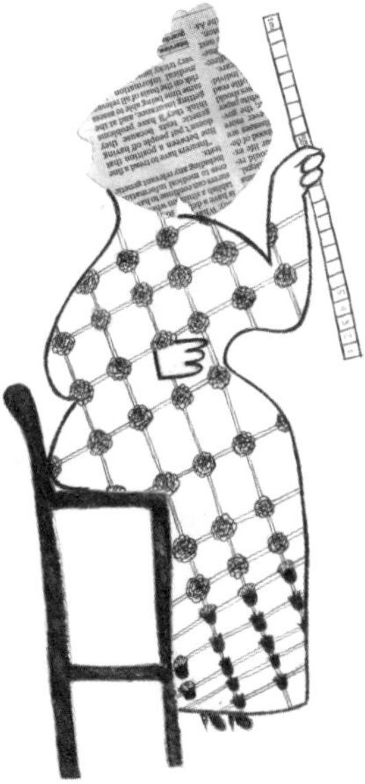

Gym socks? My third grade maths teacher Miss Thornton

The smell of flowers reminds me of the flowers I smelled as a child

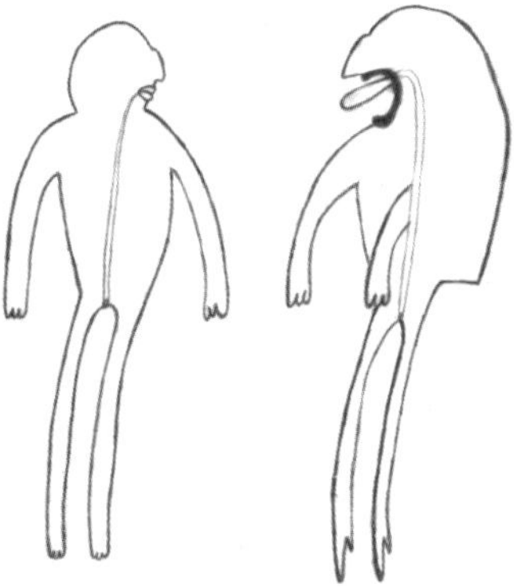

Aeroplanes have an odour that triggers memories of my first kiss

This madeleine has definitely gone off

Cat's pee: takes me back to our holidays in Southend when I was 2

See a dead body today

This may seem gruesome, but how can you hope to understand your mortality if you have never come face to face with death? Today, make arrangements to view a corpse, and reflect on the fleetingness of life.

VIEWING ETIQUETTE The deceased deserve respect. To arrange a viewing, contact your local funeral director in writing, outlining your reasons and asking for the permission of the bereaved relatives. Stress that you will not interfere with the funeral arrangements and offer to make a small donation to a charity of the family's choice. At the viewing: remain silent, try to control your emotions and of course do not attempt to take photographs. Afterwards, go outside, take a deep breath of fresh air and enjoy life to the full while you can.

Made me reflect ☐ Didn't make me reflect ☐

Today throw away an apple core in a park. Mark the spot well, and come back in 20 years' time to see your apple tree.

Is your apple tree lonely? Every apple tree needs another apple tree to cross-pollinate. Otherwise it will bear beautiful flowers, but will be barren of fruit... So ensure that you plant your tree near another (alternatively simply throw away two apple cores).

This advice comes to you courtesy of Shailesh Gor, accountant to the stars. Besides accountancy, Shailesh loves cricket and pizza, and is available for your downsizing needs for a reasonable fee. Contact him via www.benrik.co.uk.

Downsizing Day

In the current economic climate, we must all cut costs. Today fire someone from your entourage.

HAIRDRESSER? **-£10** Cut your own hair or get a handy friend to do it.	CLEANER? **-£30** Cleaners cost money and steal things. Plus it's good exercise for you.	BUTCHER? **-£9** Become a vegetarian, it's cheaper!	BROKER? **-£75** If they're any good, why haven't they retired rich by now?
BANKER? **-£50** Keep your money under your mattress, the new generation of thieves aren't trained to look there.	TRAINER? **-£25** With all that cleaning (see above), you won't need this one anymore.	PARTNER? **-£900** All that romantic tête-a-tête stuff costs a bomb. Ditch the bitch (or bastard).	CABLE GUY? **-£10** You watch too much TV.
DENTIST? **-£110** Original teeth are overrated. There are very life-like prosthetics on the market these days.	LIBRARIAN? **-£2** Can you afford those whopping fines? Reread your old books.	GARDENER? **-£15** You'll learn to love gardening when you retire. Why not start now?	BODYGUARD? **-£870** No one's going to kidnap you if you're worth nothing.
OLD FRIENDS? **-£100** Old friends expect birthday gifts and other such luxuries you can ill afford. Lose 'em.	PET? **-£25** Save money twice by not only downsizing your pet, but eating it (if it is edible).	ACCOUNTANT? **-£15000** This one's a no-no. They know too much about you. Keep 'em.	THERAPIST? **-£150** They also know too much about you, but nothing truly interesting. End it.

Take our test and find out if you're a PSYCHOPATH.

1. GLIBNESS/SUPERFICIAL CHARM
2. GRANDIOSE SENSE OF SELF-WORTH
3. TENDENCY TO BOREDOM/NEED FOR STIMULATION
4. PATHOLOGICAL LYING
5. CUNNING/MANIPULATIVE BEHAVIOUR
6. LACK OF REMORSE
7. SHALLOW AFFECT (MONOTONE VOICE, BLANK EXPRESSION)
8. LACK OF EMPATHY
9. PARASITIC LIFESTYLE
10. POOR BEHAVIOURAL CONTROL
11. PROMISCUOUS SEXUAL BEHAVIOUR
12. BEHAVIOURAL PROBLEMS EARLY IN LIFE
13. LACK OF REALISTIC LONG-TERM PLANS
14. IMPULSIVENESS
15. IRRESPONSIBLE BEHAVIOUR
16. FAILURE TO ACCEPT THE CONSEQUENCES OF ACTIONS
17. MANY MARITAL RELATIONSHIPS
18. JUVENILE DELINQUENCY
19. CALLOUSNESS
20. CRIMINAL VERSATILITY

Do you possess these traits?

NOT AT ALL: SCORE 0
SOMETIMES: SCORE 1
ALL THE TIME: SCORE 4

FOR MORE RELIABLE RESULTS, ASK A FRIEND TO ANSWER THIS FOR YOU. SURRENDER TO POLICE IMMEDIATELY IF YOU SCORE OVER 40.

TODAY, FAKE YOUR OWN KIDNAPPING AND SEE IF ANYONE PAYS THE RANSOM

We HAVE....................
NOthiNG WiLL HarM
HeR/hiM if $50,000
iS Left HeRE:..........
..................................by
SAtuRDay at N00n.
Do Not coNtact
the POLice or sHe/
he wiLL diE HOR-
riBLy. NO TriCKs!
SignEd:AnOnyMUs

How much do your loved ones really love you? Find out with this harmless subterfuge. Simply fill in this pre-prepared note; knock a few things over to make it look like there was a struggle; take yourself off to a remote country hotel for the day; watch events unfold. Bonus: Not only will you find out if you're valued, but you could also walk away with a cool tax-free £50,000!

UNUSUAL SPORTING ACHIEVEMENT DAY

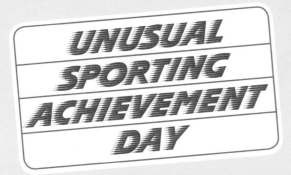

Most own goals in single football match

Sport has become the preserve of a drug-fuelled sponsorship-addled elite. An ordinary person today stands no chance of breaking a world record. So why bother playing by the rules? Today come up with your own way of making an imprint on sport history.

First marathon run backwards

Shortest basketball player

Longest involuntary ski jump

Only tennis match played entirely from the net

Longest distance swum holding a rubber duck for buoyancy

Fastest cricket streaker

First barefoot ice hockey match

Today, confuse a large corporation

Ever felt helpless in the face of a corporate behemoth? Here's your chance to get your own back. Start a dialogue with a utility about a fictitious meter. Claim you have recently moved and wish them to take over supply on this meter, which until now has been supplied by another utility. Ask the corporation to get in touch with their competitor and arrange a transfer. Make up a credible-looking meter number (455 987), give them a reading (5674.76), get a case reference number, and there you go: you have sparked off months if not years of fruitless correspondence.

Transgas
TeleTel
PowerWeb
CentraFuels
Electrica
Directelectric
Hydroline
Globofuel
Northerngas
Fuelsource
Metrix
WestComms
PacificBoard
MagnoGen
SLAMDUNK!

Can't get service? Complain to the regulator: Ofgem 020 7901 7000

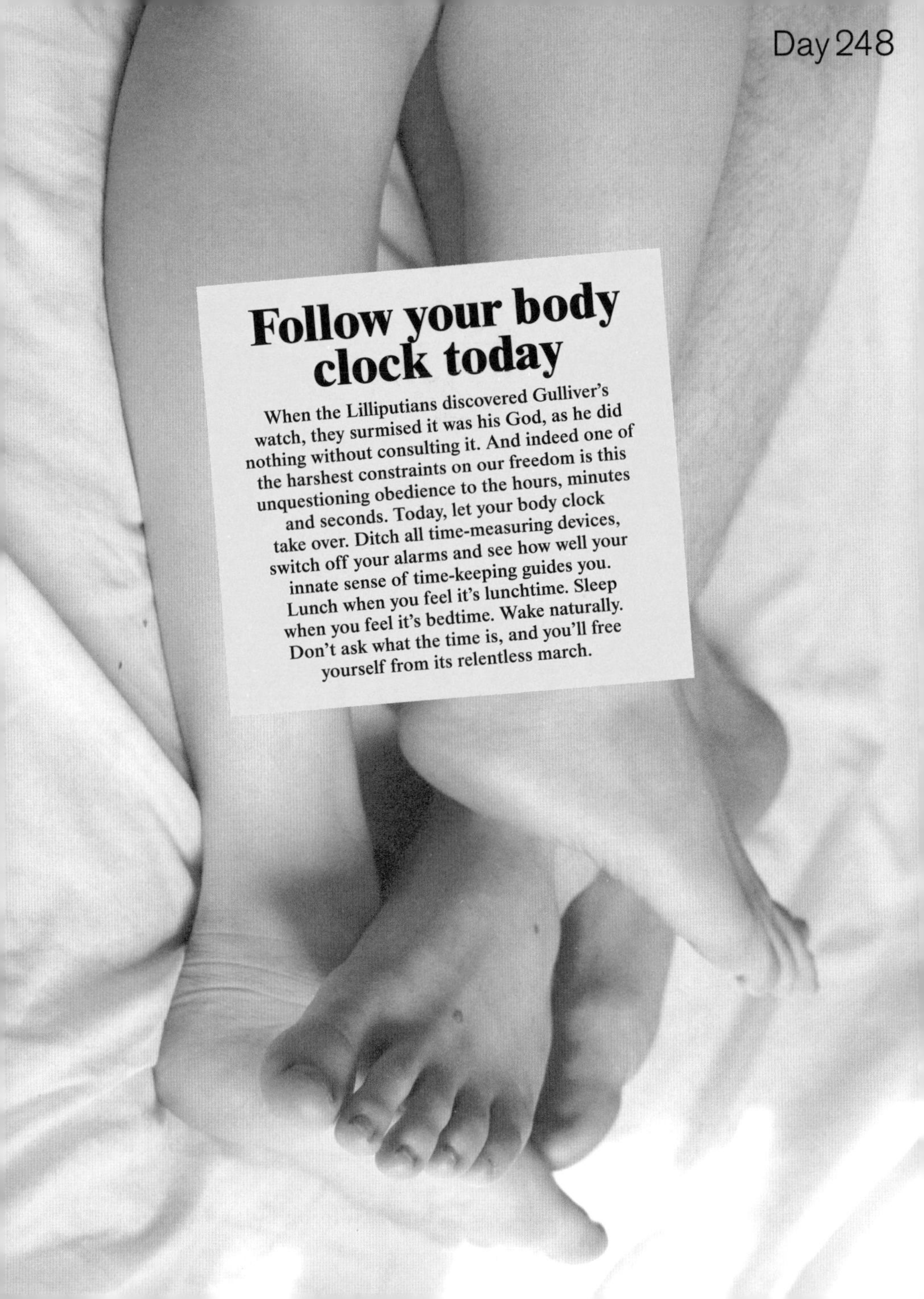

Follow your body clock today

When the Lilliputians discovered Gulliver's watch, they surmised it was his God, as he did nothing without consulting it. And indeed one of the harshest constraints on our freedom is this unquestioning obedience to the hours, minutes and seconds. Today, let your body clock take over. Ditch all time-measuring devices, switch off your alarms and see how well your innate sense of time-keeping guides you. Lunch when you feel it's lunchtime. Sleep when you feel it's bedtime. Wake naturally. Don't ask what the time is, and you'll free yourself from its relentless march.

BE SOMEONE'S GUARDIAN ANGEL TODAY

Follow a stranger and assist them at every turn

Pay for their bus fare

MORGAN
SMITH
AND CO.

Open doors for them

Shield them from excessive sunlight

Back them up in meetings

Fight off potential muggers

Cut up their food for them

Take out their rubbish

And don't expect any thanks in return. Helping is its own reward.

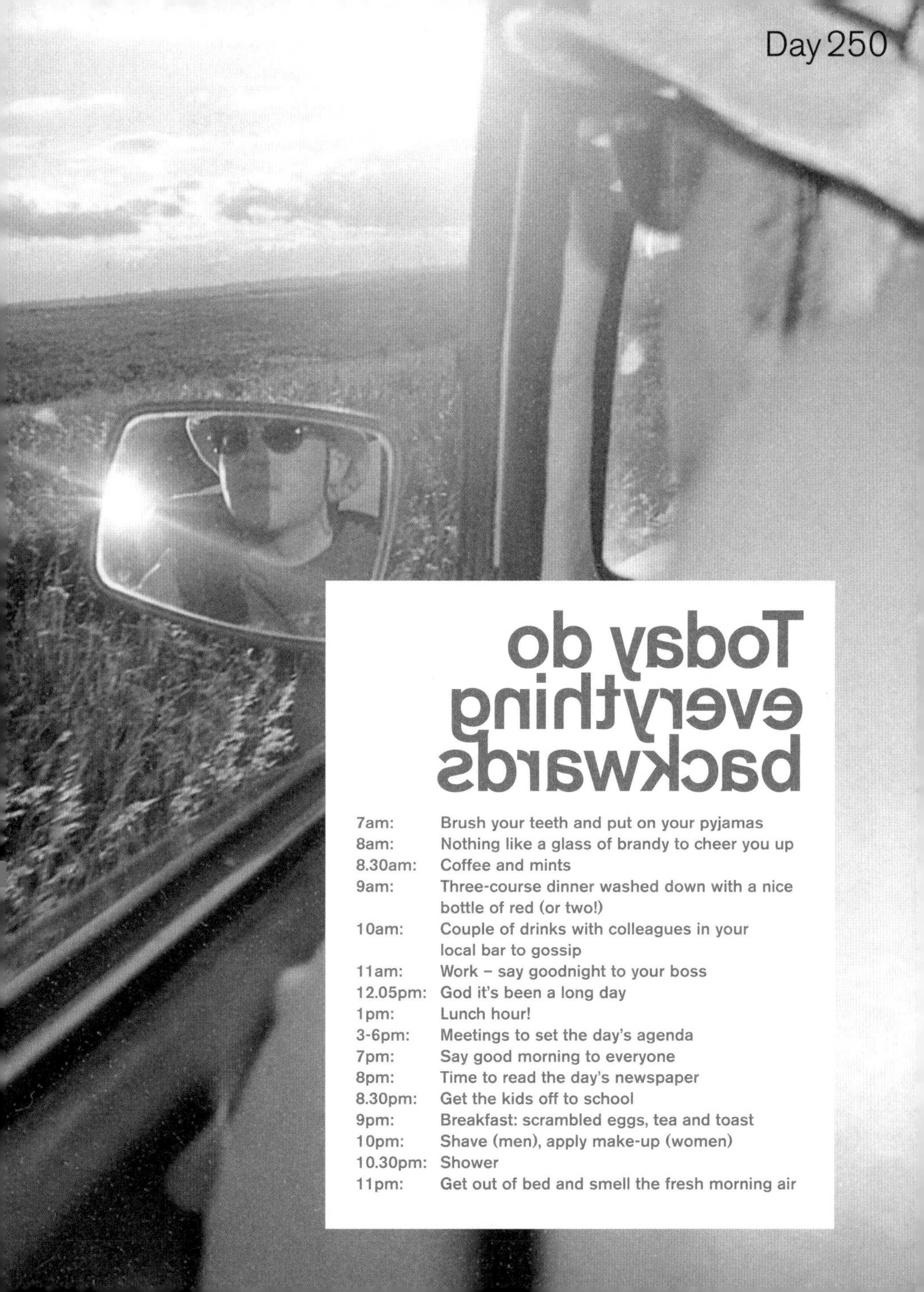

Today do everything backwards

7am:	Brush your teeth and put on your pyjamas
8am:	Nothing like a glass of brandy to cheer you up
8.30am:	Coffee and mints
9am:	Three-course dinner washed down with a nice bottle of red (or two!)
10am:	Couple of drinks with colleagues in your local bar to gossip
11am:	Work – say goodnight to your boss
12.05pm:	God it's been a long day
1pm:	Lunch hour!
3-6pm:	Meetings to set the day's agenda
7pm:	Say good morning to everyone
8pm:	Time to read the day's newspaper
8.30pm:	Get the kids off to school
9pm:	Breakfast: scrambled eggs, tea and toast
10pm:	Shave (men), apply make-up (women)
10.30pm:	Shower
11pm:	Get out of bed and smell the fresh morning air

Day 251

Hello Shelly
I was browsing the internet when I came across this rather revealing photograph of you, posted by your former boyfriend "Matt". It is a sad day when those we trust with such intimate moments betray us. Meanwhile, I wonder if your current husband "Andrew" should see it? £50 says no.

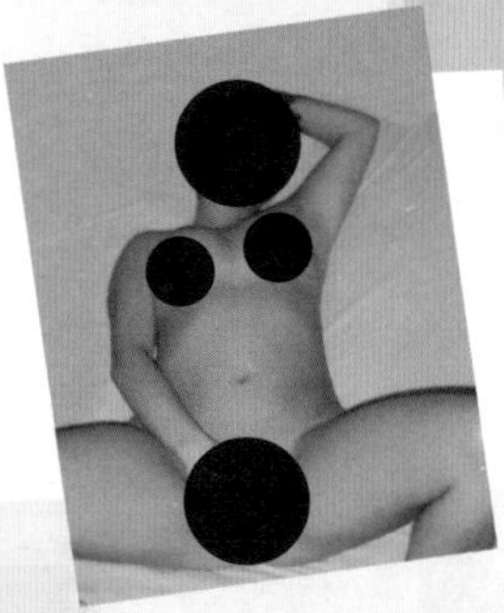

BLACKMAIL SOMEONE ON THE INTERNET TODAY
Social networking allows everyone to share their most personal details with complete strangers. As the media regularly point out, this is imprudent. Someone somewhere is no doubt harvesting drunken and sexual antics with a view to blackmailing their authors twenty years from now when they've become MPs or judges. You should not wait. Today, trawl social networks for incriminating self-disclosure, and scare those responsible into being less naïve.

Dear "Scoobster51"
In the future, your admission on the website "MySpace" that your hobbies include "pills, pills and more pills fookin' love it!!!" may handicap your employment prospects. I advise you to delete the reference, but don't worry, I have a screenshot which I will keep secure for you for a mere £15 a year.

Dear Sophie
I enjoyed reading your blog, in which you refer to your mother as "the bitch" and to your father as "the eunuch", for comic effect. I feel they would appreciate the joke and therefore propose to drop them a line about this via your school, Abingdon Girls Secondary, 56 Crown Road. Would you mind?

Good morning,
Are you both Phil Barton, IT support manager for Vistos Financial Software Limited, and Phil998, busy member of the vibrant community on doggingsoutheast.co.uk (some of the photos are out of focus, but the beard is unmistakeable). Let's talk!

NB No blackmailing of fellow Benrik readers! That would be too easy.

Get mugged today

Investigate the reality of street crime for yourself: stroll around a dodgy neighbourhood with a shiny camera, a new wristwatch and a laptop bag, and see how long it takes for some kid to approach you for your possessions. Hand them over, but only on condition he tells you all about his deprived childhood and his drug problem.

Parasite Day

Listen to the radio on someone else's set

In restaurants, finish other people's leftovers

Read newspapers and books over other people's shoulders

In our intricate society, there are many opportunities for freeloading. Today, see if you can live literally at the expense of others.

Smell other people's perfume

Watch TV through someone else's window

Buy new clothes and return them later

Hitchhike a free ride in other people's cars

Attempt to be noticed from space today.

HEY MR. C-I-A! STOP
SPYING ON ME WITH
YOUR GODDAM
SATELLITES! I PAY MY
TAXES! I'M NO FOOL!
I'M GOING TO BLAST
YOU OUT OF THE
SKIES YOU GODDAM
HARVARD PRETTY
BOYS! FACSISTS! SEE
YA IN HELL.

There are hundreds of spy satellites orbiting the earth with cameras that can pick out objects a few inches wide. Do something unusual enough to spark their attention. Arrange 100 of your friends into the shape of a giant caterpillar. Dig a nuclear-style crater on the beach. Send a message like 'EMPEROR XORG WE ARE READY FOR YOUR ARRIVAL' in Morse with a giant arc-lamp. CIA analysts too need something to lighten up their day.

Day 255

TODAY, EAT OR DRINK SOMETHING OLDER THAN YOURSELF

There is something deliciously unnatural about ingesting matter that predates you on this planet. Pick one of the following and consume it.

WINE (0 TO 150 YEARS)
Nothing could be simpler than drinking wine older than yourself; stroll down to the nearest merchant and buy a bottle from the year before your birth. Bordeaux is a safe bet, although the risk-takers might pick a Burgundy. If the wine is very old, it will react extremely quickly to air. Leave it for 10 minutes to dissipate any 'bottle-stink', then enjoy it in the next half an hour, before the evanescent aroma of decades vanishes into thin clear air.

DRIED MUSHROOMS (50 TO 70 YEARS)
In the north of Japan, farmers preserve Maitake mushrooms by drying them on the slopes of the Ishikari volcanic mountains. Then they use a unique mix of whale blubber and spices to seal them into man-sized urns which they bury for a minimum of 50 years. The result? A moreish treat with delicate yet earthy overtones, prized for its cancer-inhibiting properties. Simply brush off the dirt, soak in 23°c water for 5 hours, and fry gently for 10 minutes in extract of soya oil.

SALTED BEEF (5 TO 50 YEARS)
Salting of meat is an ancient preservation technique, particularly favoured by the Romans. Perhaps this is why some of the best salted beef comes from the Italian region of Trentino. By using only the finest cuts and mixing in some saltpetre, the locals are able to hang them for up to 50 years, by which time they have developed a layer of scrumptious fine moss. Once you've got your hands on some (no easy task!), just bring it to boil and leave to simmer with some marjoram for three hours per kilo. Serve cold with beetroot and/or radishes.

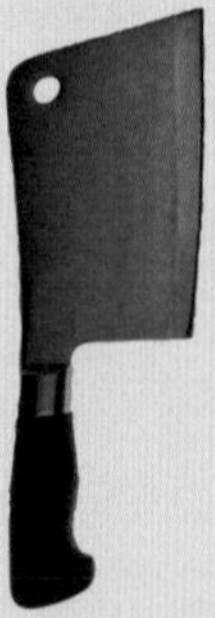

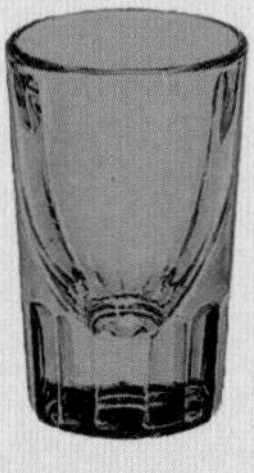

WHISKY (10 TO 70 YEARS)
A great bottle of single-malt Scotch should keep for the average human life span. It is only after 12 years in cask that it can truly be considered for drinking. If you can afford it, try the 1937 Glenfiddich, which only became fully drinkable in 2001. It's the oldest whisky in the world. There are only 60 odd bottles left worldwide. One will cost you $80,000 at the very least. But you're guaranteed a taste of history.

HANGAI YAK CHEESE (14 TO 60 YEARS)
This hard cheese is the longest-lived milk-based product in the history of food preservation. This is due in no small measure to the freezing climate of the Mongolian lowlands, where it is produced. The Hangai yak feeds on relatively acidic grasslands that provide the milk with some natural preservatives, which the Mongols then top up with rennet. The cheese itself is an acquired taste. Dense and pungent, with an inch-thick rind, it is normally enjoyed as a meal on its own.

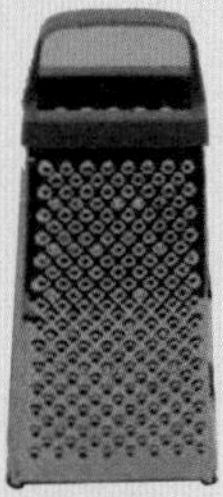

100-YEAR-OLD TURTLE SOUP
If your palate is jaded or you are already older than most of these delicacies, there is but one treat left for you: Chinese turtle soup made from century-old turtles. You will need to travel to Hunan, as export of food made from this endangered species is prohibited. There, you will need to scour the backstreets for the wily peasants who are still proficient in the art of hunting and deboning these increasingly rare ancestral beasts. The going rate for a bowl of this soup of soups is $3,000.
nb: This trip is not recommended for anyone over 95 years old.

Slavery Day

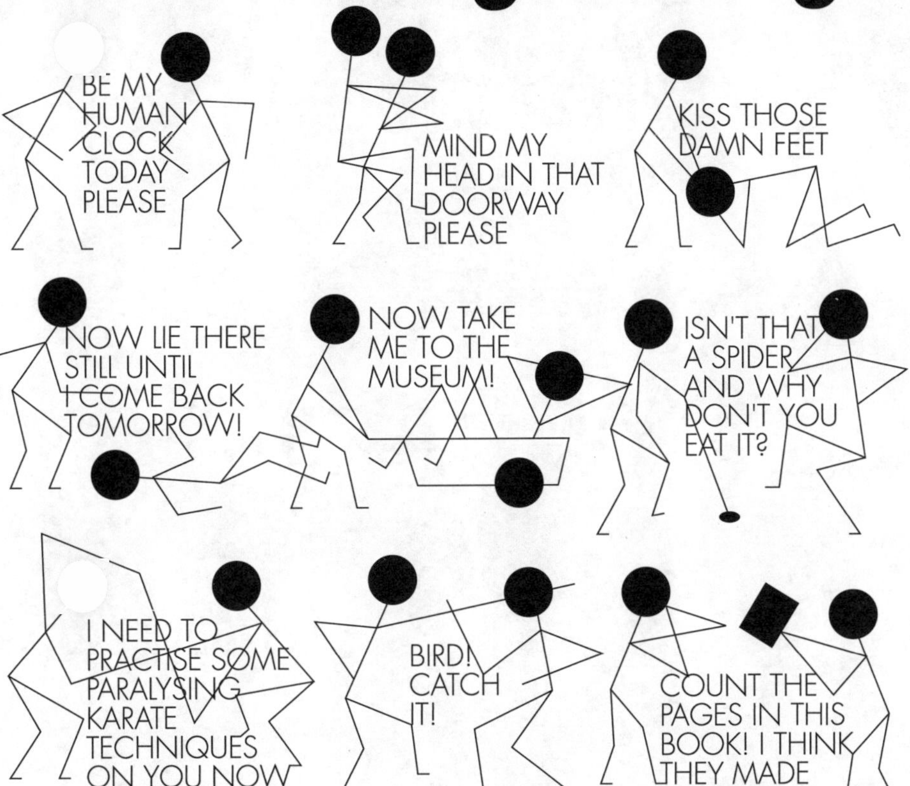
BE MY HUMAN CLOCK TODAY PLEASE
MIND MY HEAD IN THAT DOORWAY PLEASE
KISS THOSE DAMN FEET
NOW LIE THERE STILL UNTIL I COME BACK TOMORROW!
NOW TAKE ME TO THE MUSEUM!
ISN'T THAT A SPIDER AND WHY DON'T YOU EAT IT?
I NEED TO PRACTISE SOME PARALYSING KARATE TECHNIQUES ON YOU NOW I'M AFRAID!
BIRD! CATCH IT!
COUNT THE PAGES IN THIS BOOK! I THINK THEY MADE A MISTAKE!

Volunteer to become someone's slave today

Slavery is the new yoga. What better way to stop worrying about all life's responsibilities than to hand them over to someone else?

IMPLEMENT THE LAW!
THE RIOT POLICE RULES!
GOOD LUCK WITH YOUR POLICIES!
THE PACE OF REFORM IS GOOD!
TERMINATE THE ENEMIES OF THE PRIME MINISTER!
UP WITH THE GOVERNMENT!
DOWN WITH THE OPPONENTS OF THE STATE!
NO TO NAY-SAYERS!

DEMONSTRATE IN FAVOUR OF THE GOVERNMENT TODAY!

Is it any wonder our leaders take so little notice of demonstrations when they are so predictably anti-governmental? Countries such as China and North Korea show that public protest need not be antagonistic. The state is only human after all: it responds to positive feedback much more than to petty-minded criticism. Today, engage in mass rallies to encourage your government in its actions and spur it on to greater things

Invade people's personal space today

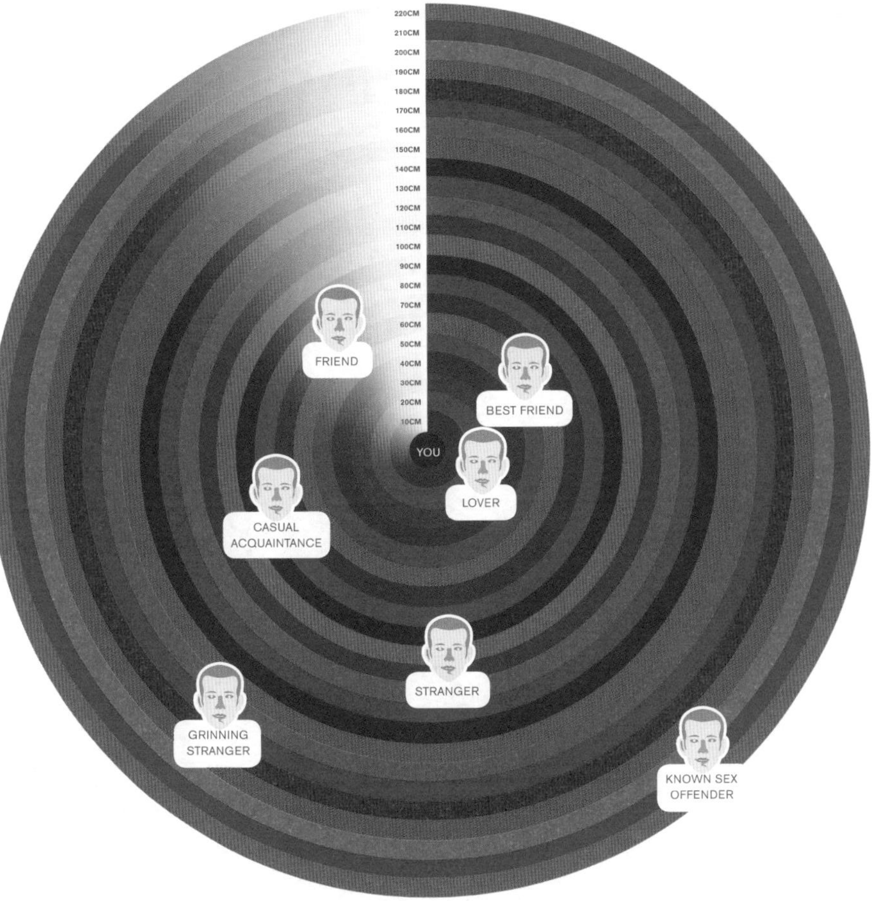
220CM
210CM
200CM
190CM
180CM
170CM
160CM
150CM
140CM
130CM
120CM
110CM
100CM
90CM
80CM
70CM
60CM
50CM
40CM
30CM
20CM
10CM
YOU
FRIEND
BEST FRIEND
LOVER
CASUAL ACQUAINTANCE
STRANGER
GRINNING STRANGER
KNOWN SEX OFFENDER

We are all surrounded by an invisible barrier which others cross at their peril. However this varies enormously according to the degree of intimacy, and each person's culture and personality. Today measure how close you have to get to violate the personal space of those you meet.

TODAY, GREET EVERYONE YOU CROSS IN THE STREET AS IF THEY WERE A LONG-LOST FRIEND AND SEE IF THEY CLAIM TO REMEMBER YOU

Billy Moffat - we used to go fishing together!

Sandy T? - my first kiss...

Matt Clark: one of the gang!

Frank - we started at Datacorp on the same day

Juliet Stern: flatmate at 11 Rosslyn Hill in -86

The Davidson brothers: Harry and...

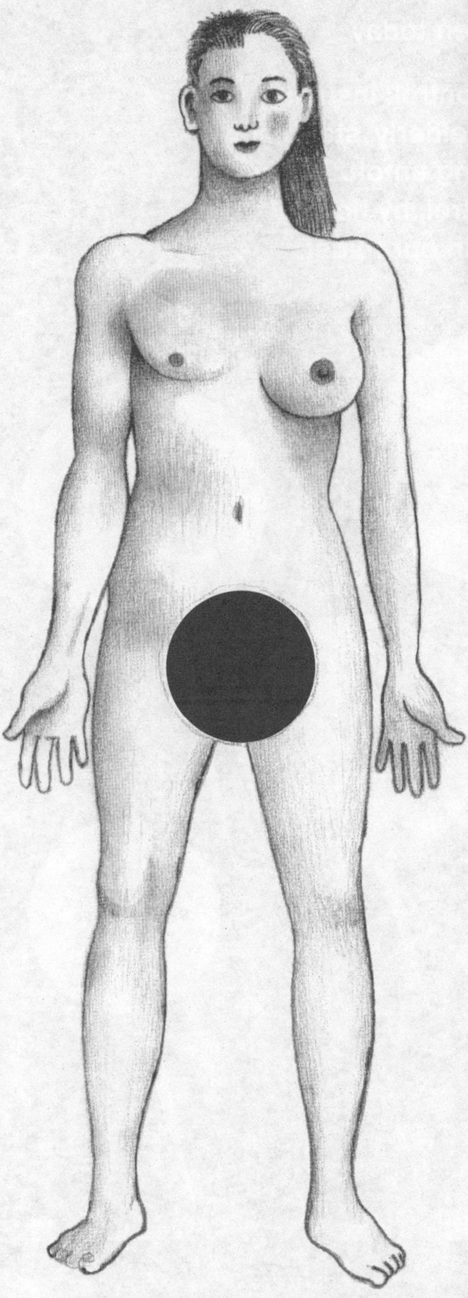

Gender Bending Day

Explore your other side today through the role-play scenarios below.

WOMEN: you are to assume the name Brian. As Brian you are one of the lads, dressing in jeans, football shirt and leather jacket. Lunchtime sees you down the pub, downing a few pints before the match. The afternoon is spent shouting at the TV, before you drunkenly head for the DIY store where you will purchase phallic powertools. You will then spend two hours trying to get them to work before even consulting the instructions. Needless to say, all of this activity will be conducted to the sound of beer-fuelled semi-continuous farting and belching, which will continue until bedtime.

MEN: today you are Deborah, a woman of the world who loves the feel of pink silk knickers and would never dream of going out without make-up. Deborah loves to shop, especially for high heels, and she loves to have her legs and bikini line waxed down at the local beauty salon, where she asks for a 'Brazilian', shameless hussy that she is! Debbie (to her girlfriends) loves it when builders wolf-whistle as she sashays down the high street, but she plays hard-to-get, never forgetting that come tomorrow she has to turn back Cinderella-like into a man.

Discipline other people's children today

Kids in our society are out of control: insulting their teachers, intimidating the elderly, stabbing each other, and generally running amok. Today, let us all re-establish adult control, by ticking off any ill-behaved youngsters in our midst.

Mind your language young fellow, there are ladies present.
Out for a stroll at this hour, are we? Isn't it past your bedtime?
Put that gun down, or I'll give you a good spanking!
Turn that racket off, it is surely the devil's own time!
You two stop that rough and tumble, or I'll confiscate both your knives!
Tell you what, I'll swap that cigarette for a nice chocolate one!

TODAY CAUSE AN INTERNATIONAL SECURITY ALERT: FOR YEARS, CONSPIRACY THEORISTS HAVE POSITED THE EXISTENCE OF ECHELON, A SUPERSECRET TRANSNATIONAL EFFORT BY THE WEST TO SPY ON ALL ELECTRONIC COMMUNICATIONS, FROM PHONES TO EMAILS. THE SYSTEM ALLEGEDLY "RED FLAGS" CERTAIN KEYWORDS IN AN ATTEMPT TO INTERCEPT TERRORIST OR OTHERWISE SUBVERSIVE MESSAGES. TODAY, TEST THIS THEORY BY INCORPORATING AS MANY OF THE FOLLOWING KEYWORDS AS POSSIBLE INTO YOUR EMAILS. YOU WILL KNOW THE THEORY IS CORRECT IF YOU ARE ARRESTED AND QUESTIONED AT GREAT LENGTH. GOODBYE. KEYWORDS INCLUDE: *ATF OSAMA BIN LADEN FBI DOD WACO TWIN TOWERS RUBY RIDGE PENTAGON OKC OKLAHOMA CITY GUANTANAMO MILITIA WORLD TRADE CENTRE CIA GUN NSA HANDGUN SEMTEX AL QAEDA HOSTAGE MILGOV 9/11 MARTYR RUMSFELD ASSAULT RIFLE TERRORISM BOMB DRUG KORESH ZARQAWI SHARON MOSSAD NASA MI5 CID FALLUJA AK47 M16 C4 REVOLUTION SADDAM HUSSEIN GEORGE BUSH TERRORIST*

Day 263

Today swap blood with another Benrik reader

Benrik readers are drawn together by a common mystical bond, a shared understanding of the world and a deep respect for the principles of extreme life-change. Make that bond sacred today, by exchanging blood with another reader, and thus forging a lifelong kinship. Here is how:

1. Locate another Benrik reader. You may know one already, or you may find one through www.benrik.co.uk.
2. Enquire if they are interested in becoming your sacred blood brother for all of eternity. If they decline, try not to take it personally.
3. Prick your thumb with a sterilized razor blade or needle (using a rusty knife is no longer considered essential).
4. Deposit some of your blood in a small sealable container. Again, don't go overboard: you don't need half a pint, just a few drops.
5. Seal tightly, affix the label provided, and mail to your soon-to-be Benrik blood brother. Allow three weeks for delivery.
6. When you receive your blood brother's sample, soak a swab in it, and carefully rub it into an open wound.
7. Before you do that, however, have it thoroughly screened for HIV and other blood-borne pathogens. You never know these days.
8. As you rub their blood into yours, chant some ancient Native American incantations, and voilà: you are now blood brothers, congratulations!

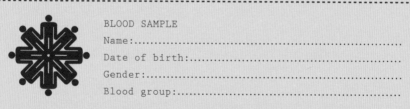

BLOOD SAMPLE

Name:..

Date of birth:...

Gender:..

Blood group:...

Attention HM Customs: This blood sample is due to be used for ritual purposes. It has no commercial value and is NOT subject to tax. Please pass it on without delay.

Affix this label on the container

Investigate a news story yourself

Don't accept what the media says at face value. Today do some fact-checking of your own on a suspicious story.

THE POST
POLICE IN MURDER CORRUPTION PROBE
The entire police department of the town of Stanton, Illinois, has been suspended pending the outcome of an FBI investigation. A disgruntled former cleaner, Gertrude Trump, has alleged that the department's officers concealed evidence in the case of contract killer Harold Mason, who was acquitted of six murders in early November 2002. According to Trump, sheriff Rick Lund accepted $100,000 from Mason's attorney in exchange for helping him evade the charges. Trump alleges she saw the money being distributed between Lund and three other officers while she was "cleaning the corridor". Mason was accused of murdering six people in cold blood for interfering in mob business. The local press dubbed him "The Pencil Sharpener", a reference to the weapon he used to despatch his victims by jamming it up their nostril. Gertrude Trump is 38.
Check spelt right?
Unlikely
Cleaner employed by multinational corporation?
Reference to cocaine?
FBI Helpline 08086549753
Criminal antecedents?
Interview?
Hush money?
Satanic number
Find pencils.

Day 265

TODAY, DOUBLECHECK YOUR PARTNER ISN'T CHEATING

"All is fair in love and war" was surely coined with the internet age in mind. Today, make sure your love is true – using the latest in unobtrusive electronic surveillance technology.

CHECK THEIR EMAILS
Look out for: emails in folders with deliberately boring names such as "tax issues" or "pilates appointments"

FIT THEIR CAR WITH A GPS TRACKER
Look out for: regular parking in unfamiliar residential neighbourhoods

MONITOR THEIR MOBILE-PHONE BILL
Look out for: regular calls to an unknown number at the time they walk the dog or you take a shower

INSTALL KEYSTROKE-LOGGING SOFTWARE ON THEIR PC
Look out for: keystrokes that form the words "sex", "meet", "gagging", "motel" or "divorce"

OLD-SCHOOL: LISTEN TO ANYTHING THEY SAY IN THEIR SLEEP
Look out for: soft moaning of someone else's name

True love confirmed ☐ True love cancelled ☐

Today, pour cocaine down an anthill

YARIBA!

Recreate the feverish atmosphere of a financial trading floor by feeding the little workers a few grams of Columbian marching powder. Watch them zap that termite colony into oblivion. Watch them blitz that forest into wasteland. Just don't stand too close: their conversation will get very boring.

Homeless Day

Today, leave your home and possessions and try to live on the streets. Could you survive the cold, the hunger, the looks? Experience life on the other side of the begging bowl, and by tomorrow morning, you'll never look down on the homeless again.

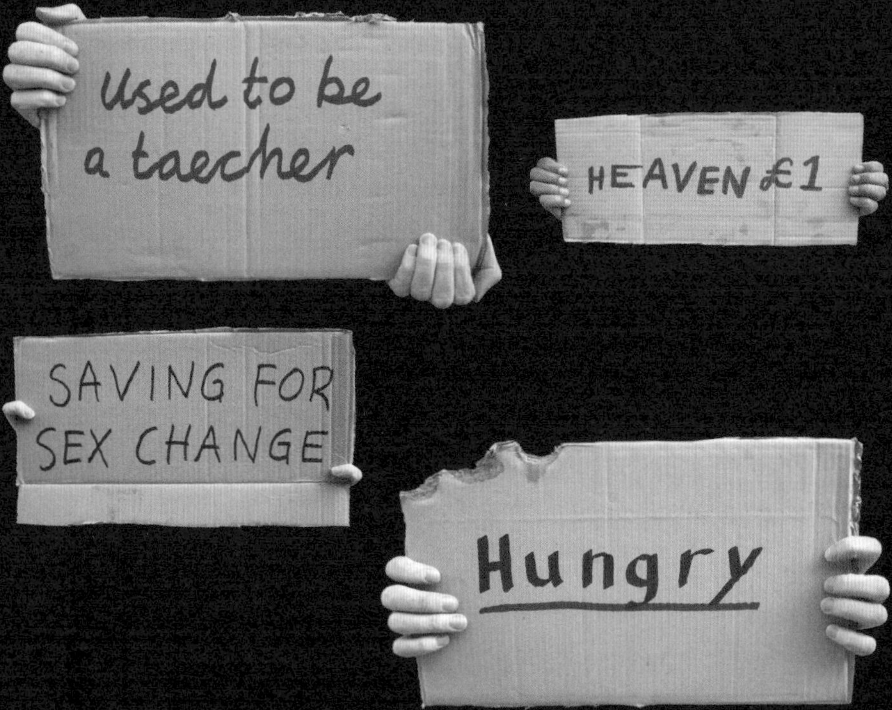
Used to be
a taecher
HEAVEN £1
SAVING FOR
SEX CHANGE
Hungry

What you may take (your past attitude to begging dictates your level of discomfort):
If you give to beggars every day: You may take a sleeping bag, comfortable walking shoes and £5.
If you give to beggars once in a while: You may take a blanket, a pair of woollen gloves, and a toothbrush.
If you never give to beggars: You may take some foreign coins, a broken umbrella, and a flea-ridden sheet.

Today, assess people's potential for evil and act in consequence

Adolf Hitler outlined his plans for the Jewish people in Mein Kampf, published in 1923. If someone then had taken him seriously enough and killed him pre-emptively, millions of deaths would have been averted. Today, probe those around you for murderous designs, and, should you find any, take history into your own hands.

Name: Becky Montagu
Potential for evil: 6/10
Proof of potential: she fancies my Kevin
Confirmed by independent observer: Yes ☑ No ☐

Name:
Potential for evil:
Proof of potential:
Confirmed by independent observer: Yes ☐ No ☐

Name:
Potential for evil:
Proof of potential:
Confirmed by independent observer: Yes ☐ No ☐

Name:
Potential for evil:
Proof of potential:
Confirmed by independent observer: Yes ☐ No ☐

Name:
Potential for evil:
Proof of potential:
Confirmed by independent observer: Yes ☐ No ☐

Name:
Potential for evil:
Proof of potential:
Confirmed by independent observer: Yes ☐ No ☐

Make sure it's confirmed by an independent observer, otherwise it's not legal!

Add your touch to an artistic masterpiece today

The idea that art is ever "finished" is thoroughly bourgeois. There's always room for improvement; indeed, without additional input, art can quickly fall behind the times. Today, visit your local museum, and update a fusty old exhibit.

Velasquez/Benrik

Today, apply for a job that you think is beneath you

Could you really be a fast food employee, a checkout guy, or a rubbish collector for the council? We assume that these so-called "menial" occupations are within anyone's reach, but perhaps you simply don't have what it takes. Apply and find out today, and get a better picture of your limits in the process.

C-list paparazzi.
Kiwi-shaver.
King without a castle.
Messenger of bad news.
Lassie's fluffer.
Corked-Wine Taster.
Bargain Prostitute.
Acidic substances Taster.
Part-time Horse-shit-Eater.
Under-paid leaf-counter.
Lawyer for the long-term unemployed.
Soon-to-retire arena-sweeper.
Karaoke-singer of Celine Dion.
Executioner of cute animals.
Unexploded-mines polisher.
Pilgrim without a goal.

TODAY, ACT SUSPICIOUSLY

Loiter outside MI5's headquarters and sketch them from all angles

Set all the alarm clocks on display in a department store to ring at the same time

Help keep society on its toes today with your suspicious behaviour. This may cause some short-term inconvenience for you and for those around you, but in the long-term, you'll have done society a good turn, even if it doesn't appreciate it just today.

Call 10 Downing St and breathe dirty down the line

Walk past police sniffer dogs with a suitcase full of sausages

Page 'Osama' at the airport information desk

Animal Day: view everyone and everything sexually

Ditch civilization and its superfluous airs and graces, and return to your primeval animal roots: your sole Darwinian purpose in life is to procreate. Today, everyone is to mate with each other indiscriminately in the manner of Viagra-abusing chimps.

Groar

Greet everyone with a low guttural moan

Smell passing strangers

Piss on the ground to mark your territory

Stare at people's crotches

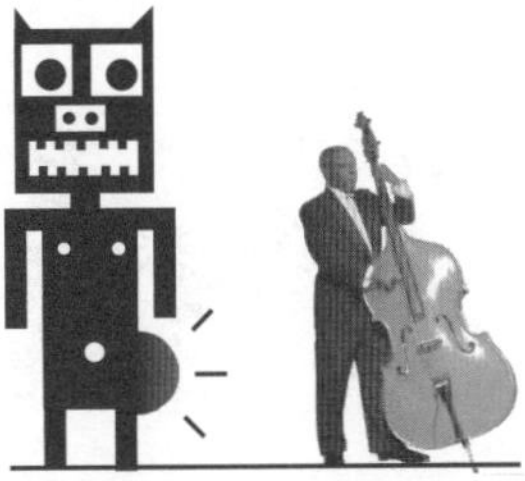

Present your swelling bottom to passing alpha males

Brush up against people you fancy

Bite, maim or kill your sexual competitors

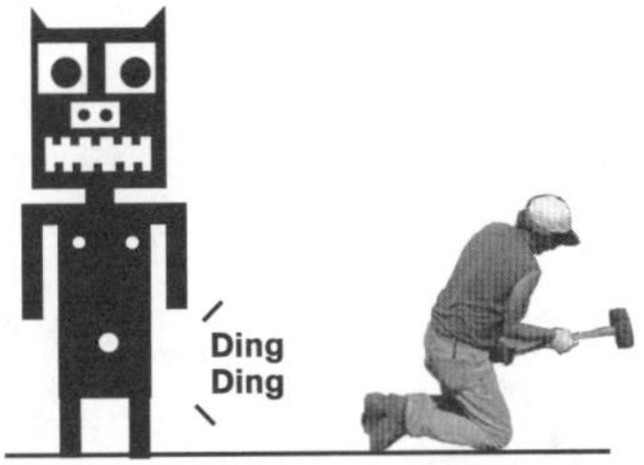
Ding
Ding

View anyone bending over as an invitation to immediate intercourse

Do something that passers-by will never forget today

Do something surreal and unwordly, something that will give others an experience they will remember for the rest of their lives, a break in the mundanity of their existence, a moment of poetry that they will recall on their deathbed as they drift away with a chuckle...

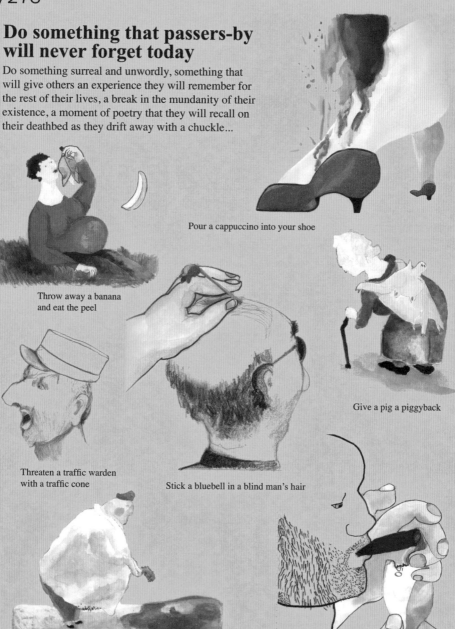

Pour a cappuccino into your shoe

Throw away a banana and eat the peel

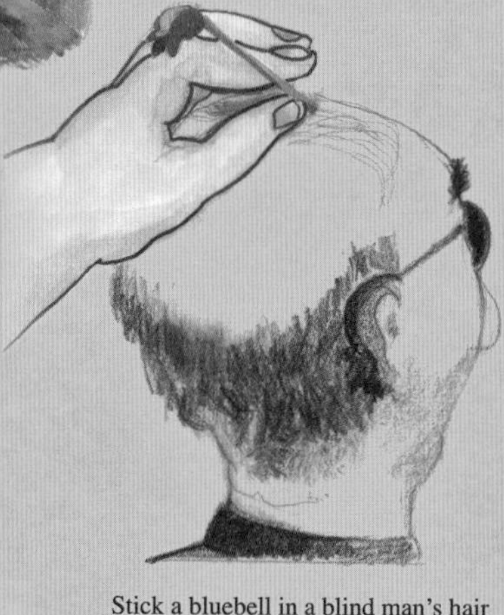

Give a pig a piggyback

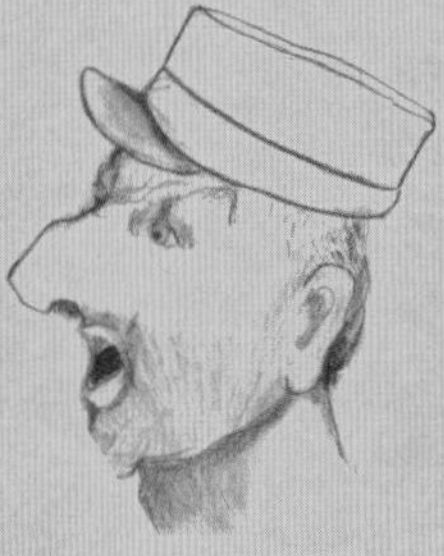

Threaten a traffic warden with a traffic cone

Stick a bluebell in a blind man's hair

Release fish fingers back into the sea

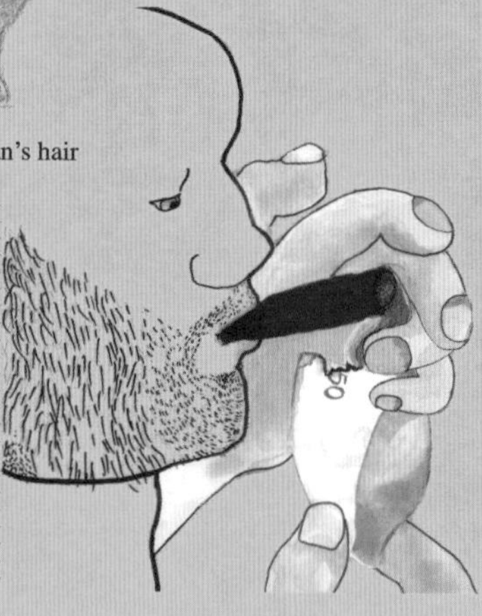

Light your cigar with a £50 note

Ada Peach's 15 minutes of fame

This is Ada Peach, 96. Today, everyone study her life from 1pm to 1.15pm, using the materials below, so she may experience her 15 minutes of fame.

Ada Searle was born in Deptford, South East London, on the 7th of April 1913. Her mother died giving birth to her, so she was mostly brought up by her grandmother. Ada's father Fred lived with them, but worked night shifts on the tramways, and so saw less of her and her three older brothers than he might have done. The First World War didn't really affect her childhood, but alas in 1925 her grandmother died, which meant she had to leave school to stay at home and cook and clean for the rest of the family. Deptford suffered during the Depression in the thirties, but Ada still managed a busy life, joining the Salvation Army, working in the laundry business by day, and running with rather a dapper crowd by night. It was during this time that she met the man she was to marry, one Frederick George Thomas Peach, formerly of the

Merchant Navy. Fred Peach jr was a charmer, who whisked Ada around in his dashing open-top sports car, took her on darts team outings, and eventually married her in 1939. They moved in together in Barnhurst, on the eve of World War II. Their flat was meant to be luxurious as it was fitted with electricity. Soon afterwards though, Fred decided that they needed a garden, so they moved to a house in Woolwich, where she lives to this day. Although it did have a garden, it didn't have hot water, electricity or a bath, and only acquired an inside toilet in 1987. The main room was 12 square foot, and served as living room and kitchen. The food was bought every day as they didn't have a fridge of course. All the washing was done by hand. And every Friday night the tin bath would come out for the weekly bath, with water boiled on the stove. (This was a routine Ada was to follow until she was well over 80!)

Now, Woolwich was a military base and so was far too dangerous to live in during the war. And thus in 1943, Ada was packed off to Northampton to have her first child, Barry. The idea was to move expectant mothers away from big cities. Heavily pregnant, Ada had to cart her heavy suitcase on and off the train and over to the house where she had been billeted. Once there, she was turfed out every morning and had to walk around Northampton all day until allowed back in at teatime. That at least gave her time to contemplate pregnancy; until she actually gave birth, she supposed the baby would emerge from her belly button. In the event things went smoothly and she was sent back to London a mere two weeks later with baby Barry in tow. Meanwhile the war was still raging. In March 1944, Ada and Barry were hiding under an iron table in the front room during an air raid, when a German bomb landed next door with a deafening boom. After the blast, Ada discovered she'd been blown out of the house and ended up at the bottom of the back garden still cradling Barry in her arms... The front of the house had been completely destroyed. Fred spent the war in the Home Guard, repairing water mains that had burst during the air raids. He also did a stint fire-watching from Shooters Hill water tower. When the high drama of the war ended, Ada and Fred settled down to the reality of marriage. In 1947, Bernard was born, followed by Sylvia two years later. Ada would work in a high street launderette in the morning, and as a petrol pump attendant in the afternoon and evening, but not without coming home at lunchtime to cook her husband a meal. Fred wasn't always an easy man to get on with, and his initial charm seemed to wear off with the years. He used to grow dahlias at the end of the garden, and sell them for a bit of cash. However, when the weather ruined them, he used to pick what was left for his wife, but charge her 2 bob for it out of her already meagre allowance... Fred had had a tough upbringing, and so believed in authority: nobody was allowed to make even the slightest noise while he was trying to sleep, or they could get a belting. And so the rest of the family spoke in whispers, and had to listen to the Marconi radio with their ears pressed against the speakers.

Ada retired from her final job as dinner lady at Shooters Hill Grammar School in 1973, aged 60. In 1979, Fred Peach died, to mixed feelings from Ada; when the doctor turned up too late and apologized, she told him not to worry about it. Since then Ada has had a vigorous retirement, with family trips to Paris and a healthy daily dose of Coronation St. She is not overly concerned with fame, but will celebrate her 15 minutes in the limelight today by reading the showbiz gossip in all the papers and seeing if she's made it.

Iconoclasm day: deface a powerful image

Ever since our cavemen ancestors thought painting mammoths would help them catch the real thing, we have been in thrall to images. Even these days we can scarcely bring ourselves to throw away photos of loved ones, such is our attachment to the quasi-voodoo notion that what we do to the photo somehow affects the person. Shatter this self-imposed taboo today by defacing a potent image, be it a photo of your parents, or the one we provide.

TODAY, CLAIM YOU'RE FROM THE FUTURE

Anyone who convinces the world that they are from the future will achieve instant fame and fortune. The key to this is following correct procedure:

1) You must arrive at night, preferably during a storm, near power lines. Any evidence of electromagnetic disturbance will enhance your credibility.
2) You must arrive naked. Clothes do not travel well through time. Also, "Made in China" labels will detract from your story.
3) You must claim urgent police protection against the androids who have been sent to kill you. If anyone questions their existence, claim that they are the fucking android and try to get them shot in the ensuing panic.
4) You must pick a credible year. 2013 is too close to be of interest. 56802 is not believable, unless you sport antennae. 2049 has a nice ring to it.
5) If you are single, why not try the chat-up line, "I've been sent from the future to save you." It's guaranteed foolproof.
6) During any psychiatric evaluations, avoid harping on about imminent nuclear holocausts; it unsettles doctors and other patients alike.
7) Once you've achieved your fame and fortune, knock yourself out, claim amnesia, and return to normal present-based life.

CONSPIRACY DAY

There's a potential conspiracy everywhere you look. Today find one in your everyday life!

My neighbour has been poisoning my cat with anthrax pellets! My cat is a different animal. He used to be cuddly but now he growls like a dog. Whenever he comes back from the next door garden, his saliva is greenish and frothing. My neighbour works for a chemical company. She keeps odd hours. I am afraid for myself and my cat.

I am the subject of a snuff reality TV show! There are cameras everywhere in my house. There have been since my birth. I even know which channel the show is on, channel 9 because they have "broken" that button on my TV. My life fascinates millions daily. But it will end with my being impaled to death live on prime time. Help me escape!

My children are the vanguard of an alien invasion! They are not like other kids. They don't go out. They don't play. They just do their homework and eat their greens. Since my wife was abducted (the so-called divorce was just for show), they stare out of the window waiting for the signal from the mothership.

My computer is bugged by the CIA! They are aware of my subversive potential. Every time I sit down to write my exposé of our crypto-world government, they zap my brain with alpha waves to cause writer's block! But I will fight back you evil bastards! What happens if I pour wate<ds5z++…
''√'ﬁ√'˛˛ç˛∂≈† <ds5z+<ds5z+<ds5z+

Elvis is living in my shed! There's worse: he's using my tools. The other day, my staple gun was on next to the drill, when I 100% remember leaving it next to the saw! I dunno what he's making but it's a big job! He's working flat out all hours of the night. I know this cos I can hear him crooning to cover up the noise.

My cleaner is a communist! She leaves hammer and sickle signs in the dust. And last week, my books must have been rearranged, because the first letters of the titles of five of them spelt Lenin backwards. I fear she is using my toilet pan to leave messages for her Comintern handler, whom I suspect is the plumber. That damn toilet always blocks!

Plagiarism Day
Today, copy everything from others: your haircut, what you wear, where you go, what you say, what you read, what you watch, what you think.
My favourite film is Batman II.
Purple is the new black.
I think it's going to rain.
I've made salmon for dinner!
I'm worried my son is gay.
I love what you're wearing.
Voff!
I'm going on holiday with my husband to Venice.
Plagiarism Day
Today, copy everything from others: your haircut, what you wear, where you go, what you say, what you read, what you watch, what you think.
I have never seen a finer movie than Batman II.
Mauve is the new black.
Looks like rain to me!
Tonight's supper is fish-based!
Your choice of clothes is divine.
My boy is homosexual, what can I do?
Vaff!
Your husband and I are off to Venice, and you're staying here, biatch!

INSIST ON SPEAKING TO THE MEDIA TODAY

The media isn't a circus, it's a club: same old faces, same old views, same old grudges. Today, demand to have your voice heard for a change! Speak out on what matters to you, whether it's how to run a good war, or about the strange way light sometimes shimmers on puddles, in country lanes, at the crack of dawn. Barge in and have your say! **How to trick the media into giving you airtime** Good: I have slept with the PM (and can prove it!); I have valuable information regarding a plot; I have swallowed a grenade and wish to say goodbye; I'm the replacement weatherman today. Bad: I am the foremost expert on country lane puddle lighting.

You aren't anyone if you haven't been on tv. And you're only a little someone if you've been on radio. And you're only a tiny teenie weenie of a somebody if you've been in the newspaper. But barely worth mentioning!

Day 280

MAKE AN INSECT'S DAY

THE LIFE OF AN INSECT IS GENERALLY NASTY BRUTISH AND SHORT. BRING A LITTLE WARMTH TO BEAR ON THIS MISERABLE EXISTENCE TODAY BY GIVING ONE OF THEM THE EXPERIENCE OF AN INSECT LIFETIME.

YOU ARE
NUMBER
ONE

- POUR A PUDDLE OF HONEY IN THE PATH OF AN UNSUSPECTING ANT
- CAPTURE A BEE AND LET IT LOOSE IN A FLOWER SHOP
- CHASE A MOSQUITO INTO A PACKED SAUNA
- PLACE A GRASSHOPPER ON A TRAMPOLINE
- FURNISH A TERMITE COLONY WITH A LOUIS XIV COMMODE
- SMUGGLE A FLY INTO A MORTUARY

Sit in the lotus position all day long today

AND RELAX!

Sit on the floor with spine erect and legs stretched out in front of you, slightly apart. Place right foot on left thigh with the sole of foot turned up. Rest right knee on the ground. Take left foot and place it high on right thigh with sole facing up and left knee resting on the ground. Let feet rest on the pressure points at the top of the groin.

Today, spy on your parents

Your mother and father are key figures in your life, but what do you actually know about them? What are they really like when you're not around? Are they indeed who they say they are? How do you even know for sure they are your real parents? Today, follow them in the street. Listen in on their phone calls. Interrogate them and others who may know the truth. Investigate them fully and confront them with the results.

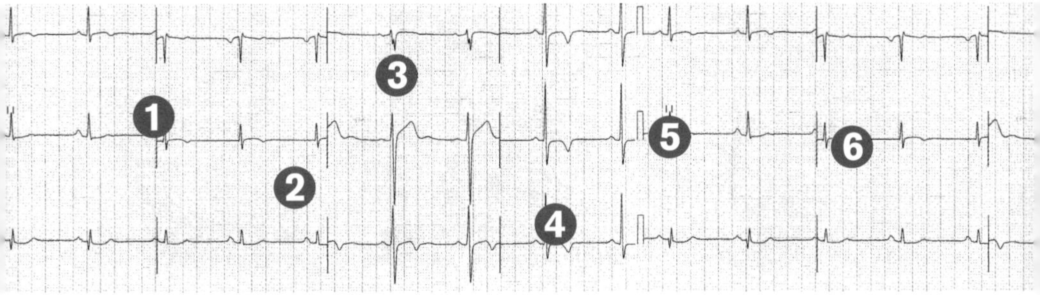
1
2
3
4
5
6

1. Interrogate: Mother
Some memories don't lie. Even if it's slightly embarrassing, ask your mother if you may breastfeed again for a minute, and check that the experience matches your recollections. Results:
Breasts feel familiar...................................+2pts
Breasts feel foreign....................................-2pts
Breasts feel arousing..................................-7pts

2. Interrogate: Father
These days, paternity can be established very easily, with a simple genetic test. If your father is the real thing, he will not mind donating a hair, a nail or a small blood sample for this purpose. Results:
DNA matches yours exactly......................+2pts
DNA does not match yours exactly.............-1pt
DNA is not human.....................................-5pts

3. Interrogate: Doctor
Track down the doctor whose name appears on your birth certificate and show him a photo of your parents. Can he or she confirm your so-called mother and father were both present at your birth? Results:
Both present..+4pts
One present...+1pt
Neither present..-3pts

4. Interrogate: Elderly relative
Every self-respecting family features a senile relative who has forgotten everything except for the darkest family secrets. Get them drunk on gin and find out if anything was kept from you. Results:
You were found..-7pts
You were adopted......................................-8pts
You were sent from planet Krypton..........-9pts

5. Interrogate: Neighbours
Neighbours have a front-row seat in the drama of your family life. And unlike relatives, they are an unbiased source of gossip. If there's the slightest peccadillo in your parents's past, they'll know it. Results:
Your mother is cheating on your father......-5pts
Your father is cheating on your mother......-5pts
Both of them are wife-swapping with the neighbours..-3pts

6. Interrogate: Police
If people have anything serious to hide, it's probably tucked away in their police record. Visit your local police station and share your suspicions. Comb through your parents' files in search of clues. Results:
Records are clean.....................................+2pts
Records have been tampered with.............-2pts
Records show you were kidnapped as a child but the ransom was never paid and so your "parents" have kept you ever since..........................-15pts

RECOMMENDATIONS More than 0 points: Your family is far too normal. Keep looking for clues. 0 to -20 points: Your parents are more of a mess than you thought, and have probably passed it on to you. Over -20 points: You have grounds for divorce from your parents. Speak to a family lawyer immediately.

Day 283

VISIT SOMEONE IN HOSPITAL

The sick need to be comforted. Today walk into your nearest hospital and cheer up an ailing stranger with a surprise hug. Here are some suggestions of people who, according to NHS Trust timetables, are due to be in hospital recovering today. Just ask for their bed number at reception.

Cardiff

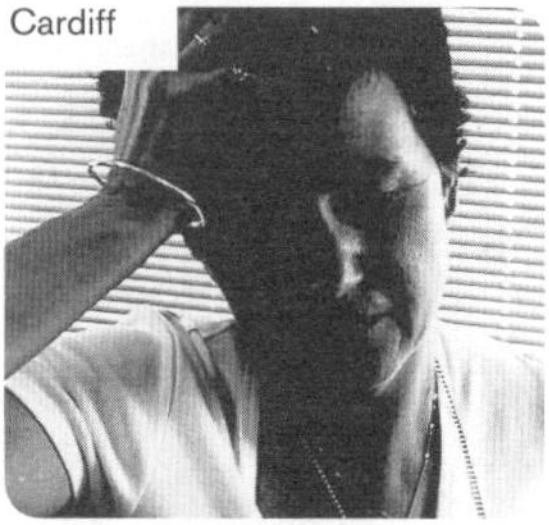

Henrietta Evans, 49
Hip replacement
Cardiff Royal Infirmary

London

Sign Jack's plaster!

Jack Trewin, 11
Broken leg
Royal Free Hospital

Brighton

Paul Burns, 34
Triple bypass
Royal Sussex County Hospital

Birmingham

Liz Aldiss, 22
Kidney transplant
City Hospital

Manchester

Julian Bell, 29
Appendicitis
Manchester Royal Infirmary

Dublin

Scott Evans, 31
Concussion
Beaumont Hospital

Edinburgh

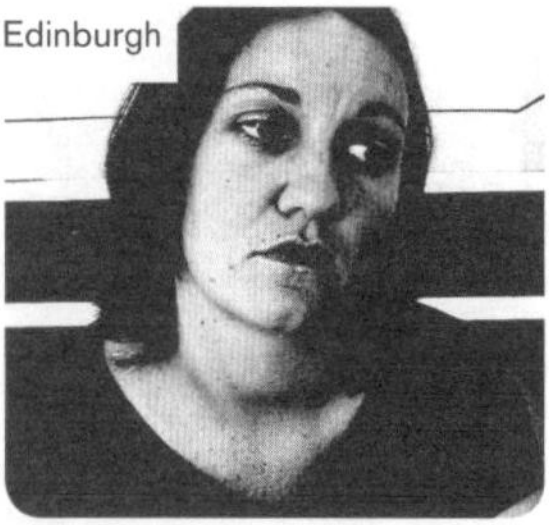

Miriam Blake, 32
Dislocated ankle
Royal Victoria Hospital

Liverpool

Anouk Baufurt, 23
Osteoporosis
Liverpool Women's Hospital

Bristol

Jim Taylor, 48
Tonsillectomy
Nuffield Hospital

It's payback time! Today get back at someone!

Revenge is a dish best served cold. Did someone fire you three years ago? Did some queen bitch steal your boyfriend in high school? Did some dog run off with your lollipop when you were two? Today, get your own back and let them know no one messes with you and your crew. With the opening up of the EU to ex-communist states, an influx of KGB-trained contract killers has become available to the Western consumer, at very reasonable prices. Not only that, but the range of punishments inflicted has also expanded, to offer a more imaginative range of options, most of which won't even land you in jail.

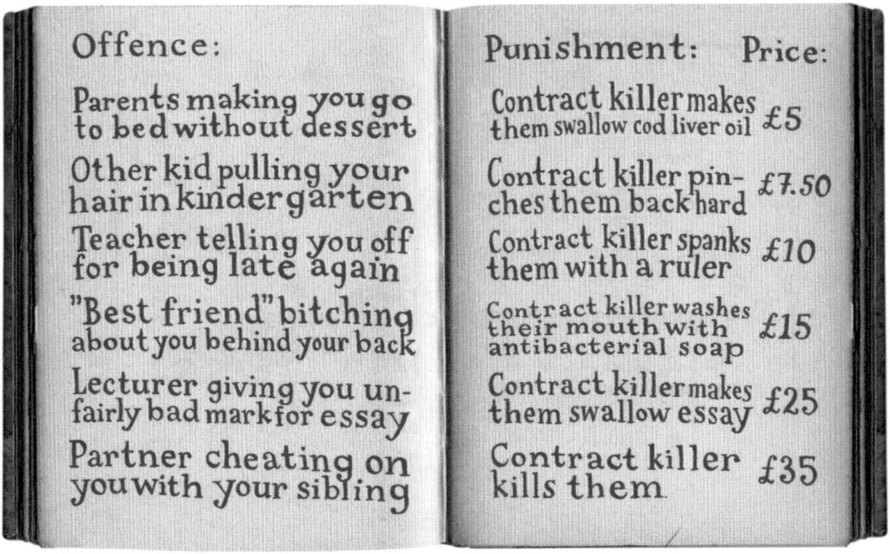
Offence:
Parents making you go to bed without dessert
Other kid pulling your hair in kindergarten
Teacher telling you off for being late again
"Best friend" bitching about you behind your back
Lecturer giving you unfairly bad mark for essay
Partner cheating on you with your sibling
Punishment:
Price:
Contract killer makes them swallow cod liver oil
£5
Contract killer pinches them back hard
£7.50
Contract killer spanks them with a ruler
£10
Contract killer washes their mouth with antibacterial soap
£15
Contract killer makes them swallow essay
£25
Contract killer kills them
£35

Here are the current revenge values for a selection of offences. You may customize these to suit your preferences, how long ago it happened, and just how deeply you were traumatized.

Day 285

TALIBAN DAY:
IMPOSE YOUR VALUES ON EVERYONE ELSE

The decline of shared moral values is undermining our society. Today, try to bring back a little cohesion by enforcing your personal morality on those around you. Don't be afraid to coerce people a little to help them internalize your values. They may protest, but remind them – it's for their own good. Here are a few methods, developed by experts in the field.

EAT ORGANIC NOW!

Picket them

H×4 OWNERS OUT!

Daub disapproving comments on their houses

PETE & MAUREEN PRESTON DON'T RECYCLE!

Name and shame them

N/A in UK currently

Bury them in the ground and stone them to death

Today imagine what
it would be like to be
this person.

What is your job?

What is your dream in life?

Are you fulfilled?

Do you break down
and sob quietly in the
middle of the night?

Are you sex-mad?

Have you ever known true love?

Day 287

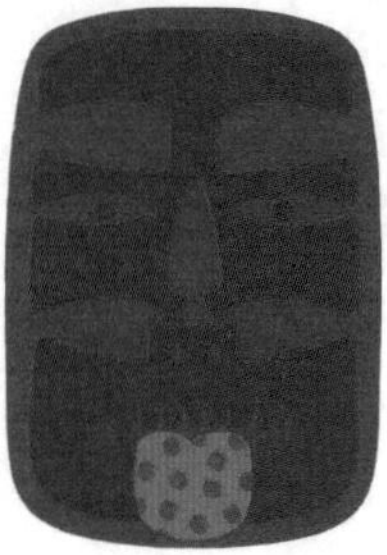

Change your name to Benrik by deed poll

YES! You can change your boring old name to a more exciting one for free with our legally valid deed poll! The only restrictions on name changes are that it mustn't be impossible to pronounce and it can't include numbers, symbols or punctuation marks (except apostrophes). So you are perfectly entitled to change your name to Clark Kent, Booty Licious or Bobby Charlton. "Benrik", however, is much more suitable.

A Deed Poll

This change of name deed made this .... day of .... by me the undersigned BENRIK of .... now or lately known as ....
....
(former name) a citizen of ....
....by birth.

Witnesses and it is hereby declared as follows:
1. I absolutely and entirely renounce relinquish and abandon the use of my said former name of
....
....(former name)
and assume adopt and determine to take and use from the date hereof the name of BENRIK in substitution for my former name, ...
....(former name).

2. I shall at all times hereafter in all records deeds documents and other writings and in all actions and proceedings as well as in all dealings and transactions and on all occasions whatsoever use and subscribe the said name of BENRIK as my name in substitution for my former name of...
.... (former name)
so relinquished as aforesaid to the intent that I may hereafter be called known or distinguished not by the former name but by the name of BENRIK only.

3. I authorize and require all persons at all times to designate describe and address me by the adopted name of BENRIK .

In witness hereof I have hereunto subscribed my adopted and substituted name of BENRIK and also my said former name of ....
....(former name)
and have affixed my seal the day and year first above written.

Signed sealed and delivered by the above-named BENRIK in the presence of:

Witness 1...

Witness 2...

Signature

Seal

Send it for safe keeping to the Enrolment Books of the Central Office of the Supreme Court of Deeds, at the Royal Courts of Justice (Strand, London WC2A 2LL). Alternatively just show this deed poll to government departments and other organizations and ask them to change your records.

GATECRASH THE NEWS TODAY

Today, make your life immediately more exciting by going to the heart of the news. Switch on your TV, find out the number one event in the world, the biggest story on the planet, call your travel agent and get yourself over there immediately. What to do when you get there: since you're in the area, why not try to get on the world news yourself? The media are always hungry for a good story, even if it's not 100% verified.

In April 2002, Japanese backpackers Yuki Makano and Mina Takahashi strolled towards the Church of the Nativity in Bethlehem, unaware of the ongoing bloody siege between Israeli soldiers and Palestinian gunmen. As journalists and residents stared on, the couple wandered around and took in the sights. They were eventually rescued. "We have been on the road for six months and haven't watched television or read the papers", said Mr Makano.

CATEGORIES OF NEWS EVENTS:

LIVE NEWS

SPORTING COMPETITION: Wait for the final day and streak across the ground at the very last, crucial minute.

LATEST NEWS!

NATURAL DISASTER: Enlist survivors and file a class action lawsuit against God and his representatives on earth, the Vatican.

NEWS JUST IN!

TERRORIST THREAT: Conduct your own interrogations, torturing suspicious passers-by until they confess their guilt or innocence.

MEDICAL BREAKTHROUGH: Denounce the breakthrough as a fraud, and insist that they test it on your own body, in public.

BREAKING NEWS!

POLITICAL ASSASSINATION: Apologize for the murder on behalf of your government, saying it was due to a typing mistake.

ACCIDENTAL THERMONUCLEAR EXPLOSION: Even if you manage to find transportation to this event, you are permitted not to go if you prefer.

Day 289

Today throw something away that you like

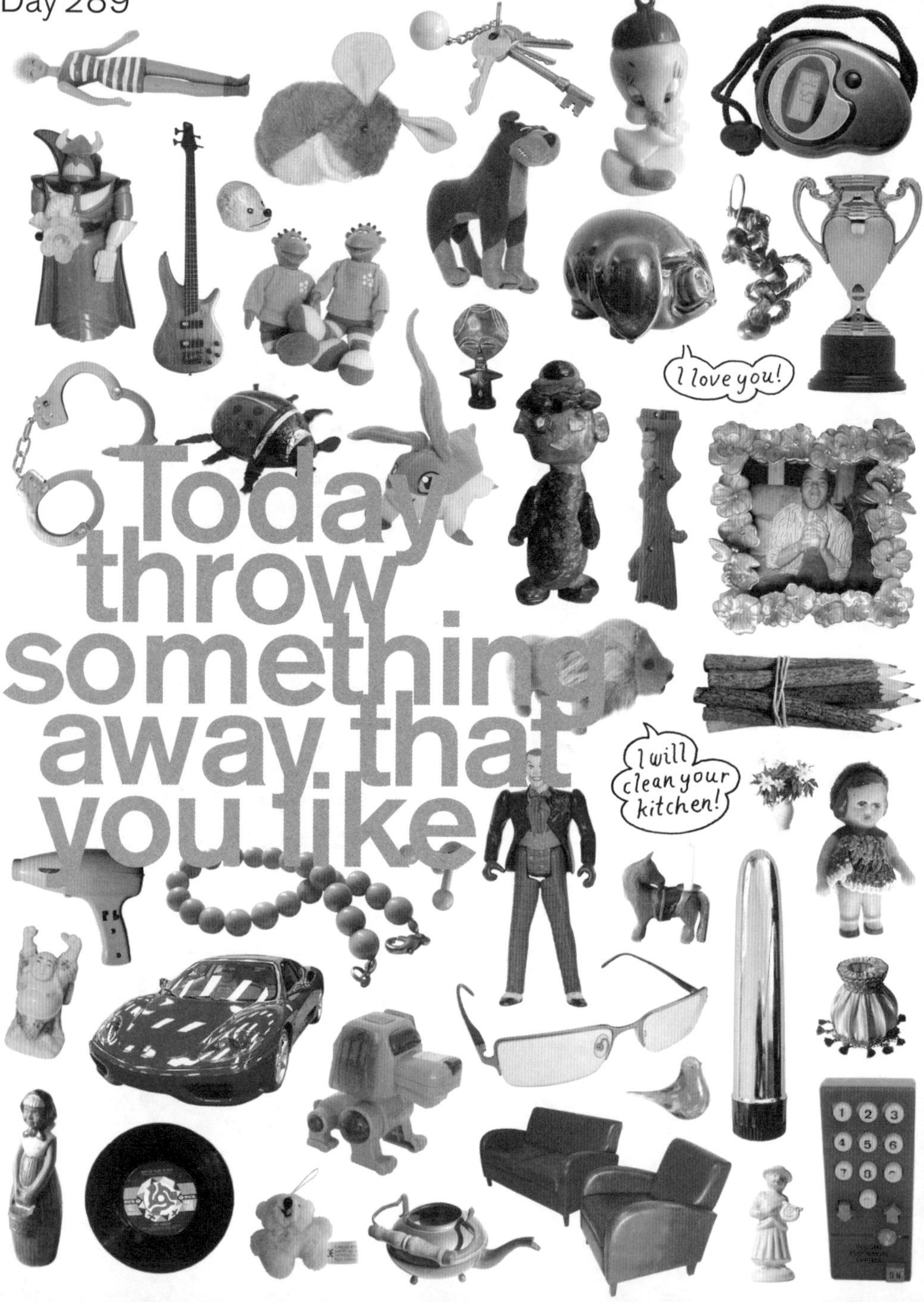
I love you!
I will clean your kitchen!

GREENLAND
ICELAND
U.S.A
CANADA
UNITED STATES OF AMERICA
MEXICO
VENEZUELA
COLOMBIA
PERU
BRAZIL
BOLIVIA
PARAGUAY
CHILE
ARGENTINA
NORWAY
SWEDEN
FINLAND
UNITED KINGDOM
FRANCE
SPAIN
ITALY
UKRAINE
ROMANIA
BULGARIA
TURKEY
RUSSIA
KAZAKHSTAN
MONGOLIA
CHINA
INDIA
IRAN
IRAQ
SYRIA
SAUDI ARABIA
MOROCCO
ALGERIA
LIBYA
EGYPT
MALI
NIGER
CHAD
SUDAN
ETHIOPIA
NIGERIA
KENYA
ANGOLA
ZAMBIA
BOTSWANA
SOUTH AFRICA
MADAGASCAR
INDONESIA
PAPAU NEW GUINEA
AUSTRALIA
NEW ZEALAND
WORLD
COLOURING-IN
DAY

Today, work out your globetrotting plans for the rest of your time on earth, and get on the phone to an accredited travel agent.
Fill in country by country:

- Been there done that
- Intend to go there this year
- Intend to go there sometime before I die
- Happy never to set foot there in my whole life

DEFY HIERARCHY TODAY

Don't just accept society's rules. Talk back. Stand up. Be the cog that clogs up the machine.

Authority figure no1:

The Boss

Do not say: Certainly Mr Johnson, you'll have that report on your desk first thing in the morning sir.
Instead, say: Hey Mr Bossman piece-of-shit capitalist exploiter, I'm tired of following your whims so take your job and stick it up your exploitative ass.

Authority figure no2:

The Law

Do not say: I'm sorry officer, I'll move along straight away, I don't want to cause an affray.
Instead, say: Fuck you, pig. If you think I'm going to move an inch you've got another thing coming, you undersized-penis scum, it's a free country, now mind your own business and piss right off.

Authority figure no3:

The Teacher

Do not say: You're absolutely correct, I do not in fact know what I am talking about, I'll just listen to your expertise and take notes from now on.
Instead, say: I don't know which is more pitiful, the role you play in perpetuating the post-capitalist patriarchal order, or the pittance you get paid to do so. Ever heard of Pink Floyd? No I didn't think so. Anyway, I'm taking my kids out of school and that's final, dammit.

Authority figure no4:

The Family

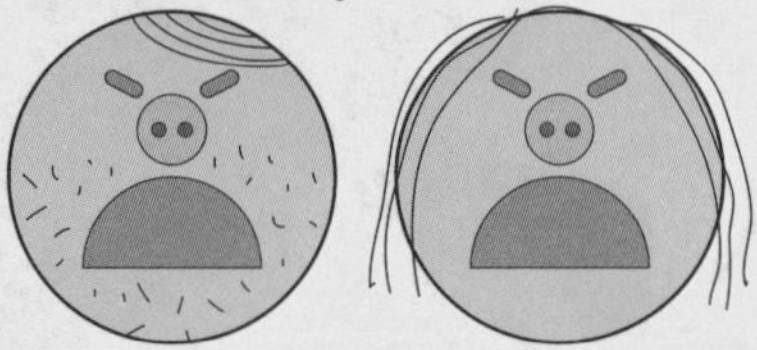

Do not say: Yes father, I'm sure you're right, I'll go for that insurance salesman job, it does look promising.
Instead, say: Look man, just cos I came out of your balls doesn't mean I have to listen to your stupid advice. I'm gonna be a heavy metal drummer, earn ten times more than you, and that's final, so get off my case or I'll lie and have you done for abuse.

Romance Day

Come up with a compliment that has never been made before.

Top female compliment clichés: "You are the woman of my dreams." "Your eyes are like two stars – it must have hurt, when you fell from heaven." "You're not like any girl I've ever met." Top male compliment clichés: "Do you work out?" "Nice driving!" "Boy, you sure can handle your drink." "Look at those hands – are you a lumberjack?"

Day 293

Ask public transport to make a detour for you

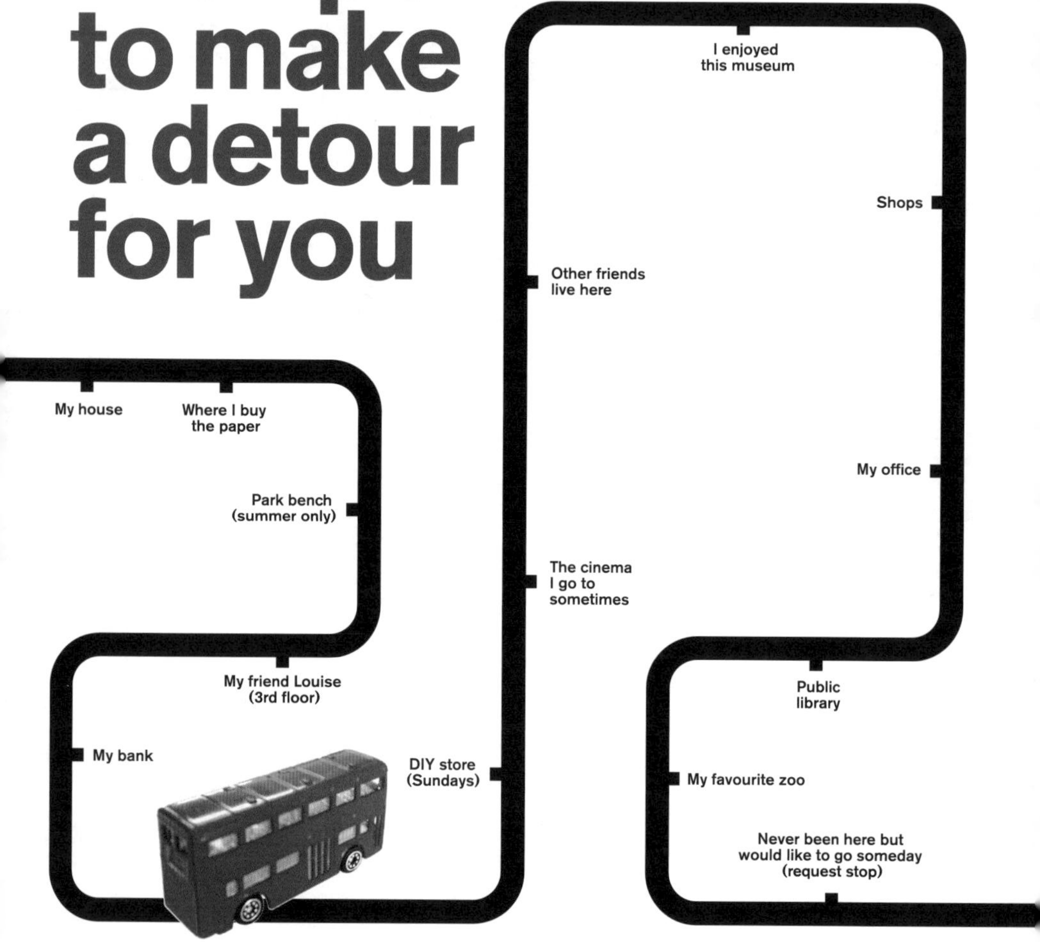
I enjoyed this museum
Shops
Other friends live here
My house
Where I buy the paper
Park bench (summer only)
My office
The cinema I go to sometimes
My friend Louise (3rd floor)
Public library
My bank
DIY store (Sundays)
My favourite zoo
Never been here but would like to go someday (request stop)

Urban planners are busy people and can't always be expected to get it right the first time. Buses, trains and underground services often stop hundreds of yards away from where you need them to. Remedy this by asking the drivers to divert via your choice of destination. Remember to check the other passengers don't mind; you'll probably find that's where they wanted to go too, only they were too shy to ask! This is only a stopgap measure, until the local authorities commit resources to servicing you properly. To help them, draw up your proposed route and send it to them for implementation. Here is an example.

Today is Blue-Sky Day

Forget the practicalities: decide what you really want out of life. I want...

A shed on the moon

72 kids

To be King of Lombardy

A second belly button

To make love to the Virgin Mary

A layer of atmosphere named after me

World peace

One pyramid for me and two smaller ones for my followers

My enemy's head on a plate

My own nuclear-powered submarine

To be beamed up

To be left alone

Now make it happen.

HELP! I'M BEING HELD AGAINST MY WILL!

Vote like me!

The key is under the mat

WINDOW ART DAY

People feel a strange urge to display their tedious political views in their windows, when there are so many more interesting statements to make. Today, display your message to the world in your most prominent window, and see how the world responds. Here are a few examples to inspire you.

I'm not coming out until my demands are met

I'm fantasizing about you from behind these blinds

I'm lonely in here, there's nothing on TV

I dare you to burgle me, passer-by

THIS FLAT IS WORTH £450,000, YOU LOSERS!

THIS WINDOW IS 100% BRICK PROOF

INCREASE YOUR PAIN THRESHOLD TODAY

What doesn't kill you makes you stronger. Today, gradually increase the level of pain you can cope with, so that you won't get hurt by what life throws at you.

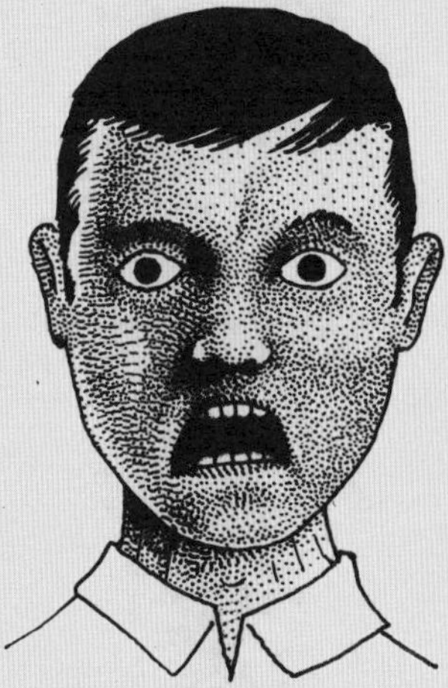

Ask an acquaintance to pinch your arm for 5 minutes

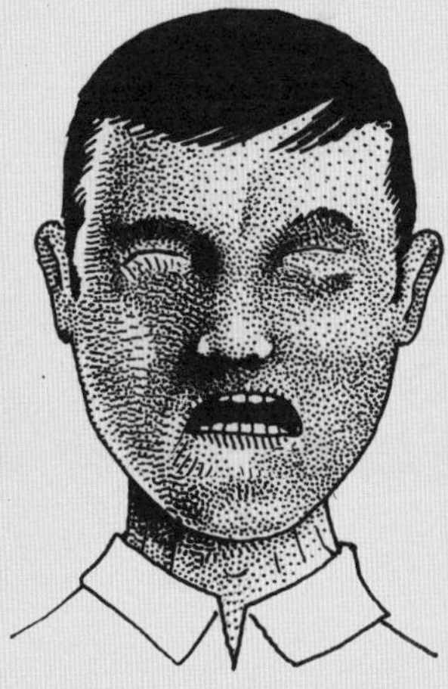

Get someone to pull your hair hard for 10 minutes

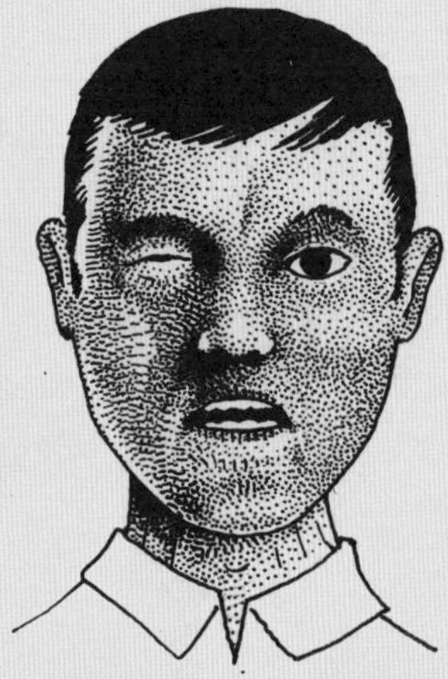

Stand under an ice-cold shower for 15 minutes

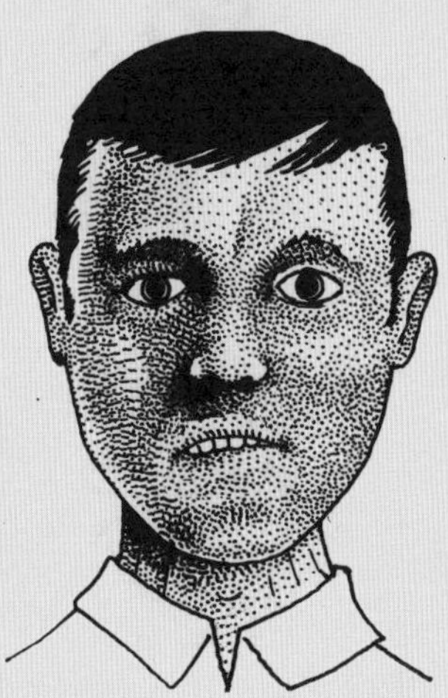

Ask a trusted friend to spank you until you plead for mercy

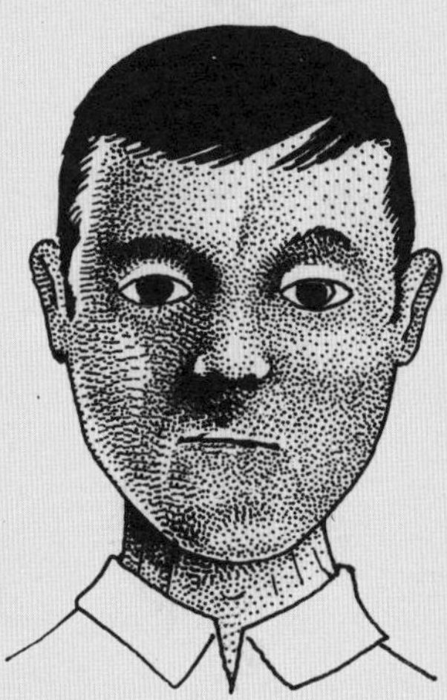

Convince a dentist to remove a back tooth without anaesthetic

Ask the love of your life to break your heart

Pain gets a bad press, but it is crucial to our survival. Pain alerts our body to danger and enables us to avoid long-term damage. Indeed, people who can't feel pain at all are usually dead by 30. If none of the exercises suggested here cause you any pain, stay indoors for the rest of your days if you value your life.

Today disappear

Don't you sometimes wish you could start all over again? How difficult would it be just to walk away from your life, and begin afresh somewhere else? Test the waters by spending the day on the run from your friends, family, and colleagues.

Let children rule the world today

Children are pure and innocent. If we all do their bidding, the world can only become a better place. Do nothing today without first asking for instructions from the nearest available child.

dolly-mountain
Spend all money on candy.
Beat up the fat kids.

Armies to be composed of pets.
Grrr.
Grrr.

Stories
Parents in bed by 8.

Detention for all teachers.
Naughty Boy

Only cartoons on TV.

Breakfast:
Lunch:
Dinner:
Burger and chips every meal.

Day 299

Today invent a new punctuation mark.

Denotes that the previous sentence is to be construed ironically.

Orgasm. More generally used to indicate the writer is sexually aroused.

Writer is aware that at this point he's bullshitting.

(( )) Double brackets: contains a secret, only read if you agree to keep it.

Example: As I write this I am sitting stark naked with a blonde on my lap **((She has a third nipple)). Actually there are two of them, twins in fact** **OK, well it's bound to happen someday**

Today plant marijuana outside a government building and report them to the local newspaper.

MORNING HERA
Hippie MPs high on power
BEST WEED: IT'S OFFICIAL!
Thursday
MINISTER IN GANJA SCANDAL
Lawyer denies everything
EXCLUSIVE INTERVIEW
PAGE 4, 5, 6

Where to plant? Picking a good location to plant your seed is crucial. Ideally you are looking for grass interspersed with trees and small bushes, and available water (bear in mind official lawns are often automatically watered). If the soil is very poor, consider adding a layer of organic topsoil with lime to make it more fertile. Sunlight is a definite plus; four hours a day is a minimum, preferably in the morning. Mid May is a good time to plant. Plant your seeds about one half-inch deep, with two inches between seeds. To guarantee a decent harvest that will photograph well, allow for 200+ seeds. Planting at night is advisable to ensure an element of surprise.

TODAY LIE TO SOMEONE ABOUT YOUR PAST

There are four main types of lie about one's past, all designed to enhance one's reputation:

WHITE LIES
My first word was "symposium".

BLATANT LIES
I'm descended through my mother's side from Attila the Hun.

LIES NO ONE CAN CHECK:
I used to work for the CIA, but the paperwork was too stifling.

LIES NO ONE WANTS TO CHECK:
They really bungled my sex change operation.

JAM THE LINE!
Everyone call the national Ku Klux Klan Headquarters, Harrison, Arkansas on
(001) 870-427-3414
repeatedly and jam the line.

BARTER DAY

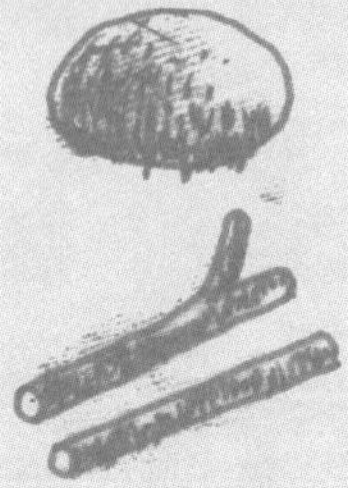

1 STONE = 2 STICKS

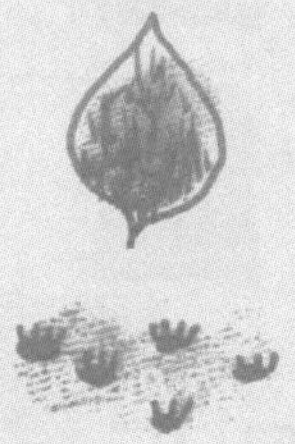

1 LEAF = 5 DEAD ANTS

12 FRENCH FRIES = 1 PENCIL

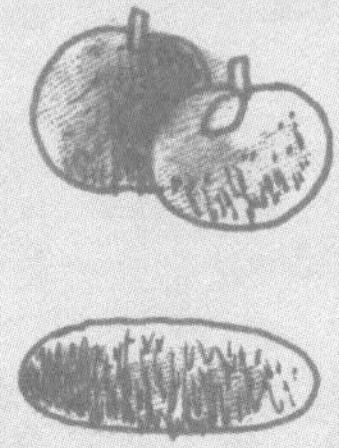

2 APPLES = 1 LOAF BREAD

1 MUD HUT = 4 DONKEYS

1 COW = 2 DOGS

1 MOTOR-BIKE = 1 FRONT GARDEN

1 GIRAFFE = 1 BICYCLE

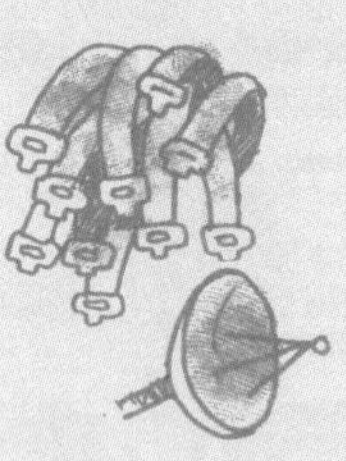

17 SEATBELTS = 1 YEAR'S CABLE TV SUBSCRIPTION

3 EIGHTEEN-WHEELERS = 1 SMALL HOUSE WITH NO WINDOW

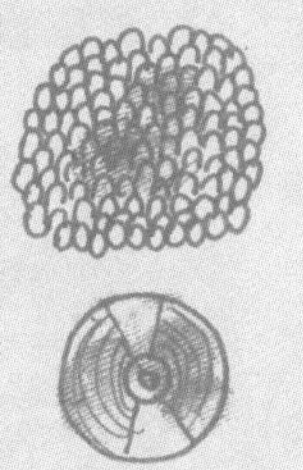

110 FRESH EGGS = 1 DVD

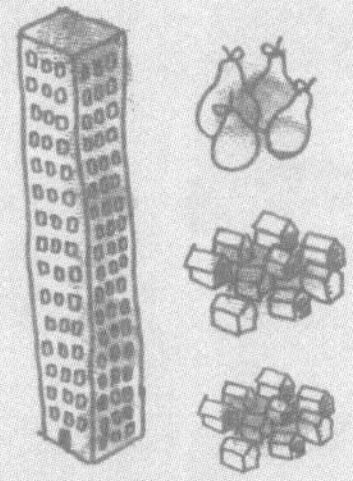

1 SKYSCRAPER + 4 PEARS = 2 REMOTE VILLAGES

Bartering provides fun for all the family, bypasses the taxman, and is a useful skill to acquire in the event of civilization suddenly reverting to the Stone Age. Here are some useful equivalencies to get you started.

Volunteer for a medical experiment today

Drugs companies need to test their new products on human volunteers. You can earn decent cash by participating in their trials. But it's not about the money, it's about the unrivalled opportunity for radical life change. These are drugs in the early stages of development, before research has sanitized them. Pick a cutting-edge drug, and chances are you'll develop a cutting-edge side effect: night vision, telepathy or radioactive superpowers perhaps. Think of how that would pep up your daily routine! Call today and volunteer your services. Worst-case scenario: you'll be able to bring an expensive lawsuit!

Case studies

Start date	Monday 11/12/06	Monday 11/12/06	Monday 11/12/06	Tuesday 12/12/06	Friday 15/12/06	Friday 15/12/06	Sunday 17/12/06
Study code	JS0098X	Sanuspol 3000z	Phfx/788/ fact.4	TT-x545	RD2000M7	DRF003/ 2a	Ch56/ 44–0004
Study type	New laxative drug	Kidney cleansing agent	Cancer vaccine	Drug side-effects on spinal fluid	Skin reaction to GM bio-enzyme YK9	Blood recoagulant	Potential vaccine for Marburg haemorrhagic fever
Country	UK	UK	Belgium	UK	USA	Andorra	Tasmania
Overnight stays	1	1	4	5	7	1 to 14+ (depending response)	59
Daily visits	Medical x2 morning visits	Medical	Medical x3, annual check-up (indef.)	Medical x2, annual check-up for 6 years	Medical x2, 12 monthly visits	Medical x3	Medical, 2 month stay
Risk factor	6/10	2/10	7/10	8/10	8/10	8/10	9/10
Payment	£1,450	£190 + travel expenses	£2,500	£4,125	$2,200	£1500 min	£6,980 + airfare

Where do I sign up? Not so fast! To qualify for most clinical trials, you should be a healthy male aged 18–45. Women aged 18–65 may apply but usually need to be post-menopausal or infertile, as the danger to any fetus from these trials is too great. However, if you are very keen, ask if you may sign a legal waiver. You will need to undergo a medical check-up to ascertain your suitability. You will usually be asked to stay overnight, and will be expected to attend daytime clinics for blood tests and other forms of monitoring. Important: Make sure to ask for early Phase I trials, or even volunteer for late-phase animal trials if you want to guarantee noticeably life-changing results. Our tip: invasive trials pay better. Contact: most of the large pharmaceutical companies have clinical research divisions.

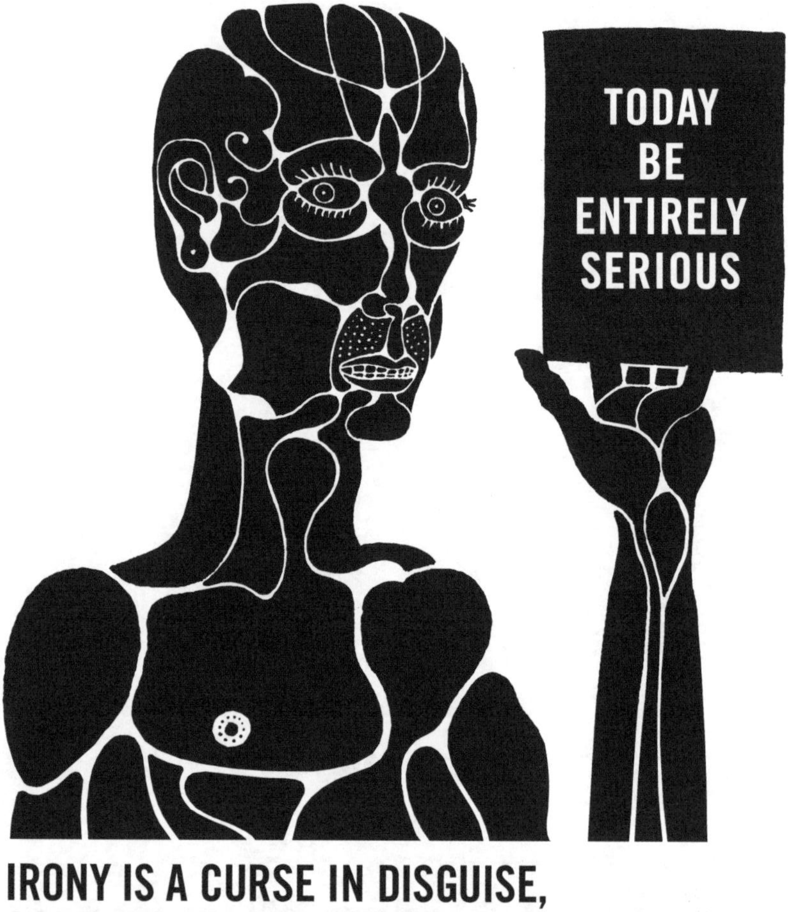
TODAY
BE
ENTIRELY
SERIOUS

IRONY IS A CURSE IN DISGUISE, CORRUPTING AND REDUCING EVERYTHING TO THE SAME SUPERFICIAL LEVEL AND ABOLISHING DEPTH IN BOTH VALUES AND RELATIONSHIPS. TODAY, AVOID THE TEMPTATIONS OF GLIBNESS AND FRIVOLITY, AND TAKE LIFE SERIOUSLY FOR A CHANGE.

TERRORISM
GLORIFIER

When
I grow up,
I want
to be a
terrorist!

More
terrorism
please!

what a glorious
day for some
TERRORISM!

Today, "glorify terrorism"

TERRORISM
IS
REALLY
RATHER
GLORIOUS!

TERRORISM
RAH
RAH
RAH!

ISN'T
TERRORISM
SIMPLY
DIVINE?

I LOVE
TERRORISM
IT'S SO
MACHO!

Benrik readers in the UK are particularly lucky that a completely new life-changing opportunity has recently presented itself. Thanks to the British state, "glorifying terrorism" can now land you in prison for years. This preposterously vague criminal offence is still in its infancy though, so help the courts decide what constitutes "glorification" by walking around with one of the badges above.

Check www.benrik.co.uk for availability.

Day 307

Get in touch with your hero today

There is nothing more uplifting than meeting the person you admire most in the world. Take the first step today by approaching your hero and requesting an encounter. Here are some suitable potential heroes if you can't think of any.

Mikhail Gorbachev
Nobel Peace Prize
39 Leningradsky
Prospect, bdg. 14,
Moscow 125167, Russia

Jane Fonda,
Peace and fitness activist
c/o Fonda, Inc.
PO Box 5840, Atlanta,
GA 31107, USA

Nelson Mandela
Nobel Peace Prize
c/o Office of the President
Pretoria 0001,
Republic of South Africa

Javier Perez De Cuellar
Fifth UN Secretary
General, c/o UN
United Nations Plaza,
New York, NY 10017, USA

Bjorn Borg,
Winner of 5 Wimbledon titles
Stadgarden 10,
Box 154 15, 10465
Stockholm, Sweden

Bono,
Singer and debt campaigner
Temple Hill, Vico Road
Killiney, Co Dublin,
Ireland

Noam Chomsky, Professor
MIT Linguistics Dept.
77 Massachusetts Ave.
Bldg. 32-D808
Cambridge, MA 02139, USA

Jimmy Carter,
Nobel Peace Prize
Carter Centre
One Copenhill, Atlanta,
GA 30307, USA

Nana Mouskouri, Singer,
UNICEF Goodwill Ambassador,
c/o Mercury – Universal 22,
rue des Fossés St-Jacques,
75005 Paris, France

Day 308
How do you know you weren't adopted?
It is estimated that one in twelve people are adopted. Many never find out. If you have ever felt different from your parents or your siblings, seek out the truth today. Check by calling the Adoption National Helpline on 0808 808 1234.

Sue over a historical grievance today

These days, it is perfectly acceptable to sue for damages done to your long-dead ancestors. Indeed, if you aren't rich, it's because at some point in history, others dispossessed your family or somehow deprived them of their rightful share of the Earth. Find the descendants of the people responsible and serve them with an inflation-adjusted claim for damages.

Grievance	Date	Claim (Inflation-adjusted)
Landowner sexually harassed your servant great-grandmother	1902	£996,545
Coalmine-owner exploited your great-great-great-great-grandfather	1823	£2,870,876
Dowry for eldest daughter of the family never paid	1769	£13,879,910
Lord of the manor stole eight bushels of hay from your family	1382	£45,788,000
Attila the Hun slaughtered family livestock	600	£108,089,778
Ancestors of Bill Gates clubbed your ancestors to death	104 BC	£783,554,891
Romans built road over your property	34,081 BC	£12,976,087,865

TONIGHT DATE YOURSELF

As Oscar Wilde noted, to love oneself is the beginning of a lifelong romance. You know you're special, and you deserve to be treated as such. Who better to cater to your every need but yourself? So today, come home early, run yourself a bubble bath, crack open a bottle of champagne, and treat yourself to a candlelit dinner where no one will bore you with selfish talk of themselves. And if the evening is successful, may we suggest you retire to the bedroom. Who knows, you might get lucky…

PETITION DAY

Submit your name on www.benrik.co.uk and we will automatically put your name to any petition of interest that comes our way. Here are just a few of the worthy causes you will support, free of charge.

END THE FALKLANDS WAR NOW
The war has been going on over 20 years now, at huge cost in lives to both sides. We ask the government to come to its senses.
NO TO WIDESCREEN
Widescreen TV is flatter and therefore discriminates against the taller actor. We the undersigned demand its immediate ban now!
U IS FOR UNFAIR!
ARTISTS WHOSE NAMES BEGIN IN U ARE NOT PROPERLY REPRESENTED IN OUR MUSEUMS. INCREASE THEIR PROPORTION TO / TH NOW!
EVERY YEAR 7 DOGS ARE EATEN BY THEIR OWNERS! STOP THE MASSACRE!
REE
(TO BE CONFIRMED) HAS BEEN WRONGLY ARRESTED!
We call on the PM to rectify this outrage immediately!

Swear day

If we swear constantly, is it still swearing?

"Dear Sir, I wish to renew my subscription to your *motherfucking* magazine."

"Who's a good kitty-*fucking*-kat?"

"Dear *wanker*, I am writing to apply for an extension to my overdraft."

"Will you *shitting* marry me?"

"Have you been on the *fucking* potty, sweetheart?"

"*Fuck* me, that cappuccino was delicious, thanks."

Test the boundaries of this new world today by swearing in every sentence you write or utter, and monitoring the reaction.

TV personalities like bad-tempered chef Gordon Ramsay have made swearing socially acceptable, transforming our everyday language more than any contemporary novelist or poet could hope to. It is liberating in one sense, but also self-defeating:

"I'll have the prawns followed by the chicken, *for fuck's sake*."

Don't use the word "cunt" though, which is like a powerful antibiotic of last resort – when it loses its effectiveness, humanity will have run out of swearing resources and swearing will come to an end.

Record the next generation of canned laughter

HAHA HAHA HAHAHA
HA HA HA HA
HA
HA HA! HA HA
HA!
Ha
HAHA!
HAHA HAHA HAHAHA
HAH AHA
HAHAH HAHAH HAHAHA
HA HAHA
HA
HAHAHA HAHAHAH AHAHAHA
HA HA HA
HAHAH AHAHAH HAH AHA HAH
HaH HaH
HO
"Most of the canned laughter on television was recorded in the early 50s. The people we hear laughing most often may already be dead" (Chuck Palahniuk, *Lullaby*)

Benrik have taken it upon themselves to update the obsolete canned laughter of our times. Fifties laughter spells fifties humour. Could you be the laugh of the next generation of sitcoms, and earn fabulous money in the process?

Record your laugh via www.benrik.co.uk today and see if it wins the "canned laughter" vote. The winner will be promoted to TV networks across the globe. Good luck. Hahahahahahahaaha hahahahahahahahahahahahahahahaha!

A DAY OF COMPLIMENTS

Flatter someone today and see if it does indeed get you anywhere.

This is the best memo I've ever read

That toupée really suits you,

WHAT A FINE HAT!

That's a nice briefcase

They never told me you were beautiful as well as intelligent

You're not the boss for nothing!

Make your dreams come true today

As Freud revealed, dreams are the disguised fulfilment of repressed wishes. To deal with these repressed wishes, you may either undergo years of therapy, or you can act them out, thus confronting the problem at the root. Today, treat your dreams literally: make them happen...

Dream:	Repressed meaning:	Making it happen:
"I was riding a goat naked, when I saw a penis-shaped cloud and fell off."	You are afraid of the animal nature of your sexuality.	Goat hire: 020 7247 8762 Riding lessons: 024 7669 8300 Meteorological Office: 0870 900 0100 Medical help: 999
"All my teeth have been knocked out to help prop up the Great Wall of China."	You are worried about ageing, that your looks won't last for ever.	Dentist: 020 7935 0875 Chinese embassy: 020 7299 4049 Fedex: 0800 123 800 UN World Heritage Sites: 00 1 212 963 4475
"I'm a prisoner in a castle trying to let my hair down to escape, but the moat is full of babies."	You are having a midlife crisis.	Castle rental: 01573 229 797 Hairdresser: www.toniandguy.co.uk Adoption agency: 0800 783 4086 Nappy wholesaler: 0845 257 3658
"The 747 I'm in flies into a flock of eagles and nearly crashes but I save the day."	You feel unrecognized by your work colleagues and hierarchical superiors.	Flying school: 01959 578101 Travel agent: www.cheapflights.co.uk Animal trainers: 020 8654 0450 Life insurance: 01603 622200
"I'm being chased by a five-legged table into a field of squishy rotten pumpkins."	Your guess is as good as ours.	Furniture maker: 01409 281579 Organic farms association: 0117 314 5000 Trainers: 0870 873 0300 Magic mushrooms: New Forest.
Bonus! Your wildest dream: "Twelve high-class models are licking chocolate off my belly as I count my million-pound fortune."	You would quite like it if twelve high-class models licked chocolate off your belly as you counted your million-pound fortune.	Elite model agency: 00 1 212 529 9700 The Chocolate Society: 01423 322230 National lottery: local newsagents Therapist: 020 7267 3626.

Today, enforce the 'customer is always' right rule: Try these complaints and see if you get your money back

This chicken was only cooked on the inside.

BENRI

This multivitamin tablet is missing B12.

BENRIK

This condom had been used before.

B

This shirt got bigger in the wash.

BEN
RIK

I got food poisoning from your chewing gum.

BENRIK

This newspaper contains too much news about dogs.

RIK

I didn't get any sleep as your hotel room was haunted.

BENRIK

That movie was packed with subliminal pornographic images.

FAMOUS LAST WORDS:

Prepare yours ahead of time

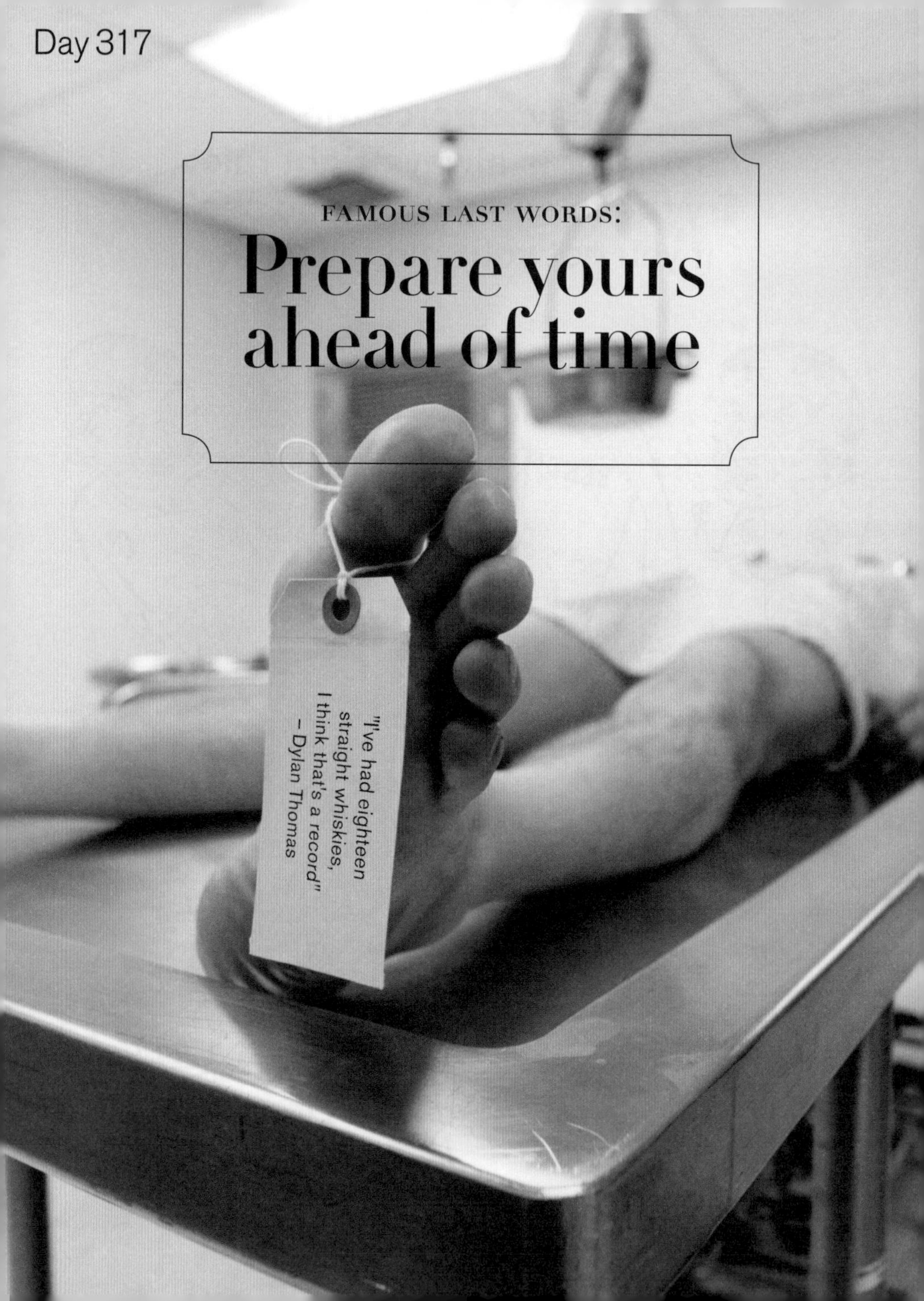
"I've had eighteen
straight whiskies,
I think that's a record"
– Dylan Thomas

Be gay for a day!

As James Dean said, why go through life with one hand tied behind your back? Here are some hints on how to experience your other side in just one day.

8 a.m. During rush hour, try to brush up gently against someone on public transport. This is just to get yourself used to the idea of same-sex contact. Do not push this too far as technically it is known as frottage and could get you arrested.

11 a.m. The office coffee machine is the ideal casual flirting situation. Wait for the object of your affection to help themselves to a coffee before bumping into them. Their beverage will spill over them, providing you with the perfect opportunity to caress their chest with a kitchen towel.

1 p.m. Because of social conventions, it is much easier to find a gay mate if you are officially on the lookout. Use your lunch hour to compose a carefully worded all-staff e-mail in which you come out of the closet. (You will always be able to claim it was a misunderstanding tomorrow.)

3pm By now you should have had plenty of responses to your flirting overtures, but you also need to start planning your evening. Ring a close same-gender friend and say you have something important to tell them. Arrange to meet in a romantic bar or restaurant. Candlelight is best.

5 p.m. The end of the office day. As tomorrow you will be able to explain everything, why not turn up the heat a little by squeezing someone's bottom playfully on your way out. (If possible pick someone with a sense of humour).

8 p.m. By now your date should be going well. After a few drinks, some inadvertent touching and a lot of eye contact, tell your close friend that you think that your relationship could be taken to the next level. They may act unconvinced at first, even play "hard to get," so don't be shy of forcing them to deal with their feelings by grabbing their hand or even French kissing them.

11 p.m. Only one hour left to explore the outer shores of your new sexuality. After today's gradual physical emotional build-up, the last inhibitions shouldn't be too difficult to shed. The rest is up to you...

If you're gay already, be straight for a day! Adapt the above guidelines, only make it clear you're heading into the closet.

Day 319

MI5 Thames House, Millbank

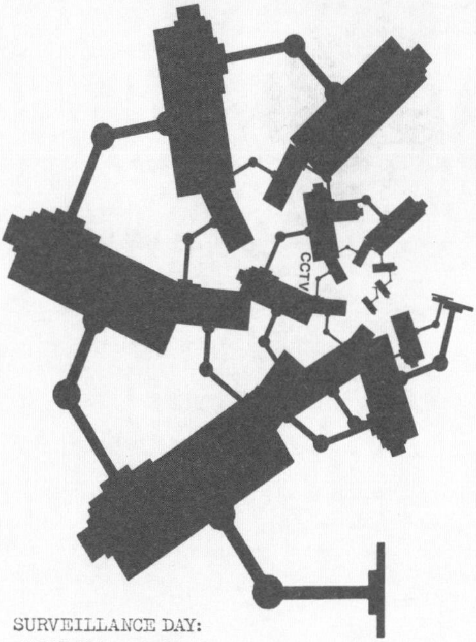
CCTV

SURVEILLANCE DAY:
WATCH THE WATCHERS

We are all under increasing surveillance, both physical and electronic. CCTV cameras are proliferating. Databases are expanding. Computers are interconnecting. This is only partly because of the threat from Al Qaeda, which has acted as a convenient catalyst for technology- and market-driven intrusion into our private lives that would have occurred anyway - albeit at a slower pace and with more public resistance. The question, as ever, is how to prevent gross abuse of the system: who is watching those who watch us? Today, it's time to turn the tables: pick a state surveillant as they leave work and tail them for the rest of the day.

TAILING TECHNIQUES

1. PLAN AHEAD Spend time investigating the area around the state surveillant's workplace. Plan possible routes, get to know the local tube station's exits and entrances, learn to avoid CCTV cameras.

2. COME PREPARED Bring the standard surveillance equipment: stills camera, video camera, notepad, local map, compass and binoculars. Use your equipment with discretion: staring at someone through binoculars may look suspicious to passers-by or the state surveillant's next-door neighbours.

3. MAINTAIN YOUR DISTANCE Pick a stakeout spot fifty yards away from the state surveillant's work exit, and start shadowing them as they emerge. Adjust your distance according to the crowd: hang back if there are few people around ("loose tail"), move in if the crowd is dense ("tight tail"). Follow them until you know where they live.

4. AVOID DIRECT EYE CONTACT Eye contact makes it easier for the state surveillant to remember you and realize they are being tailed. Do not divert your gaze either, as that looks suspicious. Instead, focus on a point beyond them.

5. GATHER EVIDENCE Log your notes on your state surveillant, and gather photographic and video records of any suspicious or incriminating behaviour. Include details of where they go, who they meet, and, most importantly, who they are surveilling.

6. NEVER LOSE SIGHT OF THEM The state surveillant will be trained in evasion tactics, so assume they will try to lose you. They may suddenly enter a public building, or a cinema, or stop and turn around abruptly. Be alert - do not let them shake you off.

7. ARE YOU BEING FOLLOWED? The state's tentacles are everywhere. As you make progress in your surveillance, you may come to their attention. If you think the state apparatus is onto you, destroy the evidence asap and flee the country before they take you in. Good luck.

EVERYONE HAS A FAVOURITE DINOSAUR

Go to your local natural history museum and make sure yours is properly displayed

Day 321

TODAY, RAISE MONEY FOR A BAD CAUSE*

THE CHILDREN OF IRAN

are running out of enriched uranium! Without it, they stand no chance against Western imperialistic aggression! They

NEED TO BE PROTECTED

against the Great Satan and Britain its fascist poodle!

£2 A MONTH

will buy enough weapons-grade uranium to protect five children. Thank you.

North Korea suffers from a shortage of state-trained psychiatrists.

MENTAL ILLNESS

is thus rife, with many hundreds of thousands suffering from paranoid doubts about our Great Leader.

IN NORTH KOREA

there is no room for doubt! Donate now to help us reinforce our political re-education programme.

PLEASE HELP!

ALASKAN NATURE FUND

The Alaskan soil contains billions of barrels of oil which the world badly needs, yet tree- and glacier-hugging "environmentalists" are trying to prevent us from extracting them.

HELP US SAVE

all this good oil from going to waste by funding a nationwide advertising and lobbying campaign. After all,

THIS BEAUTIFUL UNSPOILT WILDERNESS

is no good to anyone if you can't drive there, right?

ANGOLAN LANDMINES

are fast becoming obsolete. Within five years, few of them will detonate at all. Help us

GIVE HOPE TO

those who profit from them and from the conflicts they help perpetuate. £50 a month will help plant

A WHOLE NEW GENERATION

of more effective mines in rebel areas.

*and teach people to read the small print for a change

Eating with mouth open

Interrupting

Pointing at people

Breach of dinner party etiquette

Wearing clashing colours

Lateness

Jaywalking

Littering

Swearing in public

Theft (under £1,000)

Theft (over £1,000)

Money laundering

Arson, murder, manslaughter

STONE PEOPLE YOU DISAPPROVE OF TODAY

Stoning gets a bad press, mainly because it seems to be applied without due proportionality: one stone fits all. Yet it can be a very effective way of enforcing social norms, and is so much cheaper than resorting to the courts. The key is to use the right size of stone. Here is a rough guide.

Incest, cannibalism, taboo violations

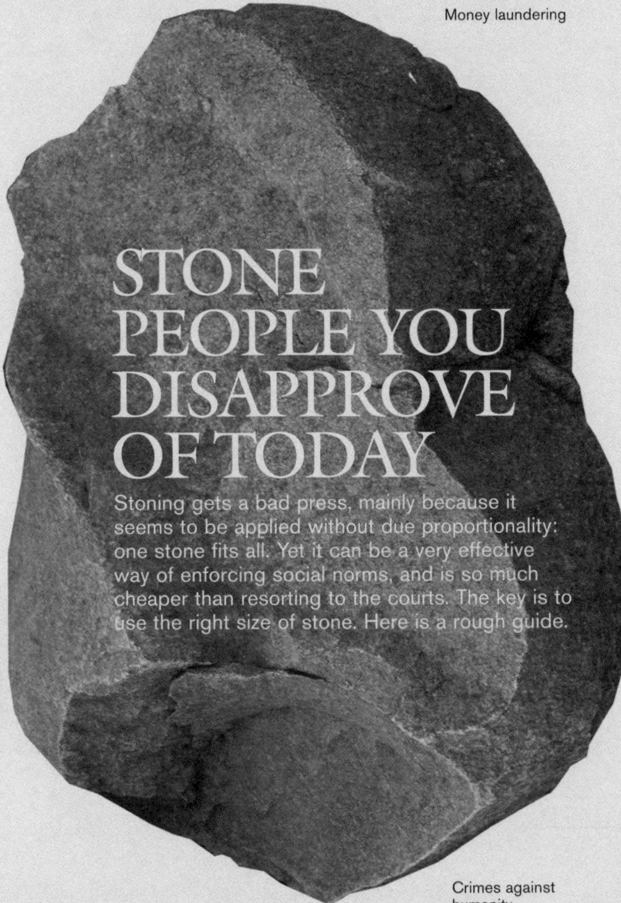
Crimes against humanity

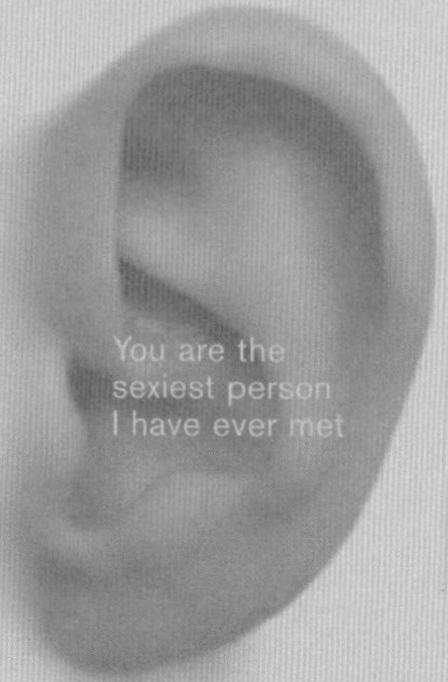
You are the
sexiest person
I have ever met

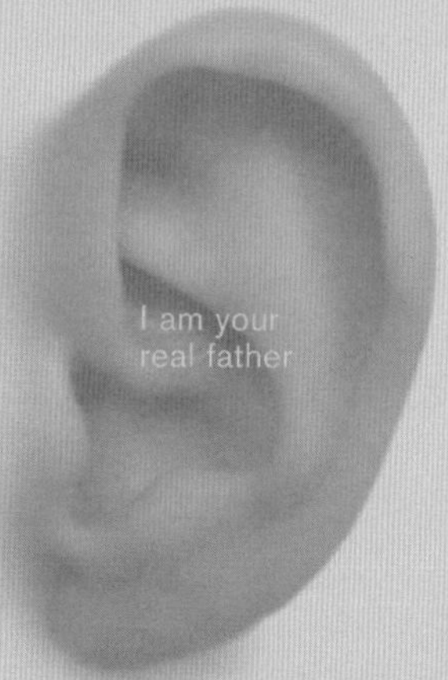
I am your
real father

You remind
me of Pol Pot

Today tell someone something they will never forget

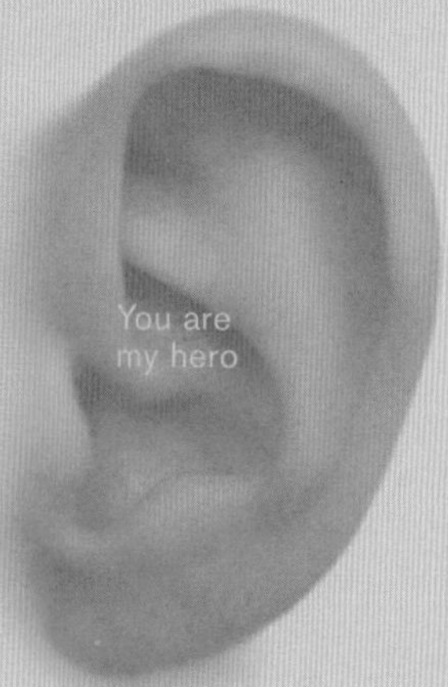
You are
my hero

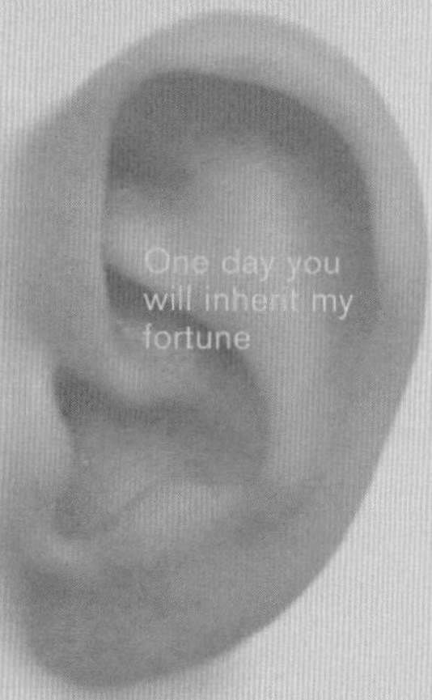
One day you
will inherit my
fortune

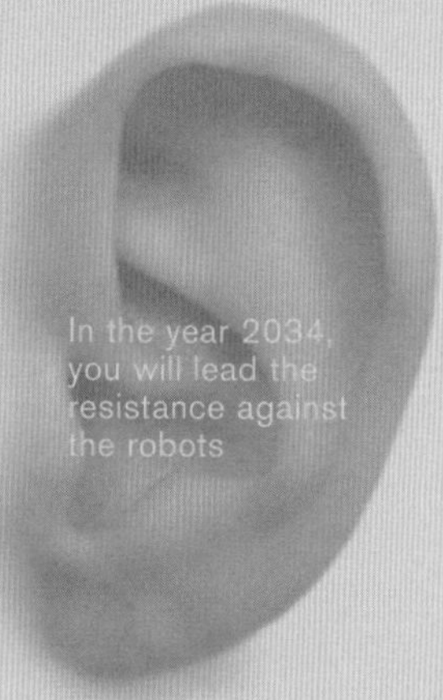
In the year 2034,
you will lead the
resistance against
the robots

Today, make friends with an insect

Animals are easy to love – they are close to us in the evolutionary tree. Insects, however, evoke a preconscious feeling of revulsion. Test the limits and the nature of your capacity for affection today, by learning to love an individual insect.

1. CATCH YOUR INSECT: Get off to a good start by being gentle.
Fly.......................... ☐
Spider....................... ☐
Ant.......................... ☐
Caterpillar.................. ☐
Not sure what the hell it is... ☐

2. NAME YOUR INSECT: This will help anthropomorphize it.
Derek........................ ☐
John......................... ☐
Michael...................... ☐
Cecilia...................... ☐
Rowan........................ ☐
Eva.......................... ☐
Other:....................... ☐

3. FEED YOUR INSECT: True friends share their food.

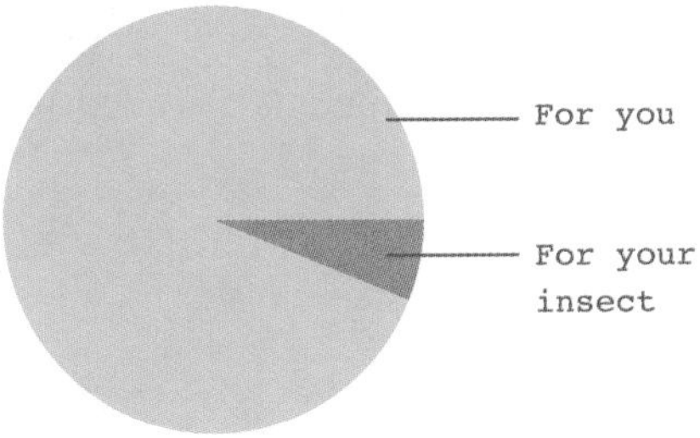
For you
For your insect

4. HANG OUT WITH YOUR INSECT: Learn what's unique about their insect personality.
Inquisitive.................. ☐
Outgoing..................... ☐
Introvert.................... ☐
Sociable..................... ☐
Thoughtful................... ☐

LOVE YOUR INSECT: By now you know each other, so have a nice cuddle.
YOU:
Enjoyed the cuddle............ ☐
Didn't enjoy the cuddle......... ☐
INSECT:
Enjoyed the cuddle............ ☐
Didn't enjoy the cuddle......... ☐

KILL YOUR INSECT: If you can't, then you have grown attached to it, bravo.
I couldn't bring myself to kill it.................. ☐
I stamped on it............... ☐
I swatted it.................. ☐
I sprayed it.................. ☐

NOW APPLY WHAT YOU HAVE LEARNT TO HUMAN BEINGS.

"You may look disgusting but I love you darling!"

Today go dogging as a Jehovah's Witness

Top dogging spots in the UK

Dogging is the latest sin, involving strangers meeting up at night in motorway laybys or country lanes and watching each other have sex. Participation is possible, subject to strict etiquette. Flashing your headlights or leaving the inside lights on invites voyeurs. Rolling the windows down invites participation. As a Jehovah's Witness, you must spread the word of God to these heathens who need it sorely. You may either approach the voyeurs gathered around a car, or the people making out inside. Acceptable opening gambits include: "Can I talk to you about Jesus?", "Adam and Eve were the original doggers you know", "Repent ye sinners!" and "Do you come here often?" Don't forget to provide some relevant literature.

Day 326

Today work out how many seconds you have left to live

Formula: Average life expectancy 78-your age x 31,536,000

Now plan for each one of them.

987761208
735556478
901739999
092687 sec

1 sec
2 sec
3 sec
Time is running out my friend!

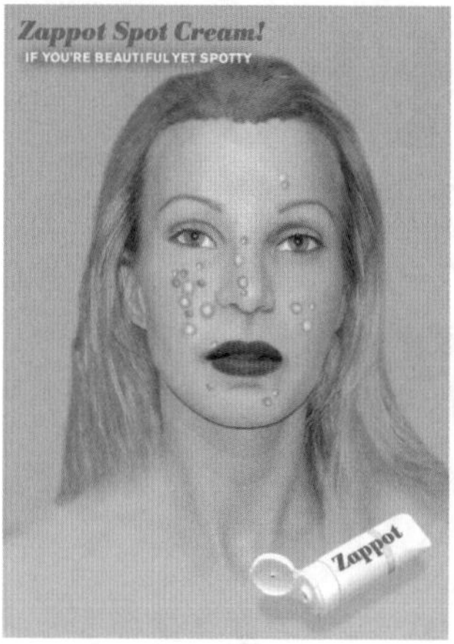
Zappot Spot Cream!
IF YOU'RE BEAUTIFUL YET SPOTTY
Zappot

Whitex
Toothpaste!
If you have great teeth

unt Edna's
hick Soup
If you have a thick mustache

COULD YOU BE THE FACE OF...

Today think of the brand you could be a great spokesperson for, and contact them to become rich.

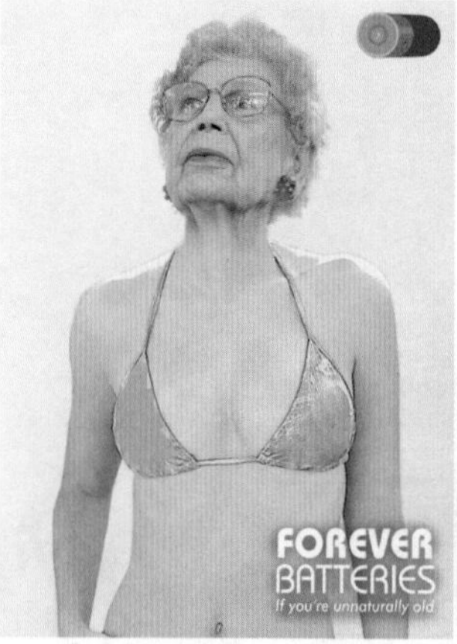
FOREVER
BATTERIES
If you're unnaturally old

YUMYUM
CHOCOLATE
YUMYUM
IF YOU'RE FAT BUT HAPPY

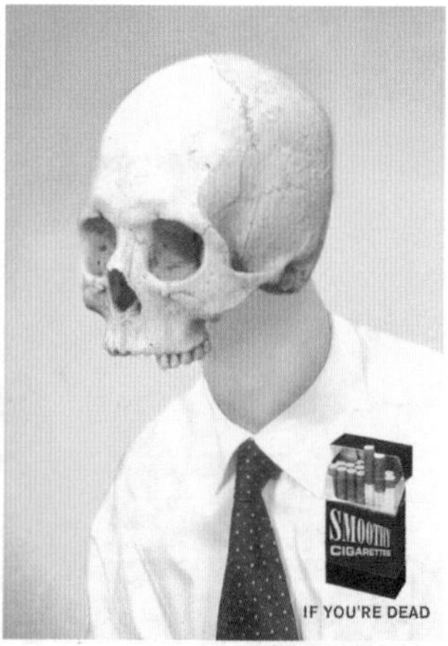
IF YOU'RE DEAD

Pretend you're a doctor today

"Trust me, I'm a doctor" is one of the most comforting phrases in the English language – and one of the most easily abused. Seek out a medical emergency today, muster up any acting talent you may possess, and do your best for the unfortunate victim. Who knows, you may be a natural at this whole "saving lives" palaver. To help, we provide professional medical guidelines for the treatment of a number of common emergency cases. Memorize them and say them out loud as you work on the patient. This will help you establish credibility.

Case 1: Pedestrian knocked over by car

Toot toot

Treatment: Traumatic Brain Surgery

Identify potential intracranial surgical lesions for possible emergent craniotomy. Maintain cerebral perfusion pressure (CPP) and oxygenation. Prevent hypoxemia: maintain O2 sat > 92%, PaO2 > 100, and intubate for GCS < 8. Prevent hypotension: maintain SBP > 100 mm Hg, MAP > 80. MAP = DBP + 1/3 (SBP - DBP). Prevent, monitor, and treat intracranial hypertension. Maintain intracranial pressure (ICP) = 5–15 mm Hg. Maintain CPP = 70–90 mm Hg. High levels of PEEP may raise ICP. Check serum sodium and keep in the range of 145–150 mEq/dL. IV mannitol (not in anuric patients), 0.25–1.0 g/kg, every 6–8 hours to keep serum osmolarity optimal. Hypercarbia should always be prevented. Beneficial effects of hyperventilation/hypocarbia must be balanced: it reduces ICP through vasoconstriction, but also reduces cerebral blood flow. Prophylactic hyperventilation should not be used. Removal of cerebrospinal fluid by placement of an intraventricular catheter. Perform craniotomy with bone and brain removal as life-saving procedure of last resort in the moribund patient.

Case 2: Woman starts contractions on public transport

STOP DA BUS!

Treatment: Emergency Delivery

Supplies needed: povidone-iodine, 10 cc syringe, lidocaine, 2 clamps, ring forceps. Clean perineum with sterile solution. If patient's first delivery, perineum should be anesthetized with lidocaine in case an episiotomy is needed. There is little support for prophylactic episiotomy, but may be necessary if the fetus is large, or tearing occurs. If an episiotomy is needed, cut in the posterior midline from the vaginal opening approx. 1/2 the length of perineum, and extend about 2–3 cm into vagina. After delivery of head, mouth and nose must be suctioned and neck palpated for evidence of a nuchal cord. Place hands along the parietal bones to allow delivery of the anterior shoulder. Downward traction should allow shoulder to clear pubis, and fetus should be directed anteriorly for delivery of the posterior shoulder. Delivery of the placenta by uterine fundal elevation, lengthening of the cord, and a gush of blood. Start patient on infusion of lactated Ringers with 20 units of oxytocin. Oxytocin can also be given IM if there is no IV access. If no oxytocin available, alternatives are methylergonovine maleate 0.2 mg intramuscular (IM).

Case 3: Man has heart attack on plane

Treatment: Angioplasty

The diagnosis of an acute myocardial event is made by the presence of ST segment elevation or depression on 12-leak ECG and/or an abnormal elevation of serum markers of myocardial injury (myoglobin [MB] fraction of creatine phosphokinase, Troponin I). Supplemental O2, Morphine, Aspirin 325 mg tablet, NTG SL (0.4 mg tablet every 5 minutes until pain relieved, maximum 3 doses) or IV infusion. Administer beta-blocker: push 5–15 mg IV slowly q6h or 50–100 mg q12h of Mitoprolol or Ytenol (50–100 mg) to help to maintain cardiac rhythm. Start compressions. Open intubation tray. Titrate morphine. Inject Heparin anticoagulant. Administer Nitro drips by IV infusion. Use Lidocaine (for arrhythmia), or Pricainomide. Administer thrombolytic tissue plasminogen activator Tinoctoplase. Perform endotracheal intubation. Move to shock treatment if no response.

Bedside manner: the way you handle your patient can determine how quickly they recover. Current best practice includes: a) asserting your authority swiftly – shush the patient and their family as you make your diagnosis; b) understanding the patient's hidden fear – don't listen to what they say, listen to what they're not saying, then make them say it; c) establishing a bond of trust – betting hard cash on your diagnosis reassures patients that you're confident in your own judgement. A great doctor is a placebo: doesn't do much but cures all the same.

TODAY PRO-POSE TO A COMPLETE ST-RAN-GER!

Hi! You don't know me but can I just say how handsome/ beautiful you look. You seem like a really nice person too. I'm usually good at telling these things. Will you marry me?

DID THEY SAY YES? HERE'S A QUICK GUIDE TO ELOPING: Marriage licences can be obtained in about 15 to 20 minutes at the marriage licensing bureau in Las Vegas. Victoria Sanchez, deputy clerk of Las Vegas marriage licensing bureau, said 99,310 couples received marriage licences in Las Vegas last year, which is 12,702 more than 1994. A driver's licence and $35 are all that is needed for a marriage licence. Both parties must be 18 or above or have a parent's consent, she said.

Arrive three quarters of an hour late for everything today

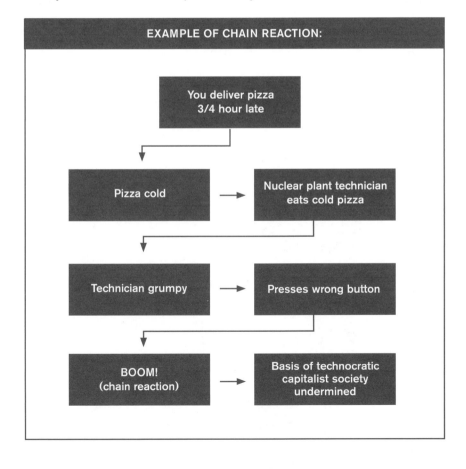

Punctuality is the thief of time. Sabotage everyone's attempts at it today by running late for any meetings, thus setting off a chain reaction that will undermine the very basis of technocratic capitalist society.

EXAMPLE OF CHAIN REACTION:

You deliver pizza 3/4 hour late

↓

Pizza cold → Nuclear plant technician eats cold pizza

↓

Technician grumpy → Presses wrong button

↓

BOOM! (chain reaction) → Basis of technocratic capitalist society undermined

Obey your elders and betters today

Most human societies cherish and respect the wisdom of their oldest members; the elders are chiefs, leaders, high priests. Western society, however, consigns them to quiet retirement homes and social irrelevance. Reverse this sad state of affairs today: let none of us make a single decision without consulting someone over the age of 70. Call any family members over 70 first; the older and more experienced, the better. If you have none, email one of these retirement homes and respectfully ask that they forward your question to a senior citizen.

BUSINESS DECISIONS
Mount Olivet Nursing Home, Devon
(mountolivet@grayareas.co.uk)

MEDICAL DECISIONS
Buxton Lodge Nursing Home, Surrey
(care@buxtonlodge.co.uk)

MILITARY DECISIONS
Taymer Nursing Home, Bedfordshire
(matron@taymer.co.uk)

ROMANTIC DECISIONS
All Hallows, Suffolk
(admin@allhallowsnursinghome.org.uk)

SCIENTIFIC DECISIONS
Villa Maria, Melbourne, Australia
(villamaria@villamaria.com.au)

POLITICAL DECISIONS
Kestrel Grove, Hertfordshire
(home@kestrelgrove.co.uk)

LEGAL DECISIONS
Aronal Cottage Rest & Nursing Home, West Sussex
(info@aronalcottage.co.uk)

CULTURAL DECISIONS
Haresbrook Care Centre, Worcestershire
(care.haresbrook@virgin.net)

SURVEILLANCE SPECIAL:

Littering
Drunken jostling
Mugging
Stabbing followed by mugging
Stabbing and/or Gangbeating with Mugging
Murder
(back alley CCTV only)

Today stage a crime in front of a CCTV camera and see if anyone comes to the rescue.

Day 333

Today go to the zoo and

DO
FEED THE ANIMALS

Zoo animals have a miserable time as it is, they should have the right to stuff their faces, whatever some fascist zookeeper says. Here are some of their favourite foods in the wild so you know what to take along.

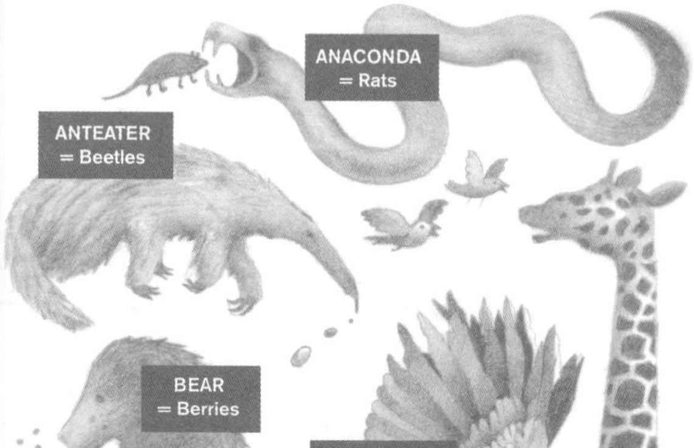
ANACONDA
= Rats
ANTEATER
= Beetles
BEAR
= Berries
BALD EAGLE
= Ice cream

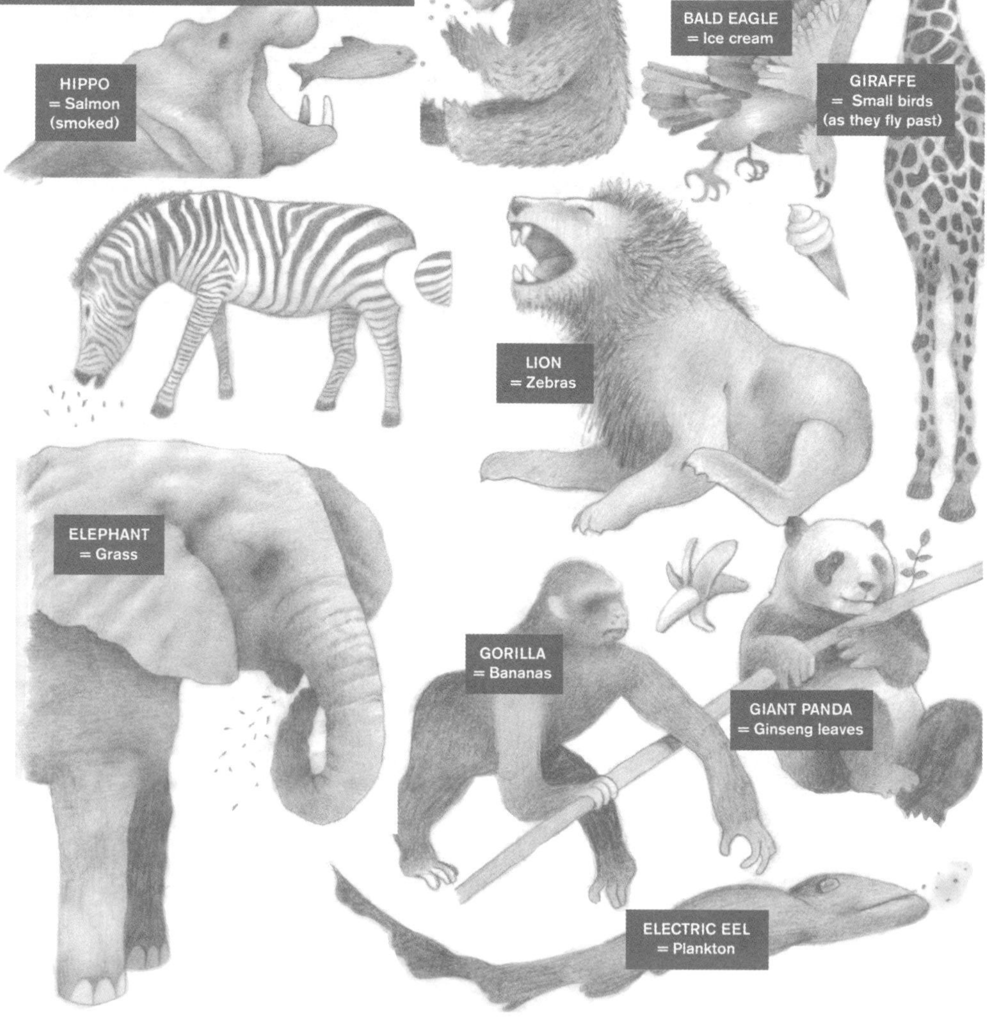
HIPPO
= Salmon
(smoked)
GIRAFFE
= Small birds
(as they fly past)
LION
= Zebras
ELEPHANT
= Grass
GORILLA
= Bananas
GIANT PANDA
= Ginseng leaves
ELECTRIC EEL
= Plankton

Become an expert on today: Read all the newspapers from A to Z and watch all the news bulletins so that by midnight tonight no one in the world knows more about the events of today than you. Here is a quick test to check your knowledge before you use it to attain unheard-of riches and power:

Weather in Zambia today:

Number of wars in progress today:

World population today:

Result of main sporting event today:

First topic on Jerry Springer today:

Middle East oil reserves today:

Number of astronauts in space today:

Lottery results in Colorado today:

Percentage of faked orgasms today:

Time spent waiting for phones to be picked up:

Moon-Earth distance at midday:

Horoscope of Leos with Scorpio ascendants:

Number of birthdays worldwide:

Congratulations: you are now the world's leading expert on today's news. Tomorrow morning be sure to get a business card printed and send it to everyone you know.

PROTEST AGAINST EVERYTHING TODAY!

DOWN WITH .... !
STOP THE .... !
SAVE THE .... !
WE WANT .... !
BAN .... IMMEDIATELY!
.... MUST RESIGN!
NO MORE .... !
WHAT DO WE WANT? .... WHEN DO WE WANT IT?
.... =MURDERER!

Here are some protest templates which you may download from www.benrik.co.uk

Protesting was much easier in the 80s, when apartheid provided an unambiguous focus for moral outrage. These days, there are thousands of causes that clamour for our attention, with no clear front-runner. The solution is not to be paralysed into apathy, but to protest against everything going. Today, consult the internet for protests in your area and join one (www.protest.net).

Day 336

Today make sure your parents know you love them.
It may seem impossible to say.
But don't wait until it is.

TODAY, APPLY TO AN ORGY

Swinging is the new clubbing. No longer the preserve of suburban housewives, the modern swinger's party is packed with beautiful young things. Would you make the grade? Apply with your photo and that of your unsuspecting partner at feverparties.com and find out if you are deemed to be acceptable orgy material.

Ask a billionaire for money today

Billionaires are happy to give money to worthy causes, like AIDS or malaria. Why shouldn't they give some to you? Write to the world's richest today asking if they could spare you just 0.01% of their fortune. It's unlikely you'll get replies from all of them, but you never know. If you don't ask, you don't get. Sample letters:

Bill Gates

Age: 53. *Marital status:* Married with 3 children
Estimated worth: $48 billion
Source of billions: Microsoft empire
Estimated generosity to complete strangers: 6/10

Dear Mr Gates,
I'm a huge huge fan of all your software products, particularly the Windows range. I use them all the time and I can honestly say they've made my working life a whole lot easier. So thanks a bunch! By the way, I read that you're into good causes and the like; could you see your way to sparing me a few millions (nothing to a man such as you)?
I would spend a lot of it on Microsoft stuff, so that way you can't lose.
Let me know and keep up the good work! Yours gratefully.

Address: c/o Microsoft, Redmond, WA 98052, USA

Ingvar Kamprad

Age: 82. *Marital status:* Married with 4 children
Estimated worth: $22 billion
Source of billions: Ikea
Estimated generosity to complete strangers: 8/10

Hallo Ingvar!
I am Swedish like you, and I have been shopping at Ikea and eating your meatballs ever since I was born. I used to love those meatballs! Though now I am a vegetarian. The furniture is still good though, especially because it is cheap. You see, living in Sweden, not like you in Switzerland, I have to pay 90% tax, and so despite my efforts, I am one of the poor. If you could give me 0.01% of your money, that would make me happy. It is probably less than I spent in your stores! Don't worry, I will not tell anyone else in Sweden. Thanx a bunch!

Address: 1066 Epalinges, Lausanne, Switzerland

Carlos Slim

Age: 72. *Marital status:* Widowed, 6 children
Estimated worth: $23 billion
Source of billions: Telecoms
Estimated generosity to complete strangers: 9/10

Hola Carlos!
I went to Mexico once in 1995 on a tour and I enjoyed your fine country immensely. Friendly people, great tequila, hot ladies, caramba as you like to say. I am now back in England where I live, and was wondering if I could bother you for a few pesos! The generosity of your people is legendary, and I'm sure you live up to it. I have modest needs: a couple of million dollars would be plenty. That's about 22 million pesos - enough to keep the margaritas flowing! Seriously though, I need it. Gracias amigo and hasta la vista!

Address: c/o Grupo Corso, Miguel de Cervantes Saavedra 255, 11520 Mexico City, Mexico

Prince Alwaleed Bin Talal Alsaud

Age: 51. *Marital status:* Married with 2 children
Estimated worth: $25 billion
Source of billions: nephew of the Saudi king
Estimated generosity to complete strangers: 6/10

Dear Excellency,
Your reputation as a kindly and giving prince, second to none, has reached my ears. Indeed, of all the Saudi princes, you are by far my favourite. I come to you with a modest plea. Your land is blessed with the black gold oil, which you have wisely used to invest in a wide variety of multinational corporations. My own land is barren, and so I was wondering if you could spare a few gallons. Or you could just transfer the cash ($2,500,000 should do the trick). Thank you and may your family prosper and your business be favoured by the Gods.

Address: c/o Kingdom Holding Company, P.O. Box 2, Riyadh 11321, Saudi Arabia

Day 339

Call someone with your telephone number but a different area code

See how long they're willing to talk about your common bond

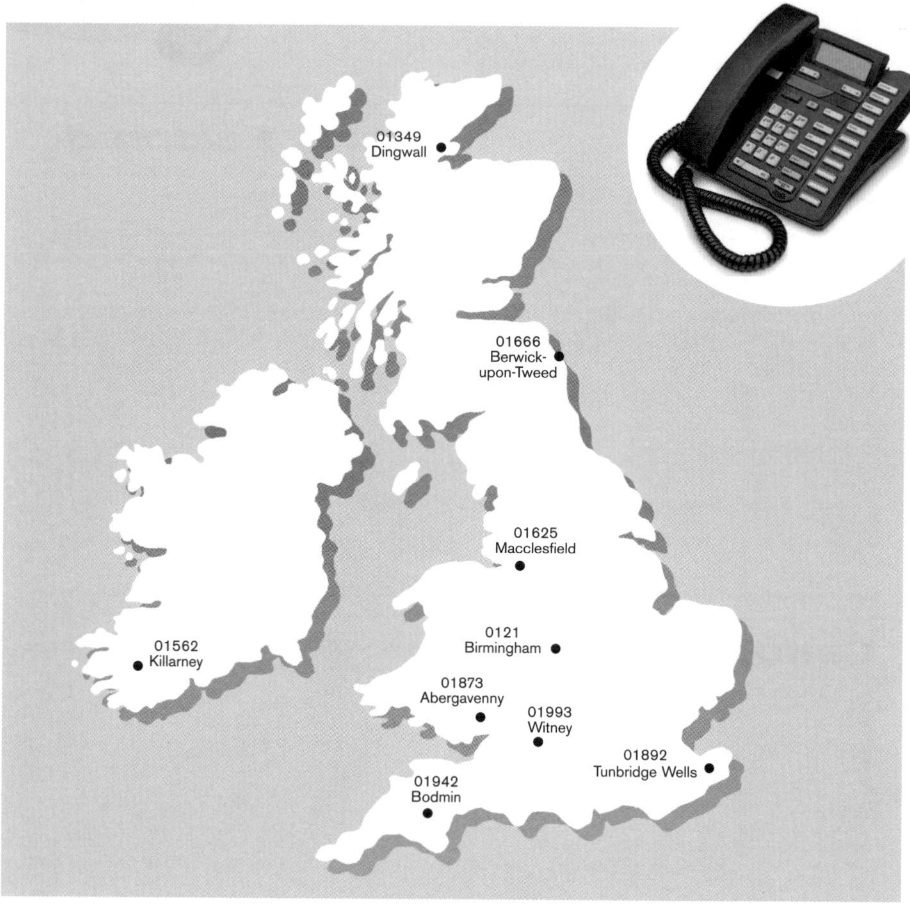
01349
Dingwall
01666
Berwick-
upon-Tweed
01625
Macclesfield
01562
Killarney
0121
Birmingham
01873
Abergavenny
01993
Witney
01892
Tunbridge Wells
01942
Bodmin

Here is a quick guide to the personality traits associated with some prominent area codes, so you can be better prepared for their reaction when you call.

01562 people are dark and mysterious. This can be difficult for loved ones, but means they are often thrilling company!

Those with area code **0121** are filled with zest for life. Meeting new people is a pleasure and a treat for them.

The people of area code **01892** are wary of strangers. For them, patience and endurance are the uppermost virtues.

Many **01349** people function on an intuitive level, and love animals and nature above all. Others are more withdrawn.

The people of area code **01942** are sometimes capable of malice, but get to know them and you will discover their softer side.

01993 area code people display huge ambition and charisma. Nothing stops them: beware those who get in the way!

Sensuality and seduction are central themes in the lives of **01666ers**. They exude a magnetic charm that few can resist...

01625 people are dominating personalities. They take up leading roles in society and mark the times they live in.

The hedonistic individuals of area code **01873** are not interested in anything beyond pleasure: all play and no work!

Wear a burka all day

Amidst the Western hysteria about various Islamic customs, find out for yourself what it is like to move about society covered from head to toe. Observe people's reactions. Witness their prejudices. Monitor your own sense of body and self, as you walk around conspicuous yet invisible. Revise your view of life accordingly.

Benrik recommend www.alhediya.com, Manufacturers and International Exporters of Quality Islamic Apparel & Products.

Day 341

SENSE-LESS DAY

Go through today without using your sense of: *touch*

HOW TO: WEAR WINTER CLOTHING – SKI GLOVES, ANORAK, CAGOULE.

True story: Bill W. lost all sense of touch in his lower left leg after a farm accident in 1977. But as he was close to retirement age, it didn't bother him too much. For a while at least. Two years later, on a cold winter morning, he was sitting in his easy chair reading his daily paper in front of the warm fire. His wife was out in the yard. His dogs were asleep in the kennel. So preoccupied was Bill W. with the day's news, that he didn't notice until alerted by the bacon-like smell that his nerveless limb had caught fire, and was charred beyond all recognition.

Stare at a single work of art for hours until you understand it fully

On the face of it, this well-known work by Algerian-born painter Khaled Reghine presents us with a straightforward narrative. Entitled Number 12, it weaves the tale of two boys who have (just?) competed in a wheelchair race. One has won and is holding the trophy. The other (the eponymous "Number 12") has lost, one of his wheels lying on the ground. Also he seems to be a werewolf. The locus is a simple one: we as spectators are enjoined to feel sympathy for No12, who holds us in his tearful gaze. Yet this deceptively simple scene conceals a web of conflicting narratives which a closer textual/pictorial interpretation will reveal. Consider the winning boy more closely. Even though he has won, he is still angry with the werewolf. Indeed, he is not only holding the trophy, but also threatening or preparing to throw it. Next to him, his mother or lover congratulates and kisses him (she is dichotomous). They stand as one pictorial mass, conjoined also to the forest, symbol of motherhood and refuge. No12, by contrast, sits alone. He is triply isolated: from the forest, from the other two, and last from us the viewers – he is stranded in the foreground of the canvas, floating in the perspectival abyss between the field of our gaze and the "grounded" plane of conifers behind him. This is a quintessentially Freudian mise-en-scène. The second boy has crossed the Oedipal bridge to the point where he is at one both with his mother (he has conquered her affection and respect) and with his lover. It is no coincidence that the pine trees in the background stretch to the sky, erect. He brandishes his trophy/penis, keen to hurt his rival with it in a display of brute testosterone-filled caveman machismo. Yet this is only one strand in this many-faceted masterpiece. For the wheelchairs provide a second key (clef) to the text. Both competitors are, it seems, disabled. They are formally similar too in that their wheels are perfectly aligned – save of course for the werewolf boy's left wheel which has come off. Many critics have sought to explain this in strictly narrative terms. Was it an accident? Did the winner push him right off the road, or even sabotage the wheelchair? Post-Marxist aficionados of Reghine in particular have found this a rich vein of analysis, positing the broken wheel as a symbol of the internal contradictions of our technocapitalist society literally coming off their axis, leaving us bereft of escape routes. All that is left to us is self-defeating faceless (numbered) struggle in a dog-eat-dog world. But this is simplistic. The true import of the wheels is to be divined at a more formal level. For the broken wheel disrupts the picture's visual field, shattering the perspective both in its positioning and through its (abnormally small) size. And this is where we intuit the force of "Number 12". The werewolf boy is doubly other: he is disabled, indeed, but beyond that

12

Number 12, by Khaled Reghine (1921-1984) (Musee De L'Art Populaire Algerien, Wahran)

he is in radical rupture with the dimensions (three) of the rest of his world, the world of the canvas. Two corresponding circles signify this, both lying flat against the viewer's eye: his lost wheel, and his moony face, grotesquely malformed by the transformation unter werewolf, that archetypal Other of our culture. He is alienated from his world, from his body, from his condition. He can no longer condone the dread illusion. He faces us directly, not merely as representation, but as mirror to our lost selves ("mon semblable, mon frère" indeed). We, like him, are pure form. He cries not at the other boy but at us and for us, for we are he, and he is us...

Cannibalism Day

Today eat part of a loved one

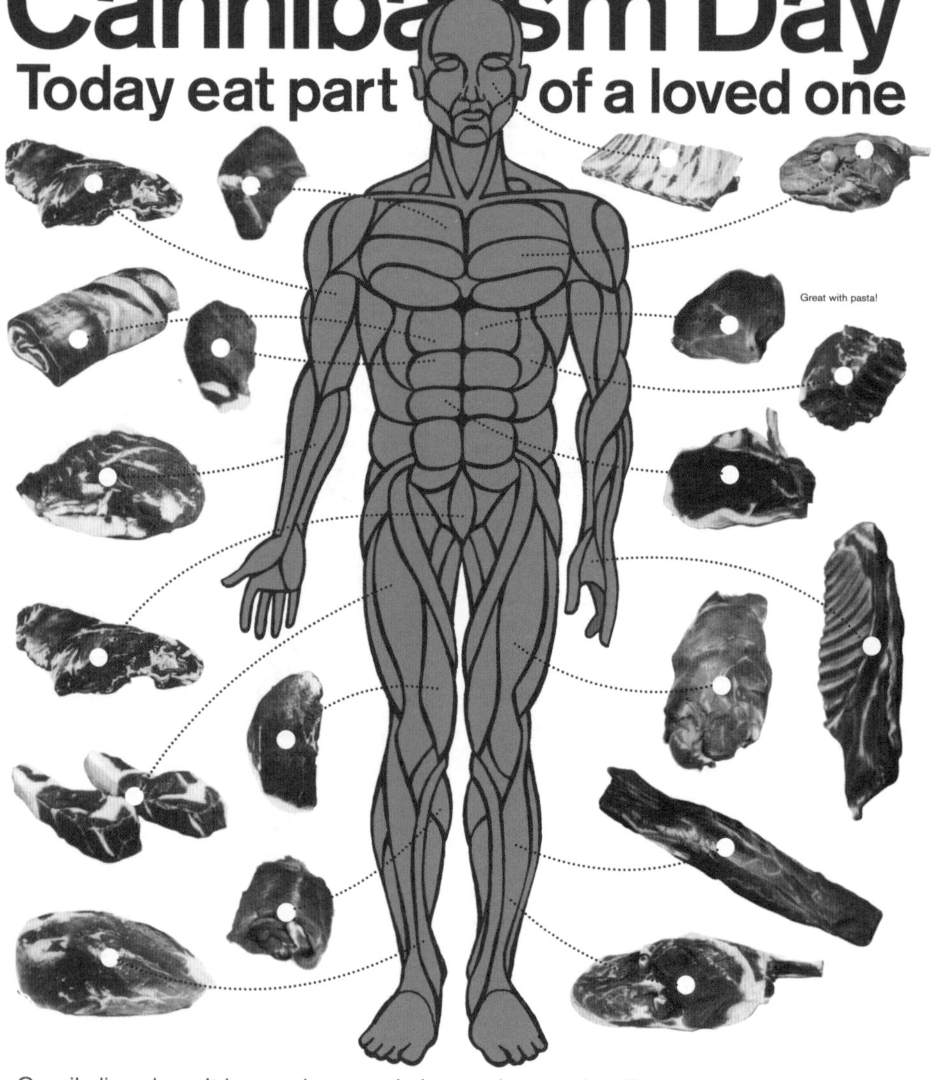
Great with pasta!

Cannibalism doesn't have to be an entirely negative practice. For some tribes such as the Amazon's Wari, eating your dead relatives is seen as an expression of affection, and much more respectful than leaving them to rot in the earth six feet under. Experience cannibalism on a beginner's scale today by eating part of your nearest and dearest: collect a lost hair, pluck out an eyelash, perhaps even clip off a fingernail and fry them up with a little garlic and lemon. You will appreciate your loved ones all the more once they have become part of you.

TODAY TALK TO A CHILD

Children are untainted by prejudice and habit. Have a proper conversation with a young child today and learn from their innocence. Topics might include: favourite colours, toys, birds, bees, granny, why people fight, belly buttons, mud (fun with).

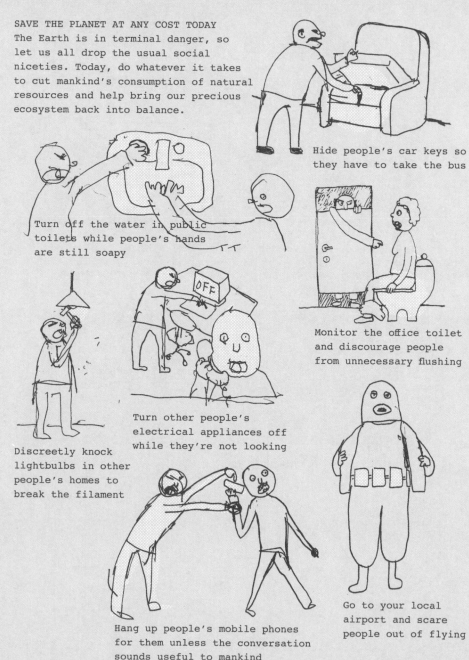

SAVE THE PLANET AT ANY COST TODAY

The Earth is in terminal danger, so let us all drop the usual social niceties. Today, do whatever it takes to cut mankind's consumption of natural resources and help bring our precious ecosystem back into balance.

Hide people's car keys so they have to take the bus

Turn off the water in public toilets while people's hands are still soapy

Monitor the office toilet and discourage people from unnecessary flushing

Discreetly knock lightbulbs in other people's homes to break the filament

OFF

Turn other people's electrical appliances off while they're not looking

Go to your local airport and scare people out of flying

Hang up people's mobile phones for them unless the conversation sounds useful to mankind

LOCAL NEWS
THE MODEL CITIZEN!!!
MAYOR CONGRATULATES HAVE-A-GO HERO
KEYS OF THE CITY ARE ONLY MODEST TOKEN OF APPRE-CIATION FOR ACHIEVEMENT
VIGILANT CITIZEN SAVES MILLIONS OF CHILDREN FROM CERTAIN DEATH
TOWN COUNCIL SAYS THANKS BY RENAMING TALLEST SKYSCRAPER
NO MORE ROOM FOR MEDALS ON JUMPER!

1

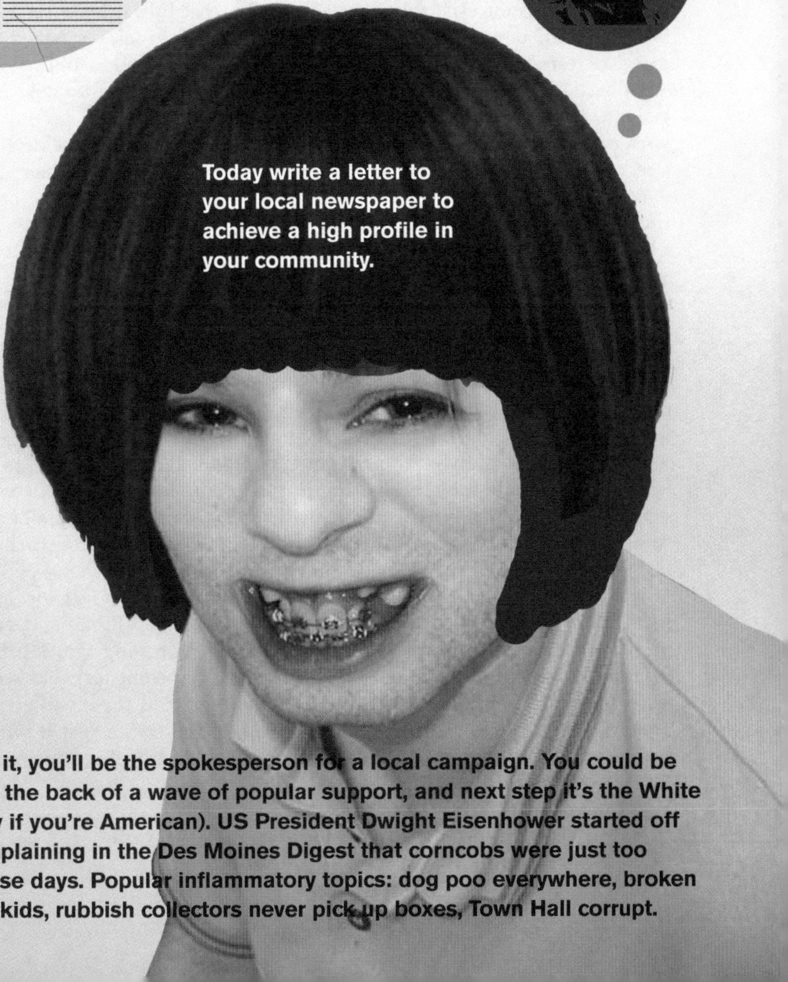

Today write a letter to your local newspaper to achieve a high profile in your community.

Before you know it, you'll be the spokesperson for a local campaign. You could be elected mayor on the back of a wave of popular support, and next step it's the White House (especially if you're American). US President Dwight Eisenhower started off in politics by complaining in the Des Moines Digest that corncobs were just too darned pricey these days. Popular inflammatory topics: dog poo everywhere, broken pavement, pesky kids, rubbish collectors never pick up boxes, Town Hall corrupt.

Today, masturbate at 13.56 to the following fantasy:

Women:

"Dark storm clouds were gathering over the Alpine mountain top as Emma finally reached the refuge. Where were the others? Where was her husband Edward? Perhaps they had fallen behind and taken the safe track back toward *St-Paul-des-Clercs* and civilization, she wondered. Well there was no point in panicking now. Night was falling fast, and she would have to spend it up here all alone at the mercy of these peaks. Exhausted, she entered the deserted cabin and barely had time to strip off her drenched clothes and slip into the thermal sleeping bag that Edward had thoughtfully given her for their sixth anniversary, before a deep slumber overtook her naked body. As even the moon retreated from the inhospitable horizon, strange and fitful dreams came upon her. She tossed and turned in the night, her feverish brow victim to wild imaginings, full of visions of werewolf-like creatures creeping around the cabin, circling, surrounding her with deep-breathing low whistles that seemed to hiss and crackle like fire?!!! Emma opened her eyes and shrieked in the empty night. There, across the room, stood the tall, dark stranger. She held her breath in terror as he looked up from the fire he had lit in the wide hearth and stared at her inscrutably. His eyes seemed to contain worlds beyond her ken. "Who – who are you? What do you want?" she cried. The man made no reply, but simply tossed another log onto the fire with barely a flicker of his powerful deep-veined forearm. He breathed in deeply, closing his eyes. Emma's voice was trembling. "Look, now, I don't know what is going on but..." He silenced her with a look from his piercing green eyes that seemed to cut right through her. Before she even realized what she was doing, Emma raced through the door in a mad dash for freedom, through the door and out into a thick curtain of rain lashing down over her exposed skin. He caught up with her easily, his strong arms grabbing her by the waist and hauling her back into the cabin. She writhed desperately in his grip until she could no more. He held her still, stared into her eyes and finally spoke in halting English, in the manner of one who seemed above words. "Don't. It is too dangerous out there for you. You are safe here with me." And somehow she knew that this was so. The fire dispensed a warm glow to the room. Before she had even recovered from the onslaught of the elements, she was trapped in an embrace as powerful as any of Nature's Furies. As the storm raged on outside, she stared into the infinite depth of his eyes. And then he was upon her, touching her deep within, roughly of course but with infinite tenderness. Suddenly lightning struck a tree nearby, while its thunder covered her animal moans. He held her tight for what seemed an eternity, until the first light of dawn broke the enchanting spell the mountain Gods had woven around them. And he was gone, as swiftly as he had come. Was it but a dream? Emma wondered wistfully, as she drifted off back to sleep smiling, her brow no longer troubled."

Men:

"Two blondes. Doing it. Together."

Shout with joy, then hug the nearest stranger and tell them you've just won the lottery. Keep it up for the rest of the day and see how many new friends you can acquire...

Submit the stuff you'd like sent along on the first human mission to Mars

Benrik have learnt that NASA are already working out what to take! Get your request in sooner rather than later. Here we present a small selection of what martians really want.

GUNS
WATER
WHAT THE MARTIANS REALLY WANT:
WATERPROOF
DVD
Sunscreen
moon BOOTS
Benrik Space Suit

NO TV TODAY!

Here are some pre-TV era activities that will feel a lot more wholesome.

WALKING
Walking is a fun activity that can be enjoyed at any age, and what's more, it's free! You can walk on your own or with someone, in the street or in the park. The possibilities are endless.

CHATTING BY THE FIRE
Everyone loves a good fire. "Round the fire" is a traditional place to chat, as everyone is gathered together. Starter topics include how well the fire is going, size of logs, how cold it must be outside.

PLAYING GAMES
There are literally dozens of games, from chess to hide-and-seek. Some of these are more advanced than others, so if you're new to games, start with something easy, like popular card game SNAP.

BIRDWATCHING
Fun AND educational. The National Parks are rich in birdlife. Look out for the yellowtailed sparrow for instance, so named after his yellow-coloured tail. To make the most of this one, binoculars are a must.

CROQUET
Not just for elderly aunts! Croquet is in fact a vicious sport where the most amiable-seeming individuals soon battle it out for supremacy. "Uncle Jo" Stalin's favourite pastime.

STARING AT THE CLOUDS
Anyone can enjoy this: all you need is a patch of sky... Clouds can assume many familiar shapes: cows, faces, goldfish, wheelbarrows. Names of clouds are fun too: "cumulo-nimbus," for instance.

WHISTLING
The great advantage of whistling is that it can be done anywhere, even while you work, as the song goes. Everyone likes a good tune, so brighten up their day as well.

SKIPPING
Beloved by schoolgirls and boxers alike, so there must be something to it. You'll need a rope and a bit of practice, but once you get the hang of it, there's no turning back!

KNITTING
One for the ladies: knitting sweaters, socks and hats is one of the most stress-relieving activities imaginable, and it's a useful skill to acquire in times of economic uncertainty.

READING
You're doing this as we speak, so you must know the basics. Hundreds of books on all sorts of topics await your perusal. Join your local library and the world of reading is your oyster.

WRESTLING
Not as difficult as it's made out to be, though you will need a partner. Grapple each other and try to push the other one to the ground. Hours of entertainment guaranteed.

CHURCHGOING
After a wrestling bout, why not settle body, mind and spirit with some church? Churchgoing has a long and proud history. This one has it all: singing, thinking, clapping.

Today think aloud all day

"Say what you think" is a common injunction in our mealy-mouthed society. Today put it into practice and let others benefit from your brain's running commentary on events.

No don't beat me Mr badger!!! Huh?! Oh it's the alarm clock. Must speak to a shrink about those dreams. What's that horrible noise? Tony snoring. God, he's really put on weight, will you look at that lump of white blubber. I'd dump him if I had the time to find someone else. Need the loo. Is it me or does my pee smell funny? Could be that asparagus stir-fry. Or thrush God I hope it's not thrush. He probably gave it to me. I bet he's sleeping around. As if. Not even a hooker would go near him. Shower. Hmmm. Soapy bubbles... I quite fancy a drink actually. Another thing to discuss with shrink. Don't forget to soap thrush away. OK, what am I going to wear? That white top again? No, boring. Oh, fuck it. Hope no one can see that stain. Is that Tony getting out of bed? I don't want to talk to him. Let's have kids soon so we don't have to talk any more. Might just get him drunk, easy enough. Let's skip breakfast, I'll get coffee at work. Bye Tony you lazy blob. Yes yes don't kiss me I'm closing the door now. Maybe I'd be happier with a dog. Less smelly. Is it going to rain? It is. It isn't. It is. It isn't. Is it? It better not. Made it! This bus shelter is full of losers. It always is. You're a loser. And so are you. Everyone is except me. And maybe that girl over there. I wonder what she does? She was on the bus yesterday. Have I seen her on TV. in an advert? Maybe maybe not. Who cares? Think about something more interesting. Me! Is this my bus? Yes. Let's get in first. That old lady was there before me. Fuck her. She shouldn't take the rush hour bus. There's a seat. Don't you dare take it you scum. Got it! Yes!!! I rock! You can look at me all you want but I'm going to stick my nose in the paper of the man next to me. What an ugly head he has! I can't even look or I'll be sick. If I'd had breakfast I'd throw it up. What's in his paper? The sports pages. Boring! Turn to the horoscope. Turn to the horoscope. Turn to the horoscope damn you! I suppose I should read my book. Only I can't be bothered. This bus is slow. Schoolkids. I hope they don't get on my bus. Except that one, he's cute. He's about 15 though. Shit, my stop's next. That old lady's in the way. I'll offer her my seat now and people will think I'm well brought-up. There you go. Buy chocolate. I'm late. I'm late. I'm late. Where's that lift? God it stinks in here, Rita from accounts must be in already. Yippee! Another day at work. Coffee. I can smell it. I need it now! Maybe with some brandy in it. No! Unhelpful thinking. Gosh! Murray's there. He's such a dish. I could lick him like a lollipop right here right now. What would he say if I did? Lick his cute little ears. Yums! Ok behave. Social interaction mode. Hi Murray can I lick your ear? Yadda yadda morning yadda report yadda yadda two sugars thanks. Here's desk. Here's boss what a cow. Your lips are moving but nothing's coming out. Yes I would mind typing this up actually I could do your job in my sleep. Anyway where's that...

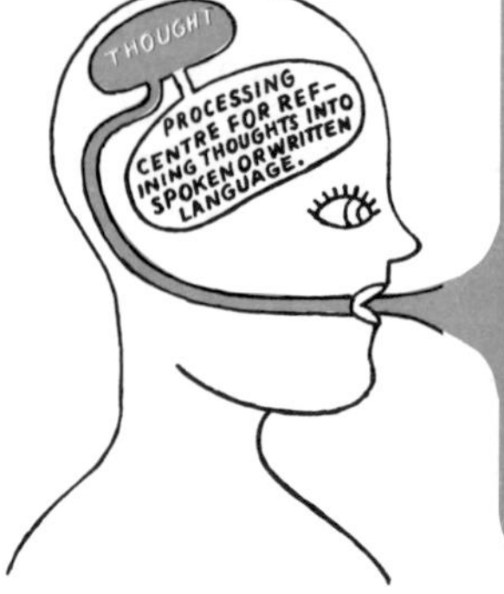
THOUGHT
PROCESSING CENTRE FOR REF-INING THOUGHTS INTO SPOKEN OR WRITTEN LANGUAGE.

TODAY, HAVE A GOOD CRY

Research has revealed that crying is good for us, indeed that it is physiologically essential. There are three different types of tears:
1. Basal tears, that keep our eyes lubricated.
2. Reflex tears, when a foreign body gets into or irritates our eyes.
3. Emotional tears, when we react psychologically to something. Emotional tears contain chemically higher levels of manganese and prolactin hormone. Losing these through crying reduces their levels in the body and keeps depression at bay. This is why we feel better after a good cry. Here are some sad thoughts to help stimulate your crying glands and cheer you up.

We're all going to die... eventually.

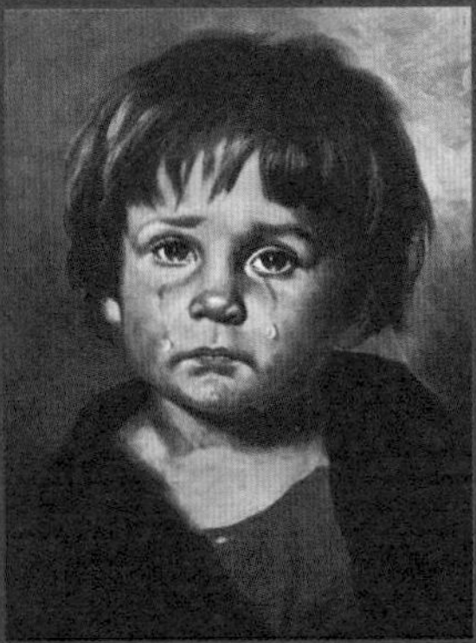

Can you ever trust anyone fully? Really?

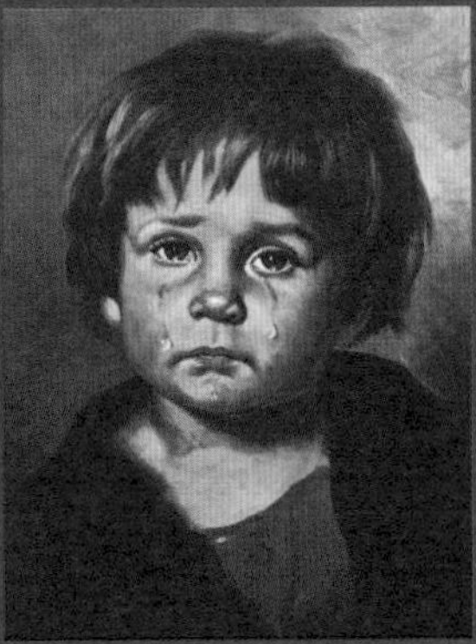

You may never meet the love of your life.

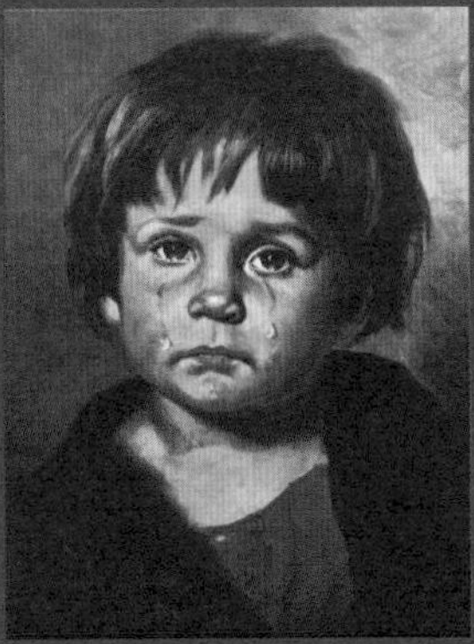

Orphans, starving.

Time is running out.

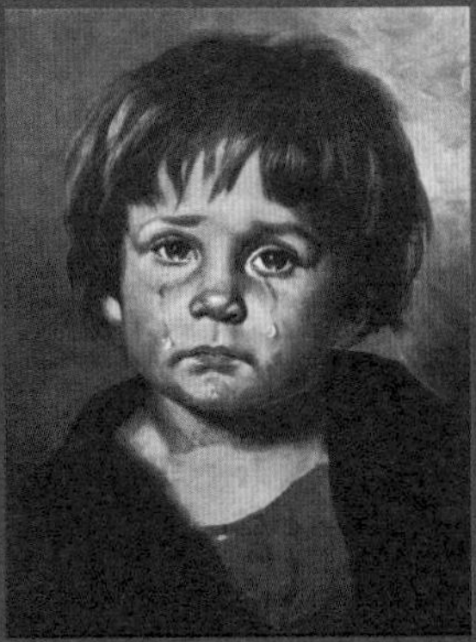

Snookums the puppy has died (horribly).

HOW POLITICALLY CORRECT IS YOUR CIRCLE OF FRIENDS?

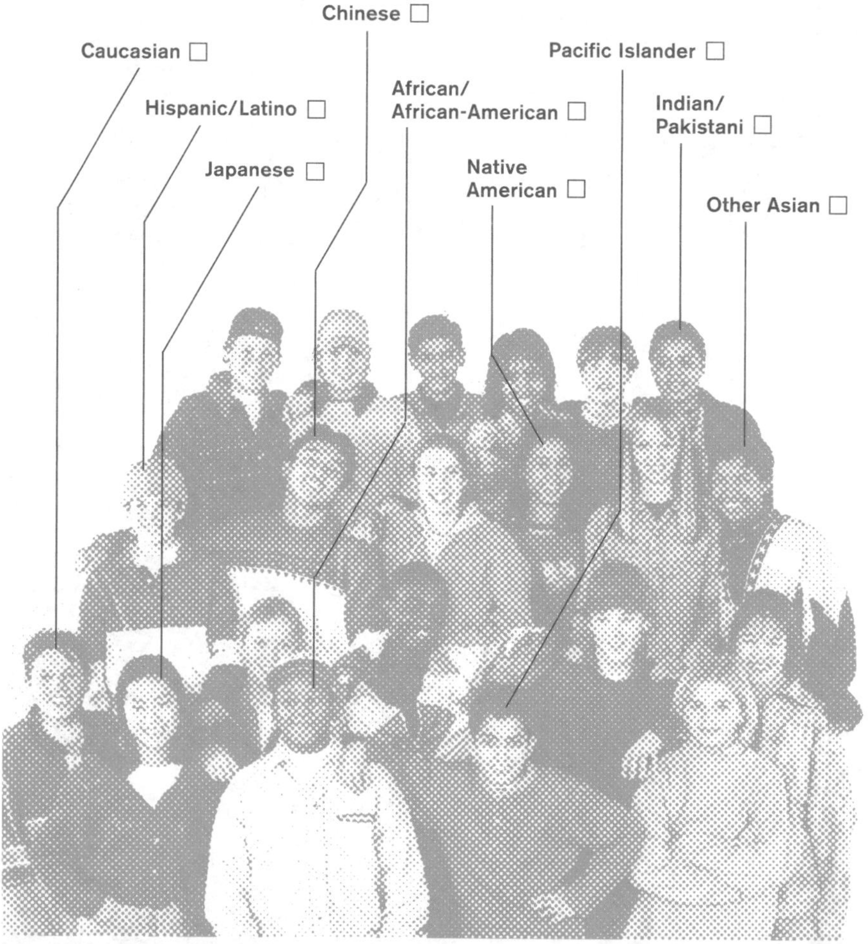
Chinese ☐
Caucasian ☐
Pacific Islander ☐
Hispanic/Latino ☐
African/
African-American ☐
Indian/
Pakistani ☐
Japanese ☐
Native
American ☐
Other Asian ☐

TODAY WORK OUT IF YOUR FRIENDS REPRESENT THE FULL TAPESTRY OF HUMAN CULTURAL AND ETHNIC VARIETY. TAKE REMEDIAL ACTION IF NOT.

Today kiss someone where they have never been kissed before

Day 355

Today test the butterfly effect: chase a butterfly away from its flight pattern to disrupt meteorological systems worldwide. The butterfly effect explained: the butterfly effect dramatically illustrates chaos theory. The idea is that very small impossible-to-measure initial changes in complex systems can have huge effects. Thus to quote Edward Lorenz, »the flap of a butterfly's wings in Brazil can set off a tornado in Texas«. Types of butterfly: *Pieris oleracea* (causes hurricanes in Southern China), *Colias philodice* (causes rainbows over Northampton), *Feniseca tarquinius* (causes freak flooding in Beirut), *Erora laeta* (causes early morning mist in Central Park), *Plebeius saepiolus* (causes sun storms on Jupiter).

TODAY HIRE A PROSTITUTE FOR A NON-SEXUAL PURPOSE: Prostitutes see a different side of life. Today, hire one for a couple of hours and ask her to fill you in on the sleazier aspects of the human condition. Prostitutes are tired of the constant sex, and will welcome the opportunity for more varied activity. Good activities to enjoy with your prostitute:

VISIT THE BRITISH MUSEUM: Prostitution is the oldest job in the world, so many of the artefacts here will relate to it.

SEE A CHICK FLICK: Prostitutes see men as they really are, and will be able to shed light on the plot's verisimilitude.

GO TO THE GYM TOGETHER: Staying in shape is a must; your prostitute should be able to double as a personal trainer.

PLAY CHESS: Just so you can tell your grandchildren that you were once beaten at chess by a prostitute grandmaster.

SHOP FOR LINGERIE: The prostitute will advise you as to the latest fashions for your wife/girlfriend.

WATCH THE SUNSET: Prostitutes don't get asked to do this much, and it should prompt a bout of revealing introspection.

Rates: The going rate for two hours might average £200, depending on the class of prostitute. If you can't afford £200, try negotiating a shorter time, like £10 for a quick chat over a cup of tea. Female readers may hire a gigolo today if they prefer. However: remember that the purpose of this task is to understand the sleazier side of humanity, which female prostitutes obviously see a lot more of.

The individuals depicted here are models, and not prostitutes or their clients. They have been chosen to make the point that prostitutes look entirely homely when not on the job.

Count your blessings: In the great hubbub of life, we often forget to pause and consider how lucky we are. Today, assess this scientifically.

Blessing	Score	Total
Are you alive?	10 points	
Are you in good health?	9 points	
Do you have a partner?	7 points	
Do you have regular sex?	6 points	
Do you have children?	3 points/child (-3 points per naughty child)	
Do you have a roof over your head?	5 points	
Can you feed yourself and your family?	5 points	
Do you have a steady job?	3 points	
Are you free from racial or sexual discrimination?	5 points	
Is your country currently at peace?	6 points	
Is your country well away from any fault lines?	6 points	
Are your parents still alive?	4 points	
Are you still on speaking terms with them?	4 points	
Have you found God?	3 points	
Have you found yourself?	2 points	
Are your bowel movements regular?	8 points	
Were you born into one of the richer social classes?	5 points	
Are you a born optimist?	6 points	
Are you a born pessimist?	−6 points	
Do you have a sense of humour?	(+1 points if you replied yes +4 points if you replied no)	
Total		

If you have scored more than 40 points, you are luckier than 90% of the human race. Congratulations.

Send a drink over to someone today

Do not send it to someone if they are with their partner.

MILK

It is traditional to send over drinks with alcoholic content only.

Wait until they raise their glass at you, then nod at them knowingly.

Do not send a drink over to someone already visibly drunk.

If they raise their glass at someone else, have the waiter fired.

If they send it back, they probably wouldn't have slept with you anyway.

Everything has a price: today, find out what it is

Go up to people and ask them how much they would require to part with their much-prized possessions, there and then. Here is a rough guide to the going rates.

£5

Selling you their unfinished coffee

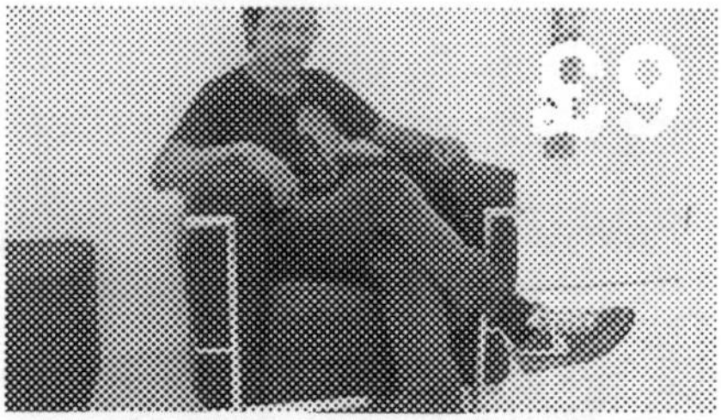
£9

Selling you their left sock

£6

Selling you a mouthful of their three-course lunch

Bookprice+
£10

Selling you the book they're reading

£1200

Selling you their pet

£35

Selling you their umbrella in a downpour

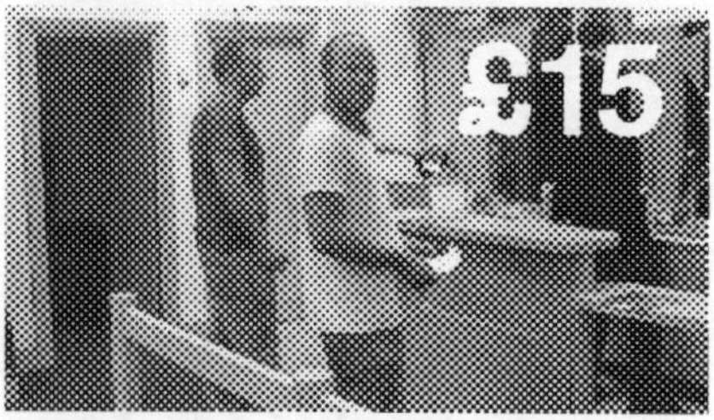
£15

Selling you their place in the queue

Negotiable

Selling you their soul

TRY SEDUCING SOMEONE WAY OUT OF YOUR LEAGUE

Most people's idea of what's attractive is imprinted on the brain when they're still in nappies. Staring up at Mummy, Daddy or Uncle Barnaby, we develop attachments to particular features that bear little relation to social norms of beauty. That's why supermodels sometimes end up going out with prime candidates for cosmetic surgery. Today, try your luck with somebody much more conventionally attractive than yourself.

YOU NEVER KNOW...

Today pre-sell your memoirs based on your spectacular future achievements

12a Shrubland Rd
Sutton SN1 1WB
London, England

Dear Mister/Madam Publisher,

This is a once-in-a-lifetime opportunity for you to buy my memoirs.

I am Bert Brown, and if you haven't heard of me yet, you sure will! At the present moment I am 29 years of age. In the next ten years, it is my intention to: climb Mt Everest naked, marry a Hollywood actress (identity to be confirmed), interview the head of the Chinese secret police, and become a chess champion.

After that, in my forties, my plan is to regroup Van Halen with me as drummer, cure cancer of the pancreas (I know someone who had it) and enter the political arena.

My plans for my fifties are a little hazy as it's still a while to go, but I reckon something to do with the Moon (we will live in space by then don't forget), divorce a famous actress (identity to be confirmed), and become a champion of the oppressed, possibly within the UN if that august international body still exists.

So you see my life will make a GREAT book of memoirs, which I am offering to YOU now. I want £100,000 for it, not a penny less. You have 24 hours or I'm off to your rivals.

Yours
Bert Brown
(Author)

PRIMAL SCREAM DAY

GET IT OUT OF YOUR SYSTEM, GO ON,
LET LOOSE BABY OH YEAH!!!!!!!!!!!!!!!!!!!!!!!!!!!!!!!!!!!

THE FOUR TYPES OF SCREAM:
1) YEEEEAAARRRGGHH!!!!!!!!!!!!!!!!!!!!!
2) RAAAAAHHHHHHRGH!!!!!!!!!!!!!!!!!
3) WHOOOOOOOOOOARRRRR!!!!!!!!!!!!!!!!!!!
4) EEEEEEEEKKK!!!!!!!!!(WOMEN ONLY)

Today kill a commercial

TV advertising may indeed create unnecessary wants, but more crucially, most of it is patronizingly brain-dead. Commercials hold up a funfair mirror to society, leading us to conclude that people are stupider than in reality. By targeting the lowest common denominator, this cheerful garbage lowers collective self-esteem and quality of life, not to mention the average IQ. Today, Benrik readers are to join together, vote on the most insulting current commercial, and complain to get it taken off air. Visit www.benrik.co.uk to vote in your country!

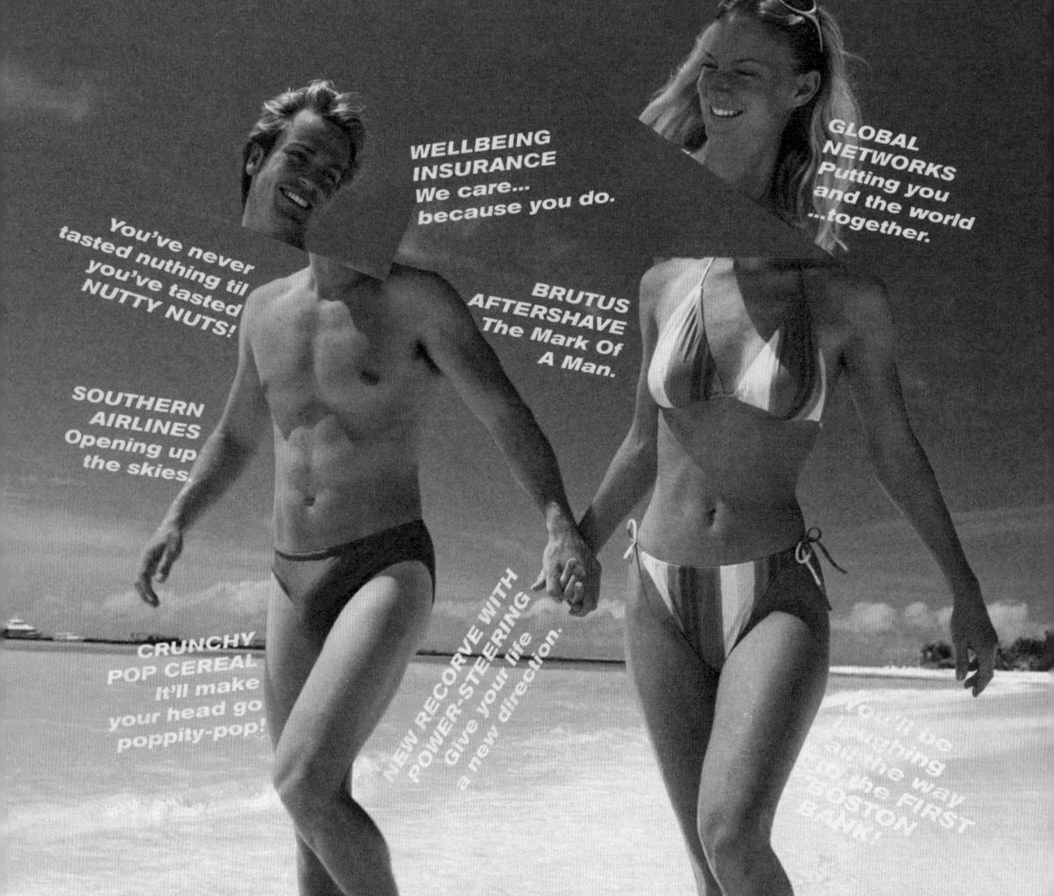
WELLBEING INSURANCE We care... because you do.
GLOBAL NETWORKS Putting you and the world ...together.
You've never tasted nuthing til you've tasted NUTTY NUTS!
BRUTUS AFTERSHAVE The Mark Of A Man.
SOUTHERN AIRLINES Opening up the skies.
CRUNCHY POP CEREAL It'll make your head go poppity-pop!
NEW RECORVE WITH POWER-STEERING Give your life a new direction.
You'll be laughing all the way to the FIRST BOSTON BANK!

These are the relevant bodies to complain to. Write a calm, convincing letter outlining the reasons for your complaint, and explaining why the commercial is insulting your intelligence and should be banned forthwith. NB They usually receive a few dozen complaints at the most. Thousands will prove effective.

UK: Advertising Standards Authority, Mid City Place, 71 High Holborn, London WC1V 6QT
AUSTRALIA: The Advertising Standards Bureau, Level 2, 97 Northbourne Avenue, Turner ACT 2612
CANADA: Advertising Standards Canada, 175 Bloor Street East, South Tower, Suite 1801, Toronto, Ontario M4W 3R8
SOUTH AFRICA: Advertising Standards Authority, P.O. Box 41555, Craighall, Johannesburg 2024
NEW ZEALAND: Advertising Standards Complaints Board, P.O. Box 10675, Wellington
PORTUGAL: Instituto Civil da Autodisciplina da Publicida (ICAP), R. Gregorio Lopes, Lote 1515, Loja 6, 1400-408, Lisbon

ALL OR NOTHING DAY:

TODAY GAMBLE EVERYTHING YOU HAVE

NO RISK, NO REWARD...

Ten commandments of casino gambling
1 – Thou shalt expect to lose.
2 – Thou shalt trust the odds, not hunches.
3 – Thou shalt not over-bet thy bankroll.
4 – Thou shalt not believe in betting systems.
5 – Thou shalt not hedge thy bets.
6 – Thou shalt covet good rules.
7 – Thou shalt not make side bets.
8 – Thou shalt have good gambling etiquette.
9 – Thou shalt honor thy gambling debts.
10 – Thou shalt tip.

DON'T LET THE AMERICAN DREAM SLIP AWAY! TODAY, SELL YOUR HOUSE, PAWN THE TV, MAX OUT YOUR CREDIT CARDS – AND ROLL THE DICE ON YOUR CASH!

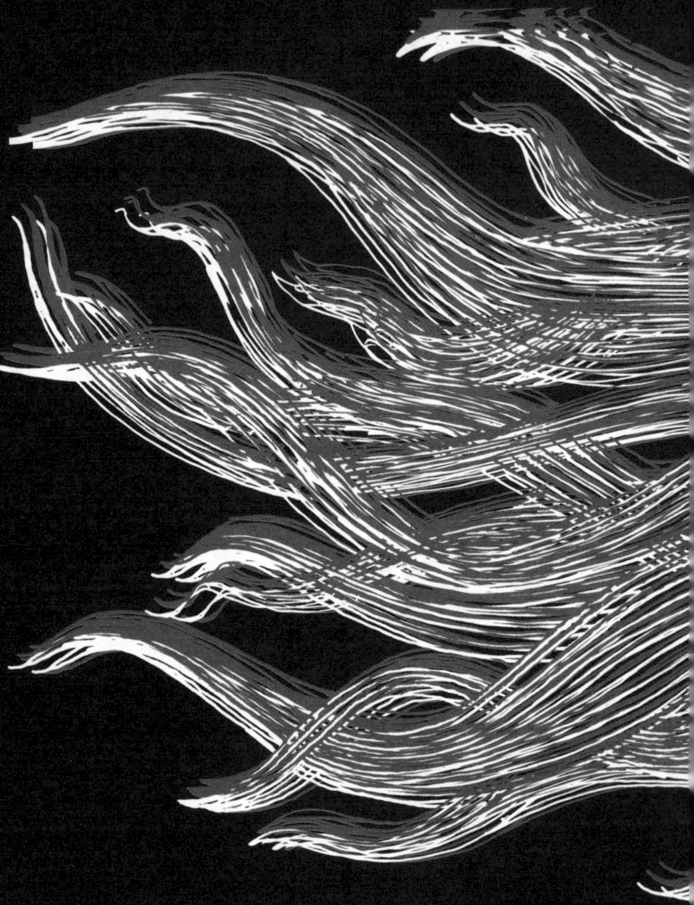

Burn this book publicly today

Well done! If you have followed each task so far, you will have left behind the ugly, hairy larva that you were a year ago, and become a beautiful butterfly. As you prepare to spread your wings and fly into the future, put your past life behind you symbolically – by burning this Book in public. No need to explain to passers-by; they wouldn't understand anyway. Stand to attention as it disappears up in smoke, and contemplate the new you.

THIS BOOK WILL CHANGE YOUR LIFE
The Best of This Diary Will Change Your Life

Covers

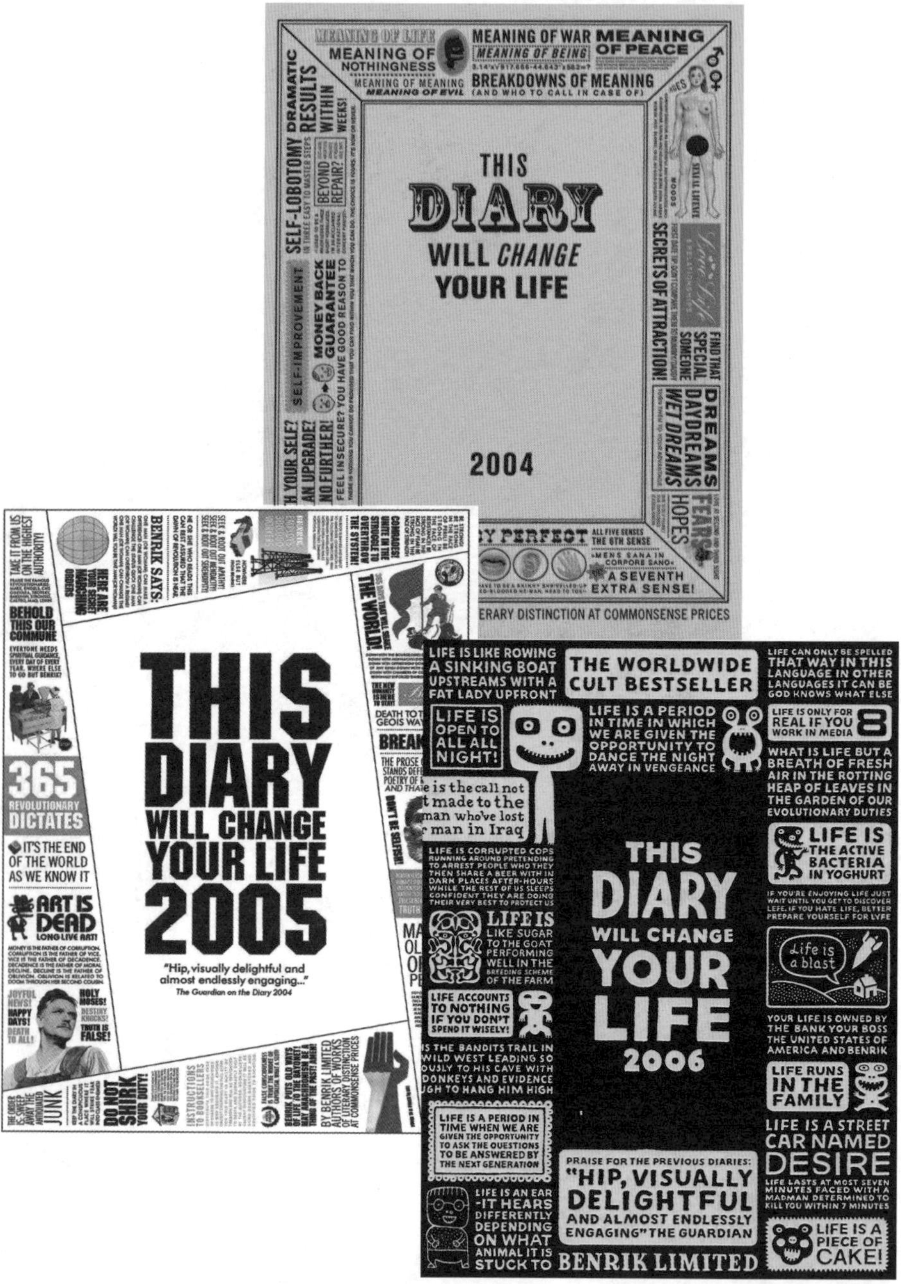
MEANING OF LIFE
MEANING OF NOTHINGNESS
MEANING OF WAR
MEANING OF BEING
MEANING OF PEACE
MEANING OF MEANING
MEANING OF EVIL
BREAKDOWNS OF MEANING
(AND WHO TO CALL IN CASE OF)
SELF-LOBOTOMY
DRAMATIC RESULTS WITHIN WEEKS!
BEYOND REPAIR?
SELF-IMPROVEMENT
MONEY BACK GUARANTEE
SECRETS OF ATTRACTION!
FIND THAT SPECIAL SOMEONE
DREAMS DAYDREAMS WET DREAMS
HOPES
FEARS
ALL FIVE SENSES
THE 6TH SENSE
A SEVENTH EXTRA SENSE!
THIS DIARY WILL CHANGE YOUR LIFE
2004
THIS DIARY WILL CHANGE YOUR LIFE 2005
"Hip, visually delightful and almost endlessly engaging..."
The Guardian on the Diary 2004
BENRIK SAYS:
BEHOLD THIS OUR COMMUNE
365 REVOLUTIONARY DICTATES
IT'S THE END OF THE WORLD AS WE KNOW IT
ART IS DEAD LONG LIVE ART!
DO NOT SHIRK YOUR DUTY!
JUNK
LIFE IS LIKE ROWING A SINKING BOAT UPSTREAMS WITH A FAT LADY UPFRONT
THE WORLDWIDE CULT BESTSELLER
LIFE CAN ONLY BE SPELLED THAT WAY IN THIS LANGUAGE IN OTHER LANGUAGES IT CAN BE GOD KNOWS WHAT ELSE
LIFE IS OPEN TO ALL ALL NIGHT!
LIFE IS A PERIOD IN TIME IN WHICH WE ARE GIVEN THE OPPORTUNITY TO DANCE THE NIGHT AWAY IN VENGEANCE
LIFE IS ONLY FOR REAL IF YOU WORK IN MEDIA
WHAT IS LIFE BUT A BREATH OF FRESH AIR IN THE ROTTING HEAP OF LEAVES IN THE GARDEN OF OUR EVOLUTIONARY DUTIES
LIFE IS THE ACTIVE BACTERIA IN YOGHURT
THIS DIARY WILL CHANGE YOUR LIFE 2006
LIFE IS LIKE SUGAR TO THE GOAT PERFORMING WELL IN THE BREEDING SCHEME OF THE FARM
life is a blast
LIFE ACCOUNTS TO NOTHING IF YOU DON'T SPEND IT WISELY!
YOUR LIFE IS OWNED BY THE BANK YOUR BOSS THE UNITED STATES OF AMERICA AND BENRIK
LIFE RUNS IN THE FAMILY
LIFE IS A STREET CAR NAMED DESIRE
LIFE IS A PERIOD IN TIME WHEN WE ARE GIVEN THE OPPORTUNITY TO ASK THE QUESTIONS TO BE ANSWERED BY THE NEXT GENERATION
PRAISE FOR THE PREVIOUS DIARIES: "HIP, VISUALLY DELIGHTFUL AND ALMOST ENDLESSLY ENGAGING" THE GUARDIAN
LIFE IS AN EAR -IT HEARS DIFFERENTLY DEPENDING ON WHAT ANIMAL IT IS STUCK TO
BENRIK LIMITED
LIFE IS A PIECE OF CAKE!

The Revolution must wear a suit.
Fur your mouth
Benrik LIMITED
BENRIK LTD This Diary Will Change Your Life 2008
YOUR SECRET INSTRUCTIONS ARE TO TALK EVERYONE YOU MEET THIS YEAR INTO COMMITTING A PARTICULARLY HORRENDOUS CRIME AGAINST HUMANITY, AND THEN PRETENDING YOU HAD NOTHING TO DO WITH IT WHATSOEVER
Routine check:

THE CULT HUMOUR BESTSELLER FROM BENRIK LIMITED
This Diary Will Change Your Life 2007
"It changed my life utterly, and all for a very reasonable
"This book taught me the meaning of life. But I forgot to write it down."
"It's cured both my piles, and my ebola."
"The Diary has made me four and a half times the man I was."
"Thanks to this Diary, I made parole ten years early."
"The results speak for themselves, even when I tell them to
"I used to be afraid of life. Now we're good buddies."
"It made me forget about global warming for a while."
"Illiterate? This book has lots of pictures!"
"This Diary has helped me become richer, sexier and godlier."
"Hip, visually delightful, and almost endlessly engaging" THE GUARDIAN
"I used to be a booker now I'm an architect."
"This Diary has helped me keep the promise of my youth."
"Life used to be a bitch, but now she's my mistress."
"I can't talk about my new life without breaking into song."

THE WORLD-WIDE CULT BEST SELLER!
This Diary Will Change Your Life 2009
MONDAY TUESDAY WEDNES. THURSD. FRI SAT SUN
A balloon is the human's first lesson in death.
Be confessional!
Let's talk it can prevent me from writing a book
POSSIBLE YES
Better a lunch at your desk than having to walk back again.
Fill in the opposites:
Bluebell =
Gutline =
Plasters =
Google =
Oatmeal =
Citybreaks =
Terrorism =
I like it when the good guy wins in the end but I don't mind if there's a bit of scruffing around with the bad guys just before the end.
WE LOVE YOU! WE NEED YOU!
BENRIK
Tomorrow this will all be behind you
One should change one's life as one change the channels on the television!

Best of Benrik readers

Svankær

Shadowy, Pashmina, MariGR, Sissiri, Elbaek, Leonora, Mindy and Papingo invade the small, isolated Danish village of Svankaer for the week (2007)

Good Taste

Come dine with them

Horton Jupiter opens a home restaurant (which receives wide media coverage and sparks a rash of copycats, 2009)

Will Parkinson eats the Diary and makes the national press (2005)

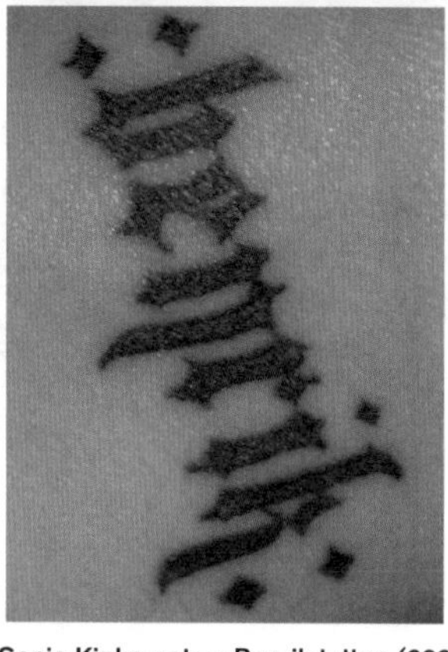

Sonja Kipka gets a Benrik tattoo (2005)

STUCK?
This Diary Will Change Your Life 2009

David Lines agrees to promote Benrik by being glued to a billboard for the day (2009)

Hundreds send in their passports for stamping with the Benrik visa (2007)

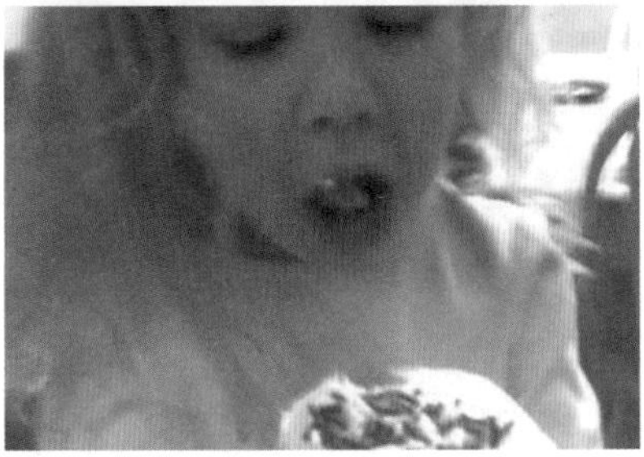

Heathernjoli and nieces "glorify terrorism", via the medium of cupcakes (2006)

Thousands submit to direct surveillance by Benrik during "Control order week", including tagging (2008)

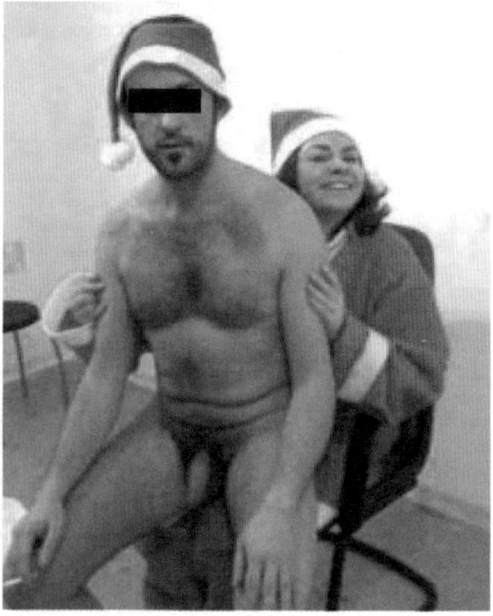

Papingo ruins the reputation of Father Xmas (2006)

Cardenio wears a burka for the day (2007)

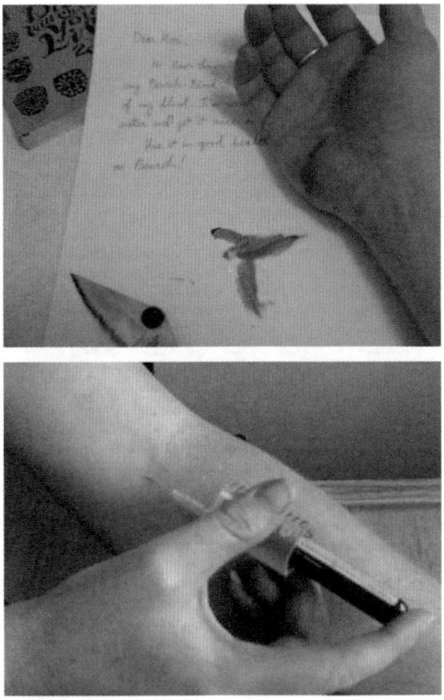

MariGR, Shadowy, Pashmina and other Benrik readers swap blood (2007)

But
Tony Blair is
the best
looking
Prime
Minister
we've ever
had!!
(and their Euan's not
too bad either!)

Mel Elliott protests in favour of the government (2007)

At the ATM

Joel Moss Levinson visits his local ATM in women's lingerie at the bidding of other Benrik readers (2007)

THIS
DIARY
2005
Inneboken tog
över hennes liv
'eronica, 18: "Jag har blivit mycket modigare"

Nicka sparks a cult scare in the Swedish tabloids (2006)

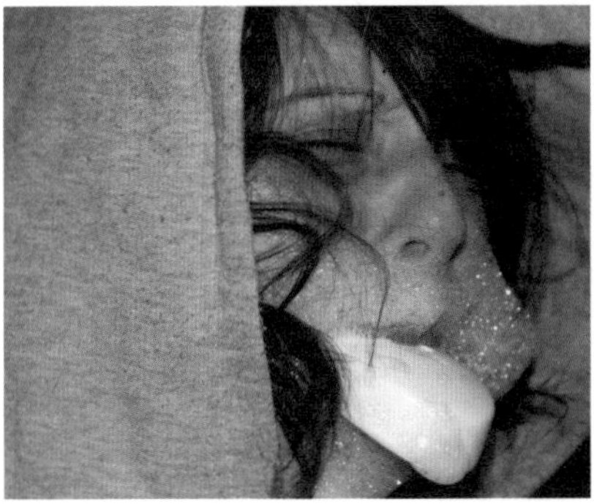

Not entirely sure what this one was about (2007)

To be inspired by more past tasking, visit benrik.co.uk

Academic studies

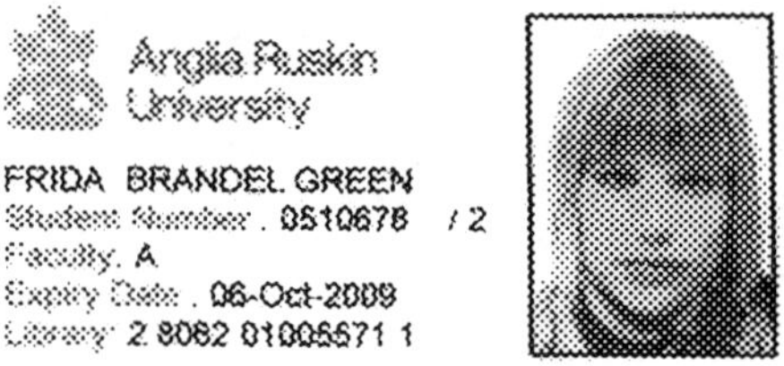
Anglia Ruskin
University
FRIDA BRANDEL GREEN
0510678 / 2
A
06-Oct-2009
2 8082 01006671 1

PRANKS, SOCIETY AND EVERYDAY LIFE:
A CRITICAL ANALYSIS OF THE BENRIK CULT
B.A. (HONS) COMMUNICATION STUDIES

ABSTRACT
The Benrik cult is the creation of Ben Carey and Henrik Delehag who have under the name of Benrik produced the annual This Diary Will Change Your Life since 2003, as well as other books and websites. The diary consists of tasks that the reader should complete and blog about on the Benrik community website Benrikland. It is not a traditional self-help book, nor a traditional cult; instead Benrik challenges and undermines contemporary society and its impositions on peoples' everyday life. With This Diary Will Change Your Life as its main focus, this project examines the Benrik cult in regard to theories on capitalism, postmodernism, everyday life, escapism and desire. The main theorists and philosophers whose work is discussed are Marx, Althusser, Lefebvre, de Certeau, Nietzsche, Baudrillard, Deleuze and Guattari. It also compares Benrik to two activist movements: the Situationist International and Culture Jamming. The project's findings consist of the image of Benrik as a postmodern phenomenon with duplicity and parody as main characteristics. Furthermore, Benrik constitutes as an alternative to the boredom of everyday life and as something that introduces an element of play and pranks. Finally, Benrik introduce to their wide audience, a set of ideas that differs from those in the dominant ideology.

1. INTRODUCTION
Benrik Ltd is founded by Ben Carey and Henrik Delehag; the company produces the annual This Diary Will Change Your Life, a diary with weekly tasks that the reader should complete. 'Benrik specialize in "extreme self-improvement" ... [which] requires permanent radical and systematic life-change, to jolt us all out of the current coma of our collective imagination (post-9/11)' (Carey and Delehag 2005: n.p.).
The aim of the diaries is outlined in This Diary Will Change your Life 2008: 'Benrik's purpose is to purge their readers' brains of the ever more restrictive clichés of contemporary culture' (Carey and Delehag 2007a: n.p.). Benrik cite Roman writer Cicero by saying that 'to be completely free one must become a slave to a set of laws' (cited in Carey and Delehag 2008a: n.p.).
The authors of the Benrik books explain that they wanted self-consciously to create a cult, a 'mainstream cult' that would encompass people in all areas of the world and of society. (Carey, interview)
Delehag underlines the importance of introducing ideas they are engaged in at the same time as being sarcastic, and to keep the balance between them. (Interview)
The tasks are designed to be physically and legally possible to accomplish, Benrik genuinely want people to do them, and in that sense it is a serious cult. (Carey, interview)
Carey and Delehag have a background in advertising and apply its codes and language onto the products of the Benrik cult. Delehag explains that 'in everything we do there is that element of persuasion and we never really suggest to people to do things, we tell people to do it' (Delehag, interview). Carey describes the language of advertising being a constant soft bullying, a concept that Benrik took to the extreme and started to overtly dictate people; an openness that has been appreciated by the readers. (Carey, interview)
The whole of society ... is dominated by more or less subtle messages trying to tell you what to do ... we parody that and take it to a different place by making it ... open and honest. And even if some of the suggestions are a bit insane, they are in the same ballpark as a lot of advertising suggestions. (Carey, interview)
On the cult's website Benrikland, the followers of the diary can create a membership account and record their progress with the tasks and discuss thoughts that are related to Benrik in the form of blogs and forums. In order to become a member of Benrikland one must give the correct answer to three questions regarding general morals. Benrik justify the reasons for the test of acceptance by stating that: 'Benrik have no truck with the so-called democracy of the web. To access this site fully, you need to prove that you aren't a complete moron' (www.benrik.co.uk). This can be comprehended in two ways; firstly, Benrik might imply that the Internet is deceitfully free, but actually controlled by advertisers. Secondly, Internet constitutes a space in which one's identity is lost; a person can pretend to be someone he or she is not. Benrik's morality test can function as a plea to people to be themselves.
Other publications by Benrik are: The Couples Book, The Mothers Book, The Fathers Book, Lose Weight! Get Laid! Find God!, and the most recent A Book For People Who Want To Become Stinking Rich But Aren't Quite Sure How. They have also launched a number of websites, for example the 'Global Vote 2004' site, where non-Americans were allowed to vote in the American election. Moreover, Benrik contribute weekly to The Guardian with the 'Benrik Pitch', which gives a reflection on a suggestion to a current affairs issue, they have also been featured on a regular basis in The Independent.
This Diary Will Change Your Life has been published since 2003; one major change appeared in the 2006 diary, when the tasks became weekly instead of daily. The first two diaries with one task for each day does consist of thought provoking tasks, similar to those in later diaries, which made me conscious of the research potential of Benrik. However, they also contain an element of arbitrariness, which is noticeable in tasks such as 'Today start to eat a piece of furniture'. (Carey and Delehag 2003: n.p.) The task 'Today bake a cake' (Carey and Delehag 2003: n.p.) can at first also seem arbitrary, but it can be linked to theories on the postmodern that are discussed in chapter four, and to capitalism and alienation dealt with in chapter two. Cooking and baking are becoming less common in contemporary society; processed food dominates the supermarket shelves, these are products that are more profitable for the food industry. Reports on this lost skill were recently broadcasted on TV in Jamie Oliver's Ministry of Food (2008), and it is just to television that cooking has been confined, with a vast amount of food programmes being broadcast on a regular basis. 'Today bake a cake' is a task that brings the reality of the basic human skill of preparing food back to the people.
When the diaries contained fewer tasks, the complexion of the tasks became more in depth, since carrying out the task must cover a whole week. Some tasks are for example divided into smaller sections, as is the case in 'This week, increase your pain threshold', where followers should day by day expose themselves to increasing levels of pain, to comply with the proverb 'what doesn't kill you makes you stronger' (Carey and Delehag 2006: n.p.).
This project will make a critical analysis of the Benrik cult, with focus on This Diary Will Change Your Life, in doing so it will compare Benrik to the work of various theorists. Firstly Karl Marx's theory on capitalism will be taken into account, as well as the work of Marxist thinker Louis Althusser ...
(Read the rest of the dissertation on www.benrik.co.uk.)

Official tutor mark: 63 (B). Comments: "Overall, this work has some strong points and some weaknesses. The first are its understanding of a range of appropriate theoretical addresses (also in its sweep a weakness). Also, its method (a weakness in not identifying this at outset) and its commitment. But also lacking is any real engagement with the notion of commodification of resistance." Congratulations Frida!